I

Reality and Subjectivity

I

By

David R. Hawkins, M.D., Ph.D.

VERITAS

Veritas Publishing
P.O. Box 3516
West Sedona, AZ 86340 U.S.A.
(928) 282-8722 • (928) 282-4789 (fax)
www.veritaspub.com

LCCN: 2002117301
ISBN: 0-9715007-0-3

Printed in the United States of America

Straight and narrow is the path…

Waste no time.

Dedication

Gloria in Excelsis! Deo!

Table of Contents

Foreword

The radically subjective state of enlightenment historically has been difficult to convey as well as comprehend. In this trilogy, a means of comprehension has been provided for the linear mind to understand the nonlinear reality of spiritual truth.

Only infrequently has a realized being been able to retain meaningful contact with the world in terms of verbal fluency or explanation that is comprehensible by ordinary human consciousness. At times, all that has been possible has been a description of the overwhelming, existent subjective state that has been revealed. Thus, the verbalizations and descriptions of awareness at that level of consciousness are often obscure or subject to misinterpretation, or they may simply sound unintelligible to the majority of mankind.

What makes this work unique is that the state of enlightenment occurred to a personality that retained fluency and, after many years of endeavor, managed to re-own and remaster the ordinary levels of consciousness in order to be able to return to the world as a teacher and function simultaneously in both the linear and nonlinear domains. This required the creation of a conceptual scheme that allowed for the intellect to bridge the gap between the linear reasoning of the mind and the nonlinear reality of spiritual truth. This work is unique in that it includes not only a full description of the inner subjective state of enlightenment, but it also encompasses the entire progression of the levels of consciousness to reach that state.

In *Power versus Force* and *The Eye of the I,* the information necessary for the spiritual aspirant was provided. In this last volume of the trilogy, that final state is described with a clear articulation.

Sedona, Arizona Sonia Martin
January 2003 Editor

Preface

This is the third book of a trilogy that encompasses the evolution of human consciousness as revealed by research as well as by subjective experience.

The first book, *Power versus Force*, outlined a verifiable scale of consciousness and revealed, for the first time in human history, a means of discovering truth from falsehood, thus overcoming the most critically important inherent defect of the human mind. *Power versus Force* addressed itself primarily to the levels of consciousness which include most of humanity. These levels progress up to the high 500s, which are often described as saintly.

The second book, *The Eye of the I*, addressed itself to the levels of consciousness from 600 to approximately 850. These levels have been considered throughout history to be the realm of the traditional enlightened spiritual teachers.

This third book, simply entitled *I*, completes the description of the evolution of human consciousness from the level of approximately 800 to its peak experience at 1,000, which historically has been the ultimate possibility in the human domain. This is the realm of the mystic whose truth stems solely from the radical subjectivity of divine revelation.

The text of the material is taken from lectures, dissertations, and dialogues with students, visitors, and spiritual aspirants from around the world who have different spiritual and religious backgrounds and varying levels of consciousness. There are relatively few references to other traditional spiritual treatises or teachers as the material is complete and sufficient in and of itself. This is not a theological text which customarily includes numerous detailed references for academic purposes. It is instead left primarily to the reader to make correlation with the world's existent literature. Thus, there is a bare minimum of Sanskrit, Christian, or Vedic terminology.

The term "artifact" is used in its customary but unique medical definition as something that is "foreign, false, or misleading." In medicine, an artifact is a fault which could be mistaken for the real, e.g., a residual stain or a speck of dust that, under the microscope, could be mistaken for a bacterium. The use of the term is therefore not the more common one that means an archeological object of antiquity; in this case, it means "spurious."

There is a purposeful repetition of certain themes and statements which is a pedagogical technique used as each repetition is in a different context and sequence.

Acknowledgements

The author expresses gratitude to the many participants and students of the classes, lectures, and sessions held around the world but especially to the devoted attendees of the monthly lecture series held at the Sedona Creative Life Center (Arizona) in the year 2002, at which many of the calibrations were publicly demonstrated and confirmed.

Special thanks are due for the dedication and skills of Sonia Martin who worked for over a year to perfect the manuscript.

We are thankful to the many organizations, spiritual groups, and churches that invited the presentation of lectures and workshops.

We are also grateful to the many enthusiasts of this collective work who have supported its promulgation through independent educational efforts via various media and workshop groups.

And, as attendees of the lectures might well surmise, the writing of the book itself was facilitated and energized by the round-the-clock help of the self and the Self of my wife Susan and her indefatigable right arm as well as her spiritual intuition and capacity for innate knowingness.

All credit is due to God whose Radiance shines forth as Creation and who, by the Holy Spirit, inspires and illuminates all understanding and realization of Divine Truth. Amen.

Caveat

The traditional religionist or the spiritually timid are fore-warned that the material presented herein may be disturbing and therefore better bypassed. The teachings are presented for the seriously committed spiritual student who is seeking God as Enlightenment.

The pathway to Enlightenment via radical truth is demand-ing and requires the surrendering of all belief systems. Only then does the Ultimate Reality reveal itself as the sought-after 'I' of the Supreme.

The material presented herein is from the perspective of the Infinite 'I' of the Self.

Introduction

Throughout history, there have been descriptions and reports of advanced states of consciousness, but often they were fragmentary, brief, cryptic, or enigmatic. Their puzzling nature led scholars to spend many years pouring over them, trying to decipher the true meaning of these teachings. Theological argument and disagreement then led to many schisms which often had severe consequences.

Many of the ancient traditions were handed down verbally from generation to generation, and some actually for many centuries or even thousands of years before they were recorded. Much was lost due to difficulties in translation. Perhaps the most difficult problems arose because the listeners to the words of the great teachers were unable to correctly interpret the meanings of the words. The nondualistic, nonlinear domain of spiritual truth does not translate easily into the reason/logic/ sequential itemization of the ego/mind, which is bound by the positionalities and presumptions of duality, such as time, duration, causality, and space.

Consciousness research reveals that enlightenment is statistically rare, and even when it does occur (level 600), the chances are only twenty percent that the enlightened being will return to an active life in the world. When consciousness level reaches 700 to 800, the chances are only five percent that the sage will again be able to relate to the world. By the time the consciousness level reaches the 900s, only one percent will be able to return to the world. The reasons for this will be investigated and explained in the chapters to follow.

Enlightenment is best described as a state or a condition that is self-revealing and replaces the previous state of consciousness. This state is complete unto itself and is also commonly termed "Self-realization." In the experience to be described, no mention was made of this occurrence for more than thirty years for it took that long to be able to recontextualize the phenomenon in such a manner as to be expressible in meaningful language. The capacity to do so was impersonal and the result of inspiration as a gift of Divinity by which means the state could be shared.

To facilitate comprehension and provide orientation and perspective, the calibrated levels of consciousness of various passages will be stated in the chapters. Following such a calibrated passage will be an explanation to clarify the meaning of the words that might otherwise seem obscure. The value of this method is that it obviates having to manipulate the understanding in order for it to be comprehended and instead allows it to be expressed as it is subjectively known.

Historical Précis

(This is an abridgement of the "About the Author" section from *Power versus Force* and *The Eye of the I* which provides historical context.)

A lifelong sequence of intense states of awareness that began at a very young age first inspired and then gave direction to the process of subjective realization.

At age three, a sudden, full awareness of the condition and state of existence occurred. The nonverbal but profound and complete understanding of the meaning of 'existence' was immediately followed by the frightening realization that the 'I' might not have come into existence at all. There was an instant awakening from oblivion to a conscious awareness, and in that moment, the personal self was born and the duality of 'Is' and 'Is Not' entered subjective awareness.

Throughout childhood and early adolescence, the paradox of existence and the question of the reality of the self was a constant concern. The personal self would sometimes begin to slip back into a greater, impersonal Self, and the initial fear of non-existence—the fundamental fear of nothingness—would recur.

In 1939, as a paperboy with a seventeen-mile bicycle route in rural Wisconsin, I was caught on a dark winter's night miles from home in a twenty-below-zero blizzard. The bicycle fell over on the ice and the fierce wind ripped the newspapers out of the handlebar basket, blowing them across the ice-covered, snowy field. There were tears of frustration and exhaustion and my clothes were frozen stiff. To get out of the wind, I broke through the icy crust of a high snow bank, dug out a space, and crawled into it. Soon the shivering stopped and there was a delicious warmth, and then a state of peace beyond all description. This was accompanied by a suffusion of light and a presence of infinite love that had no beginning and no end and was undifferentiated from my own essence. The physical body and surroundings faded as awareness was fused with this all-present, illuminated state. The mind grew silent; all thought stopped. An Infinite Presence was all that was or could be, beyond all time or description.

After that timelessness, there was suddenly an awareness of someone shaking my knee; then my father's anxious face appeared. There was great reluctance to return to the body and all that that entailed, but because of my father's love and anguish, the Spirit nurtured and reactivated the body. There was compassion for his fear of death although, at the same time, the concept of death seemed absurd.

This subjective experience was not discussed with anyone because there was no context available from which it could be described. It was not common to hear of spiritual experiences other than those reported in the lives of the saints. But after this experience, the accepted reality of the world began to seem only provisional. Traditional religious teachings lost significance. Compared to the Light of Divinity that had illuminated all existence, the God of traditional religion shone dully indeed; thus, spirituality replaced religion.

During World War II, hazardous duty on a minesweeper often brought close brushes with death but there was no fear of it. It was as though death had lost its authenticity. After the war, interest in the complexities of the mind led to the study of psychiatry and contemplation of medical school and residency. My training psychoanalyst, a professor at Columbia University, was an agnostic; we both took a dim view of religion. The psychoanalysis went well, as did the career, and success followed.

The stresses of professional life led to a progressive, fatal illness which did not respond to any available treatments. By age thirty-eight, I was *in extremis* and knew that I was about to die. I did not care about the body but my spirit was in a state of extreme anguish and despair. As the final moment approached, the thought flashed through my mind, "What if there is a God?" So I called out in prayer, "If there is a God, I ask him to help me now," and surrendered to whatever God there might be and went into oblivion. When consciousness returned, a transformation of such enormity had taken place that there was only silence and awe.

The 'person' that had been no longer existed. There was no personal 'I' or self or ego, only an Infinite Presence of unlimited power that had replaced what had been 'me'. The body and its actions were controlled solely by the Infinite Will of the Presence. The world was illuminated by the clarity of an Infinite Oneness. All things revealed their infinite beauty and perfection as the expression of Divinity.

As life went on, this stillness persisted. There was no personal will; the physical body functioned solely under the direction of the infinitely powerful but exquisitely gentle Will of the Presence.

In that state, there was no need to think about anything. All truth was self-evident and no conceptualization was necessary or even possible. At the same time, the physical nervous system felt extremely overtaxed as though it was carrying far more energy than its circuits had been designed for.

It was not possible to function effectively in the world. All ordinary motivations had disappeared, along with all fear and anxiety. There was nothing to seek as all was perfect. Fame, success, and money were meaningless. Friends urged the pragmatic return to clinical practice, but there was no motivation to do so.

There was the ability to perceive the reality that underlay personalities and that the origin of emotional sickness lay in people's belief that they *were* their personalities. And so, as though of its own, a clinical practice resumed and eventually became huge.

The practice had two thousand out-patients, which required more than fifty therapists and other employees, a suite of twenty-five offices, as well as research, clinical, and electroencephalic laboratories. There were a thousand new patients each year. In addition, there were appearances on radio and network television shows. In 1973, the clinical research was documented in the book, *Orthomolecular Psychiatry*, with Professor Linus Pauling as coauthor. This work was ten years ahead of its time and created something of a stir.

The overall condition of the nervous system improved slowly, and then another phenomenon commenced: a sweet, delicious band of energy continuously flowed up the spine and into the brain where it created an intense sensation of exquisite pleasure. Everything in life unfolded in synchronicity, evolving in perfect harmony. The miraculous was commonplace. The origin of what the world would call miracles was the Presence, not the personal self. What remained of the personal 'me' was only an awareness of these phenomena. The greater 'I', deeper than the former self or thoughts, determined all that happened.

The state that was present had been reported by others throughout history; this led to the investigation of spiritual teachings, including those of the Buddha, enlightened sages, Huang Po, and more recent teachers such as Ramana Marharshi and Nisargadatta Maharaj. It was thus confirmed that these experiences were not unique. The Bhagavad-Gita now made complete sense. At times the same spiritual ecstasy reported by Sri Ramakrishna and the Christian saints occurred.

It was necessary to stop the habitual practice of meditating for an hour in the morning and then again before dinner because it would intensify the bliss to such an extent that it was not possible to function. An experience similar to the one that had happened when a boy in the snow bank would recur, and it became increasingly difficult to leave that state and return to the world. The incredible beauty of all things shone forth in all their perfection, and where the world saw ugliness, there was only timeless beauty. This spiritual love suffused all perception and all boundaries between here and there and then and now, and separation disappeared.

During the years spent in inner silence, the strength of the Presence grew. Life was no longer personal; a personal will no longer existed. The personal 'I' had dissolved and become an instrument of the Infinite Presence and went about and did as it was willed. People felt an extraordinary peace in the aura of that Presence. Seekers sought answers, but as there was no longer any such individual as my former self, they were actually finessing answers from their own Self, which was no different from my Self. The same Self shone forth from each person through their eyes.

The miraculous happened spontaneously, beyond ordinary comprehension. Many chronic maladies from which the body had suffered for years disappeared. The eyesight spontaneously normalized and there was no longer a need for the lifetime of bifocal glasses. Occasionally, an exquisitely blissful energy of Infinite Love would suddenly begin to radiate from the heart toward the scene of some calamity and precipitate some miraculous resolution.

Profound changes of perception would come without warning in improbable circumstances. The Presence would suddenly intensify until everything and every person that had appeared as separate in ordinary perception melted into a timeless universality and oneness.

In the motionless Silence, there are no 'events' or 'things'. Nothing actually 'happens' because past, present, and future are merely artifacts of perception, as was the illusion of a separate 'I' being subject to birth and death.

As the limited, false self dissolved into the universal Self of its true origin, there was an ineffable sense of having returned home to a state of absolute peace and relief from all suffering. There was the awareness that it is only the illusion of individuality that is the origin of all suffering. When one realizes that one *is* the universe, complete and at one with All That Is, forever without end, no further suffering is possible.

Patients came from every country in the world, and some were the most hopeless of the hopeless. Grotesque, writhing, wrapped in wet sheets for transport from far-away hospitals they came, hoping for treatment for advanced psychoses and grave, incurable mental disorders. Some were catatonic; many had been mute for years. But in each patient, beneath the crippled appearance, there was the shining essence of love and beauty, perhaps so obscured to ordinary vision that they had become totally unloved in this world.

One day a mute catatonic was brought into the hospital in a strait-jacket. She also had a severe neurological disorder and was unable to stand. Squirming on the floor, she went into spasms and her eyes rolled back in her head. Her hair was matted, her clothes were torn, and she uttered guttural sounds. Her family was fairly wealthy; as a result, over the years she had been seen by innumerable physicians and famous specialists from all over the world. Every treatment had been tried and she had been given up as hopeless by the medical profession.

A short, nonverbal question arose: "What do you want done with her, God?" Then came the realization that she just needed to be loved—that was all. Her inner self shone through her eyes and the Self connected with that loving Presence. In that moment, she was healed by her own recognition of who she really was; what happened to her mind or body did not matter to her any longer.

This, in essence, occurred with countless patients. Some recovered in the eyes of the world and some did not, but whether a clinical recovery ensued no longer mattered to the patients. Their inner agony was over. As they felt loved and at peace within, their pain stopped. This phenomenon can only be explained by saying that the Compassion of the Presence recontextualized each patient's reality so that they experienced healing on a level that transcended the world and its appearances. The inner peace of the Self encompassed us beyond time and identity.

It was clear that all pain and suffering arise solely from the ego and not from God. This truth was silently communicated to the minds of the patients. This same mental block was in another mute catatonic who had not spoken in many years. The Self said to him through mind, "You're blaming God for what your ego has done to you." He jumped off the floor and began to speak, much to the shock of the nurse who witnessed the incident.

The work became increasingly taxing and eventually overwhelming. Patients were backed up, waiting for beds to open although the hospital had built an extra ward to house them. There was an enormous frustration in that the human suffering could be countered in only one patient at a time. It was like bailing out the sea. It seemed that there must be some other way to address the causes of the basic common malaise of the endless stream of spiritual distress and human suffering.

This led to the study of kinesiology, which revealed an amazing discovery. It was the 'wormhole' between two universes—the physical world and the world of the mind and spirit—an interface between dimensions. In a world full of sleepers lost from their source, here was a tool to recover and demonstrate for all to see that lost connection with the higher reality. This led to the testing of every substance, thought, and concept that could be brought to mind. The endeavor was aided by students and research assistants.

Then a major discovery was made: Whereas all subjects went weak from negative stimuli, such as fluorescent lights, pesticides, and artificial sweeteners, students of spiritual disciplines who had advanced their levels of awareness did not go weak as did ordinary people. Something important and decisive had shifted in their consciousness. It apparently occurred as they realized that they were not at the mercy of the world but rather affected only by what their minds believed. Perhaps the very process of progress toward enlightenment could be shown to increase man's ability to resist the vicissitudes of existence, including illness.

The Self had the capacity to change things in the world by merely envisioning them. Love changed the world each time it replaced nonlove. The entire scheme of civilization could be profoundly altered by focusing this power of love at a very specific point. Whenever this happened, history bifurcated down new roads.

It now appeared that these crucial insights could not only be communicated to the world but visibly and irrefutably demonstrated to it as well. It seemed that the great tragedy of human life had always been that the psyche is so easily deceived. Discord and strife have been the inevitable consequences of mankind's inability to distinguish the false from the true. But here was an answer to this fundamental dilemma, a way to recontextualize the nature of consciousness and make explicable that which otherwise could only be inferred.

It then became necessary to leave the former life and everything in it, replacing it instead with a reclusive life in a small town. The next seven years were spent in meditation and study.

Overpowering states of bliss returned unsought, and eventually there was the need to learn how to be in the Divine Presence and still function in the world. The mind had lost track of what was happening in the world at large. In order to do research and writing, it was necessary to stop all spiritual practice and focus on the world of form.

Exceptional subjective experiences of truth, which are the province of the mystic, affect all mankind by sending forth spiritual energy into the collective consciousness. Such states are not understandable by the majority of mankind and are therefore of limited meaning except to spiritual seekers. This led to an effort to be ordinary, because just being ordinary is in itself an expression of Divinity. The truth of one's real self can be discovered through the pathway of everyday life. To live with care and kindness is all that is necessary; the rest reveals itself in due time. The commonplace and God are not distinct.

And so, after a long circular journey of the spirit, there was a return to the most important work which was to try to bring the Presence at least a little closer to the grasp of as many fellow beings as possible.

The Presence is silent and conveys a state of peace that is the space in which and by which All Is and has its existence and unfolds. It is infinitely gentle and yet like a rock. With it, all fear disappears. Spiritual joy occurs on a quiet level of inexplicable ecstasy. The experience of time stops; there is no apprehension or regret, no pain or anticipation. The source of joy is unending and ever present. With no beginning or ending, there is no loss or grief or desire. Nothing needs to be done as everything is already perfect and complete.

When time stops, all problems disappear; they are merely artifacts of a point of perception. As the Presence prevails, there is no further identification with the body or mind. When the mind grows silent, the thought "I Am" also disappears, and Pure Awareness shines forth to illuminate what one is, was, and always will be, beyond all worlds and all universes, beyond time, and therefore without beginning or end.

People wonder "How does one reach this state of awareness," but few follow the steps because they are so simple. First, the desire to reach that state was intense. Then began the discipline to act with constant and universal forgiveness and gentleness, without exception. One has to be compassionate towards everything, including one's own self and thoughts. Next came a willingness to hold desires in abeyance and surrender personal will at every moment. As each thought, feeling, desire, or deed was surrendered to God, the mind became increasingly silent. At first, it released whole stories and paragraphs, then ideas and concepts. As one lets go of wanting to own these thoughts, they no longer reach such elaboration and begin to fragment while only half formed. Finally, it was possible to surrender the energy behind the very process of thinking itself before it even became thought.

The task of constant and unrelenting fixity of focus, allowing not even a moment of distraction from meditation, continued while doing ordinary activities. At first, this seemed to take effort, but as time went on, it became habitual and automatic, requiring less and less effort, and finally, it was effortless. The process is like a rocket's leaving the earth. Initially, it requires enormous energy, but then less and less as it leaves the earth's gravitational field, and eventually, it moves through space under its own momentum.

Suddenly, without warning, a shift in awareness occurred and the Presence totally prevailed, unmistakable and all encompassing. There were a few moments of intense apprehension as the self died, and then the absoluteness of the Presence inspired a flash of awe. This breakthrough was spectacular and more intense than anything before. It had no counterpart in ordinary experience. The profound shock was cushioned by the love that is the Presence. Without the support and protection of that love, it seems that one would be annihilated.

There followed a moment of terror as the ego clung to its existence, fearing it would become nothingness. Instead, as it died, it was replaced by the Self as Everythingness, the All in which everything was known and obvious in its perfect expression of its own essence. With nonlocality came the awareness that one is all that ever was or can be. One is total and complete, beyond all identities, beyond gender, beyond even humanness itself. One need never again fear suffering and death.

What happens to the body from this point is immaterial. At certain levels of spiritual awareness, ailments of the body heal or spontaneously disappear, but in the Absolute state, such considerations are irrelevant. The body will run its predicted course and then return from whence it came. It is a matter of no importance; Reality is unaffected. The body is an 'it' rather than a 'me'; it is just another object, like the furniture in a room. It may seem comical that people still address the body as though it were the individual 'you', but there is no way to explain this state of awareness to the unaware. It is best to just go on about one's business and allow Providence to handle the social adjustment. However, as one reaches bliss, it is very difficult to conceal that state of intense ecstasy.

In this final apocalypse of the self, the dissolution of the sole remaining duality of existence versus nonexistence dissolves in Universal Divinity and no individual consciousness is left to choose. The last step, then, is taken by God.

David R. Hawkins, 1995

Prologue

For convenience, a summary of the information presented previously in *Power versus Force* and *The Eye of the I* is provided.

The source of the universe and all existence is an infinite potentiality that is formless and innately Infinite Power. Out of the supreme Unmanifest arises the manifest universe as linear and nonlinear realms. Form has locality and duration; that which is formless is nonlocal and outside time.

The human mind is self-aware because of that general principle and existent reality generally termed "consciousness." It is the subjective condition that accounts for awareness of one's existence as well as the experiential content of that existence which we call life.

While the events that one presumes to be a personal life are recorded in personal memory, all events in the universe, no matter how minute, such as even a fleeting thought, are recorded in the infinite, impersonal field of consciousness beyond time, locality, and the recall of memory. It is as though space invisibly records all that happens within it for all time. This record is then discernible and retrievable forever by a simple physiologic phenomenon called the kinesiologic test. This is possible because the kinesiologic response is mediated by nonlocal consciousness.

Consciousness is an invisible quality of life which has the unique property of reacting to a stimulus that is real because it has or has had actual existence and is therefore "true." If a true statement is presented to human consciousness or silently held in mind, the muscles of the body go strong automatically with the recognition of truth. In contrast, they go weak in response to falsehood, which has no actual existence. Consciousness is therefore much like a light bulb that goes on with electricity (truth) but fails to light if there is no electricity (falsehood).

The major discovery was that, with kinesiologic testing, ***one could, for the first time in history, tell truth from falsehood about anything anywhere in time or space.*** The test itself proved to be independent of personal opinion or belief and, in fact, the innocent child was just as reliable as the sophisticated, informed adult. The response is also the same whether a statement is vocalized or made silently.

The capacity of consciousness to tell truth from falsehood meant that the invisible, nonlinear domain of spiritual truth could be researched and the reality of enlightened states could be validated. By the use of kinesiologic testing, it was possible to construct a scale of consciousness which encompassed all of humanity in all its expressions throughout history. This scale was displayed numerically. If all human possibility were displayed on a scale beginning with mere physical existence and progressing to the highest levels of consciousness that could possibly exist, the numbers would prove to be progressively huge. Therefore, a scale of 1 to 1,000 was constructed. It was logarithmic in order to make such large numbers useful in practice.

It was found that anything that calibrated over 200 proved to be true, and that anything below 200 was false. That which was over 200 was constructive, integrous, and supportive of life; that which was below 200 was negative and detrimental to humanity. Therefore, 200 proved to be the critical level that differentiated truth from falsehood and was perhaps the most important of all the discoveries.

The capacity to tell truth from falsehood was of profound importance because that is precisely what the human mind lacks. Thus, the discovery was an 'open sesame' to the mysteries of the universe and was the key that unlocked that which has been hidden from human awareness throughout history. It was the "$E = mc^2$" of the nonlinear domain. Like the discovery of the telescope, it opened whole universes for investigation that had never before been accessible.

The results of this research were presented first to the academic community as a Ph.D. dissertation entitled "Qualitative and Quantitative Analysis and Calibration of the Levels of

Human Consciousness." This was a formal presentation of the data subject to the traditional requirements of scientific proof (e.g., "P < .01," "Null Hypothesis," "Statistical Analysis," graphs, tables, documentation, and detailed references). The treatise passed academic review and, in fact, attracted considerable attention and created much excitement due to the startling discoveries that were presented.

Power versus Force described the discoveries and the implications for the various strata of society, including aspects of spiritual realities not previously considered 'real' by the limited, linear Newtonian paradigm of traditional science. This new tool for investigation allowed a rational, comprehensive exploration of the nonlinear domain of meaning and context. Initially, it differentiated that below 200 were the levels of force and above 200 were those of power. It was discovered that the qualities of force are intrinsically weak, local, destructive of life, and consume energy, whereas power based on truth is permanent, nonlocal, and produces energy rather than consuming it.

The technique of kinesiologic testing proved to be of great value in that (1) it allowed the differentiation of truth from falsehood, (2) it allowed for the calibration of the levels of human consciousness, and (3) it enabled investigation of any and every subject anywhere in time or space. What developed as a result was a means of contextualizing the evolution of human consciousness throughout time and on into its destiny, even beyond an individual physical lifetime.

The Scale of Consciousness thus allowed for a comprehensive recontextualization of mankind in all its expressions. It was observed that the lower levels of consciousness numerically encompassed the majority of mankind and that only very rarely (one in ten million people) did it reach the consciousness level of 600. Therefore, *Power versus Force* was focused on the levels of consciousness up to the level of 600.

The Eye of the I then went on to investigate the spiritual truths historically revered as states of enlightenment. It was discovered that within the states of enlightenment there are progressive strata or levels of comprehension. These advanced states represent ever higher levels of awareness. Each level represents a limitation of consciousness by an even more advanced spiritual duality that has to be resolved before the next level can be reached.

The Eye of the I described the subjective reality of the advanced mystic in such a way so as to make those states comprehensible. This resulted in a clarification of historical spiritual teachings and the resolution of ages-old mystifications and misconceptions. *The Eye of the I,* which calibrates in the high 900s, was therefore focused on very advanced spiritual truth.

In the human domain, historically, the maximum spiritual energy that could be tolerated by the human body and nervous systems calibrated at 1,000, which is the calibrated level of the founders of the world's great religions, those great teachers (avatars) of history, such as Christ, Buddha, and Krishna. The subject matter of this book is focused on the most advanced levels of human consciousness and therefore addresses the levels of approximately 850 to 1,000. No 'person' or 'personality' can write of such levels from either subjective experience or comprehension and, therefore, *I* is actually written by consciousness itself. Such levels of consciousness arise from a radical subjectivity that transcends personal identity. Consciousness at that level merely utilizes the convenience of the human mind and body to enable communication in form and language. The power of the Truth, however, exists independently of the languaging but accompanies the languaging like a carrier wave that empowers and facilitates comprehension.

Enlightenment is a state or condition that is formless but radiates its own powerful energy via a survivor of the onset and progression of that condition whose occurrence is relatively uncommon and which also, paradoxically, extracts a certain toll. These statements will be further explained and elucidated in the text that follows.

Preliminary Informational Note

In previous work, a useful Calibrated Scale of Consciousness was described which was corroborated by thousands of independent investigators and which can be replicated, starting anywhere on the scale. This verification has been conducted over a period of more than twenty-five years by innumerable individuals and research groups. At the time of this writing, this has involved more than 310,000 calibrations. If a seeming discrepancy occurred, it appeared, upon further investigation, that the supposed error was the result of a faulty technique or, more often, an imperfection in the wording of the statement to be verified.

Paradoxically, however, there were occasional complaints that the technique "doesn't work" or "gives wrong answers." A few of these complaints were worded in an erudite intellectual style and, although the reasoning sounded logical, the results were erroneous. This seemed like a puzzling paradox. Only very recently did it resolve itself by the sudden discovery that *the kinesiologic response is only valid and reliable if used by people who themselves calibrate at over 200 and whose questions are in integrity, that is, they calibrate above 200.* This discovery also demonstrates the principle that power and spiritual purity go hand in hand.

During the initial research, when it was discovered that the kinesiologic method was capable of discerning truth from falsehood about anything anywhere in the universe, there were initial misgivings that it might be misused if it fell into selfish hands. As it turned out, such a consideration was unnecessary as the technique had an unknown, built-in safeguard. Thus, the intention of the investigator plays a significant part in the reliability of the results, and the technique itself appears to be limited in usefulness to only that which is beneficial to mankind.

To restate the facts of the kinesiologic method of telling truth from falsehood:

1. Both partners (or the questioner, if a solitary method is used) must calibrate at over 200.
2. The motive or intention of the question must be integrous, i.e., calibrate over 200.
3. The question must be presented in the form of a declarative statement.
4. Calibration numbers are in reference to the published scale, i.e., "On a scale of 1 to 1,000, 'X' calibrates at over 200, 300," etc. (See Appendix B.)

5. An accurate response is obtainable without having to verbalize the statement merely by holding it (or an image) in mind. Therefore, the response is not influenced by the subject's personal beliefs or opinions. For instance, one can state "What I am holding in mind is true."

Explanation

The kinesiologic response has been confirmed by thousands of clinicians worldwide for decades. It is a replicable experiential phenomenon which is not explicable by ordinary logic or Newtonian physics. It is made comprehensible by the advanced physics of Quantum Mechanics in which the intention of the observer/questioner facilitates or does not facilitate a collapse of the wave function (the von Neumann Process I). Thus, the state of the universe (Schroedinger's equations) via the Heisenberg principle is often reduced or not (Dirac process), and therefore, the quantum response is limited to "yes" or "not yes." (See Appendix D, "Quantum Mechanics.")

SECTION ONE
THE PROCESS

CHAPTER ONE

TEACHERS AND STUDENTS

Q: How do I know if I'm going in the right direction?

A: Direction is a linear concept. What you probably mean is whether the pathway you are following is suitable and valid. This is an important question to ask and reflects a humility in the acknowledgement of the ego/mind's incapacity to tell truth from falsehood. One can verify the level of consciousness of any teaching or teacher, past or present. One can also cross-check with the kinesiologic test to determine if this is a suitable pathway at this time for oneself.

Q: Why are there so many different depictions of God?

A: These reflect the vagaries of the ego's anthropomorphic projections. Because of its inherent limitations, the ego itself cannot know God experientially. God is the absolute subjectivity that underlies existence and the capacity for awareness. God is beyond all time, place, or human characteristics. All the descriptions of the Ultimate Reality by enlightened beings throughout history have been identical. There is only one Supreme Reality.

The mythical gods of ancient cultures, as well as the demigods and deities, had limited realms or functions, such as the gods of fertility, nature, or the harvest. In the place of Divine Reality are manufactured pseudodeities with very obvious limitations that, by definition, would preclude their being the ultimate God of Creation.

Inasmuch as the Godhead, or God Unmanifest, is beyond all depiction, the Ultimate Realization is radically and purely subjective and absent of all content. To acknowledge the absolute divinity of the Infinite Supreme would be unacceptable to entities that are deluded into claiming godship. We can then say that a false deity is an entity that has declined truth for power, pride, and control over others, and has succumbed to the luciferic error which proclaims that the ego is God (i.e., megalomania). The basis for the error is the unwillingness to surrender sovereignty from the 'I' of the ego to the Allness of God.

That which is the Absolute Reality has no needs as it already is All That Is. There is no need for power when one is power itself. Infinite Power has no need to control anything. By analogy, the sky does not need the clouds nor does it create or destroy them. They arise within its all-encompassing, boundless space. The sky does not kill, retaliate, or punish clouds. The sky provides equality to all clouds as well as the context for their formation of perceptual appearance and disappearance.

Q: **The description of God as Supreme Being sounds almost impersonal.**

A: The ego thinks in terms of relationships and therefore contextualizes a relationship between two separate beings. The child in the ego's structure hopes that God will be like the idealized superparent. With this depiction, however, arises the downside, which is the fear of the parent's displeasure.

In contrast to the ego's perceptions of God, the Absolute Reality of the Self is the manifestation of God as the very core of one's existence. The Love of the Presence is ultrapersonal and experienced as infinite peace, infinite security, and the safety of foreverness so that there is no imaginary 'end' to fear. The God of the Presence imbues the joy of completion. Love is not a 'quality' of God but is God's very essence. There is no sense of 'otherness' to the Presence. God is the all-encompassing Reality of the never-ending present. There is no 'other' to fear or please.

By analogy, the sun does not play hide-and-seek when the clouds of the ego's beliefs are swept away. It is discovered that the sun has been shining all along. Its light and warmth radiate because that is the sun's innate, intrinsic essence and quality. Unlike the Earth's sun, the Sunship of God is permanent. To the Infinite, the comings and goings of universes have no meaning. That which is the Source of life and the universe is not subject to it. The glory of God has no requirements.

Q: What is the antidote to doubt?

A: The awareness of God is obscured by cynicism, skepticism, rational caution, negativism, or even ignorance. The underlying motive often reveals the answer. The ego does not like to have its world view challenged or brought into question. It protects its paradigm of reality from fear. It may feel threatened by contrary information and become defensive because it is being made to look 'wrong'. It also dislikes taking responsibility for its views because that imputes that they are held by choice.

Conflict may arise because of religious or group loyalties, or ethnic or family traditions, but the loyalty of the committed spiritual seeker is only to God. Doubt may also be a healthy signal that one is in the wrong place, spiritually speaking. As naïveté merges into spiritual maturity, discernment may flash a warning signal. If in doubt, always take 'stop'. One may also outgrow the current group or teaching; then it is time to move on.

Doubt may be motivated by the fear that there may be a loss of customary self-identity or cherished beliefs. To clear doubt, it is only necessary to identify one's motives and use kinesiologic testing as a means of verification.

The kinesiologic test is so fast and accurate with its simple "yes" and "no" responses that its reliability is limited only by the questioner's adherence to the basic rules, including careful wording of the statement. Changing even one word because it seems irrelevant can bring about a different answer. It is advisable, therefore, to ask a series of questions and cross-check them. If a seeming discrepancy appears, further questioning will reveal the source of the error. Careless statements can result in misleading responses.

For instance, Carl Jung's level of consciousness had been calibrated many times at 520 or so over the years. A questioner stated "Carl Jung is over 500," but the answer obtained was "No." When rephrased as "Carl Jung did calibrate over 500," the answer was "Yes." The answer to "Jung is over 500" was "No" simply because he is deceased.

To verify the value of a teacher or a spiritual pathway, the primary and most crucial determination is that they calibrate over level 200. Valid teachers and teachings are available for every level. A teaching in the 300s supports willingness and using one's personal power with enthusiasm. An enthusiastic and committed group may be more helpful at times than reading more advanced texts. If there is too much disparity between one's own level and that of the teacher, a great deal of useful information may be lost or not absorbed.

An enlightened sage may be at a very high level of consciousness and yet not really be capable of teaching, just as being a great pianist does not make one a great piano teacher. Teaching requires skills other than virtuosity.

The perfect teacher would have the patience to explain the truths of the various levels by contextualizing them in such a way that they become self-evident. This capacity means that the teacher is familiar with all the consciousness levels and the problems that arise in each.

In addition, the teacher is supportive of the resolution of the inherent dualities and positionalities, with resultant pairs of opposites, that stand at the gates of each level.

The teacher's knowledge must stem solely from the inner revelation of truth that accompanies and is the hallmark of enlightenment. This results in an unmistakable certainty and innate authority which only the absolute truth can convey. The true teacher clarifies that which is known by means of the Presence (classically termed *Purusha*). The teacher's source of understanding does not stem from external sources; therefore, quotes from famous teachers of history are only used for purposes of clarification for the sake of familiarity to the listener. The enlightened teacher needs no external confirmation.

The ideal teacher identifies the level of truth that is being spoken. In today's spiritual community, that level can now be precisely identified with an exact calibration that is subject to consensual validation. The source of the understanding of the teacher is inviolate and therefore needs no defense. Spiritual truth is complete within itself as it stands on its own merit. It is self-evident and requires no external agreement or props of any kind. The absolute subjectivity of revealed truth precludes all considerations or uncertainties which stem only from the ego. When the ego collapses, all argument ceases and is replaced by silence. Doubt *is* the ego. One could say that the ego is primarily a complex doubt structure that keeps itself rolling on by manufacturing endless, unsolvable problems, questions, and distractions. When confronted by the overwhelming certainty of Absolute Truth as it is reflected from the Self, the ego collapses and literally dies. That is actually the only real death possible, and only the illusory self is vulnerable to it.

Q: Even after the state called enlightenment replaces what is commonly called the ego, does not the evolution of consciousness continue?

A: It may do so but of its own accord. It is not the result of seeking or spiritual striving. In most cases the calibrated level of an enlightened sage remains the same for the remainder of that lifetime. In rare cases, consciousness spontaneously continues its evolution. It is as though the spirit within now becomes aware of a paradox at a higher level that calls for resolution. Spiritual inspiration now seeks for the resolution of the block. Like a foreign body in the skin, it draws attention to itself. It may also do this by the signal of an anguishing type of pain throughout the whole body and nervous system. Experientially, after intense prayer and meditation, this would result in a spontaneous revelation that resolved the apparent paradox, and then the pain would stop.

These painful sensations may come from a belief system that it is necessary to suffer in order to reach or serve God. With the resolution of this unconscious belief system, the pain diminishes in intensity. Through kinesiologic investigation, it may be found that the spiritual belief systems of many lifetimes are no longer acceptable to spiritual consciousness and are therefore suppressed into the unconscious, which may be harsh and strict regarding spiritual error or defect. This may result in painful sensations that feel as though the nerves are connected to high-voltage electricity. After that discovery, the burning sensation may decrease but any limitation in spiritual awareness may still make itself known by an inner spiritual discomfort that persists until the limitation becomes conscious and is resolved by intense prayer and understanding.

Q: **Cults are traps for the unwary. How can they be differentiated from legitimate, spiritual splinter groups?**

A: First, cults calibrate below 200. This may be due to the error of their teachings, or the teachings may have merit but the organization itself is not in integrity. Sometimes it is the leader who is the source of the error. Cults appeal to the innocent, the gullible, and the spiritually naïve or ignorant.

With discernment and spiritual maturity, the characteristics of cults become obvious. Primarily, they are exploitive. The leader is typically controlling; money is important; allegiance to the group is emphasized; and the cult insists on proselytizing and eliminating relationships with spouses, family or friends. There are secrets, a hierarchy, and the use of psychological pressure and persuasion that border on brainwashing. Leaving the group brings negative pressures to bear, along with psychological or even physical consequences. There may be initiations, oaths, and swearing of allegiances. The leader is charismatic, persuasive, and surrounded by a personality cult. Sex is forbidden to members, but the leader is exempt from the rule.

The leader, rather than the teachings, becomes the focus of energy, gifts, money, favors, and adulation, and the mere mention of their name brings "oh's" and "ah's" rather than simple respect. The leader often claims a special relationship with some invisible entity on the 'other side' that has a special name. This 'higher' spirit or entity gives orders and direction regarding ordinary or bizarre affairs or future predictions of great disasters. These impress vulnerable and naïve potential followers who also get caught up by cult proselytizers and enthusiasts.

Followers of cults become so brainwashed that they sometimes have to be rescued and deprogrammed by specialized professionals. Even when the pretenses of a charismatic leader are exposed, many duped followers merely resort to denial in the face of the obvious. Such examples are now commonly documented on the Internet by research groups. (For example, a cult leader recommends risky investments; another 'channels' a teacher/guide "from the other side" who, for a hefty fee, gives a spurious reading about a person who does not even exist, etc.)

To ascend in a group's hierarchy costs sizable sums of money for each step, sometimes amounting to thousands of dollars. With each step goes a title, such as first degree, Adept; second degree, Teacher; third degree, Master, and so on. Some of these organizations are structured like multilevel marketing schemes with profits going to the topmost leaders.

The teachings and activities of the group violate basic spiritual precepts by claiming exclusivity and justifying actions based on gross misinterpretations, obscure teachings, or reliance on negative scriptures such as the Book of Revelations. The teachings themselves are often bizarre. Followers are coerced into beliefs and actions that are extreme to the point of lunacy, such as waiting out in the desert to be rescued by UFOs; mass suicide; releasing poisonous gas in a subway system; mutilation of self and others, such as drilling a hole in one's skull; amputation of genitals; bizarre blood sacrifices; reliance on imaginary extraterrestrials; killing nonbelievers (infidels); suicide bombings; sacrificing children and animals; calling upon astral entities; invoking demons; dabbling in the occult; committing unnatural acts; and turning over one's earnings to the organization (as differentiated from tithing or voluntary vows of poverty).

Devotees are exploited and controlled by abuse of their naïve trust and misplaced faith. "By their fruits one can know them." In contrast, that which is of God brings beauty, love, joy, forgiveness, compassion, peace, and freedom.

Q: **Some religions or branches of traditional religions sound almost like cults.**

A: That is an astute observation. Derivatives of religions play off of the glamour, stature, and name of the original founder but then splinter into cults and even become corrupt. To recognize this is easy because there is segmentation, hostile rivalry, and overt attempts at control (e.g., Islamic terrorism calibrates at 70). They are often described as "militant" or "fundamentalist."

The nonintegrous exploitation and perversion of spiritual truth is as old as religion itself as revealed by the following important but often overlooked quotation:

"But Israel had false prophets as well as true; and you likewise will have false teachers among you. . . . They will gain many adherents to their dissolute practices, through whom the true way will be brought into disrepute. In their greed for money, they will trade on your credulity with sheer fabrications." (2 Peter 2:1, 2.)

Q: **What does it mean to be a "Christian" or a "Buddhist"?**

A: Simply one who follows the original teachings of the founding master. Truth is always the same throughout history. No group has an exclusive or inside track. By analogy, who has an inside track with the sun or the sky?

A Christian follows the teachings of Jesus Christ, which are revealed in the New Testament (Jesus did not create the Book of Revelations). There is no conflict among the world's highest teachers, only among their latter-day exploiters over the centuries, such as the current cult-like usurpers of the label "Christian."

Throughout history, there have been all kinds of prophets with strange and unlikely messages that attract the gullible. There has been and still is a multitude of messiahs and prophets; however, they simply do not stand up to a simple test which reveals the error. Baptism is of the spirit; the water is just symbolic. Of what use are claims to exclusivity? There is not a single organization that has an exclusive possession of the truth.

In recent events, for instance, one can study the visit of Pope John II to meet with the representative of the Russian Orthodox Church. The purpose was to promote benign and peaceful tolerance of co-existing religious faiths. With research, we can find that the Pope's position at the time calibrates at 590; in other words, at the level of extremely high Unconditional Love. In classical spiritual language, then, the Pope was representing the heart. In other church matters, however, various political and authoritarian positions may calibrate well below 500 and represent the downside of institutionalism.

The spiritual seeker learns to observe and become aware without judgment. One position is not better than another but merely represents a different contextualization. (The position of the Catholic Church on clerical pedophilia calibrates at 165, whereas current Catholicism itself calibrates at 510.) Thus we cannot condemn a whole organization for the acts of its weakest or worst moments. Institutions are run by fallible humans.

Much reveals itself to those who have spiritual dedication and are committed to following the road to the highest truth. Discernment is often learned through sometimes painful lessons. In classical spiritual language, this is referred to as the opening of the "third eye." It could be said that the gray hairs of wisdom have been earned.

Q: **What is the fate of the honestly deceived, naïve spiritual seeker?**

A: Krishna said that those who are pure in their devotion and intention are equally loved by God. God has no given name; Divinity is not deceived. Those who truly long for God are embraced by that Infinite Presence which is beyond all religions.

Q: What about the personal appeal of a specific pathway?

A: That is an important factor. Although, at the very highest level, they are one and the same, some pathways emphasize devotion, worship, surrender, and good works (e.g., Mother Theresa). For many, the pathway of the heart is therefore the most natural, and the way of the mind seems to be too cold or abstract. The way of the mind harnesses love into devotion to the truth and its realization. With the relinquishment of positionalities, the way is opened for the followers of the path of mind to love that which before was seen as unlovable. The way of the heart transforms dualistic perception into spiritual vision, which again transcends the opposites. There is a dedicated and interesting spiritual group that combines both paths and calls itself, with tongue in cheek, "Zen Catholicism" (which calibrates at 550).

Q: What teachers of the various religions represent their highest teachings?

A: The so-called mystics of each of the world's great religions calibrate higher than the religions themselves and are generally in accord with each other. A mystic is merely one who has bypassed the mind in order to realize the pure truth. All the great avatars calibrate at or very near 1,000. At these levels, there are no arguments. Each teacher, however, had a different style and taught in a different period of history to a different culture and geographic group.

The Great Spirit of Chief Detroit (who calibrates at 720) reflects that Native American spirituality recognizes God Manifest, with Nature (i.e., Creation) as the demonstration of the Unmanifest becoming Manifest. This is reflected in the Native American reverence for Nature and all life (an understanding which is intellectually somewhat criticized theologically as "Pantheism").

The impact of Native American spirituality, as exhibited by Chief Detroit, had a profound effect on the founding fathers of the Constitution of the United States in that the Congress is almost an exact replica of the political structure of the Iroquois Nation.

In more recent times, that Native American spirituality has been weakened by politicians and resultant exploitation. In reality, the American Indian is greatly honored everywhere. Whole states, cities, rivers, mountains, and great lakes are named after them. The greatest sports teams, noted for courage and bravery, proudly carry their name; yet, the political distortion is to declare that such honors are really defamations and politically incorrect. How such glory could be misconstrued as an indignity is beyond comprehension, but it demonstrates how truth gets distorted into its opposite for political gain. If such a demagogue were successful, imagine that the name of every region, territory, mountain range, state, city, town, road, river, sport team, as well as American product names would have to be removed and replaced by some puny substitute.

Spirituality and truth unite; falsity begets factionalism and conflict. Like the demagogue, cultism actually denigrates the religious or spiritual tradition whose name it has plagiarized and exploited.

Q: What is a true messiah?

A: The term "messiah" is used in modern parlance to signify delusions of grandeur. The modern meaning of the term plays on an ambiguity. On one hand, the term gives recognition to the validity of a true messiah and, simultaneously, to its great rarity, the term then signifies that inasmuch as the high level of enlightenment of the messiah occurs so extremely rarely, its claims to that title are false and signify an imposter unless proven otherwise.

Over the centuries, society has seen an endless procession of many self-styled seers, prophets, and messiahs. In this century, a great majority of self-proclaimed messiahs are in institutions. Messianic delusions were common when the cerebral syphilis was prevalent and untreatable. Since the discovery of penicillin, the number of messiahs has greatly decreased, with the exception of aficionados of mind-altering drugs.

Most self-proclaimed messiahs are suffering from the manic phase of a bipolar (manic-depressive) mental disorder. Political leaders are the best known messianic personalities, and they can be mesmerizing with their grandiose egomania. The world is relatively sophisticated in determining spiritual delusions but still extremely blind to political ones.

A true messiah would calibrate at a very high level, at least over 700, and most likely in the high 800s or 900s. The true bringer of light is humble, sincere, and in no need of adulation. The only gift of the true seer is the exposition of truth. The avatar reflects that truth. Religion, however, tends to adulation of the messenger rather than the message. In fact, in the name of the messenger, the truth is often trampled into the dust or the blood of the battlefield.

The true messiah brings joy, hope, liberation, and salvation to all of mankind who follow the message and the power of the message. The messiah brings a new vision of truth and uplifts the consciousness level of all mankind by restating the context of Divinity as the Source of life everlasting. The avatar, the messiah, the enlightened sage, the savior, the Christ, or the Buddha are all reflections of Divinity. These windows of God radiate the power and compassion of God to encompass all mankind to reenergize its spiritual aliveness and bring new hope and joy. Thus, the true messiah, avatar, or great teacher brings forth a renewal of faith and peace for the future of all.

Q: **The various spiritual patriarchs (sages, buddhas, avatars) then become identified with a specific culture and become 'special', leading to factionalism and sectarian exclusivity. How can this be overcome?**

A: This factionalism is transcended as spiritual evolution progresses. The collective ego of mankind quite naturally tends to form exclusive organizations and focus on the irrelevant, thereby missing the core of the teaching. At certain levels, that is probably beneficial as it gives group support and authenticity. Whether one linguistically considers God to be called Rama, Brahma, or Allah is really irrelevant. God is not limited by any positionality or ascribable qualities and is not subject to the duality of either/or, which would have to be the basis of any favoritism.

Q: **All this is obvious to an advanced teacher but it is not a common teaching in Western religions of recent times.**

A: The primary reason for religious conflict and rivalry is that religion, which is linear, tends to emphasize God as transcendent rather than immanent. This has been the traditional source of conflict for the mystic whose nonlinear experience is the reality of God as Self. It is to be remembered, however, that this is an extremely rare phenomenon, and it is understandable that it is not familiar to the churches or great religions. The average person, including religionists, feels so separated from God that the possibility that God can be experientially known seems unbelievable.

There was a time when the Church viewed the realization of God Immanent as Self as heretical. Even today, there are religious sects that view the great avatars as 'possessed by demons'. Some even deny the divinity of the Christ-consciousness of Jesus. This is based on the ego's adherence to the duality of separation, that is, man is 'here' and God is 'up there'. The limited, false gods of these fanatical sects, however, make one go weak with kinesiology, which instantly reveals their falsity.

The cults that deify these non-gods also tend to be intense proselytizers with an aggressive sectarian agenda and a strong proclivity for separation and claims to exclusivity. Such zealous aggressiveness and fervor, therefore, are signs of spiritual irrationality and may surface as political factions in some societies. Because of politicalization, some tend to become militant religious zealots, which is not a sign of spirituality but of its subversion to egotism.

Q: How do these strange belief systems arise and promulgate?

A: Each person's ego can be calibrated as to its level of consciousness. Each level represents a strata or level analogous to the light spectrum. To people in the yellow range, everything looks yellow; in the blue range, everything seems blue. The human mind tends to dissociate from levels that are too unlike its own. This tends to fragment society into classes. Each class has its characteristic language, style, vernacular, customs, occupational standards, acceptable behaviors, and norms. There is a tendency to disparage the other classes or their styles or modes of behavior. There is also denial of the reality of other ways of thinking or proceeding. For instance, science views spirituality as irrational, wishful thinking.

There are people, for example, who have never emotionally experienced depression or anxiety so they cannot empathize with such emotions as being real. Although class distinction is supposedly un-American and politically incorrect, it is actually one of the first things that people notice about each other. Thus, choice of religion often results in people with very similar world views who look at their level as the only reality.

Q: **With all the information that has been supplied, would a spiritual seeker be safe?**

A: If it is followed, that would be true. It is not a person who is the teacher but the Self of the teacher. By analogy, it is not the lighthouse which guides the ships but the light shining from the lighthouse. One is free to pursue the light, or not. Neither the light nor the lighthouse has any stake in the matter. Religions tend to deify the lighthouse at the price of the light.

Mankind's consciousness evolves. The mariner of old had a precarious life and did the best he could by the reckoning of the stars. The compass, sextant, and now satellite positioning have made the way certain for the saving of innumerable lives. Similarly, the spiritual seeker of old had only hearsay to go by. The seeker of current times now has the equivalent of a compass or a sextant. The kinesiologic test of truth versus falsehood is the first discovery of its kind to guide the seeker toward the light. It is inherently capable of saving many spiritual lives.

Q: **What is due to the teacher?**

A: Nothing at all. The listener's interest is more than sufficient. The only obligation one should accept is the obligation to one's own self to institute the wisdoms that were learned and to practice them in order to transcend the ego. Respect the teacher but save reverence only for God.

Q: **How would one characterize or term the teaching and pathway that you represent?**

A: It is the way of the mystic, and represents "devotional nonduality."

Q: **May we use that term to denote these teachings?**

A: Yes, that would be correct. It is the way of radical truth.

CHAPTER TWO

SPIRITUAL INFORMATION AND PRACTICE

Q: Is all the information that has been provided necessary to know?

A: On a certain level, yes, it is—all of it and perhaps more. Paradoxically, if one sticks to basic essentials, none of it is needed. This information is intended for the traditional spiritual seeker who, throughout the centuries, becomes inspired and then proceeds to investigate, search, and put into practice the information obtained.

There is also the path of sudden enlightenment, which may occur in a seemingly spontaneous manner or as the result of meditation or some spiritual practice, or merely by being in the presence of an enlightened teacher.

Great leaps in consciousness result from surrendering oneself to God at great depth. This is seen in our society in people who have 'hit bottom'. Willfulness/pride surrenders and transformation occurs. From the pits of hell, paradoxically, heaven is close by. We see this in so-called conversions where a former 'sinner', such as a convict, is transformed into a peaceful, loving, and almost saintly person. Prisoners frequently go through major realizations and become transformed into the opposite of their former selves. These sudden revelations also occur concomitant with near-death experiences.

Thus, many levels of consciousness can be suddenly transcended. These are often preceded by long periods of inner agony. A true conversion is corroborated by a major jump in the calibrated level of consciousness.

When spiritually oriented people are exposed to the information that has been provided, they show a measurable elevation of consciousness. Before and after each lecture, the consciousness level of the audience is calibrated, and it generally shows an increase, on the average, of between ten and forty points for the audience as a whole. This may vary individually from a low of four points to as high as hundreds of points. Within the group, however, there is great variation due to 'karmic ripeness'.

The majority of spiritual seekers goes through a variety of stages that may range from despair to high joy or even ecstasy. There are also long periods where nothing seems to be happening and the person feels they are not getting anywhere. These are interspersed with periods of what seem like stagnation, frustration, self-blame, and even hopelessness.

All these periods within the overall process are normal. Perseverance and dedication carry one through. The way is easier if a true teacher or a dedicated group is available. The pathway of nonduality, which depends primarily on meditation and devotional dedication, takes perseverance and self-discipline to achieve the necessary 'one-pointedness of mind'. If a spiritual aspirant is devotional and aspires to God through selfless surrender, much can be bypassed without necessarily understanding its structure at all.

Unknown to the aspirant is the past karma which is also an influential factor. Therefore, one cannot compare oneself to others or expect some fortuitous suddenness such as that which occurred to the well-known teacher, Ramana Marharshi. While just an ordinary teenager, he suddenly fell down and felt himself dying. He then went into a state of oneness and silent bliss that calibrated at over 700. As a consequence, he was not able to speak for two years. If we research this story with kinesiologic testing, we learn that he had spent many previous lifetimes in spiritual endeavor, and his seemingly sudden enlightenment was actually the fruition in this lifetime of that effort and dedication.

Q: So, it is not necessary to know all this information?

A: If the core is adhered to, the answer is no. Primarily, what has been provided is explanation that makes the dissolution of thought and belief much easier. To simply know that pairs of opposites are merely artifacts of positionality with no inherent reality is really only one of the tools that are needed. To make that statement comprehensible, however, it is aided by explanation. Once the explanation is comprehended, it can be discarded. Likewise, through simple meditation, one can discover and know that the Self is the substratum and source of consciousness and awareness.

The amount of information required to facilitate one's spiritual evolution also depends on the level of consciousness of the seeker. Those in the 200s, 300s, and 500s frequently request little explanation. They have a profound faith in the truths revealed and proceed to apply them directly.

The average literate seeker, however, is in the 400s and usually requires a much more detailed explanation. The level of the 400s is a difficult one to transcend because logic, intellect, and reason have been heavily energized and now have a tenacious hold.

As was said previously, only approximately four percent of the population calibrates in the 500s or above. This is the level of transcending the world of form as reality to the nonlinear reality represented by the levels of 500 (Love) and above. At those levels, Love is a way of being in the world and with oneself and one's approach to God.

Q: What is an 'advanced' seeker?

A: The more advanced seeker has heard that there is no 'out
there' or 'in here' and thus takes responsibility for all that
happens. There is the dawning awareness that all which
seems to occur really represents what is being held in what
was previously considered as 'within'. Thus, the proclivity
to project is undone. The 'innocent victim' positionality,
with all its spurious 'innocence', is unmasked.

Adversity is thus seen to be the result of what had been
previously denied and repressed into the unconscious.
By looking within, one finds the source of adversity
where it can be addressed and corrected.

Beliefs are the determinant of what one experiences.
There are no external 'causes'. One discovers the secret
payoffs that are obtained from unconscious secret
projections. One's underlying programs can be discovered by simply writing down one's litany of grievances
and woes and then merely turning them around into
their opposites.

"People hate me" stems from one's own inner hatreds.
"People don't care about me" stems from one's narcissistic absorption with one's happiness and gain instead of
that of others. "I don't get enough love" stems from not
giving love to others. "People are rude to me" stems from
lack of cordiality to others. "People are jealous of me"
arises from inner jealousy of others. Thus, if we take
responsibility for being the author of our world, we
come close to its source where we can correct it. By being
loving towards others, we discover that we are surrounded by love and lovingness. When we unreservedly
support life without expecting gain, life supports us in
return. When we abandon gain as a motive, life responds
with unexpected generosity. When we perceive in this
way, the miraculous begins to appear in the life of every
dedicated spiritual aspirant. Harmony manifests as the
unexpected discovery, the fortuitous coincidence, and
the lucky break, and finally the realization occurs that

these are the ripples coming back to oneself from the seat of consciousness.

Q: What then of simplicity?

A: To have faith in a proven teacher or pathway and to be devoted to God allows for simplicity to be sufficient. To unquestioningly follow any simple, basic spiritual truth will unravel the obstacles.

To sincerely dedicate oneself to be a servant of the Lord and ask what is His will is sufficient. The answers reveal themselves without necessarily even having to be formulated. To be 'spiritual' simply means an intention. If one is unclear about a decision or direction, one can always use kinesiologic testing for clarification. When seen for what it is, kinesiology testing is really a great gift.

Q: What if I am not adept at kinesiology or have no partner?

A: Kinesiology is in widespread use, especially among holistic practitioners of many disciplines and helping professions. There are also many organizations that keep rosters of practitioners and their diverse backgrounds. Additionally, there are numerous books on the subject and a mass of information on the Internet under "kinesiology." (See Suggested Reading/Viewing.)

Some people are able to test by themselves using the "O" of the thumb and finger of one hand and then testing the strength of resistance to opening the ring by pulling against it with the forefinger of the other hand while resisting. Holding a true statement in mind makes the "O" ring difficult to pull apart. "Not true" makes the ring weak and easily separated.

On the Map of the Scale of Consciousness, one can identify the approximate level of any attitude or emotion since they are described rather verbatim. The purpose of the levels is to provide some direction and context for understanding the nature of consciousness.

One can, by inner honesty, pretty well estimate one's own level of consciousness by identifying one's prevailing attitudes and positionalities. Thus, if we are always angry or seeing injustices, then anger/pride would be a fair level to identify with at this time. This level is easily undone by a willingness to abandon judgmentalism and see that it is merely a positionality of the mind. A quip that represents this level is "It's not fair that God loves everybody." It would seem to judgmentalism that good people were more deserving.

Q: Is there such a thing as 'spiritually deserving'?

A: Justice is inherent in the universe as a quality of its essence. Nothing escapes detection within the all-encompassing, timeless, infinite field of consciousness. Consequences are automatic, spontaneous, and guaranteed by the very structure of Creation. Everyone is at some point along the learning curve of the evolution of consciousness, and each level has its inherent characteristics. These characteristics are innate to the field of consciousness and not actually personal or arbitrary. They are not 'given' or 'taken away'.

The soul is the author of its own fate by the exercise of its own choice and selection. Each gravitates to its own concordant dimension. Spiritual paradoxes may appear in response to spiritual choice; for example, the spiritual seeker wants love and joy but that intention triggers the surfacing of all that obstructs it and prevents its appearance. Those who dedicate themselves to peace and love automatically pull up from the unconscious all that is cruel, unloving, and hateful to be healed. This may bring about consternation until judgmentalism about it is replaced with compassion, and forgiveness take its place. These were, after all, what had obstructed the love and joy, so one can be thankful that these deterrents have been brought up to be resolved by the spiritual tools available.

This process of spirituality, in which one works through the obstacles, may seem painful at times but it is only transitional. The mistakes now reappear but are resolvable and recontextualized from a higher understanding. This process is shortened and less painful if it is realized that habitual responses are not truly personal but are part and parcel of the inheritance of being human. All that we condemn within ourselves reveals itself in almost any television documentary about animal life. We see its origin, we see the lovability of the animals in their naïveté, and then we realize that these same motives arise in us from the same level of naïveté. When one accepts the structure and content of thought patterns along with their origins, one can see that it is predictable.

In reality, nothing thoughts say about oneself or others have any reality. All statements are fallacious and represent programming and positionalities. There are also positive statements about one's worth, merit, or value that are equally based on fiction. The true Self is invisible and has no characteristics by which it can be judged. It has no describable qualities nor can it be the subject of any adjectives at all. The Self merely 'is' and is beyond verbs, adverbs, and adjectives. It does not even 'do' anything.

Q: But does not the calibrated Scale of Consciousness imply value judgment or merit? Thus, is not the level of 500 better than 400?

A: The Scale does not denote 'better than', which is a program of the ego. The Scale merely denotes position or location which in turn denotes associated characteristics. A large tree is not 'better than' a small tree. Thus, the consciousness level denotes a locus on a learning curve and a stage of the evolution of consciousness. The joy of life comes from filling one potentiality at any given level. Each level has its rewards, and they actually feel the same to each person.

Goal fulfillment is self-rewarding if the goal of the aspirant is one of direction. Then a life dedicated to God is endlessly self-fulfilling, whereas, in contrast, a life devoted to gain is full of pitfalls and suffering.

Human consciousness has advanced very slowly through history. It will now probably speed up and spirituality will prevail more commonly. Even the world of business will discover that the inclusion of spiritual values is very profitable as reflected by a healthier bottom line.

Prosperity is measured not only in dollars but also in the joy of participation. Spiritual values are nondenominational and merely an affirmation of the obvious; for example, we should protect our workers because we care for them, not because the failure to do so would be a violation and bring a fine from OSHA.

It is noted that many businesses and government bureaucracies tend to calibrate at 202. From this calibration, one might suspect that they have integrity primarily because they are forced to by law. Our institutions are not noted for their mercy and forgiveness, nor for graciousness. Many seem to run on the level of a grim functionality; they are characteristically humorless and tend to be overbearing in their attitudes toward their employees and the public. Impersonality seems to be the current style; for example, an automated voice machine responds to a call to an 800 number, not with a warm "hello," but with a flat, disappointing, letdown message. The world of business needs human warmth, human presence, cordiality, and caring. It seems strange that multimillion-dollar businesses cannot afford a ten-dollar-per-hour telephone receptionist.

Historically, mankind has become painfully wary of theocracy and the invoking of the gods of religion in either the government or the marketplace. The United States Constitution, however, is quite sophisticated in that it clearly discerns between spirituality which, in simple language, merely constitutes all the known human virtues, and religion, which is sectarian and therefore undemocratic. Paradoxically, freedom 'from' religion allows for freedom 'of' religion.

If spiritual virtues are not labeled as such, they can be welcomed into all levels of society without fear and with obvious benefit. So long as Divinity remains anonymous, God can quietly sneak in the back door of societal life, its institutions, and great corporations. When this occurs, it brings about a recontextualization, with a depolarization and decrease in enmity between these polarized factions. Thus, it can be seen that despite their being demonized, the great corporations provide the very basis for our daily living as well as occupations for multitudes and incomes that support the entire social structure. Kindheartedness and concern for others and their welfare is the best business practice there is.

Q: What aspect of consciousness should be 'trained' to take the pathway of mind?

A: Intentionality perfected as one-pointedness of mind. This is the capacity for concentration and an unwavering fixity of focus. This capacity is volitional and the result of a decision and is therefore quite different from religious obsession or scrupulosity.

To effect this quality requires intense motivation and devotion which then become focused. It represents a total commitment to a task and its relentless pursuit. This acquired faculty can then be used in both the practice of formal meditation as well as in daily life.

To focus on a specific subject while attending to daily life is generally called contemplation. This can be done in two different ways, depending on circumstances or current life situations. An accomplished aspirant can switch back and forth as the life situation requires. The two methods differ primarily in their focus, with one being focused on context and the other on content.

The first practice is an unfocused, contemplative style in which the shift of focus is from central vision to peripheral vision. In this practice, one remains consistently aware of the totality of one's surroundings, with no focus, interest, or selection on anything in particular. This method is not suitable, at least in the beginning, for situations that require one's presence and participation, such as driving. Later it can be used almost constantly. By staying fixedly in the peripheral field of vision with no favoritism or rejection of what is seen or heard, detachment evolves. Suddenly, one is aware of the totality and the oneness of all that exists, and that each element is the perfect expression of its own essence. It emerges that everything proceeds with perfect serenity and total harmony.

In this exercise, the intention and focus are on the peripheral vision only and not on any thoughts or judgments about what is seen. After a period of time, one suddenly becomes the witness and then becomes awareness itself, which is functioning spontaneously and impersonally, with no 'you' even involved. Witnessing removes the 'personal' illusion of awareness. One then transcends perception, which is replaced by spiritual vision. The exercise is effortless and reveals the unity of All That Exists as an integrated, harmonious perfection and beauty of grace. Everything moves spontaneously and nothing is causing anything else. It is the harmonious dance of the Universe.

There is another exercise which is equally rewarding but begins in the opposite direction, yet it is suitable for functioning in the demanding, everyday world. In this case, the practice is to unreservedly fixate on the central focus of vision so as to be one-hundred-percent focused on the current intended action. Thus, it is comparable to target practice. During this exercise, all thought begins to stop and intentionality is allowed full focus on detail. Although the focus may shift from one object to another as required by the activity involved, the quality of absolute attention and focus remains the same, (i.e., content). There can be no selection of 'this' or 'that' as being more important than the other. It is all the same, whether one is making a ten-thousand-dollar sale or merely peeling a potato. All activities are equally important.

There is to be no holding back with thought programs. As one digs a ditch, every single shovelful is equally important, and the commitment to the activity has to be absolute and total. In due time, the faculty of awareness takes over and, again, it is found to be impersonal. There is no 'you' doing anything. One is the witness of intentionality's focusing on its own, and everything is observed to be happening of itself. All action becomes spontaneous and eventually effortless.

Either method reveals the Reality that stands behind form. The body stops being thought of as 'me' and becomes just another object in the picture. This awareness also frequently occurs spontaneously in sports or with such efforts as jogging. When one breaks through the barrier of limiting belief, the activity suddenly becomes effortless and occurs on its own. It can also happen with manual labor. When one lets go of the resistance, one can go on effortlessly, even while other workers drop out due to exhaustion. Once this barrier and how to overcome it have been discovered, it can be applied to any situation.

In this lifetime, this discovery was made while still a teenager working in a 110-degree warehouse, stacking very heavy cartons. After about twelve hours, the "I can't" barrier came up, but then a sudden inspiration flowed in, and with an absolute, unreserved resolve, there was the gritting of teeth and the absolute refusal of the barrier which was then broken. Almost instantly and amazingly, the boxes became nearly as light as a feather, and the activity was joyful and devoid of effort.

In another situation, the core of the Zen of martial arts revealed itself in a henhouse. Karate classes with a very able teacher had been attended for some time, and although the exercises were learned, the essential core, which was to be discovered, was still missing. The whole discipline of the martial arts really seemed to be a meditation, but the essential realization had not revealed itself. It became obvious that this pathway could take many years of practice, so the lessons were abandoned and karate practice was stopped.

Several years later, there was the necessity to enter a crowded henhouse and capture a specific ailing chicken that needed medical help. Upon entry, the chickens panicked and flew all around in wild hysteria. The air was full of flying chickens, dust, and loud squawking. The target chicken was cleverly elusive and almost impossible to catch or isolate from the flock. Suddenly, absolute intention arose as focus. The personal 'I' disappeared and, like a target in a telescopic gun sight, vision itself saw only the target of the chicken. All resistance disappeared and into the clear space, action exploded with absolute precision and the chicken was powerfully seized.

The secret of the martial arts had revealed itself spontaneously and with great clarity. The time delay of mentation was absent, and the intention was instantaneous in its delivery. This discovery might be called the Zen of daily life, and this one-pointedness of mind becomes perfected.

A number of such techniques are well known and constitute an important aspect of many spiritual schools. When the breakthrough occurs, it is sometimes called "satori," which can be either transient or prevail as a permanent, enlightened state. In either case, the experience is never forgotten.

Anyone can successfully meditate without the need to join a spiritual organization, with its formalities. The same two techniques are applicable to meditative practice.

The first is like the practice of peripheral vision. There is no central focus, and instead, attention is given to the prevailing state and overall conditions, with no selectivity. There is no goal to be achieved. All programs, such as 'reaching satori', are abandoned. There is, in essence, an abandonment to the mere 'is-ness' of All That Is, without mentation. The revelation that eventually occurs reveals the Allness of God, which unfolds as the awareness of consciousness as an innate aspect of the Self.

In contrast, there is a practice which is analogous to central or macular vision focus. Instead of trying to avoid mentation and the content of mental functioning, paradoxically, one maintains an absolute, intense, focused concentration on the content and the specificity of its form. This is more like the Zen of catching chickens. There is the absolute exclusion of everything except the very pinpoint of focus. Whereas, in traditional meditation practice thoughts are ignored, in this practice they are chosen to be concentrated upon and not resisted. A separation between awareness/observer and that which is observed eventually dissolves. It is discovered that there is no 'you' that is absorbed in the formal concentration; therefore, the witness is that which is witnessing; both are the same. Both practices result in transcending duality and dissolving the illusory separation between subject and object. Thus the Oneness of Reality stands revealed.

The practice of either focused or peripheral awareness in daily life or informal meditation bypasses the mental content and belief systems. There are meditation centers that refuse any descriptive labels, such as Buddhist or Christian. One merely attends and meditates. The truth that reveals itself is universal and beyond all labels. All naming sets up expectations which then become limitations, barriers, and illusory goals to be achieved or gained. To set a goal for meditation is like setting up a goal to 'be what you are' or 'try harder to relax'. (One can then see the value of the traditional Zen koan.)

Q: **Is spiritual advancement then possible by bypassing all information and merely doing the spiritual practices described?**

A: That is so. Blind faith, the truth of a teaching, and the integrity of the teacher, plus dedication and adherence to a simple practice, are all that are required. While some students have this capacity for faith and trust and proceed rapidly, more commonly, a spiritual seeker has already read widely and has had experience with a variety of spiritual groups and seminars. As a result, they have many questions and requirements for information to resolve issues. Many spiritual seekers are quite erudite and have accumulated a vast amount of spiritual education from a great variety of sources and are hoping for a reconciliation of all the diverse data. What they are really looking for is the inner experience of the reality of that which they have learned which has thus far been elusive.

Some seekers have 'been everywhere, heard everything, and visited everybody' but are still dissatisfied as the hoped-for spiritual realization has not as yet occurred. Some lament this and feel dejected, thinking they are hopeless. These seekers need their diverse information recontextualized so that it serves them rather than becoming an overwhelming morass of interesting but, so far, ineffective data. This usually means that the seeker has accumulated the data within the intellect but it has not yet ripened into subjective experience.

The basic structure of the ego still remains intact, although its content has become refined. The dismay of this group of unfulfilled seekers is based upon the training in our society that to achieve a goal, one merely has to study harder. With the realization that the intellect is no longer a useful tool but now the barrier, the seeker arrives at the ripeness which is necessary for the more focused paths to God by transcending the mind, either via the heart or via the pathway of consciousness.

A frequent problem of the relentless spiritual seeker is that they have not had the personal presence of a teacher with a high enough level of consciousness, that is, one whose aura has the power to catalyze the transformation of information into subjective awareness/experience. A truly enlightened teacher provides, via the aura, a high-energy context that illuminates and activates the student's content from the mental body into the higher spiritual bodies. The light of the teacher's illumination provides the necessary activation by the power of Grace to facilitate the transformation from intellectual data to subjective personal experience. The high energy frequency of a teacher's aura acts like a carrier wave that transmits capacity to the student's aura.

It is really simple to do both pathways simultaneously, that is, the way of the heart and the 'way of the mind'. One starts with the technique of either central, intense focus or peripheral focus, as described above, and applies it in everyday life and in meditative practice. In addition, however, one adds the pathway of the heart by making a decision to be unconditionally loving to all that is encountered with either focus. This means one has to learn to love even a garbage can.

When seen correctly, garbage cans are not only lovable but beautiful and perfect. All blocks to love surface to be removed. The mind has to be trained so that it realizes that the only reason it sees the old garbage can as repulsive is because of its innate programming.

As one meditates on the garbage can, one will realize that in Reality, there is no such thing as 'garbage'. Instead, one sees that there is a watermelon rind, and while it was on the table, it was called food. Now, when exposed there in the garbage can, it has suddenly, mysteriously, somehow changed its name to "garbage." Actually, it is still just a watermelon rind. Next to the innocent watermelon rind is a broken egg shell. No matter what you call it, it is still merely an innocent, broken egg shell.

Next to it is a nice plastic wrapper that has been subsequently ripped open and crumpled, but innately, it is still just a nice, handy piece of plastic. Now, if they are all grouped together and placed in a can, suddenly they are rejected with the epithet of being 'just garbage'.

If the inner intention is to see the lovability of all things, it then emerges that all that exists has its own integrity and identity and that all equally deserve to be honored for their service to mankind. The watermelon represents the work of horticulture. Its growth and delivery provide income. The need for eggs means that chickens live and have created another whole industry. We learn that the letting go of positionalities allows us to see the value of all that exists and its lovability in all its expressions. Whether the mouse that runs up the side of the garbage can is viewed as adorable or repulsive depends on the observer.

An easier and faster exercise than the 'garbage-can Zen' is 'Kleenex Zen'. If we focus beyond its 'Kleenex-ness', we see the beauty and grace of the form of the next tissue projecting from the box. It begins to look like an elegant sculpture, not unlike an exquisite wing or the ripple of an ocean wave.

When the beauty and lovableness of the beat-up old garbage can reveals itself, the spiritual seeker can affirm that they are well along the way. The beautiful dance of the Kleenex is the beckoning of the truth of God to proceed further as one is getting close to the goal.

Q: **Please clarify the terms "content" and "context" and their relationship.**

A: This is a critical question and one that leads to the very core of the doorways to truth. These are arbitrary but very important terms that really denote a point of view and are useful until they are transcended.

Content is an arbitrary point of focus as is the amount of data or form that is included. Context is the totality of all that which is excluded, with implied or specified boundaries, or even with none at all, such as God or the entire universe.

For example, one could select a specific star (star "A"). Then the rest of the galaxy or the entire firmament, including its evolution over time, becomes the context which also includes the observer. If another star is then selected for observation (star "B"), then star "A" becomes included in the total context of star "B." Thus, content and context are not separate distinctions nor are they intrinsic qualities but instead reflect the consciousness of the observer.

Thus the terms "linear" and "nonlinear" are categories of thought and points of intellectual reference. Form includes the formless as its substrate and is not separate from it. Consciousness as such is equally present but the information registered by awareness would be a consequence of focus.

In the transcendent state, all is continuous and nominalization or denotation are of appearance only as nothing is actually separate. All is self-evident and self-effulgent, which cannot be adequately described in language. The "Dance of Shiva" is experiential and not conceptual.

In the ordinary state of consciousness, the 'I' of the ego/self/me is content, whereas consciousness/awareness/God/Self is context. Unstated context often has more influence over the outcome than does visible content.

CHAPTER THREE

SPIRITUAL PURIFICATION

T he core of the three great pathways of 'heart', 'mind', and 'action' is the process of surrender. This is activated by intention and the attitude of willingness. Progressively, each thought, feeling, impulse, idea, or belief is recognized and then released and surrendered to God. Each is an illusion, a program, a symbol, and an impediment to the clarity of the unobstructed awareness of the Self.

Every concept, idea, image, memory or fantasy is the product of perception. All these impediments have labels that indicate judgmentalism and a positionality (e.g., acceptable versus unacceptable, true versus false, desirable versus objectionable, or good versus bad). These represent endless series of interlocking meanings and nuances of unending complexity, for they feed back into interconnecting, continuous loops that propagate further loops.

This endless stream of mental content is propagated from an underlying source that can be located and identified. Unless this font of unending babble is de-energized, it has the unbidden function of the endless proliferation of data and the obfuscation of its source and purpose. The spiritual seeker is drowned in the overwhelm and dismayed at the spectacle of undoing this endless kaleidoscope of content.

By examining the overall content of consciousness, it becomes apparent that spiritual purification of this voluminous, ever expanding, and ongoing phantasmagoria of content is impossible. Across the screen of consciousness appears an endless array of mental and emotional products that are embellished by memories and imaginings. All these are the linear, dualistic products of perception and positionalities.

It is clear that addressing the content of thinkingness would lead only to greater confusion, and the very process of doing so would automatically create the production of further content. Fortunately, there is another solution to the undoing of the dominance of the ego/mind/self, which is the identification of context rather than content.

The first illusion to surrender is the belief that there is such a thing as "mind." Experientially, one can only state that thoughts, feelings, images, and memories come into one's awareness in an endless progression. The word "mind" is therefore only a concept, as is the word "ego."

"Ego" as used hereafter generally refers to a collection of thoughts that are presumed to be representative of one's personal reality and identity, with a shading of implication that the grouping of thoughts and beliefs is purposeful. The purpose is to maintain the illusion of the personal self as the inner 'cause' of one's existence and activities, including thoughts and feelings. Again, the implication of 'ego' is that it is the self-protective collection and structure of the thought processes and is thus blamed as the culprit and source of spiritual error.

An important element of meaning of the term "ego" is the implication that its true basis is pride and narcissism, which bring in guilt about the implied selfishness of the ego. Ego is also a psychological term that generally has an implied survival value. In therapy, a patient may have the problem of a 'weak' ego and low self-esteem. In contrast, "egotism" or "egotistic" means overinflation or even grandiosity.

In spiritual parlance, "ego" implies a negative quality, an obstacle to realization because of its linear dualistic construction. In psychology, however, the term denotes coping and survival skills needed to deal effectively with the world.

Structure of the Ego

The positionalities are structures that set the entire thinking mechanisms in motion and activate its content.

Primordial Positionalities

1. Ideas have significance and importance.
2. There is a dividing line between opposites.
3. There is value of authorship—thoughts are valuable because they are 'mine'.
4. Thinking is necessary for control, and survival depends on control.

Assumptions

Thoughts are valuable because they represent 'me'. They are valuable because they have been thought by my mind. Thoughts have value because they bring rewards and expectations. Thoughts solve problems. Thoughts are entertaining and 'something to do'. Thoughts keep one occupied and feeling useful. They are necessary to make plans and achieve goals. Thoughts protect and support survival.

The context of the mental function is therefore based on two important premises: (1) Its products are valuable because they have meaning and value and, (2) its contents are necessary for survival, and the ego promises that its products will bring happiness. Thus, the Achilles' heels of the ego are vanity (being the author) because it is what ensures survival and brings happiness, and the need to 'know', with the promise of solutions.

The Process of Surrender

Spiritual seekers know that the core of all pathways to God is surrender, but to what and how are not clear. Without a decisive technique, many seekers spend years surrendering on content and complain that they are no farther along than before. The mind goes right on with its endless production and, therefore, one cannot surrender content as fast as it is produced; it is a losing game.

Next, one hears that it is not the content but attachments to the content that is the problem. This brings some relief but also brings the next question: How does one let go of attachments?

It is necessary to examine the nature of an attachment. It is based on a belief and a desire. The belief is that a mental content will bring happiness and solve problems; therefore, the attachment is to the implied promise that it is the thinking itself that is the road to happiness (wealth, success, love, etc.).

To let go of the thinking therefore seems frightening because it is also seen as the main tool of survival; plus, it is 'me'. As 'me', it is viewed as unique, personal, and precious, and it constitutes the main data base of identification of 'who I am'.

The fear of the loss of self-identity brings up resistance. As we get closer to the discovery of the source of the ego's tenacity, we make the amazing critical discovery that *we are enamored with our self.*

Even if thoughts are loaded with pain and failure and have been a disaster and source of suffering, we still cling to them because 'they are who I am', resulting in a love/hate relationship with them. To ensure its survival, the self also learned how to 'juice' satisfaction and energy from the negative emotional states. It thrives on injustice, martyrdom, failure, and guilt. The ego secretly 'loves' and clings to the position of victimhood and extracts a distorted pleasure and grim justification from pain and suffering. This can be seen in many cases as an addiction and a lifestyle. The 'loser' is an almost romanticized figure in music and folklore (e.g., Mr. Bojangles, the 'bag lady', the 'down and outer,' the rejected lover, etc.).

All along we have been 'in love' with our thoughts and we cherish them. We defend and make excuses for them. We are jealous of our beliefs. We prize them and alternately despise and punish ourselves with guilt and self-hatred. Altogether, however, it is an infatuation. The self-image gets glamorized because it is the stage upon which the drama of our life parades. To let go of what is loved brings up fear of loss. To the self, all love objects are seen as a source of happiness.

The next core problem is the difficulty of letting go of emotional love—not because of the love itself but because of the attachment to that which is loved. We think that the loss of a love object brings grief, but actually, the grief is about the loss of the attachment itself, which is due to viewing the object of love as the source of happiness. Grief is due to the illusion that one has lost a source of happiness, and that the source of happiness is 'out there'.

If one looks at the feeling of happiness, it becomes clear that it is actually located within, although the trigger may appear to come from outside oneself; the sensation, however, is totally an inner feeling of pleasure. The source of happiness is therefore actually within and is released under favorable circumstances when the mind experiences a desired outcome. By inner examination, one will discover that the event merely triggers an inner innate capacity. With the discovery that the source of happiness is actually within one's inner self and therefore cannot be lost, there is a reduction of fear.

Viewed from Reality, thoughts are actually an 'out there'. Although it may sound amazing, they can be totally dispensed with because they interfere with the achievement of true happiness.

The Critical Issue

Without undue effort, it is relatively easy to make the amazing discovery that one is attached to thinkingness because of being secretly in love with it. Because of being in love with the self, it is held in high esteem. There is fear of its loss due to the attachment that goes along with what is loved.

The next step is to discover what or who is in love with itself and when this primordial phenomenon arises. 'Something' is in love with our existence and attached to that existence, and it is noted that the ego (mind/body/self) is a love object. There is a subject and an object. There is a 'this' ('I') that is in love with a 'that' (the self, i.e., narcissism).

With contemplation, reflection, and meditation, the core of one's identifications progressively surfaces. It will be found that the true love for the self arises from something that is greater than the self and capable of totally encompassing the entirety of that self. The totality of the self is held within a larger underlying nonlinear field of awareness that is always present. It represents context rather than content. By analogy, it would be like looking at the planet Earth from outer space, where space is the context and Earth is the content.

To look within for the actual source of love leads to the discovery of the Self. Like the sun, the Self is ever present, unconditional, and not subject to thought, opinion, or attitude. The Self can only love because that is its essence. The love of the Self is not earned, deserved, or subject to limitation. The Self is the source of life and the subjective awareness of existence.

Later, it is discovered that even existence is unnecessary to the Self. It is beyond all dualities; there is no duality between the Self and existence. The Unmanifest and Manifest are one and the same. Consciousness may include content or it may not. By analogy, space is not dependent on the presence of planets or universes, yet it includes all of them.

Love is beyond duality; it does not need a subject or an object. It is a quality of Reality which is independent of circumstances.

With surrender, obstructions are dissolved by the infinite compassion of Divinity which unconditionally loves all that exists for that existence is the manifestation of God. Only illusions could make this obvious truth not apparent.

Enlightenment is merely the emergence of truth when the obstructions to the realization of that truth have been removed. By analogy, the shining of the sun is not conditional upon the removal of the clouds; it merely becomes apparent.

Q: This presentation brought about some inner, subtle change, like a release from some limitation. We calibrated the information at 998. With no disrespect intended, what accounts for that limitation?

A: That is a subtle discernment. The 'error' is that in the presentation, it sounds like love is dependent on existence. In Reality, love is independent of existence and does not need fulfillment; it is complete and total within itself.

Q: That clarifies that love as love is the complete expression of that which it is and that there is no additional requirement for an object. With that answer and clarification, the calibrated level of the information moves up to 999.9.

A: Self-identity is not an easy concept to comprehend. It is actually a subjective realization that cannot be adequately verbalized because of the inherent structure of languaging. One has to bypass the intransitive verbs of "is," "be," "existing," "doing," "acting", etc., as well as the structure of subject, predicate, and pronouns.

Q: If mentation is bypassed, how does information arise in consciousness?

A: Spiritual realizations arise spontaneously and not as a consequence of thought processes. They arise in awareness as though coming out of intuition. It is a nonlinear process through which one suddenly becomes aware that they just 'know'. The naïve person says "But how do you know that you know?" In experience, it just becomes apparent; it 'dawns on you'. Truth arises out of subjectivity and is obvious and self-revealing. This very often occurs when one is occupied with something totally unrelated. It 'comes out of nowhere' as a gift, a given. It is like the answer to an unspoken question. It is satisfying, solves an underlying puzzle, and is freeing in its effect on the psyche. It is effortless. If in doubt, its level of truth can be calibrated.

Q: What makes thinking so tenacious?

A: All mental content represents attachments, and underlying are the attachment to the self and the clinging to what is believed to be the source of survival as well as happiness. It is also one's identification. In reality, the source of happiness is the Self, and not the self.

Q: How does one actually process the content of thought?

A: First, experientially verify that one is in love with the thinkingness/self and that spiritual work is essentially the letting go of attachments to thoughts and cherished positionalities, opinions, and memories, the value of which has been inflated and over-esteemed by narcissistic identification. The core of the 'ego' is narcissism.

Second, discern the source of the love for the self. Third, be willing to surrender the objects of the love of thought, and worship God instead of the self. Fourth, become willing to surrender all attachments to the contents of the 'mind'.

Q: Is there a simple, workable technique?

A: As thought arises, it will be noted that it arises out of a primordial, silent blankness and void. It then takes form and is given an energy charge. This is associated with being emotionally reinforced over time. These recurrent opinions have come to be believed to be basic truths. Consequently, they influence and determine character traits and attitudes that trigger emotional responses which can escalate to severe degrees, as is demonstrated by the zealot. The severity of these attachments can lead to suicide, homicide, war, and physical death.

Although these basic positions are challenging to release, the spiritual payoff is very rewarding. Many of these positions were taught during childhood, so they derive authority from their parental origination and reinforcement by society. Some of these basic beliefs are magnified and become laws by which one lives. They then become identified with patriotism, religion, ethnic identity, gender, and social creeds. They come to be considered axiomatic and beyond question. To even bring them up for consideration results in defenses by the ego.

Some Basic Axiomatic Positionalities of the Ego

1. Phenomena are either good or bad, right or wrong, just or unjust, fair or unfair.
2. The 'bad' deserve to be punished and the 'good' rewarded.
3. Things happen by accident or else they are the fault of somebody else.
4. The mind is capable of comprehending and recognizing truth from falsehood.
5. The world causes and determines one's experiences.
6. Life is unfair because the innocent suffer while the wicked go unpunished.
7. People can be different than they are.
8. It is critical and necessary to be right.
9. It is critical and necessary to win.
10. Wrongs must be righted.
11. Righteousness must prevail.
12. Perceptions represent reality.

To address these types of issues, it is helpful to recall that one's only obligation is to the Truth of the Self and Divinity. This process, therefore, demands letting go of all cherished positionalities because nothing one believes is true. Actually, axioms are illusions that create suffering and result in much destruction. These 'axioms' are barriers to enlightenment and create a multitude of dualities because they arise from linear perception rather than nondualistic spiritual Reality.

From the viewpoint of Reality, not a single one of these supposed axioms contains any truth, and even if it did, it would be irrelevant. All these cherished beliefs are, at best, wishful childish notions of a make-believe world. Absolute justice is intrinsic to creation but invisible to human perception for it is the consequence of omniscience. The willingness to surrender these axiomatic propositions as well as the fate of the world to God eventually results in a clarity of spiritual vision that resolves all questions and illusions.

One of the most difficult propositions stems from the recurrent problem of the polarity of the 'duality of the opposites'. Perhaps a simple illustration will assist in the resolution of this recurrent paradox for the paradox of the opposites results in a constant either/or-ness which makes them sound as though they are alternate and distinctly separate realities or possibilities.

Actually, the opposites are not opposite at all but are merely linear gradations along the same line and not along different lines.

Example 1	Example 2
Degrees Fahrenheit	**Value**
— 3,000	— Precious
— 2,000	— Valuable
— 1,000	— Worthwhile
— 500	— Asset
— 100	— A+
— 50	— Neutral
— 0	— Unattractive
— -50	— Hindrance
— -100	— Awful
— -200	— Ugly
— etc.	— Repulsive

By examination, one can see that these are merely varying degrees of the presence of heat (Example 1) and desirability (Example 2) or their absence. One will note that there are actually no 'opposites' of hot versus cold or precious versus worthless. All are, in fact, merely along the same line and not on two different lines of gradation.

We can cite other examples:

Example 3	Example 4
Goodness	**Light**
— Heavenly	— Blindingly Bright
— Very Good	— Very Bright Light
— Good	— Bright
— Pleasant	— Very Strong Light
— 'Okay'	— Light
— Sort of 'Okay'	— Subdued Light
— Fair to Middling	— Dim
— Not Too Good	— Dusk
— Unsatisfactory	— Dark
— Bad	— "Pitch Black"
— Wicked	
— Horrible	
— Ghastly	
— Horrific	

The gradations are all on the same continuum, not on two opposing ones. There is merely one continuous quality track. One will see that there is no 'good' that is the opposite of 'bad'. The scale on the left indicates the presence or absence of Love and is therefore only about Love, just as the scale on the right indicates degrees of light and not opposites of light versus darkness.

Apparent 'facts' are illusions of truth, and it is obvious to see that such denotation actually depends totally on context. On an absolute level, total context would include comprehension of every contribution to an event throughout eternity, plus an equal knowledge of all karmic history of everything and everyone involved. This accounts for the spiritual declarations of "Judge not" and "'Judgment is mine,' sayeth the Lord." It isn't that the ego is incorrect, it is just incapable of arriving at an accurate comprehension of any seeming event.

There is a peaceful relief when judgment and criticism are abandoned because they cause constant unconscious guilt as well as fear of retribution. The self lives in fear of the very punishments and sentences that it metes out to others because, in so doing, it sets up retaliatory fears. The person, therefore, fears death, Judgment Day, and a God that is harsh and subject to one's own illusions.

Q: What of just ordinary thought?

A: Observation reveals that feelings and thoughts rise and fall away like a musical note. If focus is rigorously directed to this exact instant, a thought will be seen to arise out of a rather vague, primordial matrix. As it begins to rise, it is relatively unformed, like the swell of an approaching wave. Then the vague and as yet ill-formed primordial thought begins to take form and attract energy until if finally crests in full form where it attracts commentary, agreement and disagreement, associated meanings, and memories. Now it is in full force, with associated emotion giving it momentum. No sooner does it crest than it begins to decline and gradually lose definition and form, fading into the past.

If the focus of the sense of 'me' is on the rising crest, the person never lives in reality but is constantly poised with the expectation of control of the next instant. They are therefore constantly concerned with the future. If the focus is on the back of the falling wave, then the 'me' tends to cling to the past and editorializing. With some practice, the focus can be precisely narrowed to only the breaking crest of the wave, for in that instant, there is neither past nor future and neither regret for the past nor longing for nor anticipation of the future. Everything is witnessed to be as it is. With no editorializing or anticipation, even the illusion of 'now' disappears. Reality is actually 'always' and continuous, with no 'now' or 'then'.

Surrender is a constant process of not resisting or clinging to the moment but instead, continuously turning it over to God. The attention is thus focused on the process of letting go and not on the content of the 'what' that is being surrendered.

When this precise practice of surrender is followed, the illusion of 'rising and falling away' disappears as does the illusion of time. The ego experiences the sequence of the focus of perception which then is ascribed to time or change or being in the 'now'. There is no Reality such as 'now'.

Perception is linear, local, and limited to a fixed point of view or experiencing; therefore, from a single point of observation, there seems to be a 'here' or a 'there', a 'this' or a 'that', a 'past' or a 'future', a 'now' or a 'then', and space with dimensions and time elapses. It is important to note that 'elapse' connotes duration as well as starting and stopping points, which are obviously arbitrary.

If one could imagine what it must be like to be omni-present, the observer would then be simultaneously witnessing from every minute position in the Totality. Every point of observation would therefore be experienced as 'here'. It can be quickly seen that 'here' would then quickly become 'everywhere', and the thought of 'now' would disappear into infinity. Therefore, omni-science is the consciousness of the entire totality equally in which the world would be no particular place. Nothing would be changing, nothing would be happening, and there would be no dimension, duration, beginning, or ending.

To make the understanding more profound, realize that the 'everywhere present, simultaneous observer' actually is all that is observing. There is neither subject nor object; consequently, the Presence is completely self-knowing because it is all that exists as the Totality of Manifestation.

Q: **If the ego/self/mind is eliminated as a point of reference, are all linear concepts meaningless?**

A: That is correct. To illustrate further, imagine that you are traveling out into space faster than the speed of light, past all universes, with no reference points. If asked "Where are you," the answer would be "Nowhere" for there is no 'where' to 'be'. With no parameters, consciousness could only know itself as consciousness, for without perception, no descriptions or differentiations are possible.

Q: **Would that be the Unmanifest?**

A: No, it would be the Unmanifest manifesting as consciousness only. Out of the Infinite Consciousness arises existence, and then existence as life. (Calibrated level 995.)

Q: **It sounds foolish to phrase the question, but 'when' did all this occur?**

A: The process is outside of time and eternally continuous. It goes on forever, and that is how it has always been. Creation is continuous, always and ongoing. The comings and goings of universes are an illusion of perception. There are no universes arising and passing away inasmuch as there is no such thing as time in which universes or anything else could phase in or out of existence. That is what is meant by the Oneness of Allness. This truth can be realized but not explained.

Q: **To comprehend the Infinite, does one have to have an Infinite consciousness?**

A: There is nothing to comprehend. That would imply a duality between the knower and the known. In Reality, they are identical. The Infinite knows by virtue of the fact that it is All.

For clarification, consciousness can be understood or described as having two layers or levels. The highest layer is infinite and beyond all illusions, such as change, temporality, or sequence. The layer below has the capacity for awareness and includes recording all that transpires on the lower levels, including every thought, decision, and action of the self. It also records all decisions of the individual spiritual will, which serves as what could be called a transitional intermediary between the finite and the Infinite. A mechanical analogy would be like the differential gears of an automobile's drive train that synchronize variable action or inaction between the engine and the wheels.

As one surrenders the basic positionalities, one uncovers these basic axioms and finds that below each level of beliefs are yet deeper levels. One is brought face to face with the fundamentals of how the mind believes that it knows anything or how it even believes that it knows (epistemology).

One eventually comes to the amazing discovery that the 'mind' is not really capable of actually knowing anything at all, and that the illusion that it knows is a pretense and a vanity. By analogy, one can ask how a pair of binoculars knows what is seen through it, or how the ear knows music. Does the computer know the software programs? The mind can only 'think about' a subject. To actually 'know' it would require being the known. We can think about a cat but only a cat really 'knows' what it is to *be* a cat.

Thinking is a processing device with great pragmatic value; however, it presumes that it knows the data, but it actually has no innate capacity to know. Belief manufactures an imaginary inner 'knower' that becomes the 'me'. Likewise, it manufactures an imaginary doer of deeds, an actor of acts, and an imaginary thinker of thoughts.

The 'me' or the 'I' which constitutes the core of the illusory self (ego) is a composite of the memory of the imaginary doer of deeds, the thinker of thoughts, the actor of actions, the chooser of choices, and the maker of plans. Thinking does all this because it is set up to process dualistically, with the presumption of a subject and an object. However, when one searches for this imaginary doer of deeds, no such entity exists. When the programs have been erased, one is startled to discover that the recording tape is blank and there is no 'I' or 'me' behind all these programs.

The 'me' that is so jealously guarded and cherished is an elaborate series of layers of programs of which the last underlying program to be undone is that the other layers of programs are real and 'myself'. With this discovery, for a moment the ego/self is fearful. Its fraudulent psuedoauthority as the author of reality is being unveiled. The fear of nonexistence then arises, followed by the fear of death itself, for it is only the illusory self which is subject to actual death. At this point, one clings to the last vain belief that one is the core and author of one's life. In this claim, it is truthful in that it is the author of the life of the 'ego'. At this point, the devotee now faces the surrender of the seem-ing core of one's life to God. This is the final and ulti-mate crucial moment that stands in the way of enlight-enment. Because of its extreme importance, the subject is addressed in a separate chapter.

CHAPTER FOUR
THE 'EGO' AND SOCIETY

Social Structure as Context

Q: How should one handle the seeming conflict between the illusion called "ego," the world, and spiritual work?

A: The source of joy of spiritual endeavor stems from the work itself and is not dependent on outcomes or the achievement of goals. Each movement forward has an inner delight. There is, for instance, an inner pleasure that accompanies progress. The replacement of resentment with peaceful acceptance is its own reward. There is a progressive alteration in one's view of self and others. When this happens, one's own life story can then be recontextualized from a more compassionate understanding.

Q: If the belief system called the "ego" (self) is the source of life's pain and suffering, how does one develop compassion for it?

A: Each person who is born starts with a calibrated level of consciousness, which is shorthand for one's entire karmic inheritance. With no conscious memory of having asked for it, one is now confronted with an animal body and a literal as well as an abstract 'mind'. In addition, a whole set of conditions is simultaneously presented because one also inherits an emotional body as well as a physical one, and all these have to be integrated into the intricacies of family and social life in a complex civilization with its own innate programs that have evolved throughout history.

When one looks at the entire picture of what it means to be a human, one can develop compassion not only for society as a whole but also for the individuals who comprise it. Not only is the individual confronted by enormous complexity but also by a consciousness that is unknowingly influenced by pervasive, invisible energy fields of which they are unaware.

Within this complexity, the individual now has to cope with survival and learn complex skills on multiple levels. The individual is also aware that a single serious mistake can bring disaster to their life, or even physical death. It is as though the entity has to walk the mine field of human existence in order to survive, whether it wishes to or not.

Aside from these conditions, there is also the necessity to develop a guiding sense of self and identity. The self-image that is formed is central to all decision making. This self then coalesces all goals and ideals and integrates them with moralistic positionality. Unknowingly, an aspect of the self splits off and becomes the inner enemy, the victimizer/attacker, and the author of guilt, remorse, fear, and the relentless self-judge.

Even the most advanced computer would be swamped and unequal to the task of being the equivalent of one single human. One compelling fact that makes this observation certain is that the human entity has to contend not only with conscious data that could be put into a computer, but it also has to deal with unconscious data and energy fields of which they have no comprehension, as well as unknown individual or group karmic propensities; thus, no computer could possibly be programmed since a major portion of the most significant data is missing.

As a result, the human has a huge task to accomplish. To do so, it is further impaired by the structure and function of the brain, with its built-in reward and pleasure circuits and its naïve, easily programmable software. In an attempt to deal with the complexity of data, the mind uses the shortcut of lumping data together into classes and logical algorithms. It therefore has to be able to instantly determine every bit of input, whether it is unlike or similar to all other data. In addition, all this incredible complexity is not only handled by the mind and its software, but it is also overwhelmingly 'experienced'. There is little time to analyze experience for at the moments of its occurrence, it is already a given and included in the package which the mind automatically edits and files in the data bank of memory. The data is filed not only according to form but also according to subtle gradations of feeling that importantly determine where the information will be stored. Some is retrievable but a considerable portion is now buried and unavailable for conscious recall.

For instance, some data is stored in the "painful–do not recall" file. Some of this filed-away, now irretrievable pain data, however, is stored as potential ammunition for self-attack and painful self-torture of guilt, remorse, and even suicide. Any occurrence can trip the self-attack trigger and release a barrage of self-punishment. One mechanism the ego uses to protect itself is to disown the painful data and project it onto the world and others. The world then gets peopled with hateful enemies whose origin was actually internal, and the ego now fears attack from without instead of from within. Paranoia is an accompaniment to having an ego.

When one comprehensively recapitulates the situation of man, it becomes obvious that from his own limited resources, survival, happiness, and success are fragile. In massive numbers, even survival is not accomplished and millions of people die from multiple traps and disasters.

Even if they are not personal, one can get caught up in the ego problems of society that manifest as war, pestilence, starvation, or accidents.

Q: **If even a single mistake can be fatal, how is survival possible under these conditions?**

A: Of its own, the personal self cannot really survive, much less prosper, in such a milieu of both internal and external complexity. What has been described is actually the world of form, but the human is more than just a vulnerable ego because life is supported by the power of the nonlinear dimension of spirit. It is the overriding guidance of the spirit that enables survival, despite the ego's claims to the contrary. The spirit is like the governor on an engine, without which the engine would spin into self-destruction.

Spirit in the form of consciousness integrates the entire mass of data from instant to instant, and its output is the moment-by-moment subjective experience of life. This counterbalances the major impairment of the ego which is its inability to discern truth from falsehood.

Q: **Is survival determined by one's level of consciousness?**

A: The subjective experience of life, whatever its content, is profoundly influenced by the level of consciousness, as are the choices that appear as options. Whether the endeavor of life is satisfying or pleasant is dependent upon one's positionalities, which determine how the situations are contextualized.

If we look across the levels on the Scale of Consciousness, we can see the likelihood of choices that are open and which prevail within the parameters of a given level of consciousness. Pleasure would result from fulfilling the goals that characterize that level, and negative emotions would result from failure to do so.

The personality is complex and includes identifications and subpersonalities sometimes called "alter egos" that may lead to conflict. One subpersonality often has different goals from another. These may alternate in conscious appearance due to life's circumstances or age periods. Spiritual goals tend to synthesize the complex ego organization and give it balance.

Q: What part does the intellect fulfill?

A: Via the intellect, positionalities are refined and put into abstract symbols and languaging. All this is subsumed under the general requirement for logical, linear reasonableness. While this is operationally useful, it also reflects that the intellect can be manipulated to make any positionality seem reasonable. The intellect, however, deals not only in form but is also capable of incorporating spiritual values into its mentation. This happens progressively as one evolves up the Scale of Consciousness. When the intellect is freed of hidden motives, it is capable of refined abstract conceptualization. The basic defect, however, remains in that it is unable to tell truth from falsehood or really comprehend context, and it tends to ignore data that would conflict with its positionalities.

In addition, it mistakes effects for 'causes', which is one of its primary defects. It is unable to comprehend and contextualize the difference between the realms of the linear and the nonlinear. It also has a tendency to overcomplicate solutions to problems to the point that they become practically unworkable.

What appear on the surface of society seem to be multitudinous problems, but by use of critical factor analysis (see *Power versus Force*), they often have a common root. For example, we can make up a list of 'unsolvable' social problems, all of which are deemed to stem from different 'causes' in the world, such as poverty; crowded highways; massive immigration; rising gasoline and power consumption; environmental destruction; overwhelmed government agencies; progressive elimination of the rain forests; excessive CO_2 production; high taxation; crowded inner cities where crime and poverty prevail; smog and air pollution; global warming; overcrowded landfills; overcrowded courts, jails and prisons; overcrowded emergency rooms and overwhelming medical costs; overwhelming Social Security costs; a postal service overwhelmed by deficits; lack of dump sites; dwindling wildlife and natural resources; threatened extinction of species; pollution of the ocean; excessive case loads for all areas of welfare and human services; overwhelmed child protective services; rising costs of welfare and social services; long waits for service from all agencies; long lines at supermarkets; traffic jams; escalating police costs; overcrowded schools; teacher shortages; nursing shortages; rising noise-pollution levels; invasion of privacy on every level; shortages of raw materials; shortages of dump space for toxic materials; overtaxed energy sources; pollution of streams, lakes, and rivers; the AIDS epidemic; and starving nations and continents.

Merely listing all these supposedly diverse problems brings the awareness that they all stem from the same single basis—the very simple and obvious-to-see but unnoticed fact of *overpopulation*. Thus, we see the paradox that sending financial aid to a country results in a spurt in the birth rate and a worsening of the basic poverty level (e.g., Haiti). The already apparent burdens to society of overpopulation call into question the wisdom of unregulated immigration policies that, although they are opposed by seventy percent of the American public, are favored by eighty percent of the elitist policy makers (*Arizona Republic*, 2002).

During the last centuries, the consciousness level of the world's human population stood at 190. At this level, overpopulation was held in control by the inevitable consequences of the negativity that ensued. For example, major world wars wiped out whole generations, and great epidemics wiped out twenty-five percent of populations. (Chairman Mao's social experiment alone killed more people by starvation than World War I, and genocide killed millions more.) In the Roman era, the average life span was forty years.

In contrast, very recently, the consciousness level of mankind jumped from a negative 190 to a positive 207. Although hot spots remain, the civilized world is no longer in the mood for mass extermination. The Cold War ended, hot wars became localized, and the nations of Europe deescalated and stopped their nationalistic rampaging.

At this new level of consciousness, the mass destruction that had held the population in check became mitigated and the world population soared, as did average life spans. The most populous country in the world, China, was then forced into taking serious steps. As world population doubles and then doubles again, the time period between each doubling becomes progressively shorter. This is common to any closed-in biologic population, whether they are fruit flies, rabbits, or people. In a safer society where mass exterminations are eliminated, each generation exacerbates the proliferation. The ensuing population automatically needs more territory, more food, and more services, and metropolitan sprawl begets suburban sprawl, which means the end of more habitat in a natural environment.

The Ego and the Political Structure of Society

Q: We were looking at how the intellect falls into error.

A: We can cite examples from recent history as well as from current society. Intellectual positionalities gather favor within certain intellectual groups. There is the rise and fall of Utopian schemes, which were very common in the 1930s. One popular scheme at the time was to eliminate money and put 'work-hour' credits in its place, a technocracy. Various socialistic and Utopian 'isms' and schemes came and went, of which communism still remains. Isolationism and pacifism were popularized. "Esperanto" was touted as a new world language.

In the United States, the same groups tried to force the metric system on an unwilling population. People were not happy with Centigrade or kilometers, so they were cast aside and people went comfortably back to the familiarity of Fahrenheit and miles. The collectivist-farm idealism of Chairman Mao resulted in one of the greatest famines in history, and thirty million people died. People are not motivated to work on a 'collective' farm like they do on their own.

For a period of time, the intellectually elite had a honeymoon with the leftist extreme of communism. This resulted in sedition and even treason with the scientists becoming espionage agents for Russia and sharing atomic secrets with the KGB such as Los Alamos and the Manhattan Project; such duplicity was continual during the Cold War. This information enabled the Russians to begin planning the super atomic bomb with which all of human civilization was to be destroyed in case of defeat.

Operationally, it can be seen that in the long term, the far left political position is more dangerous than the far right in that it cloaks its intention under the sheep's clothing of pious rhetoric that seduces the naïve into opening the gates for the Trojan Horse, thus releasing the forces of oppression, war, and death.

The basic defect of faulty political positionalities is that they distort content as well as ignore context. The content may sound idealistic but it becomes fallacious under a different context. When context is ignored, an idealistic concept may become more destructive than the original problem it was meant to correct. Therefore, such idealisms are failures in contrast to wisdom, which includes context and not just content. Fanaticism is geared to capture the youth and the impressionable. Historically, as soon as revolutionary regimes gain political or military power, they kill off the educated, accomplished, professional class and the wise (e.g., the Jacobites and the guillotine).

It is important to detect and then correct political fallacies because bad politics result in bad law which, in turn, becomes a burden to the citizenry. In our current society, this can be seen in the judicial acceptance of the sophistry of blame and displacement of personal responsibility to a demonized, supposedly external 'cause' exemplified by the endless extensions of tort law, class action suits, and control of legislators by the trial lawyers associations. In some parts of the country, this trend reaches such extremes that it amounts to legalized extortion (as in Jefferson County, Mississippi). Misplaced projected blame has historically been the rationale for a majority of social distortions of which war is the most obvious.

Q: Is there a value to national identity?

A: Its downside is nationalism in the negative sense, but its upside is patriotic cooperative endeavor and the spirit of brotherhood. This was seen in the interaction of the Allies in World War II in which each nation maintained its identity but had a critical common spirit that was linked with other countries in the same situation. Interdependence serves the goal of the whole when they are spiritually united. Patriotism is simply love for one's country and should not be confused with nationalism.

Q: The ego seems to potentiate extremism.

A: Excess is the result of imbalance. The political extremes of both the far left (calibration level 190) and the far right (calibration level 90) are markedly nonintegrous, fallacious, and destructive. The far left political position represents the 'luciferic' in that it seeks to deny God, distort content, ignore context, and rely on legal force and threats of lawsuits to intimidate. It also distorts and abuses the real meaning of free speech. It then becomes the apologist and advocate for social destruction by reliance on sophistry and intellectualized distortion and imbalanced perception. It seeks power for its own sake.

The far right position becomes 'satanic' and represents the forces of moral degeneracy, violence, criminality, war, and slaughter. A coalition of the negative extremes is therefore able to bring down a whole society by the sequence of the luciferic distortion of reality that opens the door for the satanic forces. Both extremes are totalitarian in practice and attract adherents because the human mind is unable to discern truth from falsehood.

History provides endless examples of shifts from one extreme to the other. The oppression of the warlords of China was violently replaced by the oppression of Chairman Mao. The cruelty of the Russian czars (e.g., Ivan the Terrible), was merely replaced by that of Stalin. The naïveté of the public makes it susceptible to seduction by glib rhetoric ("workers unite; you have nothing to lose but your chains"). In today's world, the swan song is to demonize democracy and 'capitalism' as the 'great Satan' and thereby divide the world again into warring factions.

The Buddha extolled the wisdom of "The Middle Way." Moderation is therefore the most workable position.

Q: **The 'politically correct' activists seem to precipitate an endless series of social conflicts and strife. What is the core of the problem?**

A: They are elitist and calibrate at 180, the level of pride and vanity of egotism. The error is again one of ignoring context. Although supposedly egalitarian, they paradoxically adopt superior attitudes and pose as the high moral ground. They attempt to gain power and control over others by romanticized idealism.

There is the overemphasis of the category of "political" which ignores the totality of human reality and fails to see that the 'political' aspect of life is only one of the qualities of human life and does not take precedence over survival or emotional happiness. This is characteristic of both the 'far left' as well as the 'far right' political positions, which are equally totalitarian in actual practice, and the minority then rules the majority. (The Gestapo and the KGB displayed the true intention behind supposedly liberationist political agendas.)

Dubious political positions do not have a good history; for instance, the truth of what really went on in prior years in the treatment of the mentally ill was grossly distorted in the movie, "One Flew Over the Cuckoo's Nest" (which calibrates at 185). As a result, the elitists disassembled the entire national mental health system which, frankly, had been working quite well. Mentally ill persons now wander the streets and fill the prisons. The long-term results of the politically correct position are often disastrous for large numbers of people. For example, the current President's Commission on Mental Health Care reports that the entire mental health system is a "shambles; incapable, uncoordinated, inefficient, incoherent, fragmented, frustrating, dysfunctional . . . due to the layering on of multiple 'well-intentioned' programs that squander at least $80 billion annually and leave over 50% of the mentally ill untreated." (Sharar, 2002.)

The social consequences resulting from the implementation of any social engineering program can be predicted in advance. Those that calibrate below 200 will be detrimental. The traditional schoolroom of the first half of the last century in the United States calibrated at 405. Subsequent to the implementation of political positionalities and the influence of the teacher's union (which calibrates at 202), the average schoolroom now calibrates at 285. The huge decline is reflected in the worsening of classroom behaviors, disrespect for authority, and violence against teachers.

By calibration of diplomatic positions in international affairs, the same predictive benefit is available. This has already been utilized in consultation with foreign governments with startling success. It is possible to analyze the probable responses to any shift of position and so be able to preclude conflict and even major disasters. The United States has a negative image in many parts of the world which, by historical analysis, could well have been predicted and thereby prevented. Even today, provocation naively continues (for example, a television commentator insults the president of the largest country on earth who, in turn, adroitly and with diplomatic expertise surmounts the provocation). The attitude of superiority calibrates at 190 and is therefore antagonistic and creates enemies.

Most of the naïve positions emanate from the academic world which, classically, in its ivory tower detachment, is not exposed to the realities of human life (i.e., context). To substitute for that lack of experience, it often uses imbalanced statistical studies that are inherently defective because they exclude context, the nonlinear domain, and the all-important 'human' elements, such as wisdom. The findings are then presented to the public in an imbalanced manner so that one hysteria replaces another. Academia is heavily politically biased. Ninety-four percent of Ivy League college professors are committed to liberalism and only six percent are even somewhat conservative (*Arizona Republic,* 2002). Conservative student groups are actually excluded from student councils. Thus, in practice, liberalism denies the truth of its nominal title, that is, in truth, it is reactionary and exclusive. Secretly, it holds itself to be aristocratic.

Q: There is a constant progression of public hysterias
which represents an imbalance.

A: People panic even if a disorder affects only one in ten
million people (more people die in the bathtub). Over
the years, these formerly termed 'miasmas' included the
night air, stress, hormones, drafts, focal infections,
germs, immorality, dust, demons, bad air, particles,
'chemicals', lack of sunlight, poor nutrition, poor
sanitation, crowding, lack of sunshine, positive ions,
breast implants, yeast infections, colonic stagnation,
blood poisons, liver poisons, cholesterol, shallow breathing, sexual experience in childhood, heavy metal toxicity,
mercury poisoning from dental fillings, carbon monox-
ide, CO_2, toxic gases, mold, and more.

It has been estimated that the pollution in any big city
is equivalent to smoking two packs of cigarettes a day
and significantly raises the incidence of cancer by a large
percentage. The auto exhaust from one's own car is
putting out more hydrocarbons (another miasma) and
toxic gases than smoking a cigar. More toxins are absorbed while sitting in a traffic jam than from the smoke
of the janitor's pipe as it wafts down the hallway.

The prevalence of a disease reflects the publicity given
to it and the inviting 'deep pockets' of some demonized
industry, (e.g., 'fast food'). The human body is subject to
the mind's fears that then tend to manifest as the mind
holds the fear thought and gives it energy. This has a
suppressive effect on the immune system because the
fear triggers the dysfunction of the acupuncture meridians and autonomic nervous system; this chronic
dysfunction potentiates the appearance of actual disease
or malfunction.

The propagation of fear results in humans' developing
fibromyocitis, myocytis, irritable bowel syndrome,
chronic fatigue syndrome, environmental illness, neuras-
thenia, and various forms of hypochondriasis. The
human mind is innately innocent, unprotected, very

suggestible, and easily programmed. This has been termed the 'nocebo' effect, which has been a subject of study by institutions such as the American Health Foundation.

Q: **Much publicity is given to negative health information.**

A: Much so-called health information is distorted and merely reflects a hidden political or financial agenda. It is a self-serving positionality which the naïve public believes represents objective 'scientific' reporting. Nothing could be farther from the truth. All supposedly scientific statements represent the exposition of a positionality. The data are selective and, more importantly, imbalanced in that only part of the story is presented, and the facts that would change the influence of the report are suppressed.

Q: **What about doctor-patient relationships?**

A: Much fallacious clinical research is reported in professional journals because the impact and effect of context are ignored. This is clearly demonstrated through clinical experience as well as in our own research which shows that an investigator's bias and level of consciousness are more determinative of the seeming results than are the factors that are being studied. Thus, many physicians who are focused on the negative and emphasize negative side effects of treatments end up having much higher incidences of side effects than the physicians who have a higher level of consciousness and therefore expect positive results. In some cases, the deleterious effect of a negative context is actually more influential over the outcome than is the beneficial effect of the medication.

Because of these factors, by using kinesiologic research, it is possible to accurately predict the outcome of a research project before it even starts. This is because of two major factors: (1) Context is often more powerful than content, and (2), in the reality of the quantum potentiality, time is transcended and, therefore, past, present, and future are not sequential but coexistent; thus, the 'future' may precede the 'present'.

Q: **Many of the 'miasmas' then result in illness or symptoms?**

A: That is correct. Interestingly enough, most of the illnesses that have been mentioned above disappear under hypnosis. This has been known in psychoanalysis for many years. For example, a psychoanalyst's patient developed asthma in response to what turned out to actually be paper roses. Under hypnosis, the patient, paradoxically, had no reaction at all to real roses.

Discoveries such as this began the era of psychosomatic medicine in which repressed conflicts were linked to symptoms and illnesses. The University of Chicago School of Psychoanalysis was the leader in the field, and eventually the Academy of Psychosomatic Medicine was born. The famous author Louise Hay became known worldwide for her studies linking spiritual/philosophical/psychological mechanisms to symptoms and their unconscious bases. The psychiatrist John Diamond then linked attitudes to various organs and meridians, and kinesiology became a tool of investigation.

In those investigations, the healing effect of positive affirmations was demonstrated. Affirmations could be linked to specific acupuncture points, muscles, and meridians to positively influence the immune system whose role had been linked to suppression of the function of the thymus gland. All the above schools of research delineated in a demonstrable fashion the linking of negative attitudes, emotions, and belief systems to human pathology.

Another interesting observation is that in well-authenticated cases of multiple personality disorder, one of the personalities can have an illness while the others do not.

This lends emphasis to the intense interconnection between consciousness and the body, just as there is an innate connection between consciousness level and the pathology of society.

Q: **Are extremes the only result of imbalance?**

A: The 'unintended result' arises out of denial due to a positionality that ignores context. The hypothetical is not grounded in the real and is an abstraction which ignores the fact that everyday human life takes place quite differently. This is because the abstract is an idealization. We saw the rise of the welfare state which had a provision that welfare would not be granted to the mothers of children if there were "able-bodied men in the house." This, of course, resulted in men's leaving the children fatherless. Children proliferated on the welfare roles as welfare was paid per capita, depending on how many children there were. To facilitate the woman's welfare and that of the children, the man simply left the domicile.

Hysteria propagates by the 'could' of a hypothetical example. Imbalanced media information is picked up by the populous and the 'nocebo effect' then surfaces as a statistical change. People are very suggestible and easily programmed by fear. The conflicting reports of the incidence of cancer in women who are or who are not using postmenopausal hormones is typical.

Q: **Can the nature of a segment of society then be diagnosed by merely calibrating its level of consciousness?**

A: Very much so. It is not a matter of labeling any more than measuring the temperature of water is labeling the water. The calibrated level of a population correlates with the nature of its social problems. Hatred and war are endemic to certain regions of the world today where they hide under banners of nationalism, religion, or tradition. Even now, these so-called traditions result in death, enslavement, and mutilation.

In more sophisticated societies, negativity and violence are defended by the sophistry of deliberate distortions, such as the media's "We don't influence public opinion, we just reflect it." Catering to degeneracy is excused because it is 'profitable' or 'freedom of speech' (e.g., video games based on stalking and killing women; child pornography; gangster rock music with profane, sadistic and degenerative messages.; or criminality and violence).

A brief kinesiologic investigation into supposed causes of endemic problems reveals that they are merely the reflection of the prevailing level of consciousness of that population. There are no other external 'causes'. When the ego's limitations become politicized, social repercussions ensue, often at great cost to the populace.

Q: What about war?

A: The basic mechanisms of war are clear and simple. Generically, it amounts to the aforementioned dictum: The luciferic opens.the doors for the satanic to enter.

Political ideology sets the stage for the unleashing of primitive passions. The pen is mightier than the sword. Partisan political ideology proselytizes using rhetoric, demagoguery, and propagandist persuasion to call up support.

Favorite catch phrases heard are usually variations of proclaimed 'rights' or the righting of some perceived 'wrongs'. 'Victims' of these alleged 'wrongs' are paraded in order to arouse emotionalism and righteous indignation. The plight of the 'innocent victim' is then used to accuse, blame, and demonize alleged evil doers who can then be guiltlessly attacked and 'deservedly' ransacked and punished.

The distortions of political ideology stem from what have been traditionally described as 'luciferic' energies that seek power, control, prestige, and gain. They are often concealed under such 'sheep's clothing' banners as pacifism, peace

movements, and political idealism. These energies, like the
wolf pack, wait for signs of weakness in an intended prey.
The greater the assets of the prey ('big pockets'), the more
vociferous is the demonization. Therefore, big corporations,
industries, or institutions, including governments, that are
seats of financial and political power, are favorite targets.
The setup is like a melodrama, where the supposed knights
in shining armor save the victims from the demonized evil
doers, and in so doing, realize sizable gain, prestige, power,
and great wealth.

Like the Trojan horse, the doors to war are opened by
the justifications and persuasions of political naïveté
which then let loose the underlying 'satanic' energies of
death and destruction. The prevention of war thus
depends on the early detection of its ideologic preludes
by means of exposure of the inherent false premises (the
imbalanced distortion of data and the ignorance of
context).

Q: Can wars be prevented?

A: The preludes to war are highly visible, as can be seen in
such pre-World War I political ideologies such as Marx
and Engel's *Das Kapital* and *Communist Manifesto*, the
political writings and speeches of Lenin, Hitler's *Mein
Kampf,* and Chairman Mao's *Little Red Book.* The Nazi
occupation of Europe was justified by the political
ideologic concepts of *liebensraum* (living room), the
political ideologies for which were provided by Professor
Karl Haushoffer. These were later combined with the
philosophy of eugenics to justify genocide.

Political distortions are usually those of context, class,
or displacement in time or conditions. For example, as
society evolves, what was considered normal at one time
is later considered to be detrimental or unacceptable and
redress is then called for. Financial or military recompense is demanded of the current citizens to compensate
for what is now retroactively considered as victimization

in a past era (e.g., Hitler's play on the 'unjust' Versailles treaty). Inasmuch as everyone now living can be conceived of as suffering real consequences of some past condition, there could be constructed, therefore, a defensible view that all persons currently living are 'entitled' to recompense for the past ignorance and mistakes of a more primitive civilization. Injustice can be cited anywhere in past times.

What is ignored in claims for redress is that the current generation of descendents has already been greatly compensated by the benefits that have accrued to all citizens currently alive due to the great and rapid strides made by society in relatively recent times. Notable are the disappearance or curability of many diseases that wiped out multitudes; the benefits of technology; modern inventions; the reduction of the work week; the progression of equal rights; and the general wealth of the populous.

Even the poorest citizen of today has advantages that were not available even to the richest classes in the relatively recent past. A more balanced view would result in gratitude for being alive in today's world where provision has been made for about any single possible human condition. The rulers of the past died of diseases from which even the most impoverished are now protected by the safety nets of modern society.

Society, which is the projection of the collective ego, is on a learning curve. It is vulnerable to constant disruptions as each new complaint is unearthed by some group which then besieges the media and the courts of law or public opinion. Once the paradigm has been validated, the doors are opened for an infinite progression of demands from every segment of society. The inherent defect relies on the concept of 'causality', that great 'open sesame' to the endlessly revolving saga of victim and perpetrator in which the protagonists serially reverse roles. The factors that drive the endless schemes are blame, greed, and the concept of causality and compensation (which impress gullible judges, juries, and public sentiment). As a consequence, we live in a litigious society in which everyone is vulnerable to attack by mere accusation or by being the target of blame. One is no longer protected by reason, logic, or balance.

Q: Society primarily represents the collective interaction and expression of consciousness levels.

A: That is well expressed. Most of the difficulties represent the inability to accept personal responsibility; for example, if one eats too much, it is the fault of the restaurant. This means that the ego projects the blame on some other segment of society as the 'cause'. This propensity weakens the social fabric and leads to fallacious 'cures' that then produce further contentious conflicts because the process itself is nonintegrous. This propensity to use excuses instead of taking personal responsibility is a progressive social problem.

This trend is now being noticed and its effects are being studied and reported in the media. (Pontari et al, 2002). The authors point out that reliance on excuses for projecting blame on others leads to moral and social weakness and is destructive to the individual as well as to society. We note from kinesiologic research that reliance on blame results in a critical decrease of consciousness level and loss of power.

The displacement of responsibility also results in hatred and resentment which fuel criminality as well as class conflict and war. Thus, the wisdom of the basic axiom of the Twelve-Step spiritual groups is expressed as "There is no such thing as a justified resentment."

Q: What about legitimate social reform?

A: Power comes from integrity and accepting responsibility for the consequences of one's own actions, choices, and decisions. All choices have inherent risks, and to pretend otherwise is not integrous and is game playing for gain.

The integrity of a positionality is reflected by kinesiologically calibratable levels that denote motive and intention. Social injustice becomes correctible when presented integrously. If, however, issues are deliberately warped, they merely lead to another injustice that has to be corrected, and so on, endlessly.

The wolf comes through the door in sheep's clothing; thus, it is critically important to identify truth from falsehood when political programs are presented by some segment of society. All self-seeking schemes are hidden under pious-sounding agendas to win popular approval.

The doors to war are often opened by pacifists who provide the rationale behind the appalling but fatal constructions by which reason becomes the tool of denial. For example, the intelligence department cannot protect the public because of the restraint of political ideologies that have been enacted as legislation. Sophistry is based on psuedo-egalitarianism, mixing levels and misapplying concepts by means of ignoring context.

Q: **Can you give an illustration of what you mean from recent history?**

A: It is laid out for all to see by the preludes to World War II, where the appeasement agenda in England was represented by Neville Chamberlain (calibrated at 185), who appeased Hitler (calibrated at 125) and was blind to Hitler's real motives. The naïveté relied on disarmament and nonaggression pacts which, of course, Hitler had no intention of keeping. Winston Churchill (calibrated at 510) was widely denounced at the time as a war monger because he was not fooled by the subterfuges of naïve diplomatic negotiations. When Hitler overtly attacked, England turned back to the realistic Churchill to save them from the disaster that had been set up by the idealists. The net cost of this error was a minimum of seventy million people dead, plus the destruction of Europe. Thus, the most dangerous element in any pre-war society is represented by the idealists who, in sheep's clothing, bring about that for which mankind was warned.

The dangerous error of political extremes and idealistic oversimplifications is that any supposed reality to their progress can be supported only by ignoring context, which is the overall social reality that would negate the practicality of the political positionality. This imbalance guarantees failure and human disaster, resulting in the 'unintended result'.

The litigious fabric of society is already so weighted down with the extremes of politically correct precautionist maneuvering that it can barely function. For example, witness the gridlock paralysis of the Central Intelligence Agency, the Federal Bureau of Investigation, the Immigration and Naturalization Service, the National Security Agency, and airport security, all of which contributed to the failure to prevent the bombing of the World Trade Center.

The same attitudes that contributed to and were primarily responsible for the disaster then resurfaced again almost immediately afterward to try to block the detection of terrorists or the implementation of military/criminal justice, even if the culprits were apprehended. The contentious position demonizes authentic authority and becomes the advocate for the criminal. Thus, it becomes the apologist for that which is nonintegrous, accounting for its negative calibration. The paradox is that the luciferic distortion of truth protests the public use of the term "God" by resorting to the courts to exercise the God-given rights guaranteed by the Constitution of the United States in order to secularize society and thereby, paradoxically, remove its very source of authority for the right to freedom. (The Constitution calibrates at over 700; the 'politically correct' position calibrates at 180.) Understandably, therefore, the elitist feels 'uncomfortable' with any reference to God. (Lucifer refused to acknowledge the sovereignty of God through pride and greed for power.)

This positionality is unable to tell truth from falsehood and, due to the distortion, which is really an extremely grave failure of discernment, it results in the inability to correctly identify the perpetrator and the victim. This leads to a paradoxical switch of such roles in which the alleged victim becomes and is revealed to be the real perpetrator. The whole 'victimology' movement (and its associated pop psychology) is innately injurious in that it pathologizes the vicissitudes of life which every mature adult has to learn to handle.

Q: What would be the effect of the removal of the reference to God in the Constitution or the Pledge of Allegiance?

A: Power is a reflection of Truth which is a descriptive aspect of the Reality of Divinity. The Constitution of the United States calibrates as the highest of any nation and stands at 705. The Pledge of Allegiance calibrates at 520, which is that of love for one's country. If the word "God" were removed from the Constitution, its calibrated level would drop from 705 (Truth) to 485 (Intelligence and Reason). If "God" were removed from the Pledge of Allegiance, its calibrated level would drop from 520 to 295 (Enthusiasm and Good Will).

America is the most powerful nation on earth. To tamper with its very source of power would therefore be disastrous not only to this country but to the entire world which looks to the United States for inspiration, leadership, and example. The United States represents hope, freedom, and the opportunity for the betterment of life.

The hatred of the United States by others stems solely from envy. The wise imitate success; the venomous instead seek to destroy that which is envied out of jealousy. The far left and the far right both seek to demonize the United States. Even at this time of conflict and stress, the nonintegrous make supplicant visits to the enemies of the United States and join the demonizers. To give aid and comfort to the enemy is traditionally the role of the turncoat and seditionist who, in the end, are considered by society to represent the lowest of the low. It is interesting that even the criminals in prison are patriotic. Thus, the willful desecration of universal values is viewed as the most heinous of crimes and seen as an anathema. Traitors require special security in federal prisons; even murderers hate them.

Rationality and the Structure of Society

Q: So, reason in and of itself cannot be trusted?

A: The difficulty with rationality is that it does not take into account the downside of human nature. It presumes that a foreign national leader would not be so irrational as to destroy their own nation and peoples. This ignores the fact that the ego at its worst has no respect for human life, including that of one's own family or countrymen. 'Egomaniac' leaders have a moment on the world's stage and then bring about the killing of more of their own countrymen than does the enemy. Hitler despised the German people. Stalin killed millions, as did Chairman Mao and, more recently, Milosevich. The French Revolution killed more Frenchmen and patriots than their enemies. Saddham Hussein sacrificed a whole army. Japanese leaders forced the atomic bombing of their own country and countrymen, and Middle Eastern terrorists still force attacks on their own countries and their populations.

From this, we can see that the problem with 'decent' people is that they are naïve and project their own values onto others as presumptions. Underrating the enemy is the most notorious pitfall of countries and military leaders.

Q: How can such miscalculations be prevented? The cost
     to mankind from such ignorance is massive. Hundreds
     of thousands—in fact, millions of people—die as a
     result of the lack of simple, basic information.

A: The consequences of paradigm blindness are devastating.
     The calibrated level of each society is unique and repre-
     sents profoundly differing parameters of social and,
     therefore, political 'reality'. Each level presumes limitations
     of permitted behaviors, beliefs, and attitudes. There is not
     even common agreement as to the value of human life
     itself. Each level has different expectations, intellectual
     positions, and boundaries. When dealing with other
     individuals, social groups, or governments and their
     leaders, it is crucial to be aware of their calibrated levels
     and what that level signifies in that culture. What is 'just'
     and 'ethical' to one society is considered objectionable or
     even cowardly by another. Every politician tries to esti-
     mate such value by using polling to find out the vested
     interests of a constituency. Businesses use market research
     techniques to guide packaging and advertising.

     In international political or military affairs, the failure
     to accurately assess the prevailing 'climate' of another
     culture leads to major fiascos. For example, the people of
     Cuba did not 'rise up in protest' at a repressive regime; in
     fact, Fidel Castro has ruled longer than any other ruler
     on earth today. The thinking of bureaucrats who are in
     the 400s is usually totally incongruous with the 'realities'
     held by a populace in the 200s or 300s, much less those
     that are far below 200. Food and jobs are more impor-
     tant than a democratic form of government, which
     sounds irrelevant and impractical to those of the world
     who face daily starvation. Populations are not driven by
     logic but by passions that are often irrational or even
     extreme and destructive.

     Lack of respect for other cultures and traditions is a
     weakness. Respect for other people's cultural styles and
     their position on the learning curve of socio-political

evolution is essential to good diplomacy. To influence others, it is first necessary to 'get their ear'. This is a rule in clinical work. A principle of psychoanalysis is to "never make an interpretation in the face of a negative transference." (It will be rejected.)

Q: If the 'other side' learns of the value of the kinesiologic test, would that not be a disadvantage?

A: Interestingly and profoundly significant is that the kinesiologic test can be used accurately only by people who themselves calibrate over 200. Even more profound is that not only must the question-and-answer subjects be over 200, but the motive of the question itself (which is presented in the form of a statement) has to be integrous and over 200.

This is amazing indeed and recalls that "only the meek shall inherit the earth," and that "the wolf in sheep's clothing" now stands unmasked and revealed. Unless one is integrous and well-intentioned in purpose, this simple test does not work. Paradoxically, the test for truth is denied to those who are dedicated to falsehood. Thus, this test cannot be used for selfish or egoistic ends. The access by 'evil' to truth is denied in that truth is the essence of the Creator. Whereas mankind's innocence was previously its Achilles' heel, that innocence now returns as the royal road to the ultimate victory of truth over falsehood.

Q: How does the intention or motive limit the use of the test?

A: Research reveals that the test cannot be accurately used by those who deny the sovereignty of the Truth of God. Inasmuch as truth is a reflection of divinity, unconscious denial of God precludes its use for egotistic motives. This is a consequence of the nature of Creation and not some arbitrary, moralistic, righteous decision by God to 'punish the wicked'. God's truth is beyond attack.

These facts explain why some people who have experimented with kinesiologic testing have obtained contradictory results. A nonintegrous motive may have been the decisive factor. For instance, the most common error reported has arisen when people tried to calibrate their own level of consciousness. In this case, the motive makes quite a difference. On one hand, it could be a sincere desire to ascertain where they are in their spiritual work, whereas other people want to know for reasons of spiritual pride or the seeking of status. When done in a nonintegrous way, incorrect high numbers often occur, even over 1,000 (which is impossible). Therefore, if the motive is humility, the answers are different than if one is motivated by pride or gain. The truly spiritual seeker has no need for ranking, authority, or prestige. The primary requirement is simply that of integrity.

As an example, if a detective investigates a crime because of his commitment to serve justice and protect the innocent, the result will be quite different than if the detective was asking the question out of the motives of hate or revenge against the criminal. One time we asked if, during World War II, Churchill would have been allowed to use the method. The answer was yes. We then asked if Hitler would have been allowed to use it, and the answer was no. In this example, one can see that the power of the nonlinear domain prevails over the linear world of force.

Q: What of the atheist or agnostic?

A: We researched this and found again that it depends on motive. If the doubter held to convictions out of spiritual sincerity and honesty, the test worked. If they were motivated out of greed or hatred for God, then the motive would be nonintegrous and the test would not be available. The universe is not naïve. All consequences are merely reflections of the integrity of the all-prevalent field of consciousness. The kinesiologic test is merely a tool with which to determine if truth is present or not. Truth has no opposite, such as falsity or 'off-ness'. Nothing is hidden from the field of consciousness. Apparently, it is better to be an integrous atheist or agnostic than a nonintegrous religionist.

Q: Society exhibits such widely divergent extremes. How is it possible to not be judgmental?

A: Human life exhibits the collective karma of individuals as well as groups that express all possibilities and options from the most severe to the beatific and sublime. It could be viewed, therefore, as purgatorial in that there is the opportunity for 'bad' karma to be undone, for forgiveness to replace condemnation, and for love to replace hate. There is also the freedom to choose differently and refuse the accumulation of merit or 'good' karma.

The evolution of consciousness requires a wide range of opportunities and a playing field that affords almost unlimited options for development. If human life represents a learning process, then society is the ideal school that affords an extremely wide range of options for numerous levels of consciousness to develop, progress, define, identify, and grasp endless subtleties as well as learn more gross lessons.

The ego is extremely tenacious and therefore often seems to require extreme conditions before it lets go of a positionality. It often takes the collective experience of millions of people over many centuries to learn even what appears upon examination to be a simple and obvious truth, namely, that peace is better than war or love is better than hate.

The level of consciousness is determined by the choices made by the spiritual will and therefore is the consequence as well as the determinant of karma. Freedom to evolve requires a world which affords the greatest opportunity to ascend or descend the spiritual ladder. Viewed from that perspective, this is an ideal world and its society is constituted by a wide range of experiential options.

Freedom is the opportunity to fashion one's own destiny and learn the inherent spiritual truths that are essential. For merit or demerit to occur, the choices have to be made in a state of belief and experience that they are 'real'. Thus, even illusion subserves spiritual growth for it seems real at the time.

Human life thus subserves the spirit. The world is less painful to witness if it is appreciated as the ultimate school whereby we earn salvation and serve each other by our own lives.

Q: What is the best attitude from which to view society?

A: One of compassionate benevolence. The average person's psyche is overwhelmed by layers of programmed belief systems of which they are unaware. Out of naiveté and the belief in the principle of causality, the supposed causes and their solutions are sought 'out there'. With maturity and the wisdom of spirituality, the search becomes directed inwardly where the source and resolution are finally discovered.

CHAPTER FIVE
SPIRITUAL REALITY

Q: What is the 'structure' of the spiritual domain?

A: Although it is without structure as commonly understood, it has characteristics (analogous to the
'observables' of Quantum Mechanics) that are quite
discernible by their effects. While we can impose an
intellectual structure on these qualities, they exist only in
the mentation of the observer. Calibrated levels of
consciousness, for example, are not, in Reality, separate
from each other but are actually potentialities which we
can verifiably gradate to facilitate comprehension.

To facilitate intellectual understanding of the transition
from the macroscopic, 'objective', ordinary world of
form and logic to the subjective, 'microscopic', nonlinear
reality of subjectivity, it may be useful to summarize the
differences between the old linear Euclidian/Newtonian
paradigm of reality and the more advanced understanding of nonlinear dynamics and the science of Quantum
Mechanics and subatomic advanced theoretical physics.
(See Appendix D.) From this, we will observe that the
invisible substrate of the physically observable world is
the quantum potentiality that is demonstrably affected
by human consciousness and intention.

Newtonian	**Quantum Mechanics**
Orderly	Disorderly
Logical	Illogical
Predictable	Unpredictable
Deterministic	Free

Literal	Creative
Pedestrian	Imaginative
Reductionist	Progressive
Separate	Intermingled, Interconnected
Discrete	Diffuse
Cause	Potentiate
Atomistic	Nonlocal Coherence
Forced	Reactive
Caused	Responsive
Provable	Comprehensible
Measurable	Observable
Sequential	Simultaneous
Settled	Potential
Temporal	Time Dependent/Independent
Computational	Stochastic/Chaotic
Limited	Unlimited
Actuality	Possibility
Permanent	Altered by Observation
Constricted	Expansive
Content	Context
Objective	Subjective
Force	Power
Certain	Uncertain
Finished	Poised

In contrast to force, there is no limit to power. Power is an attribute of God and is therefore unlimited. It includes all of Creation, all its universes, and is always in perfect harmony and balance. One could say, analogously, that power automatically matches the 'demand' made upon it. An increment of merely a feather tips the scale. Although a prayer may seem like a feather, the universe responds. This does not mean that the prayer is necessarily granted in a literal way. Most prayers are made naïvely for gain or to change the course of events; however, collective, integrous prayer can have a positive effect in the course of human evolution. Prayers that include a surrender to God's will stem from a higher motivation.

Q: What about 'accidents'?

A: So-called accidents are an illusion of perception in the
    domain of form, which is based on a linear expectation.
    With kinesiologic testing, the hidden elements are
    revealed and the illusion of 'accident' disappears. The
    only hypothetical possibility for a true accident to occur
    would require that it 'happen' outside the Allness of
    Creation, which is an impossibility. For a so-called
    accident to be observable, by definition it would have to
    have occurred within the discernible universe. Every-
    thing represents the consequence of the effect of the
    entire universe throughout all time. Nothing is outside
    the karmic, balanced harmony of the universe.

    "Chaos" is a term that denotes limitation. It rests on
    the presumption that reality is limited to perception. A
    better word for chaos is "unfathomable," "unpredictable,"
    or beyond logical comprehension, statistical analysis, or
    logical probability.

    The Book of Genesis states that prior to Creation there
    was chaos, meaning dark, incomprehensible (to man),
    beyond description, and without form. The Light of
    Divinity created existence and form by virtue of the
    formlessness, which was the very source of the form
    itself. Out of darkness (nonconsciousness) arose light
    (consciousness).

    Genesis is written in language that was chosen to be as
    close as possible to describing that which is essentially
    indescribable. In essence, Genesis starts with the descrip-
    tion of the Unmanifest manifesting as Creation, thereby
    declaring and affirming that God is the sole source of All
    That Is.

    Out of the invisible nonlinear arose the linear as an
    expression of the infinite potentiality of God. That the
    Infinite Divinity was declared as the source of all Cre-
    ation was the most important truth revealed to man's
    comprehension. Out of the Unmanifest (the Godhead)
    arose Creation as the manifestation of God as Creator.

The core and substrate of that creation was the capacity for the quality of existence itself.

Consciousness was the light (energy source) of the emergence of life. The light of consciousness, as it encountered matter, evolved as biologic life which, in Genesis, evolved from vegetation to the animal kingdom to mankind. Thus it was declared that Creation and evolution proceeded from the 'top down', from the Infinite Potentiality to the actuality of literal matter, which was then imbued with the consciousness of life. The lower forms then evolved 'upwards' in their complexity to man.

The evolution from less complex to more complex life forms is a process that occurs in the nonlinear domain (i.e., the sought for "missing link") and then appears in the visible world of form as described by Darwin. The scientific explanation of evolution does not really conflict with spiritual reality because it does not address the nonlinear issues at all, such as the creation of the capacity for existence as form in the field of consciousness, or the origin of the energy of life itself. The linearity of time pertains to the realm of perception only and not to ultimate Reality. Thus, evolution is the unfoldment of Creation as it appears to perception.

The above description is affirmed by kinesiologic testing, which also confirms that evolution is the unfolding of creation to perception and that Creation and evolution are actually the same thing.

Q: **The world's religions differ in their emphasis on whether God is transcendent ('out there') or immanent ('in here').**

A: Theology (which calibrates from 480 to 485) represents the efforts of the intellect. It is thus limited to form and its contextualization of a reality that is actually beyond form and therefore beyond the reach of reason or logic. Theology utilizes concepts to try to denote realities that are actually beyond accurate conceptualization and which can be confirmed only by the actuality of subjective experience. The subjective awareness of spiritual reality is therefore called "ineffable," as was described by William James in the great classic, *Varieties of Religious Experience.*

Because only the absolute subjectivity of nonlinear spiritual experience can substantiate truth, theology lacks the authenticity and authority of the realized mystic, sage, or avatar. Theology can be quite brilliant and accurate, however, when it includes and gives adequate recognition to the truth as revealed by the enlightened sage.

To be able to address the Absolute Reality, an adequate theology has to be very erudite in its epistemology. (How does man come to know anything or know that he knows, and by what means does that occur, or is it even possible without divine intervention?)

If the subjective reality of the sage is included along with the understandings that accompany enlightenment, then it is quite apparent that God is simultaneously both immanent (as Self) and transcendent, (i.e., the Supreme). The use of the word "both" is a semantic convenience. "Both" implies two different states, whereas, in reality, God is total Oneness, and the terms "immanent" or "transcendent" are categories of perception and mentation and not representative of Reality.

Even with logic, it is obvious that a transcendent God would also have to be immanent as well or else God would be characterized as limited. This would result in a ridiculous depiction that God is everywhere in the universe except in man so that each man would be like a hole in the totality of the universe. This would be like depicting the omnipresence of God as a block of Swiss cheese, with mankind living in the holes.

Q: **Then only the actual subjective experience and realization of the Presence as Self has any radically absolute reality?**

A: That is the truth, and it is the one that solves all spiritual argument and clears up all confusion. Spiritual truth is radically subjective as is, for example, the experience of a sunset or joy or happiness. Intellectualization is basically an abstract speculation that must be confirmed by experience.

In the end, no matter how scientific or logical a theory may be, it is not proven until its authenticity is confirmed on the level of the experiential. The validity or 'truth' of an aircraft design, for instance, is not proven until the plane is actually flown, just as a recipe becomes confirmed by the actual eating of the food. The intellect is successful when it can accurately predict that which can be confirmed only by subjective experience. This is also presented by various philosophic systems which point out that unless a word denotes a verifiable reality experientially, it is not a fact but only a tautology (i.e., a hypothesis or strictly semantic intellectual construction).

Q: **It seems obvious that the hypothetical has to be confirmed by subjective, experiential verification. In view of this, why has religious argument persisted over the centuries and resulted in religious conflict and partisanship?**

A: It is based on confusion about the source of true authority. This was compounded by the statistical rarity of the ultimate subjectivity of Enlightenment. It also results in the lack of awareness of the limits of the intellect and its incapacity to inclusively comprehend the relationship between the linear and the nonlinear domains. The intellect deals with hypothetical postulations and probabilities that may or may not have the potential for experiential verification. If the intellect concludes that the nonlinear cannot be confirmed experientially, then it tends to downgrade such subjective verification as 'unreal', 'mystical', or 'unscientific'. This is the favorite epithet of materialistic reductionism.

The difficulty facing theology and religion, however, is that the information upon which religious structure is based was provided from the radically subjective experience of the enlightenment of the mystic, the sage, or the avatar upon whom a religion is founded. If the strict religious traditionalist insists that subjectivity is not real, then all religious foundations are baseless. Throughout history, Christ, Buddha, Krishna, and every enlightened Hindu sage has been self-realized for they were all transformed by the subjective Reality of the Presence/ Divinity of God.

Because of the rarity of the enlightened state, each religion then presumed that its originator and founder was 'the only one', and the possibility that there were others in history who came to the same or similar advanced states of consciousness was not considered. In fact, they were often denounced. This limitation of comprehension is understandable since it is impossible for ordinary consciousness to appreciate and grasp the profound significance of Enlightenment.

In addition to these difficulties, the ego/mind is unable to discern truth from falsehood and thereby has no absolute means to confirm the authentic from the false. To add to the difficulty, not only was the state of enlightenment extremely rare, but when it did occur, the majority who experienced it disappeared from society or, if they did not, their enlightened state was not recognized or comprehended. As a result, the illusion prevailed that it never occurred. It is characteristic of religions to act as though all truth has been at a standstill and unmoving since the time of the original founder. Because of this opinion, it was thought that there was nothing more to be known.

Whereas Truth is complete and unchanging, on the contrary, man's understanding and capacity for comprehension significantly advances and changes in all areas of knowledge. With it, significance and meaning become contextualized so that, although truth does not change, man's understanding of it certainly does.

When the consciousness level of mankind stood at 190 over the centuries (it was at approximately 90 at the time of the Buddha and at 100 at the time of the birth of Jesus Christ), the real comprehension of spiritual truth was limited primarily to the spiritually gifted. Now that the consciousness level of mankind is at 207, the way is open for spirituality to be absorbed and valued widely. There is already a widespread appreciation for the existence of spiritual values in many formerly secular areas of society. While the majority of people are still adverse to 'religion' in the marketplace, they are open to spiritual values, especially if those values are not labeled "spiritual." Inasmuch as society is now over consciousness level 200 (the level of Integrity), it will place ever greater emphasis on integrous (spiritual) values, and we will probably see the demand for spiritual ideals and standards (truth) expand within the business community and society in general.

Q: How important is the Scale of Consciousness in advancing the understanding of spirituality?

A: Kinesiologic testing and the calibrated Scale of Consciousness are remarkable because, for the first time in history, there is an objective means of verifying spiritual reality as well as its multitudinous levels of expression. This style of research is familiar to society in that its mechanism and applications are analogous to locating frequencies of energy fields on the electromagnetic spectrum. Society is also familiar with spectroscopic analysis where it is not the material but the radiation of the material that is located on a specified scale, the accuracy of which is verified over time by its consistency and usefulness. Eventually, the reliability and practical utility of such a method establishes its value and parameters of reliability. In many areas of science, a radiation spectrum scale is the primary source of information about matter, energy, and even objects that are beyond sensory detection.

There is common knowledge of the routine analysis of the radiant spectrum to discern the nature of the universe or the age of distant, unseen galaxies. Mankind is also familiar with the ordinary Geiger counter and radiation-exposure badges worn by workers in nuclear power plants to discern on a scale that which is not visible in physical form.

Whereas the familiar radiation scales have been developed for measuring the material universe and the invisible, subtle realms of form, it is not surprising that a very similar technique is available to reflect the nature of the realms of the nonlinear domain. The invisible energy fields of consciousness become identifiable by employing a style of detection that is not dissimilar to others in common use throughout all branches of science. This affords the development of a science of spiritual reality that is of great benefit to mankind.

The value of the information that can be derived from study of the nonlinear dimensions of reality is far greater than learning the details of distant stars. The Scale of Consciousness has profound significance for every aspect of human life for it is indeed the very substratum of the mind in all its activities. A calibratable level of consciousness is intrinsic to every single detail of human life in all its expressions, without exception. It is therefore the most important aspect of human life, and when fully understood, it will be seen to eclipse any other describable aspect.

Q: Consciousness level is then more important than *anything* else in life?

A: When the full implications of the effects of consciousness are understood, it becomes very apparent that this is so. Let us first look at the overwhelming and startling fact that a calibratable, discernible consciousness level is already present at birth. Therefore, to investigate and explain how this can come about in a universe where nothing happens by accident leads to a profound study of the subject of the evolution of consciousness, commonly called "karma." Like the rings of the cross-section of a tree, the 'past' of an entity is revealed.

Consciousness level is correlated with perceptual and intellectual positionality and therefore determines one's world view and experience of it. This in turn correlates with options, choices, and responses that are reflected in attitudes, decisions, vocational interests, and life goals. The perceptual level contextualizes and determines the options of values, meaning, and significance.

Consciousness level is also intrinsic to one's psychological makeup and emotionality as well as one's world view, physical and psychic health, and lifestyle. Most importantly, consciousness level also correlates with the capacity for spiritual awareness and whether one's view of God is transcendent, immanent, or both.

The capacity for spiritual awareness reflects in one's philosophical attitudes, including one's view of society, history, judicial systems, politics, and government institutions. It also influences one's innate sense of responsibility, self-esteem, and personality identifications. The psychological set that ensues then determines what mental contents are to be accepted or rejected, repressed or rationalized, projected onto others or turned against the self. In their summation, these psychological factors will classify all experiences or concepts as good versus bad, pleasurable versus painful, and attractive versus repellant. These choices have concomitant physiological consequences in the brain's automatic reward system within the central nervous system which may thereby release adrenalin or endorphins, stress hormones or corticoids, sympathetic or parasympathetic neural hormones, serotonin or norepinephrine, etc. All these in turn affect metabolic rates and energy flows in the autonomic and acupuncture energy pathways, influencing the energy supply, vitality, and functioning of all the body's organ systems, including even the focus and the moment-to-moment field of vision.

Q: **If practically everything in one's life depends on the evolution of the level of one's consciousness, it would seem that, aside from mere survival needs, developing that level of consciousness would eclipse all other endeavors in importance.**

A: That would seem to be so, but that has to be integrated into the overall context of one's life. Endeavors and activities can remain the same but need to be recontextualized and repositioned within a spiritual framework. To spiritualize one's life, it is necessary only to shift one's motive. To constantly be aware of one's actual motive tends to bring up positionality and the pairs of opposites, such as gain versus service or love versus greed. These then become visible and are available for spiritual work because one is now conscious of them.

Western countries are meritocracies in which effort is put forth for the sake of gain; this is an innate function of the brain's reward system. (As Chairman Mao found out with his collectivist farm experiment, by ignoring the innate reward system of the brain, the collectivist farmers lost their motivation, resulting in the world's greatest famine. Thirty million people died as a consequence of that political ideology.)

In spiritual work, there is no tangible worldly gain to be acquired, but there is instead an inner reward of pleasure, satisfaction, delight, and even joy. Goals replace gains as motives.

Spiritual reality is a greater source of pleasure and satisfaction than the world can supply. It is endless and always available in the present instead of the future. It is actually more exciting because one learns to live on the crest of the current moment instead of on the back of the wave, which is the past, or on the front of the wave, which is the future. There is greater freedom from living on the exciting knife edge of the moment than being a prisoner of the past or having expectations of the future.

If the goal of life is to do the very best one can do at each unfolding moment of existence, then, through spiritual work, one has already escaped the primary cause of suffering. In the stop-frame of the radical present, there is no life story to react to or edit. With this one-pointedness of mind, it soon becomes obvious that everything merely 'is as it is', without comment or adjectives.

If, in the exact passing moment of each instant, there is a complete willingness to totally surrender to it, one can suddenly, in a flash, transcend the ego, and the way opens for Realization wherein the Light of God as Self reveals the Source of all Existence and Reality. If the ego has neither past, present, nor future to focus on, it falls silent. It is replaced by the Silence of the Presence, and thus, the way to sudden enlightenment is available at all times. It occurs naturally when the fascination with the story of the 'me' of the past, present, or future is relinquished. The illusion of 'Now' is replaced by the reality of 'Always'.

Q: **If that strict spiritual practice was followed exactly, wouldn't the 'me' die?**

A: Yes, it would. When it occurs, there will not be a funeral because, in Reality, there never was a 'me'; it was simply an illusion all the time. When the 'me' dies, then the real

'I' is born into awareness, which is the Unborn—the source of consciousness and existence.

Q: If spiritual reality is of such magnificence, why would one ever choose any other goal?

A: One is simply unaware. The choices that resulted in our inborn level of consciousness, or karma, are beyond ordinary remembering. No matter what occurred before, the basic nature of the spiritual work is the same. The only difference is that karmic research would specify the origin of the content in a time dimension.

Q: Is there value in karmic past-life research?

A: There is some comfort in that explanation makes certain difficulties more comprehensible and therefore easier to accept. If one traces a life pattern back to the past, there is less likelihood to indulge in self-pity, resentment, guilt, or a feeling that life's events are unfair. One usually discovers that what is occurring in this life was done in the past to others.

   Karmic research reveals that life patterns tend to be 'impersonal' in that certain energies have been set in motion that will express themselves in this lifetime through any available, fortuitous channel. Such qualities as selfishness or cruelty to others in the past may rebound in this lifetime. Without karmic awareness, they might lead to denial and self-pity or indulging in the role of martyr or victim. When these adverse life patterns are detected, they can be undone through intense prayer and forgiveness. If this is not done, the individual's psyche will energize the unconscious inner mechanism of self-attack, guilt, self-blame, and depression. One might say that karmic research is a therapeutic effort which considerably supports spiritual advancement and comprehension.

Q: Is karmic research really necessary?

A: No. Many things can simply be lived through to their completion. However, people usually note recurrent patterns in their lives and begin to suspect that these may well have originated in some past life. Using kinesiologic testing, people are often surprised to find that what they had intuited all along did in fact occur.

If one intends to do past-life research, it is helpful to remember that the overall history of mankind over the centuries has been quite negative. When the consciousness level of humanity was below 200, there was mass negativity in the form of superstition, slavery, suppression of women, cruelty, fear, pestilence, war, torture, execution, and even obliteration of whole populations by savage hordes. At the same time, there were sizable numbers of people who did not engage in these things, but even so, their lives were influenced by their occurrence. Therefore, when doing past-life research, one has to be prepared to avoid being judgmental. Past events were an expression at the time of man's innate animal nature which was and still is inherent in the structure and mechanisms of the brain's anatomy.

At low consciousness levels, hate justified the total extermination of the enemy, even by the millions. In fact, to do so brought great glory to the conqueror. Slavery, which spared the lives of many thousands, was actually a step forward and gave value to human life. Paradoxically, slaves often lived much longer lives than did the populace from which they were captured (actually twice as long as in the American South). At the present consciousness level of humanity at 207, slaughter and slavery are seen as barbaric and reprehensible by Western civilized society, but for many centuries, they were accepted worldwide as normal aspects of human life.

Using the kinesiologic method of past-life research, one can diminish the influence of the past by taking responsibility for it as a spiritual or moral error and lack of evolution. One can now make a different choice which is more compassionate, accompanied by prayer and forgiveness. Animal behaviors in present cultures as well as in past ones have resulted in many decisions and acts based on rage, greed, hatred, killing, and pack loyalty, and all rely on force. One could say that the truly human values of ethics and spiritual responsibility are of relatively recent origin in the species. They are, in fact, so very recent that it was not until 1986 that the balance of mankind shifted from the negative, nonintegrous, and destructive behavior to the positive side. What had seemed 'just' until very recently no longer seems so in a more enlightened society.

Q: **Human life and experience express themselves in such extremes, from the unspeakably horrendous to the sublime. How can this be?**

A: This world can be viewed as a spiritual workshop wherein the consequences of past mistakes can be reworked so that, hopefully, one will 'choose differently this time'. The consequences of past actions are not due to some judgment or mechanism of 'punishment' on the part of the spiritual universe; instead, they are merely innate to its intrinsic design. They are neither good nor bad. One does not get punished by some arbitrary God for past errors; instead, one merely follows them through to their consequences and learns that what is depicted as 'sin' is essentially error based on ignorance. Civilization is evolving from primitive to evermore awareness and understanding. Whole continents still live in squalor, poverty, and chaotic destructiveness. This world could be described as purgatorial as it includes the whole spectrum of possibility, from extreme baseness to sainthood. The patterns are identifiable in the collective unconscious in which the archetypes were identified by the Swiss psychoanalyst Carl Jung.

Let us say that one carelessly drops a match in a hay barn and the barn burns down. The burning down of the hay barn is not a punishment for the careless dropping of the match; it is merely that the match put into motion a condition that set off a chain of events. If one desired to burn down the hay barn, then the effect would be considered to be a reward. If it is not desired, it would be a loss. In actuality, it is neither.

The spirit evolves over great periods of temporal time, with periodic reincarnations into the spiritual workshop of earth for growth and repairs. When all the repairs have been made, earthly life loses its value and attraction and rebirth into the human domain ceases.

Q: Can karma be 'escaped'?

A: There is not just 'bad' in one's karmic pattern, but also the accumulated 'good' karma, generally referred to as 'karmic merit', without which this lifetime would not have even occurred. The Buddha taught that to be a human is already a great good fortune and the opportunity should not be wasted; therefore, waste no time for life is fleeting. He stressed the importance of taking advantage of this golden opportunity and not to spend it in worldly pursuits, for they are ephemeral and based on transient illusions. This admonition was also repeated by Jesus, who taught that it is better to store up treasures in heaven where they are eternal, rather than on earth where they are transient and corruptible.

Karmic patterns are influential but not immutable due to the options available to the spiritual will. Correction comes about as a matter of intention by choosing a higher rather than a lower option. Temptation is the re-emergence of the old pattern which presents itself repeatedly until a decision is finalized and resolute. An unresolved karmic error tends to recur in such a way that it can be recognized and its underlying positionality identified. A most useful approach is to investigate possible role reversal—one is the victim in this lifetime of what one perpetrated on others in past lives, and now the ripples on the water are merely returning as the waves of this lifetime.

If one is uncomfortable with the concept of the term "karma," then it is equally serviceable to merely call it "the unconscious." If we do that, we could then say in psychological language that in the victim of this lifetime lies the hidden perpetrator in the personal or collective unconscious of previous lifetimes, who now unconsciously provokes attacks from others.

Rarely is a person willing to look within themselves for the origin of their difficulties because it tends to become projected onto others in the endless game of victim and perpetrator. The self-serving victim positionality of the ego is tenacious, and the ego will play the game even to the point of one's physical death. To protect itself, the ego will go to any extreme.

In clinical practice, one sees the endless parade of the deadly duos of perpetrator and victim. The pattern does not become resolved either experientially, psychologically, or spiritually until the victim takes responsibility for some aspect of their own personality, albeit repressed, that played the role of the provocateur. It is very informative to watch the degree of tenacity by which the victim refuses to acknowledge any responsibility.

In most domestic disputes, it can be seen that the victim very well knew all along the boundaries beyond which the perpetrator could not be pushed and, with a single remark, triggered the attack. The triggering remark is aimed at a specific point in the assailant's psyche which is known to be vulnerable.

For instance, a woman approached her husband and wanted to have sex, but he was not in the mood. She felt rejected and then stabbed him with a verbal knife by remarking "Well, I guess you are not much of a man." She knew his cultural heritage very well, and this comment indeed pushed him over the edge to potential violence which, in this particular case, he stopped at the last minute. Instead, he left and got a divorce. It was an insult that he could not handle. Questioning masculinity is a well-known vulnerable spot with which some women know how to trigger an emotionally unstable man.

It is always important to find out exactly what the last sentence was that was spoken by a victim prior to an assault. Again, in the domestic arena, men use silence rather than insults to push their spouse over the edge so they can say "I didn't say anything at all. She just flew into a rage and started breaking furniture."

We see the same phenomenon in the game of international disputes and violence. Each side throws bricks at the police until they get the police to shoot so that the 'innocent victim' (preferably a child) can be videotaped and used to inflame further violence. There are annual marches whereby the supposedly 'innocent' bring about retaliatory violence to their own countrymen.

Although the critical level of integrity is the very threshold of spiritual progress, one can see that by the structure of the ego, it can be difficult to achieve. The strength of the ego is such that it can be overcome only by spiritual power.

The more educated spiritual seeker takes responsibility for what seems to be happening 'out there' since inner investigation always reveals that the perception and source of the 'out there' is actually 'in here'. The interplay of society's ego programs is fascinating to the mind, which accounts for the popularity of movies where, from a safe space, the ego's subtle maneuverings can be observed on the world's stage. As one watches history unfold, one sees the seduction of the allegiance of the masses (which is due only to God) to subvert that allegiance to the inflated egos of supposed leaders. The subversion of spiritual truth to political ends is as old as civilization and continues rampant to this very day.

Q: Is there no escape from the ego and its karma?

A: Enlightenment is the only total escape, and spiritual endeavor helps to loosen its hold.

Q: Is the ego the source of karma?

A: It is its locus and repository. It is very important to realize that the ego and karma are one and the same thing. By simple kinesiological testing, within less than a minute an enormous amount of helpful information can be obtained as to the origin of a problem. However, what is important is that the problem is still present. To separate this life from others is merely an artifact created by perception. In Reality, there is only one life with periodic reincarnations because conditions are favorable for the resolution of certain problems.

   For instance, the battlefield in war affords the opportunity for souls to cross over the line of 200 (from Fear to Courage) in the face of even bodily death for a higher principle. To overcome fear, young men throughout history have been notorious for their life-threatening pursuits and attraction to high-risk occupations and sports. Bullfighting, skydiving, motorcycle racing, etc., allow them to conquer their fear of bodily death and thus conquer cowardice. Although this is a psychological accomplishment, it still lacks great spiritual merit because that leap over the energy field of 200 can be done only when the courageous defeat of fear is done in the name of a higher principle, such as loyalty, dedication to God, country, truth, or honor. This was symbolized by the knight of old when he took a glove or a rose from a symbolically significant woman and carried it with him on his quest or crusade.

Q: How does another earthly life serve one most expeditiously?

A: There are actually split seconds in which the options present themselves. These are very critical moments to watch for, and with one-pointedness of mind, they will become apparent. These moments of decision last approximately 1/10,000th of a second, as estimated by kinesiologic testing. The miracle arises in this gap. In this instant, the Holy Spirit is present and available directly by God's grace. In the ego's minute gap, the Holy Spirit empowers the opportunity, and this is the 'space' in which free will operates. It is in this moment that the warrior can choose mercy or cruelty, life or death.

Prayer and spiritual commitment give assent to the Presence as the Holy Spirit to 'create a space', as it would seem, in the progression of the sequences in temporal time for that critical instant of awareness. Based on the laws of the universe, that split instant does not open unless invited. God forces no one to choose Him. All spiritual progress is by invitation and free choice, which are consequences of prayer and spiritual intention, for these gaps are hidden gifts.

Q: Why did Jesus Christ not teach about karma?

A: The fact that the ego and karma are one and the same would make directly addressing the subject superfluous. It might have been thought to be an unnecessary diversion which, if presented, would have seemed like a deviation to the culture of the times. In a more spiritually advanced culture, such as in India and the Far East, the subject had already been accepted and was quite familiar to the people. The populous at Jesus' time would most likely have considered the subject foreign or unacceptable.

Jesus was aware that salvation depends on the voluntary letting go of the negative aspects of the ego (sin) and the striving for unconditional love and spiritual virtue. If the ego is the focus of spiritual endeavor, then its dissolution signals the end of the karma that was involved in its formation. He did teach that the fate (karma) of the soul was adversely affected by sin and, therefore, its destiny (karma) was either heaven or hell.

Both the Buddha and Jesus also knew that the ego cannot be overcome without the power and spiritual help of a teacher, a savior, or intercession by the Holy

Spirit. The need for a teacher was already a tradition accepted by Eastern religions in which the sage played a crucial role as the source or fountain of spiritual power and teaching of truth. Whether or not this is a requirement in an individual seeker's life can be discerned and clarified by the use of kinesiologic questioning.

Jesus did give recognition to reincarnation when he stated that Elias had returned as John, the Baptist (Matthew 11:7-14 and 17:10-13). As revealed by kinesiologic spiritual research, Jesus had never had previous human lifetimes, but instead had actually descended from Heaven. His purpose was to reveal the truth of the Reality of God and Heaven, and his mission was the salvation of mankind.

According to the same research methodology, a savior is necessary for all who calibrate below level 600. In contrast, the purpose of the Buddha, who had had many previous lifetimes, was to teach the way to Enlightenment, namely, to reach level 600 or beyond. Thus, the Buddha recalled prior incarnations and stressed the lessons of karma and the importance of avoiding the negative karma (sin) that would preclude the soul's going on to Heaven after physical death.

Those seekers who are more spiritually evolved choose virtue and Heaven out of love for God rather than merely avoiding sin out of fear or guilt. If sin is primarily ignorance plus animal instinct, it is counterproductive to 'hate' it and thereby become entrapped in an additional ego positionality.

Q: **For many years, you were a consultant to many religious organizations, including Catholic nuns and priests, Episcopal ministers, and a Zen monastery, and you still counsel monks and clergy. Is the kinesiologic test of practical use?**

A: In years past, there was inner spiritual experience, spiritual vision, awareness, and discernment which are still the mainstay, along with intuition. The problem that arose over the years was how to discern spiritual states from pathologic ones. They could be put in the form of a list. Differentiation is now quite simple and fast, using the kinesiologic test.

Authentic Spiritual State	Pathologic, or Non-spiritual State
Samadhi	Catatonic
Religious Ecstasy	Mania (bipolar hyper-religiosity)
Illumination	Grandiosity
Enlightenment	Religious Delusion
Piety	Scrupulosity (obsessive-compulsive)
Inspiration	Imagination
Visions	Hallucinations
Authentic Spiritual Teacher	False Guru, Imposter, Spiritual Con Artist
Experiential	Intellectual
Devotion	Zealotry, Hyper-religiosity
Committed	Obsessed, Brainwashed by Cult, Victimized
Dark Night of the Soul	Pathologic Depression
Detachment	Withdrawal, Indifference
Nonattachment, Acceptance	Passivity
Transcendent State	Mutism
Trusting	Naïve
Advanced State	Psychosis, Egomania
Beatific	Euphoria
Humility	Low Self-esteem
Spiritual Sharing	Proselytizing
Commitment	Religiosity
Inspired	Messianic

God Shock	Schizophrenic Disorganization
Spiritual Ecstasy	Manic State, High on Drugs
Genuine Spiritual Leader	Spiritual Politician, Cult Leader
Free	Psychopathic
Teaching	Controlling

Q: What is the answer to the challenge of the scientifically minded to prove spiritual 'reality'?

A: Spiritual reality is verifiable but not provable. The term "proof" is limited in application to the Newtonian paradigm of reality which is based on form and an implied process called causality. Proof is limited to content and form.

That which is 'provable' is not Reality but perception or mentation only. Reality is subjective and knowable only by virtue of identity with the known. 'Provables' belong to the classification and level of limitation and are arbitrary abstractions whose sole 'reality' is merely the consequence of selection and identification. The phenomenal is not of the same dimension as the noumenal.

CHAPTER SIX
REALIZATION

Q: **It is said that there are ten thousand ways to God, yet quite a number of religions and spiritual schools claim that theirs is the only way. How can that be?**

A: Claims to exclusivity are generally due to ignorance or are attempts to control people. If we look at the histories of all the great spiritual teachers throughout time, they arrived at their understandings through a variety of pathways. What is common to all enlightened teachers is that they totally surrendered the ego. How that came about differed for each of them, but the end result was the same. God does not exhibit favoritism or exclusivity.

Choice results from the seeker's spiritual inspiration and karmic tendencies. Everyone has already been 'chosen by God'. The Self is already present or else life and existence would not be. Acceptance is up to the individual.

The love of God is absolute and unconditional. The sky does not 'be' for some people and 'not be' for others, nor does the sun shine on only a select few who have been arbitrarily chosen. God is complete and total. Flattery is a human notion. One can worship the sun, but the sun is immune to manipulation.

Realization is not a 'gain' or an accomplishment, nor is it something that is 'given' as a reward for being good. These are all notions from childhood. God is immutable and cannot be manipulated into granting favors or seduced by bargaining or adulation. Worship benefits the worshipper by reinforcing commitment and inspiration. God is still, silent, and unmoving.

Q: What are the most valuable qualities for a spiritual seeker?

A: Start with certainty and a feeling of security instead of self-doubt or timidity. Accept without reservation that you are worthy of the quest and be resolved to totally surrender to the truth about God.

The facts that are to be unreservedly accepted are simple and very powerful. Surrendering to them brings enormous spiritual advancement.

1. The living proof of God's love and will for you is the gift of your own existence.

2. Do not compare yourself with others regarding 'holiness', merit, goodness, deservingness, sinlessness, etc. These are all human notions, and God is not limited by human notions.

3. Accept that the concept of 'the fear of God' is ignorance. God is peace and love and nothing else.

4. Realize that the depiction of God as a 'judge' is a delusion of the ego that arises as a projection of guilt from the punishment of childhood. Realize that God is not a parent.

   Christ's teaching was essentially and simply to avoid the negativity (calibrated levels below 200), and the goal of his teaching was for his followers to reach Unconditional Love (calibration level of 540). He knew that once the level of Unconditional Love was reached, the soul's destiny after death was certain and the soul was safe. This is essentially the same conclusion that is taught by the world's great religions, such as Lotus Land Buddhism.

6. Realize that salvation and enlightenment are somewhat different goals. Salvation requires purification of the ego; enlightenment requires its total dissolution. The goal of enlightenment is

more demanding and radical.

7. Clarify that it is not a personal 'you' who is seeking enlightenment but an impersonal quality of consciousness that is the motivator. Spiritual inspiration and dedication carry forth the work.

8. Comfort replaces insecurity when one realizes that the most important goal has already been accomplished. That goal is to be on the road of spiritual dedication. Spiritual development is not an accomplishment but a way of life. It is an orientation that brings its own rewards, and what is important is the direction of one's motives.

9. Appreciate that every step forward benefits everyone. One's spiritual dedication and work is a gift to life and the love of mankind.

10. There is no timetable or prescribed route to God. Although each person's route is unique, the terrain to be covered is relatively common to all. The work is to surmount and transcend the common human failings that are inherent in the structure of the human ego. One would like to think that they are personal; however, the ego itself is not personal. It was inherited along with becoming a human being. Details differ based on past karma.

11. Intense prayer augments dedication and inspiration and facilitates progress.

12. The Grace of God is available to all. Historically, the 'Grace of the Sage' is available to the committed spiritual seeker. The strength of the ego can be formidable, and without the assistance of the power of higher spiritual beings, the ego cannot of itself transcend itself. Fortunately, the power of the consciousness of every great teacher or avatar who has ever lived still remains and is available. To focus on a teacher or their teachings by meditation makes the power of that teacher available to the seeker. It is the will of every truly enlightened sage that every

spiritual seeker succeeds, and not just the members of some specific or exclusive group. Just as the individual seeker of spiritual advancement benefits all mankind, thus also does the enlightenment of the Teachers benefit the seeker. That power and energy is available to call upon. There are no requirements or obligations.

Q: Why does spiritual work often seem like such a struggle?

A: The ego has habitual modes of determining perception. They have to be identified first before they can be disassembled. One has to give up guilt about having an ego. This can be facilitated by examining its origins.

The human is in a very difficult position in the evolution of consciousness. Life on this plane is traditionally pictured as starting from the primordial 'ooze' and having primitive organisms. From the very onset of biologic life, we see that an organism is confronted with multiple challenges to survival. The basic motives and devices of the ego are simple and obvious if we merely look at the products of animal life.

Human life entails the strategies of the animal: territoriality, species competition, turf wars, group domination, hunting, killing rivals, mating rituals, protection and nurturing of the young, sibling rivalry, intimidation, and control of others. In addition, there are the fear of attack, dangers, and the fear of expulsion from the pack or the herd. These animal patterns are ingrained into physiologic and emotional responses as the so-called instincts.

Over the millennia arose a sophistication of these instincts as learned patterns of behavior that were reinforced by societal and parental input and training. These became not just individual but heavily reinforced societal patterns which were formalized into political, nationalistic, and judicial positionalities and belief systems. The intellect became an important tool for survival, and its sophistication allowed for elaboration of all these basically animal programs. Consciousness has no inherent programs; they are all inputted as software into the hardware of consciousness itself.

Although now expressed in the intellect, the basic configurations of these survival patterns arose from the animal world. Even education is dedicated primarily to survival and success. The inherent motives of the ego are therefore survival and gain, both of which are fear based.

The mechanisms of the human organism are also regulated by the neurochemistry and structure of the brain, with its inherent pain/pleasure responses. This self-actuating reward mechanism is another trap that has to be bypassed. Human ingenuity has baited this mechanism by the discovery of artificial reward/pleasure devices, such as artificial substances to which the chemistry of the brain is vulnerable and reprogrammable; thus, there is even an inherited genetic propensity to addiction which then eclipses and replaces all other goal seeking.

To make matters worse, all these levels of behavior and programmed attitudes emit an energy field in the collective energy field of all mankind. They are thus reinforced from the field of influence, which is inaccessible to ordinary awareness. These consciousness levels are further reinforced by the media and all forms of human communication that support these programs and introduce social approval and disapproval.

Although this recapitulation of the biologic roots of the ego may seem obvious, the purpose is to increase awareness of the origin and importance of these mechanisms which are inherent and inborn rather than personally self-created. Relief of guilt and greater compassion for oneself and others occur through realizing that the individual person did not volitionally create the structure of the ego, nor did anybody else. The human condition is primarily a karmic 'given'. It can be accepted compassionately as such without condemnation and is therefore neither good nor bad. Mankind lives in the realm of tension between emotional instincts and the counterbalancing power of spiritual awakening (i.e., the animal/angel conflict).

Q: If the ego is biologically rooted, genetically propagated, societally reinforced, and strongly reprogrammed, how can it be overcome?

A: It can be transcended. More important is not the nature of the ego but the problem of identification with it as the 'me', the 'I', or 'myself'.

The ego was inherited as an 'it', and is actually an impersonal 'it'. The problem arises because one personalizes and identifies with it. That 'it' of the ego structure is not unique or individual, and it is relatively similar, with karmic variations, in everyone. What really varies from individual to individual is the degree to which one is enslaved by its programs. The degree of dominance is therefore determined by the extent to which one identifies with it. Inherently, it has no power, and the power to decline the ego's programs increases exponentially as one progresses spiritually. That is the real meaning of the Scale of Consciousness.

When we see how people are dominated by the ego's programs, we realize that, without awareness or insight, they are relatively unable to help themselves. We say they are 'driven' by greed, hate, fear, addiction, or pride. It is a mistake to adopt the hypothetical, moralistic positionality that 'they ought to know better'. As a matter of fact, that is really not the case. To be unconscious means just that; thus, 'sin' can be seen really as a limitation in the evolution of consciousness. This limitation was termed 'ignorance' by both the Buddha and Jesus Christ. As evolution expresses itself in gradations, some people will be farther along the road than others. When we see this simple fact, forgiveness and compassion replace anger, fear, hatred, or condemnation. The willingness to forgive others is reflected in our own capacity for self-forgiveness and acceptance.

Q: Would not acceptance of limitation expressed in a sinful way verge on immorality or lack of ethics?

A: Compassion and forgiveness do not mean approval. Those who live in the energy fields below 200 are subject to relentless torment. In the Christian tradition, one is taught to pray for sinners. At the same time, one is advised to also avoid and dissociate from nonintegrity and negativity ('evil') rather than confront it. The 'sinful' can be seen as unfortunates whose spiritual growth is still rudimentary.

Q: Is the purpose of becoming familiar with the ego to disarm it and open the way to acceptance?

A: We see that trying to 'overcome' the ego without really understanding it brings up guilt, self-condemnation, and other negative feelings, which is one of the main reasons why many people are reluctant to become involved in spiritual work. Because of this, people are afraid to be honest with themselves and tend to project the downside of the ego onto others or even onto God. Jealousy, retaliation, vengeance, partiality, etc., are all attributes of the ego and not of God.

From a greater context, we can view that the ego is not 'evil' but is primarily a self-interested animal. Unless the 'animal self' is understood and accepted, its influence cannot be diminished. Like a pet, the inner animal can be comical and entertaining, and we can enjoy it without guilt and look forward to getting it trained and properly housebroken. This training is what is meant by the word "civilization."

Q: Why is so much attention placed on the ego?

A: Realization is a progressive process. Spiritual progress is hastened by understanding the true nature of the ego. It is not an enemy to be attacked or defeated, nor is it an evil to be vanquished. It is dissolved by compassionate understanding.

Most military and diplomatic blunders are made by not first thoroughly studying the enemy. This has been ruefully admitted by many famous military leaders. Both Napoleon and Hitler underestimated the Russians. Hitler underestimated the resolve of the British. Stalin underestimated the duplicity of the Germans, and Admiral Yamamoto said ruefully after Pearl Harbor that "We have awakened a sleeping giant."

It is therefore advisable for the spiritual seeker to be familiar with the structure of the ego and to be aware that it is not dissolved by either denial or guilt. Curiously, the ego's hold is weakened by acceptance, familiarity, and compassionate understanding; in contrast, it is reinforced by self-criticism, condemnation, fear, and shame.

Q: The ego no longer sounds as formidable when viewed with compassion.

A: The ego is transcended because it is not the ultimate reality but merely a set of survival tools from the animal world. Its emotional expressions are also displayed by children. The ego is therefore not only the animal but also the child. Freud demonstrated that the power of the unconscious was undone in psychoanalysis by the method of primarily making the unconscious conscious.

Anna Freud described the ego's mechanisms of defense. Because of her work, we are familiar with the concepts of repression, suppression, denial, and projection, as well as the action of turning instinctual drives inward against the self. Thus, the drives that were biologically innate from the animal world were hidden in what psychoanalysis called the 'id'. Control mechanisms of the 'superego' (the conscience) were derived from parents and society, and the conscious ego then had the job of reconciling these basic biologic drives with society. The 'ego-ideal' was the idealized image of what the self wished to become. It included the positive identifications with heroes, idealized traits, spiritual ideals, and personality styles. The 'persona' was that aspect of the ego which was presented to society, and its style was then the so-called personality.

The Swiss psychoanalyst, Carl Jung, enlarged this paradigm of the psyche to include the spiritual dimension of man which, curiously, like the biologic drives, is also inherent as a 'given'. Jung also saw the commonality of mankind, which he termed the "collective unconscious," that operated more by symbols than by concepts.

In later years, the nature of the self was elaborated upon by so-called "self-psychology," and the spiritual aspects were further studied as "transpersonal psychology."

The problems attendant to the mere fact of one's existence became the subject of "existential analysis," and thus, sophisticated psychology emerged into the critical area that had preoccupied philosophy over the centuries, namely, current "humanism."

Q: Is it necessary to know all these subjects to comprehend the ego?

A: No, this is just a review for the sake of appreciating mankind's struggle to know itself. These represent the efforts of the intellect to transcend the domination of the ego.

Q: From the foregoing, it becomes apparent that the intellect is not the answer to the ego but is actually its refinement.

A: That is correct. The intellect calibrates in the 400s, which is a boon to society in its expression as science, with its vast accomplishments in medicine and technology. The intellect, however, is a two-edged sword. It can save you from dying of malaria, but it can also invent nuclear weapons and poisonous gas. The 400s are still dealing with form and forces, whether they be molecules or concepts. Limitation is inherent in form itself, and its limitations cannot be escaped by refinement but only by going beyond them. Thus, those who wish to move beyond form look to the nonlinear domain, traditionally termed "spiritual." One has to move beyond force into the realm of power because the intransigent ego is tenacious and heavily reinforced.

Whereas form requires great effort, in contrast, the grace of power is its capacity to accomplish immense tasks effortlessly. It is the unique quality of power which accomplishes great effects, and not its quantity, for it does not exist in the realm of the quantifiable.

Spiritual power resembles a catalyst in that it transforms without being used up in the process. Notice in public life, for instance, how even a little "I'm sorry" can stop a whole war from emerging between nations. Most wars generate from the energy field of consciousness that calibrates at the levels of greed, hatred, or pride. The antidote to pride is humility, which does not mean to humble oneself but instead means to give up vanity and pretense and consider realistic appraisal. The benefit of true humility is that it prevents later 'egg on the face' disgrace as well as self-destruction.

Humility really means accurate, realistic assessment and awareness of limits and parameters. Thus, the intellect is not incorrect; it is merely the wrong tool to use to arrive at more advanced spiritual awareness. An intelligent intellect becomes aware of its limitations and thus seeks for answers outside itself. We also see this in the most recent cutting edge of science, which is now attempting to understand the nature of consciousness, without which it cannot progress significantly.

Q: We see that the ego is a necessary step in the evolution of consciousness. After the universe of form has been explained and studied, is the next step to look beyond form to try to find its source?

A: That is the logical progression. The study of form is fascinating to the intellect in its expressions of physics, chemistry, astronomy, cosmology, etc. Man then begins to ask where the universe came from and where is it going. Actually, this demonstrates another animal instinct that is very important, that of curiosity. In order to find food, a mate, or shelter, the animal is always instinctively searching and seems to have an insatiable curiosity. Exploration is innate to mankind, and its highest levels lead to spiritual inquiry. This brings up the questions of who am I, what am I, where did I come from, what is the origin and destiny of the self, and who and where is God.

Q: Is curiosity then an advantage to the spiritual seeker?

A: With humility, it is a useful servant. Without discernment, however, it can lead to serious pitfalls. Curiosity can lead the naïve seeker into blind alleys and useless distractions as well as snares and serious, painful traps. This is where a true teacher is necessary. Again, humility means acceptance of the indisputable fact that cannot be repeated too often: *The human mind is incapable of discerning truth from falsehood.* Were this not so, there would have been no wars in history, no social problems, and no ignorance or poverty. Everyone would be enlightened, and the consciousness level of mankind would not have remained at 190, century after century.

Q: How did this blindness come about?

A: The animal lives in the world of form. The basic elements of survival are body, food, and the ability to discern enemies. The animal brain evolves, therefore, to facilitate perception. As we look beyond the content of the ego, we come to a quality of critical importance to the seeker of enlightenment—its basic function of perception. This is of great use to the animal but it results in the creation of duality in the field of consciousness in which location, direction, and timing arise because they are necessary for the survival of the animal. For instance, to catch a prey, it is necessary to form a dualistic perception of a 'here' versus a 'there'. The limitation of form results in the reliance on the senses. Thus arise the concepts of space and distance, and the ego concludes that this perception signifies reality.

There was no reason for the animal to suspect that there was a higher reality, for its needs and their fulfillment were all within the realm of content and form. Man evolved beyond merely being an animal when the ego learned the manipulation of images in the form of thought. These images became more sophisticated and allowed for the discernment of how things were alike as well as how they were different (e.g., the classic left brain/right brain analogy or digital versus analog computer).

The forebrain enlarged to handle the now complex computational requirements of thinking in abstract concepts, symbols, and language. The forebrain, however, was an 'add-on' to the old animal brain. Thus, the new brain had the advantage but also the disadvantage of the old and the new. There was no disconnect switch between the two regions; thus, the animal emotions could flood the intellect with fear, anger, greed, etc. The intellect could also manufacture sequences of images that were associated with the animal drives.

Q: **Is it the structure of the ego and not just its content that is the major impediment?**

A: That is correct. Spiritual progress is possible because the mind, through understanding, is able to recontextualize the contents of the ego and discern its very mechanism.

Once this occurs, one is no longer blindly 'at the mercy' of the ego. This progression is depicted in the famous Zen 'ox-herding' pictures. In this sequence, first, the ego is like a wild animal; in the next picture, it is tamed and controlled. Next, the ego is transcended, and in the last picture, it disappears.

Q: **Can you summarize the critical element for the evolution of consciousness to the state of enlightenment?**

A: Note that the ego habitually takes a positionality. In the naïve person, it is usually unspoken or unconscious. Positionality then automatically creates a duality of seeming opposites. At this point, the mind is creating the world of perception, which is like a lens that distorts, enlarges, or diminishes meaning and significance. This perception is the product of belief systems and presumptions and thus becomes a distracting filter. Therefore, essence cannot be perceived from a dualistic positionality.

Input is run through the software programs that simultaneously edit the incoming programs. Reality is thus obscured and hidden behind a perceptual screen; therefore, the self lives in a perceived, edited translation of information. This processing creates an extremely small time delay (estimated at 1/10,000th of a second). This editing function of perception simultaneously interprets meaning in which the intellect and especially the memory play significant roles.

Q: **The structure and complexity of the ego's functions and proclivity to automatically edit perceptions make it seem like a formidable obstacle.**

A: If we know its structure and mode of function, then we know its susceptibility. This becomes experientially apparent during meditation; from the impersonal viewpoint of the witness/observer, we watch how it operates. The realization eventually occurs that the 'I' is not the content or the data but an impersonal field several steps removed from the content of the programs. One then realizes that one is the audience rather than the participant or subject.

Many spiritual practices and techniques have evolved over the centuries to facilitate this disidentification with the ego and its world of limited perceptual dualities of content. This is also assisted by spiritual knowledge of the nature of consciousness. One piece of correct information has within it the power to cancel out vast amounts of erroneous concepts and positionalities. The spiritual information is accompanied by a high-frequency carrier wave of great power that originates from the Self of the sage, teacher, or avatar and is therefore far more powerful than the weak energy field of the ego.

To know that the Self is context and that, in contrast, the self is content is already a huge leap forward. The naïve seeker merely keeps reshuffling the content. Lifetimes are spent struggling to overcome the ego and its sins so as to eventually reach the promise of a God who is believed to be elsewhere in place (heaven) and in time (after death), or perhaps much, much later in another lifetime if one has accumulated enough merit or good karma.

Q: **Spiritual progress can seem slow or become suddenly rapid and unexpected.**

A: Humility and surrender at great depth, as well as prayer, can shorten the process. The seeming duration of time is because one is looking for a result. Even when the ego's energies have been 'disconnected', its momentum seems to need to run out. For instance, when a giant ship, such as a great tanker, stops its engines, it often continues several miles farther before it finally comes to a stop. The ego often seems to collapse in a piecemeal fashion. Once faith in the reality of the ego as being the true self is undermined, its dissolution has already begun. When one's loyalty and allegiance is shifted from the ego to the ultimate reality of God, a space is created. Into that opening flows God's Grace as represented by the Holy Spirit.

Q: What of worldly renunciation? It is considered necessary by some teachings.

A: There is a tradition of totally leaving the ordinary world and becoming a lone recluse or joining a reclusive or even silent order or a formal monastic order. The monk and nun have been respected throughout history for their spiritual dedication which has required abstinence, poverty, chastity, humility, service, and simplicity. For even the average spiritual aspirant, some or even all these elements may be adhered to at various times, even if only for time-limited formal retreats. Ridding oneself of worldly possessions commonly occurs, as does withdrawing from the glamour of the world and moving to more serene locations and lifestyles.

In its broadest and most basic sense, renunciation means the discarding of illusion and the obstruction to the realization of truth and the Reality of God. Thus, all pathways to God renounce falsity and are devoted to that which radiates love, peace, holiness, compassion, forgiveness, mercy, and charity. It also means the choice of renouncing ignorance for Truth, darkness for Light, and the temptations of the ego, such as hatred, anger, pride, malice, greed, and selfishness. Renunciation also means freedom from the dualistic trap of denunciation, or from becoming polarized and trapped in the positionalities of the 'polarities of the opposites'. The simplest renunciation is simply refusal or nonacceptance. To choose 'up-ness', it is not necessary to 'fight down-ness' but merely to decline the alternative.

SECTION TWO
THE REALIZATION OF DIVINITY

CHAPTER SEVEN

THE RADICAL REALITY OF THE SELF

Q: If the Presence of God as Self cannot be experienced by the mind or by thought, how can it be known?

A: It is not necessary to know about the Self but simply to become it by letting go of the non-Self. The realization comes about as a subjective transformation.

Q: It is said that the seeker and the sought are one and the same. Is that correct?

A: It is actually incorrect. 'That which is looking for the Self' is the ego/self; thus, they are not the same. The Self has no need or capacity to search for that which it already is.

Q: Why is this book simply called *I?* The usual expression for God-consciousness is "I Am."

A: "Am" signifies beingness. The ultimate truth is beyond is-ness, beingness, or any intransitive verb. Any attempt at Self-definition, such as "I Am That I Am" or "I Am" is redundant. The ultimate reality is beyond all names. "I" signifies the radical subjectivity of the state of Realization. It is in itself the complete statement of Reality.

Q: Is the ultimate truth the same as "void"?

A: The term "void" has created much confusion and has misled people throughout the centuries. It implies nothingness, or nonexistence, which is not a possibility in the Real. There is no opposite to God. Only Truth has actual existence. What is more commonly meant by the term "void" is absence of form, absence of substance, or nonduality. It is often confused with nonexistence. To confuse the Ultimate Allness with nothingness/void is to fall victim to the falsity of trying to prove that nonexistence actually exists.

Q: **There are translations of the Buddhist teachings that describe the ultimate reality as "void."**

A: Here is where the kinesiologic test of truth can be of great service. The nonform of the Unmanifest is not to be confused with nothingness or nonexistence. The word "nothing" literally means "no thing," or nonform (i.e., unmanifest, the Buddha's *anatta*). It is empty of all form, including mentalizations, and thus, paradoxically, it is everything. Similarly, if you are nowhere (no position in space), then you are everywhere. If you are not limited in time, then you are timeless. That which is unlimited by form, time, or space is obviously everywhere always, and all present (omnipotent, omnipresent, and omniscient). The "Buddha Nature" is the Unmanifest.

Q: **What does it mean that power is the expression and consequence of context?**

A: It is context which defines both limits and possibilities. Unlimited context is concordant with the Infinite Unmanifest, whose power is infinite.

   In the ultimate definition, God is unlimited context out of which arises infinite power. We see its expression in the visible universes which are expanding at the speed of light. Beyond form, such conceptions, however, have no concordant reality.

Q: **Many questions that arise, therefore, are not really answerable.**

A: That is true. That is because they are often just tautologies. They merely mean what they are defined to mean but have no corollary in existence.

The mind presumes that a mentation which seems logical and intellectually reasonable must have a concordant reality. This is a major source of fallacy in human life. The specious nature of speculative intellectualization is revealed by the discovery that it has no concordant representation in actuality. The validity of truth is based solely on actual existence and therefore subjectively verifiable.

Historically, we see constant examples of this in failed social policies and political disasters. The error is the Achilles' heel of Academia whose input to society is given undue merit and status. The hypothetical is not the Real. This also gives rise to the gross miscalculations of failed intelligence agencies of various governments about the motives and probable actions of other countries. The basic fallacy is the presumption that 'other people' are ruled by ethics, logic and reason, which is a grave error. That is why this country is always 'surprised' by the response of other countries or segments of society that have very different agendas.

Academia calibrates in the 400s. Other societies and major segments of society calibrate much lower and are far below 200. Such societies are ruled by expediency, hatred, greed, selfishness, emotionality, etc. Thus, 'food for the poor' sent to other countries is customarily commandeered by the rich who feel no obligation to the 'undeserving' lower class.

Q: **If the ultimate reality is radical subjectivity, how can it be meaningfully conveyed or communicated?**

A: It is not verbally communicated. It becomes known by being it. That propensity is facilitated by the Grace (consciousness level) of the teacher. It is a self-existent identity. In Reality, there is not the triad of me, you, and a message; all are the same. The Self is the message. For example, to experience sunshine, nothing needs to be known or spoken or communicated about it. Existence is already complete and total. All definition is already an abstraction and therefore not the reality that it describes.

The source of all that exists is Divinity; thus, all that exists is already perfect. Without that perfection, nothing could exist. From the viewpoint of enlightenment, one might say that the linear is observed from the context of the nonlinear. To put it differently, existence is the manifestation of Divinity as form. In and of itself, the universe is therefore harmless. The viewpoint from enlightenment transcends the experiencer, the observer, the witness, and even awareness itself.

Q: **Why the word "Self"?**

A: The experience of the Presence is radically and profoundly subjective. It is commonly presumed by the mind that God is 'elsewhere', namely, above, beyond, transcendent, in heaven, or somewhere back in history or in the future. Traditionally, however, God is described as both transcendent and immanent. The term "Self" emphasizes that God is discovered within as the ultimate reality that underlies one's actual existence in the 'here and now' (e.g., "Heaven is within you.").

The Buddha is said to have avoided using the term "God" because of the prevalence of misconceptions surrounding it. He wanted to avoid all the limitations that that conceptualization confounds. The Self as Awareness is often referred to in literature as Light. As recounted in Genesis, the Unmanifest became Manifest first as Light, which was the radiance of the energy of God that took form as the universe.

The term "Self" also overcomes the dualistic notion that one is separated from God. Historically, the picture that there is a sinner down here on Earth and there is a God up there somewhere in heaven is the viewpoint of the ego. Thus, to most people, the term "God" implies "otherness." However, there is no separation in the Allness of Creation, so it is impossible for the created to be separate from the Creator. Enlightenment is therefore the revelation of the Self when the illusion of the reality of a separate self is removed.

The constant awareness of one's existence as 'I' is the ever present expression of the innate divinity of the Self. This is a universal, constant experience that is purely subjective and of which no proof is possible or necessary. The 'I' of the Self is the expression of Divinity as Awareness which is therefore beyond time and form. The truth of this identity is obscured by the duality created by perception and disappears when all positionalities are relinquished.

Q: How does one find Reality?

A: Truth is radical subjectivity. With the collapse of the illusions of duality, including the supposed 'reality' of a separate 'self', there remains only the state of the Infinite 'I', which is the manifestation of the Unmanifest as the Self.

There is neither subject nor object. Like infinite space, there is no distance, time, duration, or locality. All prevails simultaneously. All is self-evident, self-aware, self-revealing, and total.

Q: If Reality is without division, how does form appear?

A: Form is an expression of the potentiality of consciousness as it evolved as an aspect of Creation. The substrate of form is formless and yet innate to the expression of form as creation. Thus, form and creation are an observation.

Q: What is the relationship of the term "Truth" to God?

A: The source of infinite power is infinite context. God is infinite context, which is the unmanifest Divinity termed "the Godhead." Out of the Unmanifest infinite context of the Godhead arises God as the Creator of the manifest universe, which is therefore without beginning or end. The appearance and disappearance of universes is an illusion of perception. This illusion is referred to in the *Vedas* as "Indra's Dream." Indra, as the Supreme Reality, manifests a universe as a dream. When Indra breathes out in the dream, a universe appears, and when Indra breathes in, the universe disappears. At the next breath, another universe appears, and so on, infinitely.

Current scientific research has come up with an approximation of the age of the universe and the "big bang" theory. It claims that the big bang occurred billions of years ago, or so. In infinite time, billions of years are equivalent to a microsecond. Thus, there is an infinite series of universes and dimensions, without end.

Q: Is form then perception?

A: Perception, like awareness, is an impersonal quality of consciousness. The absolute Reality is the substrate of consciousness. Consciousness is an impersonal quality of Divinity expressed as awareness and is nondualistic and nonlinear. Consciousness is like infinite space that is capable of awareness. Conscious awareness is a quality of the Divine Essence. In Reality, there is neither subject nor object.

Q: Explain again what is meant by the term "I."

A: The statement "I" is the only complete and accurate sentence by which absolute truth can be accurately described. To add the term "am" is redundant as well as inaccurate because "am" implies beingness, and absolute reality is beyond beingness or is-ness. (Calibrated level 997.) These terms would inherently create a polarity of opposites, such as existence versus nonexistence or beingness versus non-beingness.

Q: Is the Self the "I"?

A: It is difficult for the mind to understand absolute self-identity. The mind is used to thinking in terms of a subject and a predicate in which a statement adjuncts a noun with a verb, such as beingness or is-ness or doingness. That which has existence is already total and complete or it would not exist. Existence does not require dependence on some other condition. Conditional existence is therefore an illusion of the ego/mind which believes that nothing exists except as dependent on something outside itself. Existence is self-complete and unconditional. Existence is solely by the grace of God, by Divine ordinance. (This statement verifies at calibration level 998.) Appearance reflects conditions and is therefore transitory.

Explanation

The mind is used to descriptions and definitions in terms of qualities, conditions, and presumed causes. Thus, to perception, nothing is complete or total in and of itself but is always dependent on other considerations. This is due to the dualistic mind's proclivity for separation in time and space and the superimposition of the supposed and imaginary explanation of a mysterious operant called "cause." Thus, to the mind, everything is both dependent on conditions and seen as a temporality which therefore requires explanation for understanding. Mental statements presume a separation between subject and object or conditions, namely, subject, adverb or adjective, and predicate. (Causality calibrates at 426.)

In Reality, nothing requires an explanation. Nothing is caused by anything else. Existence requires no explanation nor does it have any dependence on any other state or quality. This understanding is clarified by the realization that nothing in and of itself has any 'meaning'. Therefore, neither does it have a 'purpose'. Everything is already complete and merely self-existent as its own self-identity.

As an example, 'space' just 'is'; it just 'stands there', doing nothing at all. It cannot be measured because measurement is solely an arbitrary mentation. No reason is necessary. It would be lapsing into pointless mentation to ask "Why is space," or "What is its purpose?" There is no "why" to any reality. Nothing in the universe requires a "why," nor does any truth reveal itself by even asking the question. To pursue the "why" question is to chase one's tail and end up with merely entertaining mentations.

Let us look further into the question of "when." In Reality, which is timeless and infinite, there is no "when"; neither are there any events or happenings to be explained, nor are there any sequences, durations, or causes.

It can be seen that all explanations, descriptions, discussions, and conditions are merely abstract mentations. To escape these mentations, it is necessary to go beyond duality because the mind habitually chooses a positionality from which it creates a perceptual illusion based on that position which obscures Reality.

The Self is not conditional; it has no qualities and is not dependent or explicable. The Self has no duration, beginnings or endings, location, form, or limitations. It is the radiance of the Self that illuminates existence, without which there would be no awareness. The Self is beyond process. All descriptions are inappropriate and inapplicable to the Self.

Q: What is meant by the term "mystic"?
A: The mystic knows, experiences, and identifies the Self as both context and content, that is, context *is* the content. The content of the ego is transitory and a product of perception and, like a movie, it has no independent existence. The content of perception is an automatic byproduct of positionality and goes hand in hand with the creation of the illusions of perception. Science is the authority of the linear domain and the Newtonian paradigm; the mystic is the authority of the nonlinear domain.

Q: Since language is form, how can the mystic, who lives in the reality of nonlinear formlessness, transmit information?
A: Teaching actually takes place simultaneously on two levels. The first and most important is silent and form-

less, which occurs beyond the level of the mind and is nonverbal. This transpires as a consequence of the intrinsic power of the level of consciousness of the teacher. It could be likened to a carrier wave that accompanies the teacher's words and is a quality of the Presence as Self.

The inspiration and spiritual power of the truth of the mystic are accompanied by and are a product of Divinity, the energy field of which becomes entrained in the student's field of consciousness. This Grace has been traditionally referred to as the "transmission of no-mind," (paradoxically termed "mind," which means nonform and non-ego). This was described in *The Zen Teachings of Huang Po,* and also by the Buddha, who transmitted nonverbal awareness to his student when he gave him a flower. The spiritual aspirant's desire for truth is the assent that makes the acceptance fruitful.

The energy field of the teacher is a manifestation of the Presence. It is that field which accounts for the miraculous, for healings, for various mystical phenomena, and for sudden realizations that occur spontaneously in the presence of the teacher. The silent transmission could be likened to the phenomenon of entrainment. This is a consequence of the power of the field itself and is impersonal. The effect of the teacher's field of consciousness on that of the student is demonstrable by simple calibration (this is routinely done before and after lectures).

Q: **If Truth is formless, how can it be conveyed through words?**

A: All form is concurrently based on that which is formless, and it is the formless that accompanies the form of words which accounts for the transmission. The same words spoken as a mere intellectual learning lack the power of the carrier wave that facilitates the comprehension by the listener. Words transmitted with power bring about a transformation in the listener.

A more specific explanation is that the transmission from the teacher to the student is via the higher spiritual energy systems that are beyond that of mind, namely, the so-called causal, Buddhic, Christ, and Atmic 'bodies' which in turn have energy fields within them comparable to the chakra system. The verbal content and information is recorded via the higher (abstract thought) and lower (literal thought) mental capacities, but the higher frequency energies from the presence of the teacher activate the student's dormant spiritual energy systems.

Thus, the transmission of 'no-mind' (paradoxically called "Mind" in some literature) really means that there is a higher energy system that, like a tuning fork, is set into vibrational action by the silent process. This facilitates experiential knowingness rather than just intellectualization.

Many spiritual students are widely read and already mentally know about many spiritual truths, but the information is stored in the memory of the mental body only and thus awaits activation by the actual presence of a teacher in whom those higher spiritual bodies are highly energized.

The serious desire to reach enlightenment will drive the student until such a teacher appears. To be successful, however, the aspirant needs to be able to discern the false from the true. Many naïve seekers are mislead and with hope travel long distances to be with what they have been led to believe are true teachers because of their fame, glamour, or reputation. Many such 'teachers' who may well have even millions of followers calibrate in the high 200s or even below 200. A few do calibrate in the 400s. More peculiarly is that some widely known spiritual leaders did calibrate as high as the 500s when they began to teach but have since fallen way below 200.

The true teacher does not identify with names or titles for there is no 'person' present. Teaching is a function.

Q: Is the student's comprehension then dependent upon
    the teacher's level of consciousness?

A: The comprehension is based on the effect of the Self or
    represented by willingness, openness, intention, and the
    level of consciousness of the listener as well as that of the
    teacher. It is a common, everyday experience for people
    to know of something, but many years may elapse before
    they suddenly 'get' it. This readiness is often a conse-
    quence of periods of reflection, contemplation, prayer,
    and karmic potential.

Q: What is the benefit of learning teachings that seem
    incomprehensible at the time?

A: They only seem obscure to the intellect. They plant the
    seed, and the aspirant's spiritual aura incorporates the
    transmitted energy field of the teacher's aura. Certain
    information is transformational in itself. Exposure to
    high truth initiates a yearning in the psyche. The Buddha
    made that observation when he said that once a person
    has heard of enlightened truth, he will never be satisfied
    with anything less, even though it takes innumerable
    lifetimes to attain it.

Q: What characteristics facilitate comprehension and
    transformation?

A: Dedication, devotion, faith, prayer, surrender, and
    inspiration. When the barriers are relinquished, Truth
    reveals itself spontaneously.

Q: How is the position of the mystic throughout history
    explained?

A: The mystic has been both revered and persecuted as a
    heretic. The mystic's authority stems from the Presence,
    the Divine 'I' of the Self. This has been viewed as sacri-
    lege by authoritarian religions whose beliefs are limited
    to a transcendent God only (e.g., Meister Eckhardt);
    mystics have thus been excommunicated, burned at the

stake, or even crucified by religious authorities. Most mystics retire from society. Some, by virtue of great effort, return to the world but are silent about their inner state.

Q: **After such a major event as sudden realization, why would the mystic choose to remain silent?**

A: It is not a matter of choice but of capability. There is really nothing that can be said. To verbalize that state is difficult and requires favorable circumstances as well as some innate propensity or karmic momentum. To communicate about this state requires reenergizing form, which requires a considerable expenditure of energy. It is much easier and more natural to merely remain silent. Silence also serves in a different, peaceful way. There were many years of silence before there arose the ability to speak of these things.

Q: **Does a mystic retain a personality?**

A: This is somewhat difficult to explain. The remaining 'personality' is actually impersonal. It is an interactive 'persona' that is capable of seemingly ordinary participation in ongoing human affairs, but it is merely witnessed and allowed to do so, and it is not obligatory. It is a useful instrument or tool of the Self. The degree of participation is arbitrary and generally just serves the moment. Like the body, the personality is of no real importance; it is a transitory, voluntary, partial activity similar to going to the movies. At the movies, one can get up and leave at any time, and so it is with the persona. If participation is of service, it is allowed to occur.

Like the body, the personality is not identified as 'self'. It is actually a useful 'it'. The involvement of the personality as activity goes on of its own but can also be de-energized by simple, volitional detachment. To allow the personality to participate also requires recalling how the world sees things and adjusting to it in order to appear appropriate.

The world's affairs appear as theater which overvalues the inconsequential and ignores that which is profound. The communications of the mystic, therefore, are often reflective of the paradox, and life is recontextualized as the humor of the 'theater of the absurd'. Thus, the mystic often mysteriously laughs at what the world considers great tragedy. This is due to the absurdity of the comparison between illusion and Reality. The mystic is aware of the intrinsic reality and tries to reflect it back in a style that is catalytic to activate the latent capacity for spiritual awareness.

As we ascend the Scale of Consciousness, there is a progression of a calibratable level of power; however, even more importantly, aside from power, there is a change in the quality of the essence of that level. It could be said that the information at the lower end of the Scale is like lead, whereas information near the top of the Scale is like platinum. Lead is relatively inert; however, a minute amount of platinum can catalyze many tons of ore.

Q: **It is often difficult to understand the meaning of spiritual information.**

A: Spiritual truth is beyond meaning; it doesn't 'mean' anything. It can only be known, and that knowledge can only come about by becoming. Meaning is a mentation and a definition. Spiritual truth is a subjective awareness which is innately beyond intellection. For instance, what does a beautiful sunset 'mean'? It doesn't 'mean' anything; it is just startlingly that which it is, complete and total in and of itself. God is a direct awareness and experience, a realization, a revelation, and the absolute perfection of pure subjectivity.

Q: **What does the Self feel like?**

A: It is central, solid, profound, still, immutable, nonlocal, diffuse, all encompassing, peaceful, tranquil, comfortable, secure, emotionless joy, infinite lovingness, protection, closeness, safety, complete fulfillment, and ultra-familiar.

It is radically innate. It is the ultimate 'at home', the core of Reality and Awareness. It is the total and complete 'me' of All That Is or ever was or could be, beyond all time, place, and conditions. It is the comfort, warmth, and security of total, unconditional, and everlasting Love. It is unconditional and without pain or vulnerability. It is beyond all mentalization, question, doubt, word, or emotion. It is peace, silence, and stillness, profound and infinite. It is of the quality of Divinity, which is radiantly self-evident and all encompassing. The Love and Power of God are one and the same.

CHAPTER EIGHT
THE MYSTIC

Q: **The reality that you describe is obviously intense and total, but its description sometimes sounds almost abstract. How did it come about? What did the 'personal self' actually experience?**

A: It may be difficult to identify with a completed state and omit a description of the experiences that proceeded it. The prior experiences were very intense and profound, and a description of them may be of assistance to a spiritual seeker.

Q: **Did unusual experiences begin early in life?**

A: The onset of 'this life', as I have related elsewhere, began suddenly and astonishingly at age three, prior to which there was only oblivion. Out of this oblivion, there was suddenly the shocking awareness of existence. This condition of an awareness of existence emerged out of a seeming nothingness and actually was not a pleasurable discovery, for with it came the seemingly opposite possibility and fear of not having come into existence at all. Thus, with the consciousness of existence arose the anxiety and fear of its imaginary 'opposite' as a possibility.

The duality of the opposites of existence versus nonexistence is a paradox that actually does not present itself as a barrier to the progression of enlightenment until the consciousness level reaches approximately 840. At age three, there was no languaging or mentation about the experience; it occurred in a nonverbal but very intense, highly aware, and clear state of consciousness. However, it also set the stage for the ultimate goal of this lifetime—to resolve that paradox and evolve beyond it.

Q: **How could such an advanced state already be present at such a young chronological age?**

A: At birth, everyone already has a calibratable level of consciousness. Consciousness evolves over great expanses of temporal time, of which any given embodiment is only a chapter. (Prior to this birth, this consciousness had been a follower of the way of negation and had believed that the ultimate reality was voidness.)

Q: **What impact did that experience have and what was the life of the child like?**

A: The child was contemplative, quiet, introspective, and preferred the company of adults, having little in common with other children, who seemed overly aggressive, loud, physical, and senseless in their activities. There was an impatient waiting out of childhood, wanting to get it over with in order to get on with what was more real and meaningful.

Q: **But what about play?**

A: It was never interesting unless it led to a product or acquiring new information. There was, however, a sensitivity to aesthetics, such as classical music or the beauty of nature. Attending 'high church' in a great cathedral was a very significant and pleasing experience. The beauty of the stained glass windows, incense, the sound of the great organ and the full choir, the pageantry of the processional, and the magnificent architecture and statuary were very attractive and meaningful. Beauty was the core interest and attraction.

Q: **What about religion itself?**

A: The religious instruction was High Episcopal and, as a boy, there was service in the cathedral as an acolyte and a choir boy, but the downside of this was the development of scrupulosity.

Q: **You mentioned in a previous work about an illumination that happened in a snow bank. Was that a near-death experience?**

A: The possibility of death never occurred. Refuge from the blizzard had been sought by digging a hole in a big snow bank. Inside, there was a sense of relief and relaxation, and eventually, profound peace. Then a golden-light suffusion of Infinite Love pervaded and replaced ordinary consciousness. All location and time stopped and existence was by an Infinite Presence that was not different from the Self. There was the realization that the true Self had always existed and always would and that no threat to existence was even possible. The mind stopped and was replaced by a knowingness and, simultaneously, the body was irrelevant.

The same experience recurred later in life under different circumstances during which the profound peace, stillness, and presence of God were unmistakable. It completely eliminated all fear of death and brought about an attraction to all that is peaceful as well as a disinterest in anything that had to do with aggression or violence.

Q: **Yet, later you became an agnostic despite all these profound experiences. Why?**

A: One time, unexpectedly, the totality of human suffering suddenly appeared as a revelation within this consciousness. It was overwhelming and massive. Naively, the mind blamed God instead of the human ego for this massive suffering, which led to the rejection of the God as understood and commonly conceived of by society at that time of life. Reason and intelligence then became the guide to behavior.

Thomas Paine's *Age of Reason* replaced the Bible as a source of workable standards for behavior. Life was then lived much more comfortably without the constant fear and guilt of sin which seemed to be the focus of religion in the 1930s. Becoming an agnostic/atheist resulted in an exhilarating sense of freedom, as though the heavy chains of sin and guilt had been thrown off.

Q: Did you remain an agnostic?

A: Formally, yes, as far as the god of religion went, but intrinsically, there was a drive to arrive at the truth of reality and existence. Reading philosophy was put aside during medical school and was replaced by an interest in psychology, psychoanalysis, and in studying the nature of the human mind. This training also included an extensive personal psychoanalysis which was very effective in certain areas but ineffective in the overall drive to discover the core of existential reality.

Eventually, there was a huge clinical practice which was exhausting. Over time, multiple painful illnesses developed which finally became incapacitating. The struggle to continue functioning was very tiring.

The last major area for investigation was the spiritual domain. Because of the sin and guilt associated with Christianity, Buddha's teachings were attractive because he spoke of the existence of absolute truth without having to believe in a traditional concept of God. This led to the reading of the literature of Buddhism and visiting the first Zen Institute in New York City. This resulted in the practice of formal, seated meditation for an hour twice a day on a daily basis for many years.

Despite all these efforts, the illnesses progressed and eventually resulted in a deep despair. It was in the Hell of the depths of black despair and hopelessness that this consciousness asked, "If there is a God, I ask Him for help." That was the last, final act of the 'me', the personality/ego/mind that, after a period of oblivion, disappeared forever and was replaced by an Infinite Presence. The mind became silent; all thoughts were replaced by a knowingness that emanated from the Allness of Divinity. That revelation has been described elsewhere and became a permanent condition.

Q: **How did life in the world then proceed?**

A: The state prevailed but, with effort, it very gradually allowed for a tenuous, slow return to the world and helping patients. Functioning in the world was difficult and was comparable to getting a new set of eyeglasses. The body was now 'navigated' by the Presence and not from the prior inner sense of direction. The body's actions and speech happened on their own and were spontaneous and self-actuating rather than being directed by a central focus of a personal self. The former brief time delay between decision and action had disappeared. Instead of their being sequential, they were now simultaneous. The speech or action was the decision. That quality persists.

Even proprioception (body balance) had a different quality. Where the body was in space and what it was doing did not register with some central mental focus as it formerly had. There was no longer a sense associated with the body of an 'I' that is doing something. These required adjustments and reorientation to space/ motion/action. The supposed inner 'doer' of actions no longer existed, and the sense of self included both context and content, whereas, formerly, it only included content. The customary central focus from which normal people operate had disappeared. Action or speech originate from the entire field, which includes the totality of all prior existence.

Q: **What seems to initiate action?**

A: It occurs spontaneously as a result of the Presence in its expression as an appearance or perception. There is no such thing as time in which a specified event could occur. There is only a change of focus of attention.

Q: **What about verbal communication?**

A: Its nature changed. In Reality, nothing changes; no events occur. There are no real names for anything nor is there any seeming sequence or separation of so-called occurrences. The inner stillness of the grace of the Holy Spirit transforms the audible, spoken words of other people into a worldly meaning and interprets significance into a conceivable form.

Q: **Are these changes purely subjective or are there actually demonstrable physiological changes?**

A: The brain waves of the sage operate predominantly in the slow theta frequency of approximately four to seven cycles per second (4-7 cps), or even slower. The alpha waves of ordinary meditation are in the frequency range of 8-13 cps, and the brain waves of a normal person are predominantly in the fast beta frequencies of 13+ cps.

Subjectively, the sage lives in inner silence. The energy of another person's speech activates a quality of that silence which is at first formless but then begins to take form as a nonverbal knowingness about what is being said. This facilitates an approximate verbal response. It is as though meaning is conveyed by a translation from the nonlinear to the linear. This is done spontaneously by an impersonal capacity innate to consciousness itself. The process is not under any kind of 'personal' control. It could perhaps be likened to music being transferred into digital code and then retranslated back into music.

The process of translation causes a delay in mentalized comprehension. It appears to the world as though one is hard of hearing or absent-minded. It takes volitional effort and energy, and paying attention to the world is tiring. The preferred mode of communication is nonverbal; therefore, body language is very significant, and lengthy conversations are difficult and frequently avoided. Humor is often a shortcut to convey a shift of context that illuminates meaning without lengthy explanation. The customary communications of the world seem very laborious and frequently appear to be circuitous routes to avoid some simple, central truth. The preferred communication style deals with essence and not detail.

Q: **Does communication then become progressively nonverbal?**

A: This is true. In common language, we speak of intuition to explain the phenomenon. It is sometimes incorrectly called telepathy. "Tele" implies communication across space or distance. Although two people may appear to be distant from each other in the linear domain, in Reality, there is only one consciousness which enables one person to pick up the intent of the other person's communication prior to its being spoken. Thus, the spoken word becomes only a confirmation of what has already been sensed because in consciousness, there is no distance or space to traverse.

An example of this was a four-day experiment with twelve spiritual students (they were members of a *Course in Miracles* group) in a large house in an eastern U. S. city. Although acquainted, they were not really familiar with each other, and the vow for the retreat was to maintain silence, "no matter what." Within twenty-four hours, the entire group became 'telepathic'. Everyone's needs were met; meals appeared with no prior planning, and each knew the other's thoughts. For instance, if someone at the table merely thought the word "salt," somebody would spontaneously pass the salt, with no words being spoken. Everything progressed for four days in perfect harmony.

Everyone later described the entire experience as mystical, magical, entrancing, and beautiful. There was a great reluctance to resume speech at the end of the weekend. Speech implied diversity whereas silence implied unity. The relinquishment of the personal ego/I of speech facilitates the overlapping of the sense of Self so that a commonality of consciousness occurs. Within a few days, silence seemed much more natural than speech.

Q: **It then takes energy to verbally communicate.**

A: Yes. Verbal socialization is tiring. To be alone in nature or silently with others is preferable. All is as it is, with no necessity for explanation. It is devoid of the perceptual distancing of the ego. The sense of Self is diminished by energizing the ego/self. Comparatively, the Self is silent and peaceful, whereas the self is noisy. Verbiage is not essential for communicating significance or meaning. Witness the cat. It merely has to stand silently in front of its dish to invite the owner to fill it with food. Every motion conveys a knowingness of a condition or feeling state. The cat assumes that the messages are being conveyed. If it realizes that the message is being missed, it resorts to a vocalization of "meow" or paws the food cabinet.

Q: **How does one then live in the world?**

A: One participates but is not involved in or attached to it. One can observe without being judgmental. Detachment would require withdrawal from the world, whereas nonattachment allows participation as there is no stake in outcomes. The game is entertaining but which side 'wins' is of no importance.

Q: **What are the subjective experiences and states like at the different levels?**

A: The level of Unconditional Love, which calibrates at 540, is remarkable. It is accompanied by a sense of joy, and one is 'in love' with everything and everyone, with all of life. By the high 500s, the incredible beauty and perfection of all that exists is overwhelming and prevails as spontaneous ecstasy. Perception disappears so as to allow the beauty of existence to shine forth from what the world considers homely or even ugly. Even an alley of trash now appears like a still-life painting. A piece of Kleenex half removed from its box, with its flowing lines, now reveals a beauty of form as though it were a three-dimensional sculpture or a painting by Georgia O'Keefe. Once the stage of the beauty and perfection of all that exists shines forth, the awareness of Divinity as its essence begins to emerge. At consciousness level 600, it is overwhelming.

The spiritual truth is a recognition that dawns spontaneously and is self-obvious. Everything fulfills its own intrinsic destiny. Nothing is external to anything else, nor is it caused by anything else. What the world assumes to be 'causes' are seen to be merely means or conditions.

Q: What motivates action after that?

A: The word "motivation" no longer applies. Action occurs of its own accord, perhaps energized by an impersonal spiritual inspiration. Needs disappear and there are no gains to attain. All is complete. Manifestation appears in a harmonious synchronicity, and enjoyment replaces anticipation. An unalterable sense of completion pervades all action. Nothing in nature needs to do anything; all merely appears to be becoming that which it is. There is no doer of actions; the actions are the doer. One sees potentiality actualizing.

In duality, there is a 'this' (me) that is imagined to be the 'cause' of 'that' (action). In Reality, the action and self are one and the same. There is no thinker separate from the thoughts. It is the thoughts themselves that are the only thinker of the moment; they are not different or separate.

Q: What accounts for the peace?

A: The disappearance of time, anticipation, needs, wants, or lack. In duality, there is a constant anxiety, the classical 'existential angst', which creates a constant tension that results from the subjective experience of a sequence of time and place. Thus, the ego always feels incomplete, insecure, and vulnerable at any given moment. It also fears that happiness can always be lost, assets destroyed, or that the body may sicken or die.

Q: What were the physical changes you noticed?

A: One feels as though the brain has slowed down and is a receiving instrument for consciousness that does not originate from the brain but instead activates it. The pleasure of the high 500s is most probably accompanied by the release of endorphins. It is exquisite. Scientists mistakenly look for an area of the brain that 'causes' God consciousness or the near-death experience; however, the brain can only register that which already is. It has no power to cause anything. Extraordinary and pro-foundly transformative near-death experiences occur to 'flat-liner', brain-dead people who miraculously survive.

By analogy, fear arises from perception, and its con-comitant is a release of adrenalin. Discovering where adrenalin arises from in the body does not explain fear because adrenalin is merely a consequence and a con-comitant, not the cause, which has already occurred in the consciousness field of perception. It would be naïve to assume that to discover where joy is experienced by the brain is the cause of that joy. The brain and its physiology exist within the world of form, and spiritual states originate within the nonlinear reality of nonform. Similarly, one could assume that there is an 'inner breather' which causes the body to breathe. Actually, with very little observation, it can be seen that the body 'breathes itself' and that one is not the originator of breathing but its recipient.

Q: **What about the nervous system?**

A: Vision is different because, in the higher states, one depends on peripheral vision rather than central vision. There is a loss of the startle reflex, and nothing makes the body go weak with the kinesiologic test. The nervous system experiences distress as consciousness rapidly evolves. There may be strange aches and pains or a feeling of burning throughout the body as though high-voltage electricity were running through the wires of the nervous system. Physical discomfort increases rather markedly by the 800s or 900s. One is grateful that the Buddha described these phenomena twenty-five hundred years ago. He said that as his consciousness approached enlightenment, his body was wracked by pain as though his bones had been broken, and he felt as though he were being attacked by innumerable demons. To know that was very helpful.

Q: **Do these sensory states persist?**

A: At each advance of the level of consciousness, there was an increase in their intensity. At times, all functioning came to a halt until the intensity of the painful sensations receded. Kinesiologic inquiry revealed that the nerves take years to accommodate the higher energy. The prior peak capacity of the human nervous system was reached at the calibration level of 1,000. It would seem that, historically, it could not tolerate the stress of levels beyond that without very special assistance.

Q: **Do the physical changes make functioning in the world difficult?**

A: Yes, at times it is quite difficult and, in fact, sometimes it is not even possible at all. When there is a major jump in consciousness, there is even a loss of physical balance. There is an oversensitivity to light and a disinclination for sensory input, such as bright light or sound. The body is at times faltering, unsteady, and relatively weak, and there is a major loss of appetite and resort to a liquid diet. If the body persists, it is due to a strong spiritual commitment to keep it going for some higher purpose because the world of form has lost importance as such.

Q: **Is there a correlation between the brain wave frequency, the functioning of the nervous system, and the prevailing level of consciousness?**

A: Beta-wave frequencies (14 cps) are adaptive to the requirements of the ego to respond rapidly to the changes in form of content. The wave frequency slows to the 8-13 cps Alpha range in meditation states where action and decision making are not required. In the enlightened state of approximately calibrated level 700, the EEG frequency slows to the Theta range of 4-7 cps as consciousness is aligned with unchanging context rather than being focused on form. At even higher levels of consciousness in the thoughtless silence of the Presence, the Theta brain wave frequency may slow to even 2-3 cps, and the electroencephalogram tracing is characterized by low amplitude and low voltage.

CHAPTER NINE
THE LEVELS OF ENLIGHTENMENT

Q: **The consciousness levels from 600 to 1,000 indicate that there are actually different levels of enlightenment.**

A: It has been historically presumed that there are only two possible states of consciousness: unenlightened (the ego/mind) and enlightened (beyond ego), also termed "no-mind," Mind (i.e., the mind of God), the Buddha nature, Truth, Reality, Self, the Presence, God, the Ultimate, or the Supreme. Through consciousness research as well as inner experience, it can definitely be stated that this is not the case. There are indeed levels between levels 600 and 1,000.

The higher levels of truth can be calibrated as easily and accurately as any of the others. Each level represents a strata of consciousness that is also represented by historical spiritual teachers and spiritual traditions.

Calibrated Scale of Consciousness:
The Enlightened and Divine States

The Supreme Godhead—God Unmanifest	Infinity
God Manifest as Divinity/Creator	Infinity
Archangel	50,000 +
"I" as Essence of Creation	1,250
"I" of Ultimate Reality	1,000 +
Christ, Buddhahood, Krishna, Brahman	1,000 +
Avatar	985

God (Self) as Logos	850
Self as Beyond Existence or Nonexistence	840
Teacher of Enlightenment	800
"I"/Self-Divinity as Allness (Beatific, Vision)	750
Sage—Self as God Manifest	700
Self as Existence	680
"I Am"	650
Enlightenment	600
Sainthood	575

In this and prior works, the emergence of consciousness level 600 has been described in some detail because it is the classic hallmark of enlightenment about which spiritual seekers have heard the most. This is understandably so as the transition from the high 500s to the 600s is both dazzling and spectacular at its onset, and then it becomes profoundly peaceful as it settles and ripens.

Often this state is accompanied by a disinclination to remain in the ordinary world, and, according to consciousness research, only fifty percent of such beings will continue to live in a physical condition. Of those who do persist, only a few will speak, teach, or write. Most seek seclusion or a spiritual retreat. Destiny as karmic momentum plays a role in the outcome and the decision to function in the world again, which is admittedly somewhat difficult.

Q: How can higher levels be differentiated?

A: Each level of consciousness is not only a calibrated level of power but also has a characteristic quality. The logarithmic consciousness level numbers are really a shorthand, a generality, and a manner of denotation. The numbers cannot really be studied mathematically because as they rise, they denote changes in quality. Therefore, an attempt to compare the numbers mathematically would be like comparing platinum and lead by their atomic weights. Lead is relatively inert and nonreactive, whereas platinum is powerfully catalytic. A gram of platinum can catalyze tons of ore. Similarly, H_2O at a low temperature is a solid; at mid-temperature, as water, it is a liquid; and at a higher temperature, it is a gaseous vapor. There is, in fact, a triple state where, in a vacuum, all three can occur simultaneously.

Therefore, a meaningful description has to include context. Power is a manifestation of context. As power increases, descriptions that were pertinent at lower levels are no longer appropriate.

A helpful analogy of the field of consciousness is to compare the calibrated scale with an electromagnetic spectrum. Beginning at the lower end, there is infrasound, which only elephants can hear, and at the other extreme, there is ultrasound. There is light which goes from invisible infrared through the color spectrum to ultraviolet. Beyond that, there are X rays; radio waves; gamma, beta, and cosmic waves; photons, and more. Although numbers can denote frequencies, the numbers are only a small aspect of adequate description. Estimates of power in the nonlinear domain are by nonlinear calibrated definition and not literally measurable by linear standards.

Another example would be the use of biologic phenomena as measuring devices. For example, instead of a thermometer, temperatures can be determined by the rate of growth of bacteria, and time lapse can determine the reproductive rates. Similar types of tests are actually used every day in forensic science laboratories.

The calibrated levels of consciousness are a shorthand way of denoting a major stratum of human development which stems from a point of view that determines perception and what is significant, meaningful, or real at that level. In general, calibrated consciousness levels imply the capacity to comprehend spiritual truth; social, emotional, and intellectual attitudes; occupational capabilities; goals; and interests. The levels also relate to psychological or physical health and longevity as well as to ethics, morals, social and private behaviors, the likelihood of criminality, and the capacity for comprehension.

The consciousness levels also relate to worldly affairs, such as income, skills, assets, personality, attitudes, responsibility, types of goals, family orientation, socio-economic status, and even such things as response to commercials, advertising, and buying habits. The levels also imply the capacity for happiness, satisfaction, and love. They even relate to styles of socialization, selection of entertainment and reading material, preference for television channels and programs, habits, and recreation.

With the awareness of the importance of the levels of consciousness, any aspect of human life can be examined at different levels. While all the above are significant to earthly life, they have even more importance for spiritual destiny when physical life ends. Consciousness both precedes this physical life and continues long after it.

It could be said that within a certain context, the only real significance of this earthly life is the consequences that ensue to one's spiritual reality, which has a timeless trajectory. The destiny of the spirit will be for better or worse, depending on the choices and decisions one makes. This statement is in agreement with the teachings of every major religion and true spiritual teachers throughout human history.

Great historic cultures focused primarily on the destiny of the soul and preparations for its transition to other realms. Egypt certainly stands out as a striking example with which everyone is familiar. The great pyramids are symbolic of man's comprehension of this ultimate destiny.

Q: When the consciousness level goes over 600, does it usually just remain there or continue to progress spontaneously?

A: The condition above 600 is self-sustaining and usually remains stationary. No energy is required. Some beings at that level cease functioning except for having visitors, and some remain silent, merely conveying their blessing on spiritual seekers. The state feels and is complete.

Q: If this is so, why would spiritual endeavor continue?

A: It is really not a 'personal' choice. The power of the Presence acts like a magnetic field. If the consciousness of the enlightened being has the capacity to move on, it does so because it has the innate qualities required for the stresses that will ensue. The spiritual commitment and dedication have to be absolute with resolute resolve, one that sustains by the love of God and Divine inspiration.

Q: To continue on, are there other obstacles to be met?

A: There are the 'confrontations with the opposites' that are precipitated with each increase in the level of consciousness. They are often unexpected and appear suddenly, without warning. There are also the confrontations from the forces that dominate the 'dark side' of the fields of consciousness. Apt descriptions of such events were recounted by both Christ and the Buddha.

At the lower levels, these forces are aptly described as 'satanic', personified as "Mara" (the evil one) by Buddha. Satanic energies are those that surround the classic temptations of seduction, glamour, addiction, sensation, and excitement, as well as bloodshed, crime, war, killing, and thrills in all their forms. At their lowest end, the satanic energies are expressed via the 'spleen' of envy, hatred, jealousy, and revenge, which prevail and dominate energies in all parts of the world. Thus, peace or a powerful source of peace on the planet is considered to be a threat by these energies. This can be understood when it is seen that they control entire populations, nations, and cultures for extended periods of time (e.g., the barbarian hordes, Nazi Germany, and Islamic zealots).

The satanic energy is also called demonic when the forces possess the consciousness of an individual, such as a serial killer. When this happens, the 'possessed' person may go into amnesia, during which times the satanic energies result in savagery. Sometimes the possessed person understands that there is a possessing energy and even gives it a name. When this happens after a crime, the person will honestly state that they personally did not 'do it'. Many claim that they were obeying 'God's voice' (command hallucinations).

It was necessary at one time to calibrate what turned out to be a rather strange case in which an insistent visitor from a foreign country was inappropriately persistent and aroused suspicion by the oddness of the request. Sometimes the person calibrated in the high 300s, and at other times, he calibrated extremely low (at 70). Inasmuch as a calibrated level of consciousness does not fluctuate in that manner, it was finally determined that two different consciousnesses inhabited his body. One was definitely satanic, whereas the other was a normal person in the high 300s. When the personality in the 300s dominated, he was reasonable and a very positive kind of person. When the other personality took over, he would hear 'God's voice' telling him to do very horrible things to the point where he was literally quite dangerous.

The satanic energies also hold dominion and sway over many activities of sensation and pleasure, including many video games and media productions involved with violence, seduction, and murder. These seductions are obvious snares that a spiritual aspirant will intuitively bypass. They also dominate the regions usually meant by the word "sin." Despite the obvious warnings, it is not uncommon for erstwhile 'gurus' to fall into the trap of seduction and become involved with followers. The satanic energies affect the lower chakras.

The less obvious challenges and traps stem from the more sophisticated and subtle energies best described as "luciferic." They have to do with power, control, fame,

wealth, importance, and prestige, as well as cold calcula-
tion, which require the rejection of love, compassion, or
concern for others. These energies prevail in some areas
of academia, bureaucracies, and corporate worlds where
human values and the quality of life are sacrificed for
political and financial gain. This kind of thinking is
exemplified, for instance, by a corporate decision that it
is cheaper to pay off the injured or killed rather than to
improve the product.

Whereas the satanic energies are directed at the lower
chakras (base, sexual, and spleen), the luciferic energies
are directed at the higher chakras, namely, solar plexus
(greed, gain, and pride), heart (sell out love for power or
advantage), throat (distorted speech), and the 'third eye'
(distorted perception and capacity to discern truth). The
luciferic energy of pride is also directed at the crown
chakra where surrender to God is replaced by the pride
of the ego and selfish self-centeredness.

The luciferic energy's primary tool is distortion of
truth. Thus, it is directed at the mind and relies on false
promises and half-truths.

While the mind can defend itself against the satanic
energies by reliance on simple morality, it has little
defense against distortions of truth convincingly presented because the innate innocence of the substrate of
mind lacks the innate capacity to discern truth from
falsehood. Whether one's destiny is for better or worse
can depend on the interpretation of even a single word
or phrase.

In current society, various political/social positionalities are reflections of pride (they calibrate at 190).
These distortions of truth depend on denial of context
and partialization of content

It is the luciferic energy of power and prestige which
traps the unprepared spiritual leader when they reach
the level where they are tempted to exercise the control
of spiritual power over others. We see this demonstrated

in the endless power struggles among the world's religions over the centuries.

When the spiritual level of a dedicated seeker becomes quite advanced, it seems to trigger a response from those energies that perceive advancement as a threat. These threatened forces may even literally surface and take the form of a direct confrontation in the form of a presence which seems to overtake the consciousness of a person to whom one is speaking.

Q: Did you ever experience such a situation?

A: As one evolves, one is, as the Buddha says, beset by demons of all sorts as well as by psychic attacks. And they do indeed manifest, sometimes directly in a worldly form and setting.

One peculiarity of such confrontations with either the luciferic or satanic energy is an amazing degree of what can only be called 'overt stupidity'. This mark should never be ignored for it is an infallible sign and a dead give-away of the presence of a luciferic or satanic energy. For example, a seemingly intelligent and articulate person will suddenly say and do things that are totally incongruous and even outrageous, such as declaring that they are "higher than Jesus." This ridiculous claim has been said blatantly, even by famous 'gurus' with many thousands of followers and worldwide reputations.

This was actually experienced in a conversation with a relatively well-known spiritual leader who suddenly stated, in a different voice, that not only was he "higher than Jesus" but that "Jesus and Buddha were just astrals." The overshadowing energy that accompanied these statements was indeed horrific. The astral entity then went on to insist that sizeable amounts of money should be charged for spiritual teachings and that truth should only be sold for a price. He also stated that industrialists were higher than Jesus or Buddha.

One can also suddenly meet the temptation on the nonphysical level when it tries to persuade one to use one's power over others for the sake of the power itself and not necessarily for any external gain. This can sometimes be cloaked in the form of a persuasive innocence. Power for its own sake has been a pitfall for many who could have instead surrendered it to God for the good of all mankind.

The so-called 'dark forces' are made up of entities who refuse or deny God and therefore deny Love and Truth. They are the "People of the Lie" as described by M. Scott Peck, a psychiatrist, in his book by the same name, written in the 1980s.

The luciferic energies are adept at destroying the power of truth by propagating distortions, misunderstandings, and sophisticated, subtle warping by twisting content or shifting content into another context. This is commonly seen in the error of 'Monday-morning quarterbacking', that is, the content is shifted into another time frame. This is commonly done in socio-political intellectualizations when current social mores are projected backwards in history and past events are thereby made 'wrong'. This is exploited shamelessly by politically motivated groups with an axe to grind that try to make the current generation feel guilty about how society functioned in the distant past. Such distortions are purposeful, nonintegrous (calibrating below 200), and play on the victim/perpetrator model. It propagates because it is seen to be politically and financially lucrative or implies a morally 'superior' position. Such time shifts ignore that every aspect of former societies was more rudimentary and underdeveloped.

Q: Is there still a motive to evolve through higher levels?

A: No. It comes about not as a motive but from the Allness of the Self, which then encompasses all mankind. The compassion is for the consciousness of humanity as a whole. One is inspired to the perfection of being a perfect mirror to reflect God's grace to be shared by all. True spiritual authority is rooted in Truth and thus has no need or desire to be authoritarian. It has no argument nor does it have a desire or a need for acceptance. It would be a misuse of spiritual power to try to use it to control the minds of people. Authoritarianism is intrinsically insecure and therefore has to insist on agreement with its belief systems; it is the antithesis of freedom.

Religions become totalitarian when they seek to force people into agreement. Spiritual truth is benevolent and grants freedom to everyone. Coercion is foreign to spiritual truth. If a spiritual teacher states that negative motives and actions will have subsequent deleterious spiritual consequences, it is merely a statement of fact and not an attempt to use that information to control others. A true teacher has no desire for power and is beyond gain or loss and therefore respects the rights of others to fulfill their own karmic destiny.

CHAPTER TEN
THE NATURE OF GOD

Throughout history, man has heard about the "Will of God," the "Word of God," the "Laws of God," and the "Commandments of God," and these have often brought about consternation rather than hope. We should therefore investigate exactly how man has actually come to know of the reality of God and what can be believed and verified.

Traditionally, the main avenues of knowledge about God have been by revelation, illumination, inspiration, and introspection, as well as by intellection and deduction. Theology has been the province of the specific study of religion and the development of man's intellectual knowledge of God.

Theology is primarily an historic examination of the elements whereby knowledge arises and blends into epistemology and the philosophy of metaphysics. The basic elements necessary for any form of knowingness have thus become the focus of analysis as well as speculation.

Religion has presupposed that the comprehension, much less the experience of the truth of God, is beyond ordinary mortals. Thus, historically, religion has been society's primary source of information about the nature of Divinity.

The truths of every religion originate from the awareness of the mystics who were the avatars upon whom the religions were founded. These were uniformly God-realized spiritual geniuses who were able to share their experience, information, and knowledge for the benefit of mankind. When we confirm their level of enlightenment with the described technique of calibration, we arrive at the following examples:

Christ	1,000
Buddha	1,000
Krishna	1,000
Christian Apostles	930
Moses	910
Zoroaster	860
Mohamed (at the time of the writing of the Koran)	740

We can also confirm the truth of all the great enlightened teachers, masters, saints, and sages throughout history, as well as the calibrated level of authenticity of all the sacred scriptures and teachings during that time. We thus arrive at a very solid core of reliable information with cross-corroboration that encompasses all racial, ethnic, or religious boundaries, as well as identification with a concordance that is verifiable over the centuries from totally different cultures.

Collectively, the verifiable, authentic sources for man's knowledge of the nature of Divinity are actually quite impressive in their unanimity and correlation. There emerges a substructure of irreducible truth that is sovereign to all knowledge and which, in addition, is now verifiable by recently discovered calibration techniques so that the teachings can be understood, languaged, and represented to modern man in a manner that is comprehensible to the ordinary intellect. A modern-day theology is now available which is logical and capable of affirmation.

It is important to be aware that Truth is not provable nor subject to proof, nor is it in the category or province of knowledge that is measurable, such as the subject of Logic. Truth is only that which is verifiable by the realization of subjective, experiential reality. 'Provables' are merely propositions, whereas truth, like space, merely 'is' and consequently, is not arguable. Descriptions can be challenged but not the reality of subjectivity.

From the totality of authentically verifiable sources of spiritual knowledge can be distilled an absolute, irreducible quintessence, a core of absolute validity that transcends all positionalities or editorializing for either advantage or gain. From the source of the subjective reality from which these words emanate, as well as the derivation of man's spiritual experience throughout history, the following statements can be made with absolute certainty:

1. God is both manifest as the Totality and Allness of Creation and simultaneously unmanifest as the Godhead, the Infinite Potentiality and source or 'voidness' prior to form.

2. God is infinite beyond time or depictions of space or locality, without beginning or end.

3. God is omnipresent, omnipotent, and omniscient.

4. God is the source and substrate of consciousness, awareness, knowingness, and sentience.

5. God is the sole source of the energy of life.

6. God is the source of evolution and Creation, which are one and the same.

7. God is the source and presence of peace, love, stillness, and beauty.

8. God is beyond all universes and materiality, yet is the source of All That Is.

9. God is the sole source of existence and the potentiality of beingness.

10. God is the ultimate context of which the universe and all existence is the content.

11. God is the *a priori* formless source of existence within all form.

12. God is not within the province of the provable or the intellect.

13. God is the source and essence of the subjective state of 'I-ness' called Enlightenment.

14. God is the radical subjectivity of Self-realization.

15. God is descriptively immanent and transcendent.

16. The human experience of the Presence of God is the same in all ages, all cultures, and all localities.

17. The effect on human consciousness of the experience of the Presence of God is subjectively transformative and

identical throughout human history. It leaves a timeless mark that is verifiable as a calibration of a recorded level of consciousness.

18. The essence of God does not include human frailties, such as partiality, the desire to control, favoritism, duality, judgmentalism, wrath, righteous anger, resentment, limitation, arbitrariness, vanity, revenge, jealousy, retaliation, vulnerability, or locality.

19. The variabilities of the depictions of Divinity reflect the variabilities of human perception and the projections of the impediments of the ego and its positionalities.

20. The purity of the Presence of God is traditionally the essence of the ineffable quality of holiness and is the basis for the depictive term "sacred." That which is devoid of content is the equivalent of Innocence.

21. When the obstacles of human mentation, emotionality, and the ego's structures from which they are derived are transcended, the Self as God Immanent shines forth of its own accord, just as the sun shines forth when the clouds are removed.

22. God is the context and source of the karmic unity of all Creation, beyond all perceptual descriptions or limitations, such as time or space.

23. Truth is verifiable only by identity with it and not by knowing about it.

The absolute truth of these statements about the Reality of Divinity was publicly corroborated on July 13, 2002, before an audience of over two hundred people during a public lecture. The audience divided into one hundred kinesiologic test teams. The truth of each statement was then tested by the whole audience simultaneously. The confirmation of each statement was one hundred percent (calibrated level 1,000), and the procedure was video taped. The purpose was to present credible documentation of Truth in today's world to provide validation that does not depend on historical accounts or ecclesiastic authority which are often the subject of doubt in modern society.

Traditionally, states of self-realization have been referred to as illumination or transcendent awareness which, by Grace, is comprehensible in essence by human consciousness when it is devoid of obstructions. The witness of the state of realization or illumination can only report its occurrence. As strange as it may seem, at that point, it has no 'meaning' as such. Significance and conclusion are then subsequently derived.

If the totality of the content of human consciousness is illuminated, then the consequences and derivations of the levels of consciousness become apparent, much like a map allows the fate of certain pathways to become clearer. Thus, the sage or avatar merely points out the consequences of going in various directions based on the revelation of the certainty of the absolute karmic unity and divinity of Creation which, in predictability, are comparable to the physical laws, such as those of gravity.

The sage then confirms that the karmic laws of Creation supersede all the illusions and errors of the ego. The message to be conveyed by spiritual teachings is that just as the physical body is subject to the laws of Newtonian linear physics, the spiritual body is subject to the laws of the nonlinear spiritual truth, which are quite different. Because of the rudimentary level of the evolution of man's consciousness, the avatar, mystic, or sage has been illuminated in order to teach the difference between the two domains.

Human life seems to represent a staging process or dimension by which life as consciousness evolves from the simplest life energy, such as the cells of the body through elaboration as form, and progresses up through the animal kingdom, on through the complexity of the primate and the evolution of an intelligence to enable comprehension. As intelligence develops, it becomes capable of investigation and comprehension of meaning and abstract derivation of essence apart from form, that is, content vis-à-vis context. Out of context arises the inference of and search for source in the capacity for spiritual awareness.

The animal knows and loves that it is, but it has no knowledge of its source or destiny. The spiritual sage emerges as a consequence of that level of consciousness which discovers its source and proclaims the discovery for the information of all. The spiritual information then illuminates the possibilities of the soul's destiny at the cessation of human physicality.

When mankind hears of the news, some individuals become very excited or fearful and therefore become authoritarian. They form into groups, and various individuals report unique or strange experiences. They then part from the group and start their own interpretations of what has been revealed. In addition, they nominalize their declarations as 'rules', 'regulations', or authoritarian pronouncements that become 'canon', 'law', or ecclesiastic doctrines.

Some of these deviations over time are given such undue emphasis that they actually obscure and eclipse the truths from which they were derived. Some become so distorted that they end up being and conveying the exact opposite of the original, for example, that it is God's commandment to kill the innocent, the infidels, or Americans in the name of God.

Thus, the innocence of consciousness is, at the same time, its Achilles' heel and vulnerable to attack from the energies that actually refuse spiritual truth. What we can conclude by surveying all the verifiable spiritual information available to man is that the karmic unity of all Creation, beyond all time or expression, is immutable in its manifestations and concordance with its unity which we call God.

SECTION THREE
THE OBSTACLES

CHAPTER ELEVEN

TRANSCENDING THE WORLD

Transcending Duality: The Polarity of the 'Opposites'

To successfully transcend the seeming 'opposites', it is only necessary to see that what appear to be two different or opposing concepts are actually just gradations of possibilities that change quality as they progress along a single base line of perception. We have previously used temperature as a model to disassemble the seeming opposites of 'hot' versus 'cold'.

In order to facilitate languaging, the mind chooses some point along a progressive scale from which to segregate all measurements or qualities into two contrasting groups. They are then perceived dualistically as 'opposites' and become a source of conflict. In nature we see that there are no opposites as they are merely mentations with no external existence.

As conditions change, so does appearance. At a low temperature, water is a solid called ice. As it warms up, it turns to a liquid called water. At a higher temperature, it boils and turns into a gas or vapor. At an even higher temperature, water (H_2O) turns into the separate gases of hydrogen and oxygen. We do not say that ice and vapor are 'opposites' or that hydrogen and oxygen are 'opposites'. At best, labeling is a linguistic convenience that has a limited but useful pragmatic or utilitarian purpose.

While the above explanation may seem obvious and mundane, it is actually of considerable importance because it displays the basic principles by which one can disassemble the perceptual errors that result in duality. Upon examination, seeming social polarities also simply dissolve into progressions, such as rich/poor, have/have nots, educated/ignorant, healthy/sick, smart/dumb, strong/weak, and liberal/conservative.

What would be considered 'poor' in the U. S. would be viewed as 'very rich' in other countries. As possessions increase, there is an imaginary dividing line between rich and poor. This is an arbitrary definition that depends on economic conditions and political bent. These merely represent positions along a gradient scale, just as tall is not the opposite of short, nor is strong the opposite of weak.

Emotions are another common example of gradation in that happy is not actually the opposite of unhappy as there are various gradations of all emotions. Love is not the opposite of hate nor is greed the opposite of generosity. To make such statements would require denoting degrees and progressive value judgments, such as how much irrationality would be required to discern sanity from insanity.

In Reality, there are no opposites. Positionalities are merely arbitrary mentations. When sunlight passes through a prism, it diffracts the light into a color spectrum. It would be foolish to say that infrared is the opposite of ultraviolet.

In the subjective, experienced emotions of daily life, one reacts to preferences via the pleasure principle, which is innate to brain function, so that the most simple and often heard personal remarks have to do with likes and dislikes. These then become socially codified into seeming opposites.

The Paradox of 'Good' versus 'Evil'

To transcend the great classic seeming opposites of good and evil, it is beneficial to appreciate again that all seeming opposites are the illusory consequences of collective labeling from an arbitrary point along a scale that includes only one variable, not two. We can construct a scale of 'desirability' of human actions, behaviors, and events which starts at the top with "wonderful" and declines through "undesirable" to "awful," and finally, to "horrific" and "catastrophic."

This could be modified to apply to any area of human life, depending on the desired result or value (e.g., business profit, farm production, personal happiness, moral conduct, etc.). The consequence of any event would then automatically become descriptively classified or termed "good" or "bad," depending on its influence on the desired result. From this observation, we can confirm that what is considered 'truth' depends on context.

From the traditional historical religious viewpoint, to disobey God (Garden of Eden) was at the top of the list of possible evils, followed by fratricide (Cain versus Abel), which was then followed by patricide, matricide, infanticide, and the defiling of the innocent. Farther down the list came torture, cruelty, enslavement, mayhem, manslaughter, rape, and assault and battery against persons. Then followed offenses against sovereignty, property, money, and articles of value. Added to the list were offenses against human values, such as freedom, dignity, and personal choice, as well as ethical and moral values, and moral rights, including entitlements, and finally, emotions.

Lack of clarity about rules, laws, and standards of behavior have reflected lack of certainty about context. Context itself is very complex and often vague or unspecified, which results in jurisprudence to define nuances of the gravity of offenses. The seemingly simple definitions of 'right' versus 'wrong' often defy the best of human intelligence. Discernment reflects the output of complicated and intricate interacting factors, such as education, age, IQ, and maturity, as well as ethnic, regional, and historic elements.

Consequently, the mantle of officialdom does not rest easily on the shoulders of responsibility. Morality and ethics shift with viewpoint that, in turn, reflects the input of society at an evolutionary point of history and the development of civilization. Even a seemingly minor scientific discovery in a laboratory can change an exhaustively derived verdict from 'guilty' to 'innocent' (i.e., DNA testing).

When we view the extreme complexity of trying to define

context, it would seem that wisdom counsels to avoid glib and facile statements or judgmentalism. What appears to be a seemingly obvious truth can, in seconds, be turned into its opposite by a simple discovery of a more advanced mathematical process produced by a computer.

It would seem that what is considered to be 'truth' fluctuates from second to second, and with that fluidity, there is a correlate variability of ethics, morality, and the subtleties of good and evil. As an example, we can look at current brain research which demonstrates that psychopaths (the chronic criminal recidivist) have defects of the frontal lobe cortex which are genetic in origin. They have a genetic inability to learn from experience, or to delay gratification, or to surrender short-term impulses for long-term goals. Should these genetically impaired individuals be viewed as evil, bad, criminal, or wrong and be punished? For instance, a very famous criminal, who cut off the arms of his rape victim so she could not defend herself, was released after some eighteen years in prison, and within twenty-four hours he had raped and murdered another woman. Paradoxically, he had pleaded to not be released as he knew that he would be compelled to do it again.

We note that what is very animalistic is often labeled as evil. Thus, the unspoken context of all depictions of good versus evil reflects the positionality that all events that support human life, the common good, and spiritual values are good and those that have the opposite result are termed bad or evil.

If we examine the arbitrary scale of good versus bad from beyond the human condition to its effect on life, then all morality and dualistic judgmentalism falls away within the larger context. Life itself has no opinion; it just 'is'. Life effortlessly diverts quickly from one form to another without innate reaction or resistance. It does not even register a reaction to change of form. Life, like light, is innately formless and beyond preference, resistance, or reaction.

The moral dilemma is solved by comprehending the teachings of Jesus Christ that evil is in the eye of the beholder; yet, paradoxically, to transgress results in serious consequences to the human who ignores spiritual reality and willfully commits sin. Spiritual evolution brings with it new responsibilities and karmic consequences.

With kinesiologic research, it was discovered that animal life is generally oblivious and barely notices when it 'dies' because it merely continues on uninterruptedly in its etheric body. The animal is apparently not attached to the physicality of form; thus, when a fly is swatted, it goes on flying in its etheric form and does not even notice the change. The dreaming cat or dog does not differentiate between dream life and physically experienced life, nor does it value one more than the other.

Death is not possible to life anymore than a shadow can kill light. Truth is not impaired or negated by falsity, and only its expression can be misunderstood or misrepresented. There is no opposite to life, to God, to Truth, or to the Allness of Reality.

From the analysis of the origin of the concepts of good and evil as perceptions of human consciousness, we can understand the answer to the question often posed throughout the ages: "How can a good God create a world that includes evil?" The answer, of course, is that He did not. The seeming opposites exist in the mind of man as perceptions and positionalities.

As human consciousness evolves, all depictions of good, evil, and value judgments reflect a level of consciousness that is calibratable and relatively predictable. If consciousness evolves, it takes on evermore advanced moral, ethical, and spiritual responsibility. What is seen as a virtue at one level of consciousness can be seen as a fault at another level. Thus, kindness, consideration, and forgiveness are values of the higher levels and could be contrarily seen at lower levels as weaknesses, defects, or faults. We see the same switch of values when there is a major shift of context, such as the rules of behavior during wartime are different from those in peacetime. Whole countries and cultures alternate between being friends or enemies over long courses of time, and the ally of one decade becomes the enemy of the next and then reverts back. The scintillations of human life and society reflect the shifts in content, context, and positionalities of perception, all of which interface and reflect back again the prevailing, calibratable level of consciousness.

Moralistic polarity is traditionally the greatest conflicted area of civilization. It is responsible for the killing of more people than any of nature's catastrophes for it segments mankind into hate, guilt, revenge, murder, suicide, and more. It also sets up the ideological basis for all the pseudo-religious wars that parade under the banner of some religion, yet it completely disregards and violates all the premises of the religion under which the persecutions and terrorist attacks are conducted, ostensibly in the name of God.

Even 'heaven' and 'hell' are not opposites but merely quite different spiritual regions. The same phenomena occur in political ideologies, such as communism versus democracy, totalitarianism versus freedom, and communism versus socialism. If we examine much of what the world traditionally calls evil, what we discover is not evil, which is an abstraction, epithet, and label; instead, we see behaviors that could be described as primitive, infantile, egotistical, narcissistic, selfish, and ignorant, complicated by the psychological mechanisms of denial, projection, and paranoia in order to justify hatred.

In much criminal behavior, 'evil' can easily be seen as a form of insanity and the acting out of infantile impulses and irrationality. Religious or political excess is acted out as righteous indignation, which supposedly removes all personal responsibility; that is, the basic excuse is the rationalized so-called 'principle'. The ego loves to act out of the vanity of 'principle'. As amazing as it may seem, upon inspection, entire populations, countries, and civilizations can be easily persuaded by propaganda to give up their lives and property, and even their families and children, to some banal slogan. Out of infantilism, the immature psyche seeks external authority, which often is merely the consensus of public opinion under the sway of demagoguery. The real defect can be more correctly identified as a lack of the evolution of consciousness, plus the innate defect of the human mind and its inability to discern truth from falsehood.

To get to the core of the issue, one has to look at the fact that the matrix and underpinnings of belief is willingness. The propagandist understands very well that the populous is eager to believe a lie for the sake of the emotional payoff experienced by the ego. Secretly, people enjoy the pleasure of 'righteous' anger, hatred, self-pity, etc. Over time, this has become labeled as 'temptation', which has been alleged to be 'out there' rather than 'within here'.

Temptation stems from within; it is merely the desire to experience the ego's payoff and satisfactions of an impulse, even if it is only a curiosity or a wanting. The ego gets a secret thrill, excitement, and a temporary sense of self-inflation or importance, even if it amounts to killing one's classmates just to 'see what it feels like to kill people'. We see that the location of the temptation is within the ego itself, and the external world simply provides an excuse, an attractive stimulus, or an opportunity. All self-responsibility, guilt, and blame are relieved by projecting the origin of the problem onto the external world as "they" or "my past made me do it."

Just as there is no 'thinker' behind thoughts nor 'doer' behind actions, there is also no actual inner 'tempter' as such. The ego likes to pretend that evil exists 'out there' and seduces the hapless, innocent ego into inadvertently falling into the trap of seduction. The real tempter is the ego's desire for gain, whether that be sensation, excitement, advantage, prestige, or the pleasure of controlling others.

To realize the truth of the above releases one from the bondage of guilt and hate that ensues from the classic duality of good versus evil which has prevailed since the allegory of Adam and Eve. The presumed devil represents the ego's own proclivities and repressed desires. Man is therefore the victim of the inability to tell truth from falsehood as well as the seductions of the ego.

The calibrated levels of consciousness reflect the degree of the presence of Love, just as a thermometer registers the presence of heat. Each level represents an energy field that has innate characteristics and which is identifiable by the presence of those attributes. Each level also has its own culture in which there are leaders or symbolic representatives. Within each level, there are 'prominence' and 'success' as determined by the differing criteria and definitions of that level of consciousness.

From the infinite power of the Supreme beyond all universes, the Unmanifest manifests as the Light of Creation and all life. This radiates down through the heavens and celestial realms and appears on Earth as the great avatars, the enlightened sages, and the saints. Then there are the devoted people whose lives are dedicated to goodness and the relief of suffering. Next is the lovingness inherent in the average person that becomes conditional. Then occurs the consciousness that is devoted to intelligence and the intellect. The world of man is supported by the willingness and sociability of the populous and the integrity of the daily worker.

As dedication to Love diminishes, pride, selfishness, and anger become more overt. Self-centeredness and selfish egocentricity replace love, and darkness ensues. The energy fields devoid of love are consequent to the refusal of God and become denoted as 'lower astral', wherein reign the luciferic and satanic entities that envy and hate goodness and love as their enemies and seek to dominate or destroy the vulnerable. True evil is the result of a choice of the spiritual will and has grave spiritual and karmic consequences. At its worst, extreme evil is chosen for its own sake because it is evil. This characterizes the truly demonic.

The psychological source of seeming evil is primarily the naïve childishness of the primitive animal instincts of the infantile ego which tends to go into rage if its impulses are blocked by external authority. The same oppositional rage or narcissistic rebellion characterizes the criminal, the adolescent delinquent, the warmonger, and the puritanical moralist; they are all the same.

To fear evil is to fear lack of control over one's impulses. The average heroin addict starts out as being just one of the crowd and does not want to appear to be 'chicken' but then discovers that even one dose is sufficient to begin the lifetime entrapment. The addiction is actually not to the drug itself but to the euphoria that surpasses other possible human experiences. Addiction is a psychological, social, and physiological phenomenon born of naïveté and denial.

The spiritual aspirant, therefore, is wise to detach from all positionalities and opinions and be willing to surrender the ego's temporary satisfactions for a higher goal. Human history is the drama of the interaction of the collective egos of a population within which the general majority calibrates below the level of Integrity.

Q: This helps to clarify the teachings of Ramana Marharshi who says there is no point in trying to save the world because the world one perceives does not even exist. He recommended surrendering the world to God and concentrating instead on self-inquiry.

A: He was clear that the appearance of the world is the result of dualistic perception and the intrinsic mechanisms of the ego. All one can actually see within the world are differences and preferences. If one looks at a forest, one sees large and small trees, bent and twisted trees. There is no purpose in going into the forest to try to straighten out all the crooked trees. There is nothing 'wrong' with crooked trees or those that seem to be falling over.

Q: Is the enlightened sage beyond karma?

A: Yes, but only in the ordinary sense of personal human karma, which stems from the ego. However, all that exists is included within the overall karmic patterns of the entire universe and Creation. All is still within the Presence of God as Self. All that comes into existence does so by the 'karma' of having been created by God. The basic karma of the Reality of God forms the ultimate context of the Manifest.

The possibility of the evolution of consciousness is man's karmic inheritance. It is universal and not personal. One is free to make choices and is also free to refuse God. The lower astral realms are made up of such entities that are not put there by God but are there by their own choice.

The dandelion seed floats in the air and its destiny is set by the interaction of its form with prevailing winds. Like the dandelion seed, man has a given bodily structure, but he differs from the dandelion in that he has the rudders of mind and spirit and can thus influence direction and take responsibility. Until only very recently, however, although man had rudders, he did not have a compass and his responsibility was thereby diminished by ignorance. Man did have historic command to be obedient to God but he did not know who God was or what He was like. Over the centuries, spiritual truth had become so distorted that even the most willing servant of God could be led far astray by false beliefs into such extremes of behavior as the sacrificing of innocent children and civilians to appease or please God.

It is not necessary to use the label "evil" as it is an inflammatory term. One does better by describing the behavior for what it is—narcissistic selfishness, ego aggrandizement, ignorance, mass hysteria, or psychopathic/criminal acting out of animalistic impulses. These behaviors are characterized by the absence of love.

Q: **How can one stay detached from such human catastrophes?**

A: A more expanded context allows for a more detached view. Human consciousness evolves from the animal and infant to curious adolescence and mature adult, but only very rarely to that new branch of humanity that we could call *Homo spiritus*. Although spiritually inspired and gifted individuals and groups have existed for thousands of years, their numbers have not been large and their overt influence has been limited and impaired by opposition and distortion. One can observe the ebb and flow of life as fluctuations that are not needful of pejorative labels. Human life is a great school.

Detachment from positionalities, and especially the positionalities occasioned by labeling, leads to serenity, freedom, and security. Greater serenity arises from relating to the context of life rather than to the content which is primarily a game board of interacting egos. This broader style of relating to life leads to greater compassion and emancipation from being at the effect of the world.

It is well to keep in mind at all times that the ego/mind does not experience the world but only its own perceptions of it. The media exploit emotionality and sensationalism in images and languaging to elicit sentimentality, indignation, or outrage, or to satisfy prurient curiosity. When seen for what they are, these invitations to reactivity can be declined. All life ebbs and flows. Everyone is born, suffers afflictions, and dies. There are happiness and sadness, catastrophe and success, increase and decrease. The stock market rises and falls. Diseases and accidents come and go. The karmic dance of life unfolds in the karmic theater of the universe.

All reactions to life are subjective. There is nothing happening that is awful, exciting, sad, good, or bad. It is pointless to hold a position that catastrophes shouldn't 'happen' or that the innocent 'didn't deserve it', or 'isn't it awful', or 'it must be somebody's fault'. With a broad view, one can remain unperturbed by either the content or the context of life. That requires giving up judgments, expectations, or 'sensitivities'.

The potentiality for events can be modified by changing conditions so as to effect the balance of propensities one way or the other. As an example, following a forest fire, a wise observer was quoted as stating in a newspaper article that "Fires are neither good nor bad. They reflect local conditions." (Paxon, 2002.) What is considered 'bad' by residents is healthy, natural and 'good' for the forest over the long term.

In Reality, there are no events; there are no beginnings or endings. The backdrop is silent, still, and undisturbed by the movie. One's reality is the context and not the content. The oneness of life appears to perception as multitudinous. What makes the appearances of the world seem real is a projection of the Radiance of the Self. The movie itself has no intrinsic reality as perceived. The actual locus of the sense of realness lies totally within consciousness as subjectivity. Even if there were such a thing as an independent, objective reality, it would only be knowable because of one's internal subjectivity.

Q: That statement is really saying that the only Reality is God.

A: God can only be known and not proven. Beyond subjectivity, no world exists. Without the presence of God, nothing could be known or experienced, including even one's own existence. Existence as subjectivity is complete, total, and whole, and it is the very basis of joy. The Self is the Presence of the Source of Existence as the Infinite 'I'.

Q: What is the subjective experience or realization of Allness like?

A: It is an awareness of a condition that has always been present. The novelty of sequential experiencing disappears as do expectation, regret, or the desire to anticipate or control. Existence *as* Existence is total and complete. All one's needs are already fulfilled. There is nothing to gain or lose and everything is of equal value. It would be like all movies being equally enjoyable because the pleasure stems from 'going to the movies', and the movie that is playing is irrelevant.

With the elimination of preference, all form is seen to be equal in value; in fact, its common value is only that it has form. The weed is the same as the diamond—each may differ in appearance but not in intrinsic value. Their beauty is equal because it is innate in all form. Everything is equal by virtue of having existence. Nothing is in the process of 'becoming'; it already is its own identity, complete and perfect. Existence is never incomplete.

An 'instant' is an artifact of attention and has no independent reality. There are no 'instants' in the world. The unfolding of Creation is continuous; it does not go from incomplete to complete but from complete to complete. In one instant, it can appear to be completely 'this', and in the next instant, it can appear to be completely 'that'.

Everything exists outside of time and not within it; therefore, nothing exists in time nor is subject to it. Time is merely a style of perception. If one looks at a chair, one just sees a chair and does not see time. If one looks at a clock, one sees change but not time. Time is an abstract concept projected onto observable form.

The descriptive quality that we call "time" actually stands still. Events seem to move, but time is unmoving. Time does not exist, change, or have duration. It is stationary. Measurement moves, planets move, but the contexts of space and time are stationary. There is no self-existent reality such as time, and because time is stationary, it is therefore always that which is beyond here or now. Time never changes because there is nothing to change. Change requires form; time has no form.

Time is a concept of measurement, and concepts exist only as mental phenomena. Without the presence of the human brain, even a concept such as time could not occur. The mind assumes that nothing can exist unless it exists in time, which is a mind game.

If time is nonexistent, then so is the notion of 'place'. We can see spatial relationships, but there is no such thing as 'place'. 'Place' has no independent existence; it is a mentation.

'Space' is a concept. The mind imagines that if something exists in a place, then that place must be a space. Like time, 'space' is an imagination. There is no 'place', there is no 'where', there is no 'here', and there is no 'there'; neither is there a 'when'. Existence is independent of form, time, space, or location.

"Now" is also a concept. There is only foreverness—that which is the Self is felt/known as a quality of always and is not experienced as a current instant that would be analogous to a place or episode in linear time. In the nonlinear Reality, there is no time track upon which to position a moment or an instant denotable as "now."

CHAPTER TWELVE

THE EMOTIONS

Commitment to the highest spiritual goals tends to bring up the ego's defects, which is to be expected. Defects are inherent in the ego's structure and should not be taken personally. The ego is not the real 'you'; it was inherited as part of being born a human. It basically originates from the animal world, and the evolution of consciousness is through primitive stages of mankind's evolution, so it could be said that to seek enlightenment is to recapitulate the history of human evolution.

The seeking of Enlightenment is a very major commitment, and is, in fact, the most difficult of all human pursuits. It can be alternately arduous or exhilarating, exciting or tedious, demanding or inspired. There are great breakthroughs as well as exasperating, seemingly impossible obstacles. It is to be expected that this pattern is par for the course. The ego puts up resistances and it struggles for survival. Therefore, when its proclivities arise, they should be viewed as a sign of success and not of failure. Instead of dismay, the surfacing of the ego's resistances should be taken as a sign of accomplishment. The inner search that characterizes the spiritual pathway is a recapitulation of the evolution of the ego from prehistoric times up to the present, but this time there is the gift of freedom to choose differently.

Thus far, we have addressed the higher levels of consciousness that calibrate above 200, the intrinsic structure of the ego, and the means by which to transcend positionalities and undo the paradox of the 'opposites' at the various levels. With some modifications, the same principles can be applied to the consciousness levels below 200. These tend to recur as hidden aspects of personality and may surface only in certain specific activities or relationships. These are often referred to as character defects or emotional problems. Some may be persistent and aggravating, requiring specific remedies.

Pride

There is a normal, benign level of pride that is more correctly termed "self-esteem" or "self-care." This refers to putting one's best foot forward and the normal satisfactions that result from successful effort and achievement. These forms of a positive self-image are the result of effort and are therefore appropriate and not necessarily inflationary to the ego. They have been earned and have a realistic foundation.

Pride as a spiritual defect refers to pridefulness as an attitude and a positionality. It is an arrogance that can apply to beliefs, thoughts, opinions, and the general attitude of being better than others. This is an overvaluation of self-worth and is commonly referred to as egotism. Since it is not based on accomplishment and is unearned, it is fragile.

Because pride is vulnerable, it has to be constantly defended and can be accompanied by a "chip on the shoulder" attitude. Its weakness is usually recognized in the common saying "Pride goeth before a fall." The vulnerability occurs because it is an arbitrary positionality. Pride is an ego inflation and like a balloon, it is easily punctured. Flattery feeds pride because pride is vanity. Vanity is egocentric in that it is psychologically based on narcissism. Its downside is that it decreases the capacity to be compassionate and loving towards others.

Pride, in its strictest spiritual sense, refers to the refusal to surrender to God as the Supreme Source of one's existence. It is therefore a subtle attitude of competition with God for sovereignty.

Underneath spiritual vanity is the refusal of humility because, to egotism, humility is misunderstood as submission, inferiority, and humiliation. The truly humble are immune to

humiliation. False humility is based on the same misunderstanding. True humility is based on an accurate assessment,
without ascribing value or worth. A truly accurate and humble
scientist, for example, is quite aware of both the upside, the
downside, and the limitations of the scientific method, including logic and reason. A truly humble person can derive great
satisfaction from even great achievements without pridefulness
and can therefore take credit without assuming the secretly
prideful position of psuedohumility.

The best antidotes for pridefulness are gratitude, satisfaction,
and thankfulness. True humility allows one to say, without
pride, that facts are just facts. One can be humble and, at the
same time, admit that yes, they are indeed the greatest and best
in their particular field, at least at the present moment. This is
possible if there is no ego inflation involved. If egotism is
involved, then the person feels that they have to adopt a
psuedohumility and pretense to appear humble. Society
recognizes greatness, major accomplishment, or status but
without necessarily introducing pridefulness. Greatness
realistically accepts the importance of a position or accomplishment without becoming inflated by it. To do this, the
person often separates the personal self from their role, position, or function. The personality that bases pridefulness on
narcissistic ego inflation tends to have an 'entitled' attitude that
has not been earned by personal accomplishment.

Entitlement as an emotional/psychological position stems from
unresolved infantile, narcissistic egocentricity. It is the hidden
'baby' behind the raging emotional sensitivity of the borderline
personality disorder as well as the egotistic dictator who callously
brings about the destruction of his own country and its population. The entitled attitude is also the trigger springboard for
domestic violence and heinous crimes. The habitual criminal feels
entitled to forcefully take that which is desired at the cost of the
suffering and violation of the rights of others.

The ego inflation of entitlement makes it the very core of
what is seen as evil in society. It is the wellspring of domestic
strife and crime. It is the secret 'Divine Right of Kings' attitude

which is demonstrated by the excessive cruelty and slaughter perpetrated through the ages of the military conquerors and dictators who decimated the populace.

Egotism is accompanied by sensitivity to slights that make the subject feel invalidated and therefore angry and paranoid. This volatility is seen in the chronic 'rager', the bully, and the militant whose paranoid sensitivity results in seeing 'slights' in all social situations. Many such people become litigious and petition for redress of 'wrongs' that are merely the distortions of perception of borderline attitudes. Some become chronic protesters and can be seen at every protest rally or parade.

The sensitivity and over reactivity to real, imaginary, or delusional slights can release enormous rage that is dangerous and massively destructive, such as the killing of many others, setting fire to houses and forests, shooting employers ("going postal"), murdering spouses, and going on berserk rampages.

Pride of entitlement also produces the characteristic lack of remorse seen in criminals as well as gross perpetration of genocide because entitlement is accompanied by the conviction of being 'justified'. That attitude is openly displayed in street gang cultures where being 'disrespected' justifies even murder.

That 'low self-esteem' is the cause of antisocial behavior has been a pet illusion of sociological, psychological, and political positionalities for decades. On the contrary, criminals and other deviants have inflated and often grandiose self-esteem. This easily observable clinical fact is now even reaching public awareness as reported in the media (Sullivan, 2002).

Conquerors in war feel justified to pillage and rape the vanquished, and 'justified resentments' daily spoil the happiness and peace of the ordinary person. The same egocentric positionality foments as jealousy and envy, which are innate to the negative emotional melodramas of the human condition. Thus, the actions and emotion of spite undermine emotional security for many people who spend their lives nursing grievances and self-pity as well as fantasies of revenge.

Egotism leads to inflated expectations and, therefore, the person is constantly disgruntled at not being treated as 'special'.

Society reacts negatively to the associated vanity and excessive demands. The 'entitled' person can be vengeful and vicious as well as exceptionally vain, competitive, jealous, and prone to hatred.

The entitled attitude tends to be tenacious, rigidly defended, and often uncorrectable by any known means. This attitude is basically psychotic as the inner grandiosity is essentially delusional. The recalcitrance to correction explains why true criminality is unaffected by incarceration and the psychopath characteristically is unable to learn from experience.

Pride is undone by the inspiration of devotion that willingly surrenders its vanity to God. With spiritual evolvement, even self-esteem is no longer a necessity nor even a meaningful concept. Both pride and shame arise out of a self-valued judgmentalism. In Reality, 'worth' is not a consideration. All is as it is, with no explanations or adjectives necessary. To advanced consciousness, what the world thinks or believes is of no real significance or importance.

The human psyche becomes attached to qualifying and rating everything on arbitrary social scales of desirability, appeal, or value. Whole lives can become devoted to pursuing some mystique in which subtle distinctions become inflated and sought after for their social symbolism. This can lead to an endless seeking of status, possessions, wealth, and symbols of distinction, as well as the need to be 'right' about everything.

So-called spiritual pride is also status seeking but in a different classification system. There is even a pride in being a spiritual seeker who is then 'better than' crass materialists (e.g., the paradox of being prideful of one's humility). This can be undone by seeing that everyone is working at mastering a certain level of consciousness so that they can go on to the next. It is said that one is not done with this world until one has mastered it. Thus, the Calibrated Scale of Consciousness does not indicate levels of 'better than' others but merely 'different from' others as a transitory evolutionary progression.

Paradoxically, it is also spiritual pride to hold a negative judgment about pride, spiritual pride, a vanity, or to look down on status seekers or worldliness. Although pride is a deterrent to enlightenment when it is based on real accomplishment, it is a useful motivator for a large portion of the population. It can be dropped later when it is no longer needed since inner fulfillment no longer requires it.

In the classic Eastern spiritual traditions, the Sanskrit terms "tamas," "rajas," and "satva" are used to broadly classify the major levels of influences in the universe, including the human psyche. The level of tamas is characterized by laziness, lack of desire, lack of ambition, carelessness, lack of caring, lack of motivation, oppositionalism, resistance, refusal, selfishness, negativity, slough, poverty of mind and spirit, and lack of positive emotions. The prime characteristics of tamas are inertia, resistance, and lack. The way out of tamas is often through the arising of desire, greed, or even anger, and the final arising of pride.

Rajas indicates the level of activity, action, accomplishment, gain, and the fulfillment of goals. The next step, 'high rajas', is the level of maximal functioning, which, in the spiritual progression, is transcended and finally leads to satva, the level of tranquility, peace, and satisfaction. At that level, one no longer has to prove anything, and goals become progressively more spiritual and internalized rather than external.

In tamas, one doesn't have a sweater to wear or else it is dirty and full of holes. In rajas, the sweater is new, neat, and clean. In high rajas, one has a collection of cashmere sweaters. In satva, one can again wear one's favorite old sweater that has moth holes in it; however, it is clean.

One of the unseen effects of television is that it brought up desire and anger in those who were in tamas, and it tended to move them up to rajas and the desire for possessions and a higher lifestyle. Thus, each level has its own purpose, useful-ness, and value, and when seen in the context of being a stage in spiritual evolution, it can be observed compassionately without judgmentalism.

Society is constantly learning better methods to motivate people who are stuck in tamas. Those who live in hopelessness and despair lack energy and need uplifting by the input of interest and by education and the learning of more effective coping styles.

Desire

Desire is a wantingness that can be obsessive and, when excessive, is called greed. It is, however, an important drive in human affairs and motivates the whole economy to a considerable degree. Normal desire tends to run its course until the wants are fulfilled. Its primordial origin is the hunger of the animal organism. Fulfillment results in a sense of completion so that the psyche is free to turn within and pursue spiritual values. In and of itself, desire, like pride, need not be condemned as wrong for it is socially useful if it is channeled into beneficial activities such as education and health. Greed is condemned primarily because the motivation is seen to be selfish and therefore exploitive of others. It leads to the desire to control others and therefore represents an attachment.

Desire is fueled by the illusion of lack and that the source of happiness is outside oneself and therefore has to be pursued or acquired. The importance of the object of desire is thereby inflated and overvalued by its symbolism and mystique. The pleasure of the sense of the Self is blocked by desire. When that desire is fulfilled, the ego ascribes the resultant sense of joy to the acquisition of an external. However, this is a clever illusion because the actual source of the pleasure is that the block to experiencing the joy of the Self has been temporarily removed. The source of the experienced happiness is the radiance of the Self that shines forth when it is not shut off by an ego distress.

In addictions, desire is very powerful and results in the obsession and compulsion of craving. Drugs or alcohol actually calibrate very low; however, they sedate the lower vibrations of the ego so that the higher Self can be experienced. The drugs or alcohol are not capable of creating a 'high'; the 'high' is the radiance of the Self. The ego ascribes the pleasurable feeling to the drugs themselves.

Joy calibrates at 540 and up; drugs calibrate at only 80 or less. So, how could a substance that calibrates at only 75 'cause' an experience that can be in the high 500s? The obvious answer is simply that it does not. By analogy, the drugs briefly dissolve the clouds so that the sun shines forth. The naïve ego ascribes the ecstasy, joy, and happiness to the drugs themselves. The addict is actually addicted to the experience of the joy of the Self and therefore repeats what is believed to be the only way to have that experience. Even a single such experience is unforgettable. The craving is for the 'high' of joy, not for the drug itself.

To the spiritual aspirant, desire and attachments are deterrents to progress, and as they arise, what they symbolize can be surrendered to God. At the same time, the positionalities that they signify can be identified and surrendered because they become progressive burdens. Frequently, at a certain phase of spiritual evolution, it is common for aspirants to walk away from all possessions. Later on, possessions are no longer seen as a hindrance or an asset because the sense of ownership disappears and illusions are no longer projected upon them.

To undo the endless sequences of wanting and craving, it is useful to disassemble them by doing an exercise called "and then what?" I want (a better job, more money, better car, college degree, or whatever), followed by the question "and then what?" It will be found that the answer is always the final belief that "and then I will be happy."

In ordinary life, fulfillment and desire bring temporary relief, but soon the wantingness merely switches to a new desire. Success and money are the most frequent illusory goals and not infrequently do they become an obsession.

It is helpful to understand that if one is not happy with present circumstances, the chances are that happiness will still be elusive when conditions change to meet one's current desire, that is, if happiness is elusive now, it will continue to be so in the future because the ability to locate the source of happiness has not yet been found.

The value of asceticism is that one discovers the capacity to be content and happy with only the barest minimum of essentials for survival. There is great joy in the realization that one does not actually need anything at all to be happy, not even external stimuli, such as television, music, conversation, or the presence of other people or activities. At a more advanced level, one learns that even the amusement of mental activity and thoughts can be dispensed with and that the awareness of existence itself is sufficient. There is an even greater happiness as the Self shines forth as the Allness that precludes all lack or otherness. There is then nothing left to desire and no source of desire because the Totality is complete in its identity as the Infinite 'I'.

In ordinary life, desire for success and status as ambition is considered normal and represents the quality of rajas activity; it is therefore a sign of the evolution of consciousness beyond the resistance of lethargy. The spiritual seeker notes that it is not the successful activity or position which is the hindrance but the underlying pride and attachment. One can transcend these aspects by surrendering and dedicating all actions to God. The joy of excellence is internally rewarding, and success is accompanied by gratitude rather than pride.

With the further evolution of consciousness, the illusion of the personal 'I' behind performance disappears and the activity is experienced as being autonomous and effortless. This is a common experience that comes to endeavors in sports and the arts. The jogger breaks through the "I can't" barrier and experiences an effortless run. The dancer dances without effort and is inexhaustible. The worker goes into effortless motion that is beyond exhaustion. Any activity can result in the sudden discovery of selflessness, which is joyful and can even become ecstasy. The realization that the Self is the author of one's actions and not the self is a transformative joy.

The spontaneity of life is an expression of essences interacting effortlessly. The miracle of Creation is continuous, and all life shares in the Divinity of its Source, for nothing comes into existence except by Divine ordinance. Once the sacredness of life is revealed, there follows the knowingness of what is meant by the phrase, "Gloria in Excelsis! Deo!"

It can be seen that any so-called spiritual defect or obstacle can be the very springboard to its transcendence. By recontextualization, what was a negative becomes a positive and an avenue to the discovery of God. Every defect contains a hidden treasure, and all supposed defects are doorways.

Guilt

This is perhaps the most feared block to spiritual endeavor and the one that frightens many people away from embarking on a spiritual quest. People declare that they are afraid to look within themselves for fear of what they might discover. Guilt is the source of everyone's fear of Judgment Day, for it conjures up frightful images of sin, hell, and God's righteous wrath. The fearsome downside of being a human is subsumed as sin/guilt/judgment/condemnation/punishment/death/hell. It is the pall that hangs over human life which is then lived on the stage of the trapdoor to hell. Death is feared as the trigger that releases the trapdoor at any moment. One hears that, at the last moment, life passes before one in review like the Spirit of Christmas Past, whose ghostly finger points accusingly. "O woe, Spirit," humans say, "have you no mercy? We have seen enough. We hear the clanking chains. What will be our fate?"

Thus, much fear is based on guilt because the unconscious projects into the unknown its imaginations of that which it has condemned. Past self-judgments become projected onto a fearsome God whose angry vengeance is mighty and too horrible to even think about. These are the underpinnings of the fear of death, which is seen as God's ultimate, righteous justice, but even death is not enough, for the wrathful deity may now throw the soul into hell forever.

As a consequence of this fearsome scenario, frightened people resort to denial and scoff at any spiritual reality. They pretend that there is no God, no soul, and no afterlife and thus hope that this terrible scenario is thereby escaped by going into a merciful oblivion. "After death, there is nothing" is their dream of being saved at last from spiritual responsibility. They

keep their fingers crossed and keep the door to 'all that imagination stuff' tightly closed. Friends respect these desires and
wish them luck.

Everyone (except psychopaths) is familiar with the various
forms of guilt, such as shame, regret, self-accusation, self-
condemnation, low self-esteem, self-hatred, and subtle
intropunitive twinges of remorse. The religious person has a
traditional means of alleviating guilt by confession, penance,
absolution, prayer, and the resolve to do better, and one can
compensate additionally by renewed dedication to good works.

Guilt is based on three major positionalities. These should be
understood before the whole subject of guilt is tackled to a
major degree. (1) Like any aspect of the ego, guilt is based on a
positionality that creates a perceptual duality of the opposites.
(2) The hypothesized is believed to be a reality. (3) The actor of
the action is believed to be real.

The typical guilt statement is as follows: "I (error #3)
shouldn't have done that (error #2); therefore, I am a bad
person (error #1)." The hypothetical ideal is held to be realistic,
whereas, in fact, the person did what appeared at the time to be
possible or reasonable in the context of the time, with the
strengths and weaknesses that were then operative.

One's definition of self as the 'me' or the 'I' is not fixed but
variable. Because it is variable, the context of the action has an
equally variable influence. If the self thinks "I am desperate," it
will do things that it would not do if the self thinks "I am safe."
The idealized self is not the same self that plays on the field of
life. The ego/self fluctuates from moment to moment. At one
instant, it is benign; at another, angry; at another, selfish, and at
another, generous. The self of actions is illusory, just as the self
of the present moment is also illusory.

Decisions stem from a great multitude of underlying con-
tributing factors. Action is therefore determined by a complex
interaction of programs, both conscious and unconscious,
which also include the unseen effect of the dominating field of
consciousness to which one is subject at the time.

These factors are intrinsic to what is termed "situational ethics," which is a more advanced understanding than literal black-and-white morality and judgmentalism because it includes context rather than just content. Even courts consider mitigating factors (i.e., context) when evaluating a case, and in some instances, the mitigating factors are so strong that they outweigh even legal responsibility. Any act reflects the expression of human consciousness throughout all its evolution in the total context of the universe. This accounts for the saying "It seemed like a good idea at the time."

The ego is a set of programs in which reason operates through complex, multilayered series of algorithms wherein thought follows certain decision trees that are variously weighted by past experience, indoctrination, and social forces; it is therefore not a self-created condition. The instinctual drive is attached to the programs, thereby causing physiological processes to come into play. The intellect in the forebrain can be genetically impaired or easily bypassed by strong emotions surging up from the more primitive, deeper layers of the brain. The act is also influenced by the life phase of the individual as well as unseen karmic forces.

It is beneficial to examine the motives that lead to a regretful action. There is usually fear, such as that of loss, of being controlled or dominated, of lack or failure, or of loss of status. In addition, there are impulsiveness and a lack of sufficient information upon which to act, such as the difference between truth and falsehood. All this is subsumed under the generality of 'human weakness'. From the hypothetical, moralistic viewpoint, one is not supposed to give in to 'weakness', and who is to be blamed for the fact that the evolution of consciousness has not brought one to saintly resolve, a healthy brain, and beneficial genes? We could blame the rhinencephalon, that old animal brain that is rapacious in order to survive. We could blame parents or society. We could blame the Pavlovian conditioning of the media. We could blame the DNA and the human gene pool from which some people are born literally without the capacity to even have a conscience and who feel entitled to whatever they want. Testosterone can certainly be blamed for a lot of missteps in life. (It is a clinical fact that castrated men actually live nine years longer than normal men.) We could blame the media for corrupting the morals and glamorizing evil.

In this kaleidoscope of interacting factors, who should we blame? Who should wear the sack cloth and ashes and beat their breast? When any single act is disassembled, it will be found to have no single determinative cause, and the 'who' that ostensibly performed the act no longer even exists. But, the mind says, isn't all this just rationalizing away guilt? There is the belief that suffering and contrition will make people better.

We can see from the inherent complexity of even a simple act that only the omniscience of God would be capable of judging; thus arises the spiritual dictum "Judge not." It is vanity which leads the ego to think it is capable of judging others or itself.

There is no indication from any source of higher truth that God is influenced or assuaged by guilt. The great sages of history do not speak of guilt but instead refer to "sin" as being due to ignorance. They teach that certain acts will result in the soul's transition to unpleasant realms, whereas virtue leads to higher realms after physical death. They merely make these as factual statements; they are not attempts to threaten, intimidate, or frighten.

Past errors are to be looked at with compassion as well as responsibility, which is the only way to correct an error. One has to clarify the intention of the act at the time as well as the difference between guilt and regret. Regret is often more appropriate for past actions that did not turn out well. True guilt applies to intention, whereas regret refers to unfavorable outcome.

It can easily be observed that the mind is often not rational or dependable, nor does it have the necessary facts to justify any actions. It jumps to conclusions without having first investigated a situation. In addition, circumstantial pressures are operative, and the mind is subject to frequent episodes of 'microinsanity' when it actually becomes quite irrational. This is a common observation. People often say "I must have been insane at the time." Although the mind will usually cancel out 'insane' options or choices, it cannot be counted on to do so absolutely. That is one of several reasons why businesses require two signatures on checks of large amounts.

Experientially, guilt is an operational 'reality' until the underpinnings of the ego are removed. Spiritual seekers are sometimes prone to look back critically on their past actions from their newfound spiritual position. All self-examination should be done with compassion. Past errors arose within a different context. The best resolution of guilt is to rededicate oneself to God and one's fellow man and to the forgiveness of self and others.

Suffering is not a gift to God anymore than is a rain cloud a gift to the sky. Guilt can become a self-indulgence. It uses up energy that is better turned into service to one's fellow man. It is necessary to be forgiving to oneself as well as others or else the ego becomes reinforced with self-condemnation. Self-hatred needs to be surrendered to God and given up as an egocentric, narcissistic self-centeredness. It is a clinging to the past where Reality is not discoverable.

Anger

Anger begins in infancy where it stems from the narcissistic frustration of wants. Its primordial basis is seen in the animal world, where fighting and arguing over food, territory, and mates are innate. In more sophisticated adult life, this anger becomes elaborated and applies to social issues and positionalities, such as right versus wrong, guilt versus inno-cence, and frustrated expectations.

Anger arises when perception signals a threat to the ego which then regresses to a basic animal response. In the child, anger can be directed towards the adult figure who is seen as frustrating its wants. Although the origin of anger is intrapsy-chic, it is commonly projected outward or is meant to intimi-date and control others.

With a shift of focus from the subjective participant to the observer, one sees the narcissistic emphasis on expectations as an ego positionality that makes the individual a petulant or anger-prone person. The angry person secretly feels entitled to its wants and desires and has impossible expectations of life. Anger can also be an attitude and a vulnerable ego positionality. It leads to aggression rather than the healthier alternative of self-assertion.

The basic antidote to anger is humility, which is the counter-balance to the egotism that feeds it. The infant within the angry person rails against the unfairness of life, which is actually the perception of the petulant, spoiled child. Narcissism engenders the belief that one deserves to get what one wants, for the narcissistic core of the ego is concerned only with an inflated self-importance. When it dawns on the infant that the universe is indifferent to the ego's wants, it goes into a rage that trans-poses into patterns of interpersonal conflict. Anger then becomes the futile attempt to control others who become objects to be manipulated or blamed for frustration.

The best defense against the development of anger is to see others as equals, lessen expectations, and via humility, surren-der the fulfillment of one's wants to God. With progressive detachment and relinquishment of the ego's demands and expectations, anger diminishes.

So-called righteous anger and indignation are moralistic inflations of positionalities and expectations of others. With hatred, the anger fixates on an external enemy that is actually the ego's projection of its own inner hatred tendencies onto sym-bolic representations. The 'hatred of sin' is still just hatred, and because it is still just hatred, it is not morally superior. The 'hatred of sin' creates the absurdity of an error's condemning an error. There is not much gain in shaking one's fist in indignant wrath at sinners other than the self-servingness of demagoguery.

A major source of spiritual error is to mix diverse realms as though they were on the same plane and levels of reality. The whale does not do battle with the tiger; they exist in different worlds. The concept of God doing battle with the forces of evil is an impossibility created by guilt-ridden, fearful fantasies. In Reality, there is no possible threat to heaven or to God or to the purity of Absolute Reality. The Real exists and the unreal does not, and the Real is not threatened by the unreal.

The only place where an encounter and interaction between the forces of good and evil could be possible is in the lower astral realms or human imagination. The human imagination, like a movie, treats impossibilities as realities and gives them graphic interaction, such as in a movie like "War of the Worlds."

It is helpful to recall that the mind is totally unable to tell truth from falsehood and that the primitive mind is even less capable. The myth, the fable, or the epic satisfy the need to express certain human fears and hopes about its destiny. They are poetic but not factual, nor do they reflect spiritual reality, much less absolute truth. The unreal need not be denounced, for only that which has existence is capable of being denounced. The unreal only needs to be disenfranchised by Truth.

The Book of Revelations (which calibrates at 70) has been exploited by religious demagogues for centuries. Its author, John, calibrates at 70. The credulous naïveté of the populous is fertile ground for manipulation and intimidation. Over the centuries, up to and including the present, numerous psychics, mediums, and prophets have tapped into the whole drama of the lower astral realm. Repeatedly, the gullible prepare for the 'end times'. Various religious cults and sects become enamored of the apocalyptic legend which arises again and again, surfacing and capturing the imagination of the impressionable. The whole legend is based on man's collective guilt, fears, and spiritual ignorance, plus the hopeful pride of being among the 'elected', and the specialness of being selected as one of the favored few.

Falsity is based on force and fear; truth is based on power. Falsity is fearful because it is based on illusion. Truth is beyond fear or attack. Falsity gains influence only by allegiance for it has no intrinsic power. The fearsome 'end times' refers to the lower astral realms where false illusions are given validity.

Fear

The ego's prime supports are pride (ignorance), desire (to propagate its continuance), and fear (of death). Of these, the most primordial is fear, because the ego's vulnerability is that its seeming reality is illusory and therefore subject to disillusion.

The most prevalent conscious fear is that of physical survival because the body is believed to be the primary reality of life. The body is also evidence of being separate, unique, and individual; therefore, the mind becomes the instrument that primarily serves physical survival plus its accoutrements of comfort, status, and security. Therefore, the schemes and efforts to ensure survival or success take up the time and energy of most people. The ego identifies with all these elaborations, and the fears and defenses become innumerable and unending.

The ego's investments take the form of pride and identification with belief systems; therefore, these also have to be defended. This results in a hyperalertness to danger, like that of the animal in the wild. All that is valued has to be defended; therefore, danger lurks everywhere. The ego is ever watchful of every slight, slur, or encroachment on its turf. The mind is paranoid, and collective paranoia can dominate whole countries, such as Russia during the long Cold War.

Because of the ego's investments, innumerable positionalities, and false identifications, its fears are endless and continuously propagate. They subside only when the identification of 'me' with the positionalities is withdrawn and the fears relating to physical survival and being separate diminish as a result of total surrender of one's life and survival to God.

The endless everyday fears are subsumed under the common human conditions called worry and anxiety. This is so prevalent that it is accepted as part of being 'normal.' Numerous activities are motivated by the desire to escape fear, and often the majority of life's activities become unconsciously fear motivated. Jesus Christ said that fear was the last, final negativity to be surrendered.

The Buddha enumerated the basic fears 2,500 years ago as those of "sickness, poverty, old age, and death." Thus, they are all the fears of loss that become pervasive and color all activities: loss of privilege, position, title, reputation, relationships, youth, possessions, influence, power, love, money, strength, skills, sexual attractiveness, status, comfort, opportunity, mental faculties, and more.

The general trend of fear is that of the loss of assets which, in turn, means the loss of pleasure and satisfaction or the means of survival. Self-confidence is the normal safeguard against multiple fears, and that capacity is enhanced by the often painful learning of life skills in the course of events.

The common element of most fears is that they are based on the illusion that happiness is dependent on externals and therefore vulnerable. To overcome the illusion of vulnerability brings great relief and the correction of being run by fear so that life becomes benign and filled with satisfaction and an easy-going, confident attitude instead of constant guardedness.

Cessation of fear is the result of learning that the source of happiness and joy is from within. It stems from recognizing that its source is the joy of one's own existence, which is continuous and not dependent on externals. This results from surrendering expectations and demands on one's self, the world, and others. The thought "I can only be happy if I win or get what I want" is a guarantee of worry, anxiety, and unhappiness.

Fears are eliminated by graceful acceptance of the qualities inherent in the human condition which brings to awareness the comforting realization that one's discomforts are shared equally by all. This results in a healing compassion towards all life. To become loving brings an end to the fear of loss of love, for lovingness engenders love wherever it goes.

Survival fear is eliminated by the knowledge that one's ongoing survival is already determined and guaranteed by the Self and one's karmic inheritance. The exact time of death was already set at birth. (This statement tests "true" with kinesiology.) Realize also that no 'accidents' are possible in the universe.

One can also do a simple exercise called the "death-bed certainty principle": Project ahead in time to the inevitable scene of one's inevitable demise and appreciate that to have gotten to the end, one must have survived the duration of what was necessary to get to the end. All fear is eliminated totally by the realization of the Self, for in that state is the absolute knowingness of immortality—that that which is one's actual Reality is not even subject to birth or death, much less vicissitudes.

A profound fact that eliminates survival fear is the realization that one's survival is actually maintained from moment to moment by the Self which is infinitely all powerful. The ego/mind/self does what it does to survive because it is under the 'supervision' and 'control' of the Presence of God within. The ego takes credit for its life-sustaining activities and ideas without realizing it is directed to do so by the powerful influence of the all-powerful field and context of life, the Self of Divinity.

Life is sustained by the Source of life itself which is ever present. The reason we take vitamins is because the quality and principle of the Self enhance the attraction of that which is life enhancing for so long as it is appropriate. When the prescribed duration of life ends, then the Self sustains the existence of the Spirit life instead of the body life.

Life itself is not subject to cessation but only to change of form. The Source and essence of life is God who is not subject to demise. One cannot lose one's source. Death is the end of one chapter of a series of stories that finally only cease when the ego-author surrenders to its source.

The Self is like one's inner grandmother who watches over a child so it does not forget to take a raincoat or forget to mail the rent check. God is not ominous but loving. Fears arise from the imagination.

When examined, it will be found that most of life's activities are basically related to ensuring physical survival by means of sophisticated techniques, such as education, health, success, possessions, houses, cars, money, and status. The totality of these efforts becomes an endless bondage and source of constant anxiety.

People who have had an out-of-body or near-death experience remember the surprise of the profound sense of freedom and peace that accompany loss of the ever present existential anxiety of having a physical body. The same release from survival anxiety occurs when consciousness level 600 is reached. At that level, the identification of self with the body ceases, and the body is witnessed to become completely autonomous.

The fears to be overcome relate to the ego's self-definitions with positionalities, identifications, and physicality. When these have been transcended, the ego faces the death of the illusion that its presumed identity is the source of its existence. The one and only real death that it is possible to experience is the surrender of the illusion that one is the author of one's own existence to a god that is really experientially unknown and unknowable until that final event occurs.

The ego fears the loss of conscious existence, and its final surrender means facing 'the great unknown'. The last step, therefore, requires great courage, faith, and the conviction of the truth of the great teachers. The core of the ego is then relinquished by Divine Grace, and the revelation that it ensures erases the last vestige of fear because its source has been removed.

Grief

The loss of that which is valued due to the attachment of identification results in a unique, painful, emotional response that first appears in the evolution of consciousness at the level of the higher animals. The dog, the cat, the wolf pack, and the elephant family all mourn the loss of a companion, mate, or group member. This vulnerability is most severe in the infant, for whom the loss of the mother is crucial and life threatening.

Loss brings about physiological reactions and changes in the brain's neurotransmitters. There is a decrease in the brain's serotonin levels and a depression of the immune system. In addition, there is a decrease in physical energy, a loss of appetite, and changes in the sleep pattern. The anguish, however, is primarily emotional/mental, and when severe, brings on thoughts of suicide. It is as though one has lost an irretrievable part of the self and an irreplaceable source of happiness. The grief can deepen to a severe, immobilizing depression and become life threatening, requiring professional treatment.

The mind clings to thoughts, memories, and imagery of the lost person, object, or condition. The basis for grief and loss is attachment, which can include anything that is valued, such as status, position, youth, title, belongings, group membership, or even details of bodily configuration or appearance.

The offset of loss to the spiritual devotee is the realization that loss represents an opportunity for greater freedom. An attachment is a tie and a fetter of the ego. Although the relinquishment initially feels like an emotional stress, there awakens the realization that the bondage would have to have been surrendered to God in due time in the process of letting go of the illusion that the source of happiness is external. The true source of happiness and joy is the Self and not the identifications of the ego/self. Through close examination, it will be found that the fulfillment of desires quells the ego's painful sense of lack, and in the quiet that ensues, it is really the happiness of the Self that was then experienced and not the ego's acquisition. The source of the pleasure was not from the thing, action, or event itself but from the fact that in quieting the ego's feeling of distress, the presence of the Self could be sensed.

This is the mechanism behind all ego gains—the painful wantingness or clamor of the desirous ego is silenced and thus the inner Self is pleasantly experienced. The mind's error is that it ascribes the source of the feeling of happiness to 'out there' instead of 'in here'.

The pain of loss is therefore not due to the loss of the person or object but is from the attachment itself. Attachment is an investment of emotional energy. In due time, it reinvests itself either to a substitute object or, more hopefully, in devotion to God.

Shame

To be ostracized or rejected by society or family is feared by 'normal' people. The conscience of a psychologically intact person becomes the internalized (introject) of parental and societal standards of behavior. This is expanded to the inner judge of self-worth as lovability and again projected onto God as the ultimate Judge.

The sense of self shrinks with disapproval and expands with approval. Shame can be experienced as chagrin or embarrassment and thus has a wider societal base than does guilt, which tends to be more localized or intrapsychic. Shame results in low self-esteem, and the ego seeks to hide or avoid others. Shame can be societal in origin and relate to general characteristics, such as age, sex, color, ethnic origin, class, economic circumstances, intelligence, personal appearance, hair color, stature, religious affiliation, etc. It can be painful in young adults who feel shameful about body weight or facial and bodily features. In some cases, the degree of fixation reaches delusional and pathological proportions.

To undo shame, it is helpful to realize that it is based on pride. The loss of status is painful to the degree that the ego relies on pride as a prop to self-esteem. Were it not for narcissistic pride, a mistake or negative feedback would be experienced only as a regret and ascribed to human frailty and fallibility. Mistakes help one to retain humility.

Loss of that which has been valued can result in remorse, sorrow, sadness, mourning, bereavement, and loneliness. Loss stems from attachment as well as the illusion that the object person or status was an 'out there' source of happiness.

A source of regret and loss is the unrealistic expectation of self and others. Nothing in the world of form is permanent. Eventually, all has to be surrendered to the will of God. To succeed at surrendering, it is necessary to realize that God's will is not personalized to suit individual wishes. The will of God is really the karmic design of the entire universe. To surrender to God's will is to surrender to the truth that nothing other than the Ultimate Reality is permanent. All that arises in form passes away. A loss is an opportunity to become freed from an attachment.

Loss represents a clinging to the past and substituting memory for the awareness of Reality. In any single instant, there is neither loss nor gain, both of which arise from making a story of one's life.

Apathy

As denial of the reality of the Love of God as absolute truth proceeds, it turns into hopelessness and finally into the dejection of apathy. If the ego is the primary focus of identification as 'self', then its failures bespeak worthlessness and failure.

Self-hatred brings up thoughts or acts of self-destruction and suicide. Escape may be sought through drugs, alcohol, or frank psychosis with hallucinations, paranoia, and delusions. The despair weakens resistance to negative entities that are attracted to the vulnerable prey and thus suggest murder or violence. Possession by lower astral entities can lead to grotesque crimes such as serial killings, which are characteristically savage and gruesome. (Serial child killers calibrate between 7 and 35.)

The lowest levels of consciousness (tamas) are expressed in society collectively as squalor, crime, poverty, indifference, sloth, coarseness, abusiveness, early death, high birth and infant mortality rates; drunkenness, gross language, overt hostility and defiance; lack of education; defilement of beauty, peace, and Nature; and disdain for the sacredness of life. Cruelty is rampant, and ugliness is celebrated by grossness of musical lyrics, profanity and sacrilege.

Responsibility is rejected and replaced by blame. There are rat bites, accidents, rapes, shootings, drownings, auto crashes, suicide, theft, burglary, drugs, guns, fights, and weapons.

We say of all the above "how horrible," "like goes to like," "if you sleep with dogs, you get flees," etc. Thus, in the unconscious is the subtle awareness that there is a central attractor field to this as well as every other level of consciousness. Not just neighborhoods but whole geographic regions and subcontinents are the homes of these energies. The true criminal is a recidivist, and the majority eventually gravitates back into prison as though attracted and at home with grossness and violence. The horrific quality of life in the famous penal colony of French Guiana was created by the inmates, the prisoners themselves, and not by the penal authorities.

It is interesting that sociology has lately discovered the nature of this underlying attractor field and has labeled it "the broken-window principle." Unless early signs of decline are corrected in a neighborhood, they attract further abuse, damage, and neglect, and the rate of decline accelerates as though there were a magnet-like attraction to all that is negative. It starts with graffiti and eventuates into gang turf warfare, drugs, shootings, and arson (e.g., the South Bronx and Brownsville in Brooklyn, New York; the East End of London, etc.). Thus, the attractor fields of consciousness levels act as though they have a magnetic attractor or repellent effect on other energies, almost as though they were charged or polarized. It is the attractor field of the negative energy of apathy that attracts the classical social expressions of poverty, crime, overpopulation, and structural decline.

Thus, poverty is not basically a financial condition but is instead a concomitant and consequence of a specific level of consciousness that cannot be cured simply by financial assistance. More often, financial aid worsens the poverty as it gives a stimulus to the already excessive birth rate which then brings even further poverty

In apathy/depression, the immune system is suppressed, which leads to accident proneness and lowered resistance to disease. The brain's neurotransmitters (i.e., serotonin and norepinephrin) are suppressed as is the function of the thymus gland. The loss of appetite leads to anorexia and death by starvation.

The classic stress response was first described by physiologists as "fight or flight" (i.e., anger or fear). Later, Hans Selye defined the stages as (1) alarm, (2) resistance, and, finally, (3) exhaustion. The three stages have concordant emotional, psychological, physiological, and spiritual characteristics. Paradoxically, the 'black night of the soul' can lead to the relinquishment of the basic egocentricity which underlies it. It is also the great spiritual opportunity of 'hitting bottom' and totally surrendering the ego's willfulness to God. This results in seemingly miraculous recoveries and spiritual rebirth.

Judgmentalism

This is primarily a pride-based human failing and less rooted in primitive animal behaviors than the more basic ego responses that have just been discussed. However, even in animal groups, aberrant behavior results in rejection by the herd or pack.

In humans, social conditioning establishes acceptable versus unacceptable behaviors or belief systems. Pejorative denunciations and condemnations are institutionalized, and judgmentalism is supported and encouraged. Behaviors are identified with morality and ethics and simply classified as good versus bad or right versus wrong.

Because judgmentalism can be, and often has been, so extreme in its destructive expressions and consequences in human history, it bears close examination. From a purely spiritual viewpoint, paradoxically, judgmentalism itself is something that is judged as 'wrong' or 'bad'. At the same time, nonjudgmentalism is described as wrong or bad. These arise from a position that judgmentalism is necessary to society where boundaries, norms, and limits are seen as needed for societal survival.

The way out of this dilemma is to recognize that judgmentalism is a good/bad moralistic view. It is a superimposition on desirable versus undesirable behaviors that could be viewed conversely as acceptable, workable, integrous, and constructive versus unacceptable, unworkable, nonintegrous, or destructive. There is that which leads to God, life, truth, and love, and there is, simply put, that which leads in the opposite direction. Thus, one is actually free to support or reject alternatives without condemnation.

Mankind's immersion into the pitfall of judgmentalism is energized, supported, and propagated by the religious axioms and presumptions that God is the ultimate basis and justification for judgmentalism. This is, in fact, one of the main bulwarks of major religions based on authoritarianism.

At the level of the child or domestic animal, certain behaviors are rewarded and errors are not rewarded. This results in a Pavlovian conditioning, the content of which depends on social circumstances, including parental capability. Its success also depends on the innate capacity of the cognitive system which is genetically transmitted. The success of the reward/no-reward conditioning system is further influenced by the emotional matrix in which the reward of love may or may not be more important than the fear of punishment. In the most successful outcome, the reward of love becomes predominant.

At the lowest levels of the evolution of consciousness, right versus wrong is equated primarily at the animal level of gain versus loss. At another level, the motive becomes fear of negative consequences, including guilt. As consciousness progresses, the motives for behavior include social approval, self-acceptance, and self-esteem. This then merges into the level at 200 of integrity and moral responsibility. As this occurs, we speak of character formation and self-respect.

As egocentricity and selfishness diminish as motivators, the capacity for concern with the happiness and welfare of others gains dominance, and thus love (level 500) and its gain or loss become dominant. As this propensity matures, lovingness becomes the expression of what one has become (level 540) and is unconditional. Love then becomes the field and the context as well as the content of intentions and actions.

Thus, it becomes clear that as consciousness evolves, it no longer needs judgmentalism or the polarities of good/bad as a guide to behavior. The choice of that which is integrous and loving occurs spontaneously because it is the natural expression of an evolved comprehension of life. Spiritual discernment then transcends the need to rely on the black/white dualistic perceptual system of a less evolved ego. Morality becomes supplanted by Reality and spiritual discernment.

Recontextualization of the Levels of Consciousness

Each level represents an impersonal field of energy that can be identified by calibration techniques. The levels represent the progression of the evolution of consciousness and is concordant with the challenges and tasks appropriate to that level. Each thus serves its own purpose like stepping stones. Each level may appear to be an impediment or even detrimental to those who have evolved beyond it, but in turn, each level represents progress and an improvement over the levels below it.

Thus, the human world represents a purgatorial-like range of opportunities and choices, from the most grim to the exalted, from criminality to nobility, from fear to courage, from despair to hope, and from greed to charity. Thus if the purpose of the human experience is to evolve, then this world is perfect just as it is.

CHAPTER THIRTEEN

"MIND"

W hereas the majority of mankind still calibrates below 200 and is therefore dominated by primitive emotions, such as apathy, desire, hate, fear, anger, resentment, and revenge, as consciousness evolves in more civilized societies, one crosses over the level of Integrity at 200 and people rely progressively on the intellect to solve their problems with logic, reason, and education. Modern civilized societies calibrate in the 300s and the 400s (America currently calibrates at 431); thus, the blocks to the advancement of spiritual awareness are not primarily those of heavy negativity, but instead, reason itself becomes a block to enlightenment.

While only eight percent of the world's population operates at the consciousness level of the 400s, we note the statistical rarity with which consciousness levels exceed the 400s. Only four percent of the population calibrates at over 500, and only .04 percent calibrates over 540. Thus, the 400s represent the great avenue to the higher spiritual levels. The great geniuses of the intellect, historically of science and discovery over a period of centuries, calibrate at exactly 499.

Most of the greatest scientists of both the present and the past were quite religious, and some even wrote well-known religious dissertations. It is a common characteristic that the most brilliant intellects, including those of famous scientific geniuses, included the belief in God. As genius advances to its highest development, the fact of the existence of God becomes increasingly apparent and acknowledged. Why, then, does consciousness at that level of awareness stop at specifically calibration level 499? There must be something about the intellect itself that accounts for this recurrent phenomenon.

Although consciousness level 400 is reached by eight percent of the world's population, and educated, literate, intelligent people in modern, advanced societies consider intelligence and education to be the 'norm', that is obviously not the case for the majority of mankind for whom reason and logic play a minor role in the motivations of everyday life.

Calibration level is set by spiritual will, decision, intention and dedication. It is the level that 'rules' behaviors and expectations of self and others. It becomes the yardstick by which values and motives are set and judgments are rendered. The standards of a given level then dominate consciousness and the ego's complex set of operations of endeavor, value, and human energy.

Reason, logic, information, and its expressions as science, technology, and industry become the dominant institutions. They thus become the authorities that are beseeched and prodded to solve the problems of collective society, and the science of psychology is expected to hold the resolution and answers to emotional and personal conflicts. This faith in reason is compounded by the rapid developments of the science and technology of the computer age in which all problems will eventually be vanquished by that great hope of human society called "research."

Thus, the intellect, reason, and logic are the recipients of the faith of modern man. In the modern world, although a sizable portion of the population is ostensibly still religious, the primary thrust of society emphasizes progress in the advancement of the intellect. Man is confronted with the challenge of daily survival in the here and now and thus religion, which is viewed as derived from the ancient past and then again is projected to the hypothetical distant future, is put on the back burner. The serious pursuit of religious truth is thus often deferred until later in life when one becomes older and it therefore seems more pertinent.

Until the very recent advent of consciousness research, religion seemed to be intellectually irrelevant because it was related to history and events that occurred thousands of years ago in foreign cultures. The only information that could be called really interesting was the periodic discoveries of archeological artifacts, or fragments of historical documents, or geologic confirmations of some ancient scriptures. Church teachings focused on chronological events in the long-distant past, and thus, to modern man, historical religion, aside from the set of rather obvious moral precepts, seemed to have little relevance to modern life. Dissatisfaction resulted in the emergence of more recent nondenominational churches that emphasize the activation of spiritual truth and religious concepts experientially in daily activities.

The seeming inadequacy of religion to answer the challenges of human life led to emphasis on the development of the intellect and reason as we can see from the emergence of the brilliant intellectual advancement represented by the great philosophers of ancient Greece. The mind itself became the subject of investigation of philosophy, of which epistemology became its greatest branch. "Know thyself" was the call that led to the investigation of knowledge itself. How does the human mind know and how does it know it knows, and can its capacity to know even be proven or demonstrated?

It was out of ontology, metaphysics, cosmology, and the inner inspections of the workings of the intellect that the laws of science and logic emerged. Paradoxically, modern-day physics is the end product of the dissertations of supposedly unscientific metaphysics. In recent times, the puzzles of quantum mechanics (see Appendix D) and advanced theoretical physics have reawakened interest in the philosophical basis of scientific thought for without it, comprehension reaches the limits set by context. Facts are interesting and intriguing but the real question then arises, what do they mean?

Of considerable interest to the student of philosophy and epistemology is the ubiquitous question throughout the ages of the relevance of reason, logic, and the intellect to the reality of God and the nature of Divinity. The question has been recurrently expressed as "Is man's capacity to think, know, and reason actually a quality of Divinity?" Thus, the philosophic debate leads to the examination of the qualities of consciousness without which there could be no discourse or knowingness to even address the subject.

In the end, the finalization of all scientific/philosophical/ metaphysical/ psychological/intellectual/religious/spiritual or semantic dialog dissolves into the awareness of the substrate of awareness called consciousness and subjectivity. The final realization is that consciousness itself, the capacity to be aware, know, feel, sense, or even argue, is *a priori* to all human experience. With that realization comes the recurrent, crucial question: Is the source of that consciousness a personal self, or is it a quality of the Presence within man, a quality of Divinity? The answer that one arrives at then spells the difference between the calibrated levels of the 400s and the 500s.

It is interesting that, characteristically, extremely brilliant, well-known and published researchers and writers on the scientific basis of consciousness research calibrate in the very high 400s. This indicates that the consciousness of the researcher identifies self as 'mind'. Thus, understanding is contextualized to be the product of one's own thoughts rather than as a gift from Universal Mind, that is, God as the Logos, the substrate that makes all awareness or comprehension possible. (The realization of God as Logos calibrates at level 850.)

The level of the 400s tends to identify the self with thought, thinkingness, 'mind', reason, and logic. It therefore distrusts intuition and the nonlinear domain, even though that domain is the very source or substrate of mind itself. The trap of the intellect is that it sees itself as the source of survival rather than as merely a mechanism or a tool by which the Self sustains existence in human form.

The unaware intellect presumes that the source for its capacity to think and be aware is the physical brain, which again is merely the means, the mechanism, and the tool whereby the linear and the nonlinear interact. Whether one believes that the source of life is the material or realizes that is the spiritual differentiates the 400s from the 500s.

If we explore the relationship between mentalization and the brain using consciousness research techniques already described, we find confirmation that thoughts exist independently of the brain. The brain is activated by thoughts and is their correlate within the physical domain of form, much as the physical body is the correlate of the etheric body. (They are isomeric.) Like a radio that converts unseen energy waves into intelligible sound, the brain is a receiver instrument of the energies of thought forms. Thus, the attractor fields of the nonlinear domain of consciousness influence many 'minds' and brains simultaneously. Like an unseen radio transmitter, the attractor field radiates a field which is accessible to those instruments with which it has concordance. (Note that the mechanism is concordance and not causality.)

A calibratable level of consciousness then exists as an independent field that contains concordant thought forms attuned to the 'frequency' of that attractor field. The field therefore sustains, supports, and gives a 'home' to similar thought forms. If an individual mind attunes to that level of consciousness, the field tends to potentiate the emergence of associated thoughts. This may result in the phenomenon of entrainment as the associated emotions increase the energy of alignment and commitment to the field and its personification as 'me'.

Thus, we see great masses of people emoting and behaving in concert as though hypnotized. The most spectacular examples are the historic crowd responses to Hitler's exhortive public addresses and the periodic mass public demonstrations that to this day erupt in response to demagogues.

The contagion of mass hysteria is legendary and has been the favorite tool of the propagandist. The same suggestibility, which is displayed by crowd behaviors, is exhibited in less obvious ways by public response to other forms of information and communication. Ideologies become popularized and tend to self-promulgate. News media trigger mass responses and hysteria, as do advertising, movies, and television programs, such as sports and publicized world events. It is as though the collective psyche of the public is a giant, potential response field that is merely awaiting a tune to set it marching off in one direction or another.

The masses are so easy to manipulate that the masters of the game of manipulation play the public like a giant musical instrument. The formulas have become standardized; for example, the stock horrendous shock movie with gross butchery; the sentimental, sad little-girl tale; the 'tots' drowning in the family pool; the indignant insult to the country's honor; the wicked prelate; the degeneracy of youth; the celebrity murder; or the latest anxiety-provoking medical discovery. There are the routine righteous political story, the latest war horror story, and the latest 'rights' violation, complete with protest march. The political slant of the news media then simply gives more seconds or minutes of exposure to one side of the story or the other. (The current favorite is to focus the television news camera on the innocent civilian victims of one side of the conflict or the other, and the selection of which side of the conflict is victim and which is perpetrator is determined by the political slant of the news editor.) The media thus view humanity as a collective, with predictable triggers and responses, and each segment can be manipulated and orchestrated by the use of appropriate symbols, slogans, and positionalities.

Q: **While 'mass delusions and the madness of crowds' have been well-known for centuries, what is the significance of all this for the individual who is endeavoring to transcend the ordinary levels of consciousness in the search for enlightenment?**

A: The study of mass psychology reveals to the spiritual student the illusory nature of belief systems that had been naively considered to be personal and unique.

Each level of consciousness is held in place by its basic positionalities. If their public expositions are examined, they are much easier to identify and see as impersonal aspects of a general field, rather than as a personal attribute of one's self. The field of each level of consciousness is sustained by basic postulates and belief systems that have been enumerated elsewhere. What have been naively believed to be personal opinions can then be seen to be simply products of a field. It can also be observed that many basic postulates have such wide acceptance that they are automatically uncritically subscribed to. We can call this phenomenon "being at the effect of the postulates," which, in the unaware person, occurs primarily outside awareness. To the spiritual student, this awareness is of critical importance because each postulate establishes a context that is a constraint and limitation, with its resultant dualities of perception and belief.

Some common examples that illustrate the principle of limiting postulates are:

1. There is a right side and a wrong side to every conflict.
2. There is a cause for everything.
3. Someone is responsible for everything.
4. Someone is to blame for unfortunate events and accidents.
5. There is an answer to every question.
6. Everything has an opposite.
7. Everything has a meaning.
8. Everyone is capable of reason.
9. Everyone's reality is really basically the same.
10. Some things are better than others.
11. Time marches on.
12. Some things are more valuable than others.
13. Reason is a reliable tool.
14. Logic is proof.
15. There is a self-existent, discoverable, objective reality 'out there'.
16. Man is superior to animals because he can think.
17. Everyone knows right from wrong.
18. The guilty deserve punishment and the good deserve rewards.

While these postulates may seem different, they are actually inherently all the same in that they create a restrictive structure and limitation to transcending the dominion of form and the ego structure itself. We note that level 500 denotes not only a major advance in power but, like ice turning to water at 32 degrees F., it denotes a change of quality as well. What begin to gain importance are qualities such as mercy, forgiveness, forbearance, tolerance, patience, nurturance, aesthetics, warmth, friendliness, openness, flexibility, joviality, concordance, humor, surrender, letting go, overlooking, affection, love, transcendence, open-mindedness, compassion, peace, gentleness, faithfulness, grace, and charity. There then appears the capacity to suspend judgment, relinquish positionalities, and resolve conflict through surrender so as to be able to intuit and apprehend rather than logically comprehend. There is greater tolerance for ambiguity, and it is no longer necessary to be right or to win or feel superior to others. The 'spirit' of an enterprise becomes predominantly important, and there is a heightened sensitivity to intention, with increased capacity for spiritual discernment.

The awareness of context becomes progressively more important than content. It becomes obvious that the end does not justify the means and that integrity has greater pragmatic value than expediency. (The proposition that "the end justifies the means" tests out as false and makes one go weak with the test for truth.) The source of happiness is discovered as an innate inner quality rather than something to be obtained. The innate beauty of all that exists becomes progressively apparent. All things become of equal value so that all life and all that exists are honored for their presence and the sheer fact of their existence. The perfection of all that exists stands forth, and the illusion of imperfection dissolves. Each and every thing is the perfect expression of its essence manifesting as its innate existence, simply by being what it is.

Everything reveals the miracle of existence and, therefore, everything, without exception, is equal to everything else by virtue of its existence. The miracle of
existence is a quality that supercedes all others. The
holiness of the Allness of Creation stands forth as self-
evident, and the manifestation of the capacity to exist
demonstrates its innate divinity. When presumptions are
no longer projected onto the observed, the radiance of
Divinity shines forth from the world as well as from the
Self. The Radiance of God as Self shines forth as the
Infinite 'I'.

Independent of content, the capacity to be, to know, to
exist, and to be aware are the *a priori* substrates to life in
its expression as consciousness. To exist and be conscious of existence supercedes all logic, reason, or proof.
Awareness is aware that it is aware. To know God, it is
only necessary to know and fully comprehend the
significance that one exists. Realize that even the animal
knows that it 'is' and loves its own existence. (On testing,
that calibrates as a true statement.)

The pathway of the heart then bypasses the intellect
and puts its faith in the perfection of love rather than the
pursuit of the intellect and reason. To love, the intellect
and logic are merely tools but they are not 'who I am'.
'Mind' cannot transcend mind by pursuit of the mind,
but only by the surrender of the illusion of mind as
savior. It is by the heart of Love that one is saved from
the limitations of mind by love itself. Only love has the
power to overcome beliefs. At this point, historically, the
seeker is counseled to "Throw away all the books and
just be. Surrender all to God without reservation. Stop
struggling and allow the realization of that which you
already are."

The letting go of identification of self as thoughts is
facilitated by disengaging from the content of group
beliefs, with their well-known and predictable agendas
and reactions. One can refuse to identify with them as

'me'. To surrender identification with that which was presumed to be 'me' allows the real Me to shine forth as the immanent quality of Divinity that is the source of the unencumbered reality of 'I'.

Q: We note that your lectures always start with the same opening statement, "Everything is happening of its own; nothing is causing anything else."

A: The belief in linear causality is a basic axiom of the whole structure of the ego/mind dualistic belief system. To see through that illusion is the most important and greatest leap available for getting closer to comprehending Reality.

It is critical to grasp that the illusion of linear causality as an explanation for the observed phenomena of life is the major and most profound limitation of thinkingness. It is the major block that cannot be transcended even by intellectual geniuses who characteristically calibrate at 499. The intellect which serves to aid the progress of civilization becomes entrenched in the psyche and becomes the major obstacle to Realization. Although causality (calibration 426) is a major illusion, it is really not a difficult one to solve once it is disassembled.

Mentation, reason, logic, and language are all structured dualistically, based on the axiom that there is a subject and an object, that there is a 'this' doing or causing a 'that'. Reason strives to find a connection between a witnessed phenomenon and some antecedent which is most commonly located in prior time. Logic then concludes that what precedes an event must somehow be its 'cause' or explanation. It confuses temporal sequence with causation.

The term "cause" is an abstract hypothesis, a tautology, an intellectualization which has no concordant substrate in reality. It is at best an operational supposition to satisfy the mind's requirement for an 'explanation'. Fallacy arises out of the mind's proclivity to ask the redundant and fatal question "Why?"

We have stated elsewhere that there is no 'why' to anything in Reality and, in fact, no 'why' can be answered and still stay within Reality. All answers to "why" questions are intrinsically fallacious as they require a jump from verifiable observables to hypothetical suppositions which are all mentations.

Events and conditions have a source or origination but not a cause. The concept of 'cause' limits comprehension to context only, whereas in reality, all content is subject to context. This is the very crux of the understanding that allows consciousness to jump from 499 to the 500s.

Neither God nor Truth can be found within the limitation of content only for, by simple observation, content is only definition or description whereas context supplies meaning, significance, and concordance with the reality of existence itself. This is important to comprehend not only in spiritual work but also in everyday social and political policies.

To fail to properly contextualize content has historically been the basis for the slaughter of millions of people in every century throughout human history. To ignore context is the greatest source of catastrophe for every generation of man, and it continues on in the present time with the same catastrophic consequences. There is no greater lesson that needs to be learned to reduce human suffering and bring ignorance to an end.

Q: **If the concept of cause is so misleading, how else can phenomena be explained?**

A: That is the most important and critical single question to examine. All observed phenomena arise out of the totality of the evolution of Creation as it unfolds to perception as progressive observation. Nothing arises solely of its own but only within the field of context. What appears to be change is the emergence of potentiality out of essence into manifestation (calibration level 750).

Context means prevailing conditions that are ever changing and unfolding. What was legal, sane, normal, acceptable, ethical, and appropriate two hundred years ago is no longer the same today. What we consider 'normal' today will again be discredited, ridiculed, and considered abhorrent a century or two from now. Thus, context includes all of life and civilization, the state of the world, and even the universe.

Q: How does this apply to everyday life?

A: The 'cause' of anything is always the same. It is the totality of all that exists now or ever has existed throughout history. Context is the total universe. We can find a source and an explanation but not any specific, identifiable, hypothetical item that can be credited with the implied power or faculty of being termed 'cause'. The 'cause' of anything is not an identifiable single element but always a composite which constitutes the actual source that accounts for an observed phenomenon.

Events are the products of propensity, facilitation, timing, probability, potential, likelihood, alignment, momentum, promulgation, selection, randomness, condition, control, favoritism, public sentiment, the weather, economic conditions, morale, political climate, availability, supply, need, affordability, emotional climate, social morality, etc. To ignore the composite of context is to invite disaster, as history has demonstrated over and over.

Q: How does this apply to specific individual behavior?

A: The belief in linear causality results in naïve presumptions about the supposed 'causes' of behaviors. In popular psychology, for instance, it leads to looking to a person's childhood for explanatory 'causes'.

The activation of certain behaviors is a result of a person's psychological constitution as it exists in the present and not how it was or might have been in the past. For example, abuse in childhood does not 'cause' criminality in the present; instead, the same energy field of consciousness that favored abuse to the child is now favoring the selection of criminal behaviors.

In understanding human behavior, the most important factors to consider are the influence of the prevailing levels of consciousness of both the person and the locus in society. These factors outweigh all others in degree and extent of influence on choice and outcome. Only by inner spiritual growth and choice can an individual transcend the influence of the prevailing personal as well as the social level of consciousness.

Q: Then the 'karma' or collective consequences of past actions is primarily the determinant of choices, actions, and events?

A: That is exactly the answer. Both content (i.e., an individual choice) and context (social conditions) are in accord with their calibratable level of consciousness. The social phenomena that we observe on a daily basis are the result of interaction of dominant energy fields having characteristics that profoundly facilitate as well as limit concordant freedom of choice or behaviors and that are dependent on prevailing conditions. These are the product of multiple factors that reflect the history of the universe and are the ongoing source of prevalent energies.

Q: It is simple to see that if the same attractor field holds dominance, then behaviors will not change.

A: Let us say that an infant at birth calibrates at only 90. As a result, it is born to abusive, neglectful parents who calibrate at 90 and who live in a community ridden with poverty and crime. As an adolescent, the child gets involved in street crime as well as drugs and adopts the prevailing antisocial, anti-educational, and anti-responsible attitudes, which also calibrate at 90. After arrest, the individual is incarcerated in a very low energy field with others who constitute a subpopulation of like-minded antisocial persons calibrating at 90. After release, the personal alliances and group loyalties of the low energy field prevail (still calibrating at 90). Recidivism is therefore the rule rather than the exception. (It is often seventy-five to eighty percent, or even higher.)

The sociopathic personality is unable to learn from experience, is unable to control impulses, and has a genetic defect of the frontal cortex so that the threat of punishment does not have a deterrent effect. Therefore, prison terms merely result in the criminal's expending greater effort to avoid detection rather than ceasing criminal activities.

The nature of criminality is why the California "Three strikes and out" policy has reduced so much crime. It takes the career criminal off the streets. What the protesters of the policy fail to realize is that criminals are really only arrested and convicted for a very small minority of the crimes they actually commit.

The publicized case of convicts' doing life for 'just stealing a bicycle' ignores that the ostensible 'victim' of an 'unfair' law has actually been committing crimes in the hundreds, going back to early adolescence. The flagrant defiance of lawfulness by that type of criminal is why police stop people for improper tail lights. They know that criminality is a chronic lifestyle.

A recent study in a medium-sized southwestern city found that an amazing eighty-five percent of hitchhikers had criminal records. Sexual predators have usually molested scores or even hundreds of children before their current arrest. The same pattern is seen in drunken drivers or rapists who finally get caught.

Thus, to ignore context leads to supposed but futile solutions because the problem stems from long-standing patterns that reflect the influence of a dominant energy field of consciousness.

Q: The examples clarify the importance of understanding the relationship between content and context. Seemingly different events are not coming from separate 'causes' but all can have the same current ongoing source.

A: The expression of events is facilitated or hindered by prevailing conditions that affect probabilities. Choices and decisions are not determined ('caused') by the past but by the totality of conditions in the present. The major importance of chronologically past experiences is the degree to which they are still currently operative. The past does not 'cause' the present; instead, the same conditions (i.e., level of consciousness) currently present potentiate the likelihood of recurrence. Thus, the common human admonition to "learn from experience" implies a willingness to evolve and change for a greater satisfaction and a higher degree of happiness.

Q: How does one best apply the understanding of the relationship between content and context to serious spiritual endeavor?

A: The self (ego) focuses on linear content and specifics and identifies with form and limitation. Spiritual work involves withdrawing attachment to or identification with content and then progressively realizing that one's reality is context. The briefest explanation is that 'self' is content and 'Self' is context.

We can see by the basic dualistic structure of thought itself how the belief in a separate self (ego) arises, which is then reinforced by parents and society. There are a subject and a predicate connected by a verb that states or implies 'cause'. Therefore, all action implies a central causal agent—the personal 'I' of content which is the personal self reinforced by having a name and being the recipient of reward and punishment.

This same identity builds up to be imagined as the thinker behind thoughts, the doer behind deeds, and the actor behind actions so that all which occurs becomes self-referential. It then becomes imbued with emotional attitudes and gradations of judgmentalism. The personalization focuses all attention on the inner self which becomes progressively energized as a supposedly independent, sole entity.

The process of mentation reflects the concordant level of the evolution of consciousness. At the level of lower mind, emotions color vision and dominate or influence thought. At the level of higher mind, emotion is transcended and intellection becomes subject to evermore abstract, sophisticated accuracy, precision, and reliability. Eventually, the pretence of the mind's alleged capacity to 'know' anything is transcended by the progressive inclusion of context so that intentional content is replaced by gnosis, which is the spontaneous effulgence of the Presence as Self.

In the Reality of the mystic, there is no space or room for the ego to edit or distort as the knower and the known are one and the same. Radical subjectivity is thus the source of Truth by virtue of the fusion of Self with Divinity and the Allness of Reality. That is what is meant by the Sanskrit term "Purusha," which is the source of the knowingness of the enlightened sage or teacher.

The oneness of Self-identity is the substrate of the phenomenon known as Revelation or Realization. Enlightenment is the finalized state that ensues and is unconditional, total, and complete.

Q: **This explanation brings with it a feeling of satisfaction and completion. We note that the recitation calibrates at 999.9. What does that mean?**

A: There is a loss of 0.1 percent in the process of the Unmanifest becoming Manifest as form in consciousness, yet the formless is innate and constitutes the very source of form.

As an analogy, one could use the process whereby an exposed photographic film contains the potentiality for form which only appears when the film is submersed in the developing solution. The nascent form becomes manifest as a consequence of the favorable condition of intentionality, which is a function of the will and choice. This in turn would be reflective of context, such as karmic potentialities.

CHAPTER FOURTEEN
CONSIDERATIONS

Q: What are the knowable facts about physical death?

A: The fear of physical death underlies many other human anxieties, and some clarification of what it is all about is therefore helpful. There are two important facts not widely known that are really quite important to know.

The first is that one does not really experience one's own physical death, for at the moment of the body's expiration, the experiencer/witness/awareness faculty instantly and painlessly leaves the body and one immediately feels free and greatly relieved. The surprise is the discovery that one isn't dead after all, but quite alive. The former body is witnessed as not even being attractive or desirable. The reborn self now becomes entranced with its rediscovery of immortality and the new potentialities to which one awakens. The body was like a cage from which one is now liberated. The body was never the source of the sense of 'I' or existence but merely part of its identification with content.

The second interesting and liberating fact that eliminates a lot of anxiety about death is that the time of physical death has already been karmically set. Although the timing has been determined at birth, the nature and circumstances surrounding the event are not preset but are influenced by other factors and choices. These may involve psychological processes, such as the underlay of guilt, the choosing of symbolic mechanisms of death, risk taking, health decisions, cultural patterns, and, importantly, belief systems held by the ego/mind.

Just to know that one does not and, in fact, cannot experience one's own physical death, and that the time is already preset, relieves a lot of needless worry. The only real 'death' which is actually possible to experience is the final death of the sense of self as the ego. Even that ordeal need not be experienced because it can be refused for as long as one wishes, and even that actual death cannot occur without one's inner consent.

Because the ego presumes it is a body, it believes that 'nobody has ever survived death to tell us what it was like'. That is a fallacious belief which disappears beyond consciousness level 600, where previous incarnations and physical deaths are not only easily remembered but the circumstances and significance of each death are recalled very clearly.

In general, if the consciousness of the entity is below 200, death may be the occasion for reactions of grief, anger, resentment, or loss. Above 200, death represents a learning opportunity that serves to uplift awareness. At the higher levels, death presents an opportunity for major leaps in awareness.

It is not the physicality of prior lifetimes that is important but the spiritual lessons that were learned. In looking at a sequence of lifetimes, one can see the evolution of consciousness through its various stages of learning.

It is said that after physical death, it takes the average soul approximately three days to completely disidentify with the body and detach from it, including working through the stages of denial, grieving, and letting go of attachment. Therefore, a wait of three days is generally recommended before burial or cremation to avoid interruption of the separation process. In each case, the appropriate time can be determined by kinesiologic testing.

If we state in general with kinesiologic testing that "It is wise to wait three days before disposing of the body," the answer we get is yes. Less evolved souls generally take longer to make the transition than do those that are more highly evolved.

Q: **The core of the ego is often identified as selfishness, whereas the spiritual goal is selflessness. Are these opposites?**

A: All seeming pairs of opposites are the illusion of polarity that arises automatically from a positionality. What determines the nature of an act is intention. The intention of selfishness is that of getting and gain, and its purpose is survival, whereas the purpose of selflessness is serving and giving. In considering these contrasting motives, one needs to avoid another positionality, that of labeling selfishness as wrong or bad and selflessness as good or right. They merely represent different degrees of the evolution of consciousness and are alternatives, not opposites.

The origin of selfishness is seen in the animal world and functions out of the residual animal-brain structure inherent within the human brain. It becomes overtly expressed in young children. It is part of the survival instinct that seeks gratification of wants and desires as well as appetites and biologic drives. These drives extend in human life as they do in the animal world to food, water, territoriality, boundaries, possessions, mates, etc. In the adult, these become expanded into acquisitions, symbolic prizes, and the endless seeking for gain and advantage. In excess, they become defined as greed and being driven, and one sees the display of the animal-pack mentality in rivalry for the position of the 'alpha male' or 'alpha female'.

From a biological and psychological point of view, there is a healthy self-interest that is essential for survival and self-esteem, but it becomes pathological narcissism when the ego is self-reflective in that all actions are self-referential. The basic premise of selfishness is "I want." This wanting can escalate to obsessive craving and addiction.

As consciousness evolves, like the infant, it learns to give up the infantile illusion that the ego's wants or its hypothetical rights and expectations have to be met in order to thrive successfully. The infantile, narcissistic ego then moves from the level of the baby and its relationship to the mother and discovers that survival and success depend on giving up infantilism and learning cooperation. In return, the ego now receives love and approval for learning how to share and be patient, and the transition is supported by the reward systems of adequate and responsible parenting. If that type of parenting is lacking, infantilism persists, along with concomitant resentments, anger, and self-pity. Maturity means that one has learned to find gratification from the nonlinear domains of meaning and love. There is then the discovery that happiness is not an external gain but an inner self-satisfaction so that at full maturity, gratification stems from what one has become, not from what one has or does.

The infantile ego hopes to gain by grasping and getting. Later, it learns to gain by performance (good grades in school, etc.), productivity, and the inner pleasure that accompanies the fulfillment of nonlinear spiritual values. As it progresses, it becomes more independent and stops trying to control others.

Egotism and selfishness are very vulnerable and lead to endless defensiveness and desire for approval and agreement. The more mature ego becomes increasingly independent and finally learns that its source of happiness and security stems from within. With this realization, spiritual goals tend to become increasingly important and integrity becomes the yardstick of happiness. This leads to the evolution of consciousness in which the

ultimate goal becomes the perfection of one's relationship with God.

Although, at first, God may be believed to be 'without',
the source of life is simultaneously sensed to be 'within',
and finally, the Presence reveals itself as the Self, which
transcends any differentiation between 'inner' and 'outer'
but is All Present. The Supreme is simultaneously
immanent and transcendent.

We could call this evolution of consciousness, which
tracks the patterns of the ego, as the 'self' pathway to
God (in which the progressive relinquishment of the
narcissistic core of the ego leads to the discovery that the
real source of happiness, fulfillment, and joy is the Self).
The many expressions of the ego, including its vanity of
ideas, beliefs, etc., can be viewed as an expression of
grandiosity in that it clings to the insistence that its
thoughts are valuable and its positionalities are correct
and important. Selfishness is the basic underpinning of
vanity and illusion.

Q: **It is usually stated that selfishness, desire, and greed
stem from lack.**

A: That statement could be turned around to its opposite,
that selfishness results from an excess of vanity and
wanting. There is no lack of expectations or demands.
Excessive desire creates the illusion of lack, just like
seeming money problems are created by spending faster
than income.

Desire based on a realistic need leads to a feeling of
completion when it becomes satisfied. It is a feeling of
fulfillment and peace. In contrast, the person who is
driven by cravings is unable reach satisfaction, and we
say that they are 'being run by their solar plexus', because
wantingness as a predominant level of consciousness
cannot be satisfied.

Aside from the usual greed for wealth, position, and
possessions, desire can focus on many other things, such

as new experiences, novelty, relationships, sex, excitement, fame, winning, admiration, credit, power and control over others, and a multitude of symbols.

Q: **What is the difference between normal self-interest and self-esteem from selfishness?**

A: Healthy self-interest includes concern for the welfare of others, whereas selfishness disregards others. Self-interest is not destructive to others and is therefore integrous and increases self-esteem. Egotism is separatist and seeks gain at a cost to others, leading to a loss of inner self-esteem. It is therefore vulnerable, nonintegrous, and an illusory self-inflation that leads to loss of self-respect.

An illusion that drives desire and craving is that the object of desire has become imbued with an exaggerated importance and significance, resulting in an inflated value and attractiveness. Once the object has been acquired, it loses its magical aura and that seductive image is now projected onto the next object of desire. This is well-known in the area of sexual relationships where conquest is the goal and the attractiveness of the desired object of infatuation quickly fades.

The object of pursuit, therefore, does not exist in Reality, and what is pursued is the illusory promise of inflated value. The seductive glamour of attraction is a projected inflation from the ego that uses the desired object as a source of happiness. As the true source of happiness stems from within, the wantingness or desire cannot be satisfied because it is a constant projection of specialness onto the external and is therefore the pursuit of a fantasy. As one desire becomes fulfilled and satisfied, the focus then moves on to the next object of desire in an endless procession, like a carrot on a stick.

As consciousness evolves through progressive surrender of positionalities, the mechanism of desire eventually subsides and gratification arises from the realization of inner goals. The feeling of self-sufficiency replaces neediness when the source of happiness is found to be within. What need to be surrendered are not the objects of desire but the quality of desiring and the imbuing of the objects with the magical inflation of value. Upon investigation, this inflation will be discovered to be merely an animal energy. For survival, the animal is constantly seeking externally. The majority of supposedly human behaviors does not differ from the display one can observe in any primate community. The main difference one will see is that although primates vocalize, they rely more heavily on body language for communication.

Q: Of what value are breathing exercises?

A: These are especially useful upon the realization that one is 'stuck' on a lower level and too much energy has accumulated in the lower chakras. To utilize breathing exercises, it is necessary to have some simple understanding of the etheric body and the chakra energy system. Sexual energy can accumulate in the base chakra. Hatred, envy, jealousy, revenge, and spite are energies in the spleen, while ambition, gain, control, aggression, and selfishness are energies centered in the solar plexus.

The heart is the center for love and forgiveness. The throat relates to communication, expression, and creativity. The third eye or brow chakra relates to spiritual vision, and the crown chakra relates to God-consciousness.

The basic spiritual/life energy is usually referred to as "chi," or kundalini energy, and runs not only up a special channel in the spine but also along the body's acupuncture and nervous systems and down the twelve main meridians that eventually supply life energy to all the body's vital organs. These energies and acupuncture points are simultaneously related to all the specific muscles and muscle groups. This is the basis for clinical kinesiology, which is used both diagnostically and therapeutically. The distribution of the energy flow is altered by attitudes and mental positionalities. In clinical kinesiology, the weakness of a muscle group reveals which organ is being pathologically affected and relates to a specific acupuncture point. The negative attitude or belief system is uncovered by further kinesiologic testing and a reparative affirmation is prescribed.

Overall, the energy level of the spiritual/acupuncture energy system is mediated by the thymus gland, which lies just behind the upper sternum. The function of the thymus is to support the body's immune system. It produces so-called 'killer cells', or T-cells, which destroy invading organisms. The energy of the thymus is depleted by internal and external stresses caused primarily by negative emotions and attitudes that calibrate below level 200.

The most basic, simple, and effective breathing exercise consists of breathing the spiritual energy up the spinal channel, through which it flows from the base or lower chakras, up to the heart, the Third Eye, or the crown chakra. This is the basic technique used in many spiritual schools in which one simply pictures the energy flowing up the spinal channel with each inhalation. At the same time, the energy is willed to flow to a higher locus. The practice is often used during the initial phase of formal meditation but it can, in and of itself, constitute the meditative practice.

As one pictures the light of consciousness as energy flowing up the spine to the higher chakras, one will almost immediately feel a shift of energies and a change of inner sensation. In addition to the traditional bodily chakras, there are spiritual energy bodies above the crown chakra. One can pull the energy up through the higher chakras and picture it going through the crown to the higher spiritual bodies and on up to God. The energy is usually pictured as light or illuminated love energy of divine origin.

More intricate and specialized breathing techniques are taught by the various spiritual schools. Before these are chosen (e.g., pranayama), they should be checked by kinesiologic testing to determine their calibrated energy level and suitability for the practitioner.

Q: **The existence of the spiritual energy system and breathing techniques may sound foreign to Westerners. Are they really of practical value to the aspirant?**

A: Yes, and generally, they are beneficial. There are also specific problems where breathing exercises can be very useful. For example, a person who is obsessed with sex may find relief by breathing up the energy from the base chakra to the higher energy centers. Similarly, a person caught in seemingly unsolvable hatred, jealousy, blame, resentment, or revenge will find relief by breathing up the excessive energy which has become blocked in the spleen chakra. The overly ambitious, materialistic, or greedy person will benefit by decompressing the energies that have accumulated in the solar plexus. The heartsick will get relief by breathing up the energy from the heart to the third eye or the crown chakra so that the energy of personal love (where the loss has been perceived) is transferred to the love of God, which can never be lost. The person who lacks spiritual comprehension, awareness, or vision needs to breathe up more energy into the brow, or third eye.

There are the classical and time-honored techniques (the classical yogas, not hatha yoga) which depend almost entirely on breathing-practice meditation. There are many interesting books on the subjective experiences that arise from these techniques which influence the so-called kundalini (spiritual) energy.

All spiritual practices are inherently more powerful than the naïve seeker realizes. They should be approached with respect and the seeker should obtain adequate preparation information. There are a multitude of spiritual practitioners and healers of every variety. The dictum *"caveat emptor"* applies and should be heeded. The naïve seeker is often pressured by enthusiasts to participate in faulty practices and to visit charismatic, so-called healers, psychics, aura readers, channelers, spirit birthers, transmediums, prophets, and spokespersons for famous dead celebrities.

There are also persuasive invitations to join various exclusive sects, mystical cults, and the like, and become an initiate, thereby being privy to ancient secrets and mystical powers. It is important to remember the high teaching "Swear not nor take any oaths, nor make any pledges or binding commitments, nor commit any other bondage, for there are within them hidden, unseen consequences and karmic entrapments." Remember that allegiance is due only to God, to one's relationship with God, and to purity and holiness. No organization has any special favor with God, and all organizations as such are based on ego premises and illusions. To bind oneself to illusion can have unseen karmic consequences. These are detainments and pitfalls to be avoided by the wise. It is obvious on the face of it that the purpose of an oath is to bind. The ego is already laden down with commitments and bondages to a multitude of illusions and does not need to be impaired by another one.

Groups that require oaths of fealty or the swearing by oaths (some of which include description of demonic consequences if the oath is broken), promise a specialness and an exclusiveness, such as secrets or an inside track to God and special favors. It is important to realize that there are no special secrets or favors to be granted. All that needs to be known is already available. God has nothing to hide nor does the avatar. The enlightened sages, the advanced spiritual teachers, and the saints have nothing to hide. The pure in heart and the honest have nothing to conceal.

Secrecy is the cloak, the tool, and the modus operandi of the 'forces' that calibrate below consciousness level 200. Truth has nothing to fear and therefore has no reason to hide. That which is purposely hidden is obviously not in integrity, and the motive of secret information (mantras, symbols, rituals, etc.) is, frankly, to sell it for a price, which is either monetary or power over other people.

The organizations that promise specialness are merely appealing to the vanity of the ego. The ego will stop at nothing for it respects no boundaries due to its narcissistic core. Throughout history, monarchs and dictators have willingly demolished their own populations to satisfy the ego's vanities. The ego's megalomania chooses suicide rather than to admit it is wrong.

People are very resistant to modifying their views. In fact, the last president of the Flat Earth Society just recently died. Organizations are slow to adapt to change because change implies that their previous position was wrong.

The Buddha taught that the basic attachment was to the senses, sensation, and the objects of the senses, including thoughts. Therefore, asceticism is common to many spiritual disciplines that emphasize the value of being free of possessions and worldliness.

Q: **Sex and money are the temptations that are emphasized by many spiritual groups as the traps to be avoided.**

A: That tradition has value but also ambiguous results. First, it creates an aversion and a sense of sin or guilt about the issues. It also inflates their importance, thereby creating a fear. It is not sex and money that are the problems but the attachments to them. In the nonattached state, there is neither attraction nor aversion. Teachers such as Ramakrishna forbade both sex and money to his young male students. He held that they could be contaminated by even just the energy of sex or money.

Inasmuch as greed and desire calibrate below 200 (they are at 125), avoidance was an attempt to forestall attachment. However, the desire for sex or money stems from within and can remain within the ego, even though it is not indulged in or acted upon. At beginning levels of spiritual training, avoidance may well be the best course because desires are so strong. The mere willingness to sacrifice sensual pleasure or worldly gain is already of value in learning how to transcend attractions and instinctual drives, and the intensity of spiritual commitment is enhanced.

Throughout history and up to the current time, there have been a number of well-known 'gurus' who became addicted to sex, power, and money, and who covered up their actions with clever rationalizations. Those who exhibit wealth, a veneer of spiritual trappings, and who approve of sexual acting out attract many followers.

The basis for this paradox was revealed through spiritual research. Often, the early writings of a famous or popular guru calibrate quite high (usually in the high 400s to middle 500s). Then, after much success and acclaim, the calibrated level of the guru drops precipitously, sometimes to even below 200. Thus, it is not uncommon for there to be a wide disparity between the early writings of a teacher and the teacher's later level of consciousness. In some cases, both recent and current, the resultant misbehaviors create scandal and dismay, and residual followers have to resort to denial to rationalize their continued obedience to a cult or group of adherents. Although the erstwhile guru's own calibration may have fallen significantly, the calibration of the original writings remains the same.

Devotion to the now fallen guru personally, however, is obviously deleterious. This fact may bring about painful dismay to former devotees, but the pathway to enlighten-ment is strict. Devotion is due to God and not to person-alities. As the Buddha said, "Make no images of me."

A most curious and highly significant example is that of the Islamic prophet Mohamed who calibrated at 740 when he wrote the Koran. The Koran calibrates at 700. At age 38, Mohamed's calibration suddenly dropped to 130, and he took up the sword. Interestingly, almost as soon as Islam was established, its fundamentalist mili-tant sector became an aggressive invader of other nations and slaughtered 'infidels' by the hundreds of thousands. This began during Mohamed's lifetime when he was a participant and leader of this faction.

To this day, Islamic nations calibrate very low and their societies are characterized by misogynistic repression, overt cruelty, and hatred. It is to be emphasized that that which is truly holy and of God brings only peace and love. Thus, Mohamed and some branches of Islam were captured and dominated by the satanic form of negative energy.

The basic danger of the fundamentalist branch is its attraction to the lowest elements of society that desire the ego-inflationary sense of instant empowerment when they become a warrior of Jihad and are given license to kill in the name of Allah. Thus, the gun becomes the social symbol of God's favor and religious fervor, resulting in the spiritual absurdity of the 'holy killer'.

The progressive fall of Islamic culture has been studied and documented by modern scholars (B. Lewis, 2001; P. Watson, 2002; McGeary, 2002). Even a child can see the absurdity of slaughtering people in the name of "Allah, the All Merciful." In contrast, as mentioned previously, the Koran calibrates at 700. Therefore, it is spiritually integrous to follow the Koran but not zealots who subvert its truth for political power.

Q: **The ego and society are beset by innumerable traps. It seems as though success at spiritual purification is arduous or even discouraging; the array of obstacles seems imposing.**

A: There is a solution which is common to all. Simply find the underlying positionality, illusion, or drive; surrender that underpinning, and the many seeming problems fall away. The common drive, or the ego's attraction, is basically the desire for pleasure. It is therefore not the egotism or vanity which is the problem but the pleasure that is derived from egotism in its expressions as vanity, self-righteousness, being right, success, feeling superior, etc. It is not vengeance and hatred which are the problems but the pleasure and satisfaction gained from these attitudes.

At the level of nonattachment, desire and anticipation or need for gratification no longer are a pressure. Physical enjoyment arises spontaneously out of the activity itself as a passing pleasure and can be interrupted and instantly dismissed without a feeling of loss or disappointment because each moment is total and complete within itself. If the music stops, it is not a disappointment, nor is incompletion experienced as a loss. It is irrelevant whether an experience continues or not. The presence of the Self is complete, permanent, and totally fulfilling. It has no needs. Everything occurs spontaneously as an expression of its intrinsic essence. There is nothing and no one to 'cause' anything to happen.

As an example, when one watches the combatants in the Middle East attack and counterattack, one can see the immense pleasure and satisfaction that are derived and which continue to feed the endless conflict and mayhem. There is a covert glee in hating, punishing, getting even, and killing one's enemy because one can, at the same time, feel superior, virtuous, and even as a martyr. There is secret pleasure in provoking an attack so that one can bask in being the innocent victim. Hatred is then guiltless because it is justified and glorified by patriotic, psuedo-religious or nationalistic slogans.

Q: **For sheer excitement, glamour, and seduction, how can such a 'rewarding' package of motives be refused?**

A: The combination of factors, plus historical precedent, lead to an addiction in that the egos feed off the conflict and have a need to propagate it. The egos of those involved in social conflict are fed on both sides and inflated by media attention. Publicity adds fuel to the fire of fanaticism which reaches its dramatic height and absurdity through acts of suicidal attacks. These truly constitute the 'theater of the absurd'.

It can be seen that peace would be a threat to this melodrama and all its conscious and unconscious payoffs. Peace would also be a threat to the leaders and the multiple gains involved (money, publicity, importance, etc.). The polarization is therefore carefully nurtured by both sides, and when peace threatens the game, one side or the other is driven to cite another 'outrageous provocation', with the usual outcries and calls for retaliatory action. All this melodrama exploits the gullibility of the general public and the media, which feeds the emotionalism by giving detailed, graphic attention to the endless atrocities that have actually been deliberately manufactured to manipulate public sentiment through sensationalism.

The tragic video shown of the dead infant child and the wailing mother is practically routine. The whole melodramatic scenario is a gross manipulation that is an orchestration designed to inflame passions and escalate the drama. It is theatrics on a grand scale that, in the end, are self-defeating because of the lack of inner integrity.

Q: **That was a detailed description and analysis.**

A: Yes, because it exhibits on a grand scale exactly how the ego works so that one can identify the same phenomena within the secret plans and plots of one's own ego. Its surreptitious gains are essentially the same as this external drama. The ego gets a grim pleasure and satisfaction from suffering and all the nonintegrous levels of pride, anger, desire, guilt, shame, and grief. The secret pleasure of suffering is addictive. Many people devote their whole life to it and encourage others to follow suit. To stop this mechanism, the pleasure of the payoff has to be identified and willingly surrendered to God. Out of shame, the ego blocks out conscious awareness of its machinations, especially the secretiveness of the game of 'victim'.

The coin of the realm of the chronic loser, martyr, innocent victim, and hopeless sufferer of endless catastrophes and maladies is repetition of the same disasters. Prisons are populated by recidivists. People rebuild homes as quickly as they can after the water drains away from the flooded plain. They rebuild on the paths of the volcanoes and on top of earthquake faults, on the hurricane-swept beachfronts and on the mud-slide slopes, and on the waterways below the dams. Dangerous jobs do not lack workers nor do extreme sports or sky divers lack enthusiasts. There is an endless procession of mountain climbers climbing to their deaths or creating a need for their rescue. The negatives, therefore, are pleasurably attractive. That perversity is one of the ego's strange twists by which people become addicted to the pleasure and excitement of risk and the pleasure of the fear of death and injury. The secret pleasure of horror is an attraction to the ego to which such endeavors have become imbued with a larger-than-life magical quality or meaning.

Q: Then the programs of the ego do not continue unless they are secretly pleasurable?

A: That is the secret about secrets. The payoff is a gain of a pleasurably satisfying reward. The ego has learned to be very clever in order to survive. It is capable of resorting to any lengths or ruse of self-deception and camouflage. The world we witness is merely the drama of the collective egos acting out on the perceptual stage of form and time.

For endless centuries, the human drama has been a maudlin game built on the secret pleasure of the nonintegrous game of falsity. This would be likely when one realizes that the consciousness level of mankind was below 200 for many centuries. Now that the level is up to 207, the falsity of the game begins to reveal itself. Until now, mankind did not have even the most rudimentary capacity to tell truth from falsehood. The great con games of human life are now subject to exposure.

In the early 1990s, the egos of eighty-five percent of the world's population fed off of and perpetuated negativity, but by the year 2003, that percentage has already dropped to only seventy-eight percent, showing that the replacement of falsehood by truth is inevitable.

Q: The negative lie game is self-perpetuating?

A: That is the very reason for its prevalence and duration. The majority profit in both gross and subtle ways. The satisfactions of the ego are more pleasurable and addicting than the preservation of human life, much less dignity. Characteristically, all that is required are a few parades, some bombastic rhetoric by a demagogue, plus an appealing slogan. In response, we can watch forty million people enslave themselves and march off naively to their deaths and destruction. This involves not only the destruction of their personal selves but also their homes and families.

To 'die for the cause' is the call of the Pied Piper who leads the blind mice over the precipice. Unfortunately, fanatics are willing to sacrifice not only themselves but take others along with them. Recently, a female revolutionary was asked whether she felt any guilt about all the innocent who were slaughtered in the mayhem, and she remarked, "Unfortunately, some have to be sacrificed for the good of the cause" (cause meaning 'her' cause). Every dictator is only too happy to have his populous sacrifice their lives for some popularized slogan. As yet, the world cannot differentiate between a true leader and a megalomaniac dictator, nor between a statesman and a vain politician.

Q: How can such calamities be prevented?

A: By adhering to the spiritual truth that obedience, allegiance, and surrender are due only to God. Because the mind is incapable of telling truth from falsehood, following this dictum is the only safety that it can rely on.

Q: What perpetuates illusions of the world?

A: The pleasure of profit, power, prestige, and money of the charismatic, politically savvy game players who have learned how to manipulate the egos of the populace and play on human ignorance perpetuates the illusions. This is facilitated by the mastery of the media, which is the latest game board on which image is used to control and seduce. The media have discovered that it is not even necessary to have any reality whatsoever behind images. The so-called 'nonlinear' (here used differently than in the foregoing) imaging techniques simply bypass reason and the intellect and directly program the mind of the populace without any interference. Reality is now considered to be irrelevant. (In current discussions, it is bantered about whether an objective reality even exists.) By Pavlovian conditioning, the naïve mind is quickly programmed and does not even realize that it is being programmed. To the nonintegrous, such values as peace honesty, caring, genuineness, and love are merely images to be exploited. Distortion is currently the most favored manipulation in which images bypass reason.

Q: That sounds pernicious.

A: No, it is merely a reminder of where society has been until the very recent past. It is only recently that any large-scale level of integrity is being discovered as having an intrinsic and reliable value that sizably shows up on the bottom line. Many very successful corporations, however, have known this all along and have been built on integrity and honesty. They have a long and respected tradition of their own.

In *Power versus Force*, Wal-Mart was cited as an example of the successful implementation of integrous values in the everyday world of retailing and corporate management. These values were established as pragmatic operating standards by Wal-Mart's founder, and the accuracy of the statements made in *Power versus Force* was confirmed through correspondence with Sam Walton himself. Now, some years later, Wal-Mart, with over one million employees, has become the largest and most successful corporation in the entire world. Its success, therefore, is a demonstration of the consequences of integrity as a standard of business.

In contrast to Wal-Mart (which calibrates in the high 300s), there is the concurrent, woeful example of the collapse of multiple corporations that were apparently run by greed, deception, and disregard for the welfare of employees, shareholders, and the public (They calibrate at 90).

The striking example of these contrasting businesses succinctly demonstrates the practical, 'real life' impact of spiritual values that are acted upon and put into practice. Such an example certainly seems to offset the criticism that spirituality is "airy-fairy," impractical, or just idealistic wishful thinking. Integrity shows up on the bottom line.

In contrasting these corporations, it can be seen that it is not necessary to employ judgmental terminology or terms such as good/bad or right/wrong. Simply stated, integrity is strong, 'works', and is constructive and successful, whereas its opposite fails. Integrity is therefore practical; its absence leads to weakness and collapse.

The concept that integrity is a strength worth pursuing is slipping into government agencies which are currently going through various cleanup campaigns. The chicanery that can prevail at consciousness level 190 is no longer acceptable nor is it so easily hidden at a consciousness level of 207. (For example, realize the significance of the fact that federal agencies routinely 'lose' billions of dollars.)

In the past, the yardstick of success was gain or profit, and morality or ethical principles were sacrificed to the all-important 'bottom line'. The new measure of worth, however, is integrity by which corporations, government agencies, schools, and public officials are now being rated and examined. This is a consequence of the level of consciousness of mankind rising from 190 (pride) to 207 (integrity). The demand for integrity is toppling public figures and changing the operations of many social institutions, from accounting firms to bureaucracies, and even the Catholic Church. Even the media are being called upon for more balanced reporting and greater social responsibility.

Q: **Social phenomena and history are often cited in these discourses.**

A: Yes, because they are very informative. Society is merely the collective ego in action. It is easy to observe and study for it is really the externalization and dramatization of the ego. One can more easily identify error if it is considered to be 'out there' rather than 'within'; however, with awareness, information, and compassion, the same errors can be discovered to be within without undue guilt or shame. The ego is merely the human condition. It is simply a construct and not really personal except to the degree that one identifies with it and terms it 'me'.

CHAPTER FIFTEEN

KARMA

Q: Elsewhere you gave an explanation of karma. Can you
    elaborate on it?

A: The entire universe and all that it contains operates as a
    unitary, karmic unfoldment of God Manifest in that
    each and every element in it becomes the fulfillment and
    expression of its own essence. Thus, the experience of
    life is the interactive dance of all these fields, which is the
    consequence of the divinely ordained capacity for
    existence.

    That which has existence may also be created with the
    capacity for life and thus become a 'being'. 'To be' is to
    exist with the consciousness of life itself as the light that
    illuminates the capacity for awareness.

    Inasmuch as the entire universe and everything in it is
    a karmic unity, the Allness of Reality is the realization of
    enlightenment. If all is a karmic unity that originates
    from the same source, then to see any separation is an
    artifact of perception. In Reality, the one and the many
    are the same.

    Anyone who is familiar with kinesiology can easily
    answer all questions about karma. In essence, individual
    karma is an information package (analogous to a
    computer chip) that exists within the nonphysical
    domain of consciousness. It contains the code of stored
    information that is intrinsic to and a portion of the
    spiritual body or soul. The code represents a condensa-
    tion of all past experiences, together with associated

nuances of thought and feeling. The spirit body retains freedom of choice, but the range of choices has already been patterned.

It is obvious that propensities would tend to recur but, at the same time, afford opportunity for change; for example, to transcend the paradox of opposites. The soul may choose physical reincarnation, become a discarnate, or explore the astral realms and thus struggle in hells and purgatories or, more hopefully, follow into the heavens because of the support of and surrender to Love, Truth, God, and/or a Savior.

The choice between pride or humility has a considerable bearing on one's karma. With kinesiologic questioning, it was clarified that the purpose of the Buddha was to teach enlightenment. In contrast, Christ came as a Savior to the souls of all those who had not accepted their spiritual reality. The Buddha taught enlightenment and Christ taught salvation.

Without the understanding of karma, earthly life appears to be unjust and cruel. To the naïve, the wicked appear to go "scott free" while the innocent are slain. Therefore, faith is the crutch relied upon by most people to explain this paradox. Faith is the conviction that there is a divine reality beyond appearances. From our own research and experience, it is well-founded.

Q: Why can some people recall past lives?

A: Below consciousness level 600, there is usually amnesia for past lives because of the identification with the body/mind as the reality of 'I-ness'. This amnesia can be transcended in altered states of consciousness, out-of-body experiences, dreams, hypnotic states, near-death experiences, and spontaneous flashbacks. The clinical practice of past-life regression is well-known and can be very effective clinically for uncovering past-life traumas and errors that manifest in this lifetime as illness or psychological problems. The therapeutic use of past-life regression can indeed produce spectacular healings and results. In addition, young children also speak spontaneously about past lives, and some even recall their prior existences in verifiable detail.

Above consciousness level 600, past lives are accessible because the identification of self is with the witness/experiencer/awareness of consciousness. With recall, one can see that there is a concordance with major significant spiritual events of past lives and the events, attitudes, and psychological configurations of this lifetime. Upon reflection, a pattern emerges that reflects what might be called the journey of the soul.

The Buddha recalled numerous past lifetimes, but this awareness is not part of traditional Judeo-Christian tradition, although it is a major understanding of other world religions that stretches back into antiquity. Spiritual research reveals that although the Buddha had many past reincarnations, Jesus Christ did not, and He did indeed 'descend from Heaven' without having any prior human lives.

A pathway that excludes awareness of karma must then rely heavily on faith or there would be no other spiritually integrous way of explaining the events of human life. The downside is that if faith or belief are lost, the disillusioned spirit is then vulnerable to either sinking into despair or latching onto a substitute for God. In the Western world, this is a very common occurrence and accounts for the fact that the intellect, in its expression as reason/logic/science, is now the main hope for the betterment of life. When this occurs, the mind and reason become deified and treated as though they were a religion. People become dedicated with great fervor to social and political causes and intellectual positionalities that are then elevated to become the new supposed saviors of mankind. That proclivity is characteristic of the consciousness levels of the 400s, which are rarely transcended.

We see that ninety-six percent of the world's population never transcends consciousness level 499. Intellect, however, need not totally displace spirituality; thus, many people in the 400s, although they place great faith in the intellect, are simultaneously involved in religious or spiritual pursuits. The wise know that the intellect can take one only so far, and beyond that, faith and belief must substitute for knowledge.

Q: **What are the various karmic potentialities of consciousness after death of the body?**

A: They calibrate as follows:

Consciousness Levels below 200 = Various Levels of Hells and the Lower Astral Domain

Consciousness Levels 200-240 = Inner Astral Planes

Consciousness Levels 240-500 = Higher Astral Planes

Heavens; Persistence of Form

Consciousness Levels 500-600 = Celestial Realm

Consciousness Levels 600+ = Higher Heavens (Nonform)

Research reveals that the heavens are the destiny only of souls that calibrate over 200 and that there are multiple heavens which reflect different spiritual groups and their belief systems. Historically, various religions have specified certain 'requirements' necessary to 'get into heaven'. It is as though each group then goes to 'its own' heavenly region but naively assumes that it is 'the only one'.

It is reassuring to discover that there are multiple provisions for spiritual destination. That each 'goes to its own' is in accord with the overall characteristics of consciousness. Faith and dedication bring their own rewards. To recognize that there are multiple heavens and that each is in accord with its own adherents means that religious conflict and rivalry could be dispensed with out of respect and humility. It is the naïve claim to exclusivity that results in the discord between religious groups.

All the great teachers proclaim the seriousness of 'avoiding sin', which means to avoid behaviors, attitudes, and affiliations with the energy fields that calibrate below 200. They teach that these are the pathways to the spiritual realms of great suffering which are therefore called "hells." Hells refer to spiritual torment and despair, and most of the people in their current earthly lives have already experienced at least some of the upper levels of the 'hell' of despair, depression, fear, terror, loss, and anxiety.

It seems obvious that guilt would result in a penitent realm of suffering in which one can reach great depths. The levels of hell were accurately depicted by Dante. Artists such as Hieronymus Bosch generally illustrate the upper levels of hell in which form predominates. Much more grim are the lower levels of hell which become, paradoxically (like the upper levels of consciousness), increasingly formless and finally sink into timeless, insurmountable, nameless dread and hopelessness.

In the lower regions, time stops and suffering is experienced as eternal and never ending. Thus, as one enters the lower levels of hell, there appears the knowingness that may be visually experienced as the sign "Abandon hope for all eternity." There the soul goes into the infinite hell of timeless despair as though being shut off totally and forever from the Light of God.

In this lifetime, such was the actual experience. Some-how, out of the formless, timeless depths of hell, some aspect of the spirit survived and prayed "If there is a God, I ask Him for help." This was followed, mercifully, by oblivion. After an indeterminate period of temporal time, consciousness returned, but it now entered a completely different and stunning realm of splendor in which all prior sense of self was replaced by an Infinite

Divine Presence. The mind was silent in awe of the splendor of the revelation of Divinity as the source and essence of all that exists. Spiritual truth shone forth with profound clarity. All sense of a separate personal self had been obliterated, and the only reality that remained was the Infinite Allness of the Presence. Many years later came the recall of the Zen saying that "Heaven and Hell are only one-tenth of an inch apart."

The power of the experience took thirty years to integrate in order to be able to even speak or write of it. There was nothing to say and nothing that could be said until the work occurred that allowed for an explanation, which resulted in the writing of *Power versus Force.*

Prior to the transformation, there seemed to be a central self which the ego assumed to be the cause of actions. This was totally wiped out by the Presence, and subsequently, the illusion of cause disappeared and was replaced by the awareness that all is occurring spontaneously as a result of its essence as created by Divinity. All is happening spontaneously because of its own innate nature interacting with the innate nature of everything else. There is no 'cause' of anything. Action is an interactive dance of the responsiveness of life.

Explanation

The statement "There is no 'cause' of anything" calibrates at 999. The Buddha's Law of Dependent Origination or Interdependent Co-creation calibrates at 965. The Buddha's law pertains to the evolution of form or existence, that is, the Manifest. However, the Buddha stated that the Ultimate (the Void) was beyond form and there was nothing that was permanent (i.e., the Law of Impermanence, or Anatta). The soul is the nonphysical residual of the ego, and as the ego dissolves, even the personal soul, with its karmic propensities, dissolves into the Unmanifest Oneness of the Ultimate Reality. Inasmuch as no separate 'things' exist in the Nonlinear Reality, no explanation such as 'causality' is necessary. By analogy, once a drop of water falls into the ocean, it becomes one with the ocean.

Q: Why were these extreme states at both ends of the spiritual spectrum never shared with others?

A: There was no context in which they could be explained. To speak of such matters to others would have been meaningless. There was once a spontaneous meeting with a stranger on the streets of New York City in which the enlightened awareness of the truth of the Self was wordlessly exchanged and mutually recognized. Some years later, there was a brief encounter with Swami Mutkananda, and sometime after that, there was a lengthy exchange over several days with Ramesh Balsekar. This entailed discussion on the significance of transcending the opposites of existence versus nonexistence. Ramesh Balsekar had become enlightened as a result of being Nisargadatta Maharaj's translator and close associate for more than twenty years.

Q: Was the state of awareness that presented itself as the Presence stationary?

A: It was stationary for some years during which there was a relearning of how to be in the world. This was occasioned by the fact that there was now nonattachment rather than detachment. Had there been detachment, there would have been no return to the world. With nonattachment, the personality is free to interact. It has no effect on the state of awareness.

Years later, however, consciousness began to evolve again and progress. This required leaving the ordinary world for many years. Seemingly abstract dualities of advanced spiritual awareness presented themselves. Any impediment to the advancement of consciousness was accompanied by an intense, burning pain that was experienced as an incessant torment. Once the gates of the paradox were transcended by a higher recontextualization, the distress disappeared. It became apparent that these were some of the seeming 'demons' that had 'attacked' the Buddha. They represented the collective energies of the lower ego states that had accumulated in consciousness over great expanses of time. It is as though the very foundations of the ego are strongly defended, and the defense increases in intensity as its survival is threatened.

The psychic opposition to spiritual progress became extremely intense. It then progressed, and each progression was accompanied by a recurrence of what could be termed 'psychic attack' by the seeming opposite of the more advanced truth. It was as though dominions were being threatened by the advance of truth.

On one occasion, there was no worldly presence, but on the consciousness level, there was an encounter with a more rarified luciferic presence that promised great power if one went into agreement with it. When this was refused, it retreated. This occurred at what might be analogously referred to as a high-altitude fail/pass test. One could see and know that Christ had passed through that temptation and had also refused it.

It was also obvious that not every entity that had reached this fail/pass test had refused the temptation. In itself, the temptation was craftily presented nonverbally as an understanding that "now that you realize that you are beyond all karma, you are free, without any consequence, to reign with great power because there are no consequences for your actions, and no longer are you subject to consequences."

It was clear that the great avatars had passed purely through this temptation, and it was also clear that it was at this point that a number of aspirants had fallen. Thus, this consciousness countered, with an absolute declaration, that the condition could never be used for gain. With the rededication of the power of that level to the service of God, the tempting energy/entity/consciousness disappeared. (The luciferic error is that although a spirit has evolved beyond ordinary human karma, it is still subject to the karmic laws of the universe and God.)

The luciferic temptation that occurs at this level is subtle and sophisticated. It plays on advanced but as yet incomplete spiritual knowledge and understanding. The presentation is as follows: "Now that you are released from the attachment of love and realize that all karma was only based on illusion and that there is no fearsome, judgmental God or any 'others' to be encountered, and now that you are beyond form and therefore beyond karma and totally free, your power is unlimited. Own that power as yours." The offer is to join the power for power's sake and reign in the luciferic domain. The temptation is to the spiritual ego to obtain God's power but to reject God's love.

Historically, Jesus recounted that Lucifer requested him to bow down before him. Then he would own the power over all the world. The meaning generally inferred by Jesus' description was to surrender to Lucifer instead of God. The Buddha also described similar temptations. The realm of Lucifer is devoid of love.

The absence of love is also a requisite for membership in the high ranks of the satanic realm. This surfaced visibly in the training of Japanese soldiers in Nanking during World War II, and also again in Cambodia during the reign of Pot Pol. Sympathy or compassion for the defeated enemy or captives was reviled. The supreme demonstration was by a soldier who gleefully bayoneted an infant to death in its mother's arms. It is the satanic energy that surfaces as torture. The conversion to the ranks of 'evil' are complete when the recruit gets pleasure and satisfaction from the pain, agony, and suffering of others, especially if they are innocent and helpless. War is the ultimate recruitment center for satanic beings who are also lured by rape, pillage, arson, and mass destruction.

Q: What can be explained about the so-called astral realms?

A: There are an infinite number of universes that exist in infinite dimensions. The world is merely one possible expression of Creation which we call physical from the positionality of the human point of view. Because the world as viewed from this human positionality, with its innate human egocentricity, is considered real, it is then considered that other universes are fantasies, or unreal.

We now have a reliable method to investigate these areas of uncertainty. Historically, sacred scripture has not said that such realms are unreal but has, instead, warned us to avoid the supernatural and other realms. The astral realms are domains that are dangerous to humans for a variety of reasons. They are invisible and cannot be verified by consensual validation and are domains that are unknown to the average person. They are occupied by entities whose energies and intentions are unknown. They are extremely clever and able to seduce innocent humans to yield to their influence. The lower astral realms also include extremely dangerous entities that have the capacity to 'take over' the consciousness of weaker humans. The lower astral domains contain an endless number of energies that sound pious and spuriously claim to be spiritual guides, with names such as "Master," "Baba," "Brother," etc. The human is gullible because of the thought that anything nonphysical, mysterious, and mystical must be 'spiritual'.

There are an infinite number of astral planes that claim spiritual authenticity. Innumerable channelers have made contact with them and written many books about them. Each of these domains typically has a spiritual hierarchy, some of which even claim to include Jesus Christ. They also include trainings and initiations and are cult-like in their exclusivity and possessiveness. Some of these realms claim to impart 'ancient mysteries' or state that their teachings originate from ancient mystics, prophets, Biblical characters, Egyptian priests, etc. Many include heavy reliance on mystical symbols and rituals.

To the naïve, all these claims sound impressive. The seduction here is one of glamour and specialness, such as to become an 'initiate' in an ancient mystery school. Even if this were so, one finds an instant difficulty here in that these entities are in a dimension different from that of the human. Even if their claims were valid, the fact is that you as a human are not going to become one of them at all. These entities are living on obscure astral planes. They may give some accordance to this fact and invite, instead, that one's soul 'travel', with promises of meeting the god of their domain who frequently has a somewhat bizarre-sounding name. Then one discovers, if one continues, that beyond the 'great god', there are other, more vast domains, infinite in number, each of which is again ruled by another entity with a mysterious-sounding name. The requirement is often an oath of secrecy, plus a substantial monetary fee. (Note that in Reality, the Supreme is beyond name and form.)

In researching this phenomenon, something rather interesting was discovered. The lower astral planes are inhabited by entities that have refused and hate God. They are jealous of God and have learned how to mimic human personalities, ambitions, and spiritual teachers. Their ploy is to control humans and divert them to a deliberate pathway on which they are blocked from access to God. During this research session, it was not asked why they had refused God, nor were further inquiries made. It is known that many entities on these planes are experts at deception and that their favorite target is a genuine spiritual seeker or even a relatively evolved aspirant who falls for an astral entity that claims to be higher than Jesus Christ.

It is also known from widespread media publicity that extremely negative demonic energies do, in fact, temporarily inhabit physical bodies, often resulting in grotesque criminality and serial killings. It is not uncommon at all for mentally ill or intoxicated persons or people who have had recent brain injuries to publicly proclaim that they hear Jesus Christ or God telling them to act in ways that are obviously the opposite of all verifiable spiritual teachings, exemplified by the current 'religious' terrorists.

It seems then that to be born a human is a great gift and opportunity, for humans do have access to salvation, heaven, and enlightenment. It appears that this progression is not a spiritual possibility for entities in other dimensions. Apparently they have created alternatives to God that lack spiritual reality, such as the devil, Satan, Lucifer, or a variety of spurious 'gods' who reign over their limited domains as demigods.

It appears that no real benefit can come to a human who dabbles in the occult or astral and supernatural realms. In fact, serious harm can result. Observe the fact that even in the ordinary world of human life, the human mind cannot tell truth from falsehood, even about simple matters. If so, what chance does the human mind have to discern the truth or falsehood of unknown entities with hidden agendas?

The conclusion of the investigations into the matter therefore arrived at the same conclusions as those of spiritual tradition: Avoid (and that means to not even 'dabble' with) the supernatural by whatever name it calls itself. Let us realize that this world has been blessed indeed by very great spiritual teachers and teachings, all of which are complete and total, and there is no need for any psuedo-teachings from 'other realms', no matter how impressively, piously, or seductively presented.

The Infinite Supreme is the same for all mankind throughout all time. The God of all human religions is one and the same and transcends all the tribal gods of old. God is both transcendent and immanent, both in heaven and within us. The realized Self is the knowingness of God Immanent, which is in accord with Christ's teachings that heaven is within us. The infinite, timeless Reality has also been historically referred to as the "Buddha Nature," "Christ Consciousness," the "Supreme" of Krishna, etc.

The naïve initiate needs to know that there are false pathways and clever deceivers who stand to gain by engaging the unwary. Christ warned to "beware of the wolf in sheep's clothing." That is a distinction that can now be made with certainty and consensually validated verification. This research is therefore dedicated to that teaching.

Q: **At the time of the publication of *Power versus Force*, some of the calibrated estimates were done in 1994. Have any changed since then? For example, at that time, there were only twelve persons on the planet who calibrated at 700, while eighty-five percent of the world's population calibrated below 200.**

A: As a result of the progression of the consciousness of mankind, these figures have changed. At this time, only seventy-eight percent of the world's population is below 200. That is indeed a huge advance, with profound implications. Another change is that the number of individuals calibrated at 600 also increased.

The information obtained is not the result of mathematical calculations but of spiritual awareness and consciousness research. As consciousness evolves, entire nations or cultures are undoubtedly going through transitions. These movements affect the consciousness of the whole of mankind.

It is necessary to transcend the illusion of separation and realize that all humanity is one, and that those endowed beings who calibrate over 600 belong to all of us; they are part of us. They are simply the peaks of the waves on the ocean. Those who do calibrate over 600 identify themselves as all of humanity, which they see as beloved and sacred. Their energies are available to all. Out of all-inclusive, unconditional compassion comes the healing of all mankind.

Q: Does karma determine the soul's destiny?

A: The soul gravitates to the realms which it has chosen by its own actions. Every act of the spiritual will is strongly determinative. An analogy is that all acts of the will are entered into the computer-like consciousness (comparable to data bank/memory file/floppy disk/CD), which is a permanent track in the soul body within the universal consciousness. These are minute frequency patterns. It was estimated that their energy content was extremely minute by worldly standards (e.g., log 10 to the minus 400 microwatts, etc.) These figures were arrived at by kinesiologic testing and not by mathematical means or experiments in a physics laboratory. (They were reconfirmed in September 2002.)

People are familiar with the term "watts" because they pay their electric bills based on megawatts consumed every month. The purpose of the figures and references is merely analogous to denote in a comprehensible way the registering of actions in the nonlinear domain. The physics and mathematics of the Newtonian paradigm do not apply to the nonlinear domain, and it is naïve to try to inappropriately apply the tools of one domain to another.

Although, in *Power versus Force*, some means were provided to straddle the two realms, the tools of one domain are not strictly applicable to another because different realities stem from different contextual origins. Thus, a questioner said "Nothing could be smaller than a photon." What he meant to say was that nothing smaller than a photon could be found in the physical domain where measurability is a significant concept. In the nonlinear, nonphysical domain of spirituality, such a statement has no significance or reality since the nonlinear is, by definition, nonphysical, beyond form, nondefinable, nonmeasurable, and beyond Newtonian mathematics.

Perhaps the closest approximation of the crossover from the microscopic, Newtonian, measurable world to the submicroscopic, invisible, underlying Reality is afforded by Quantum Mechanics in which 'observables' are subject to influence and change by the mere act of observation (the Heisenberg principle). The infinite quantum potentiality deflects the interaction of consciousness and the substrate of matter, namely, the wave/particle potentiality and unpredictability in space or position. 'Observables' replace 'measurables' and are therefore seen to be selections of the intuition of the observer rather than a self-existent, fixed, 'objective' reality. (See Appendix D.)

If a thought is smaller than a photon, obviously it cannot be measured in Newtonian terms. However, the fate of one's soul rests completely in this realm of unseen power in which all that is or ever was stands trackable beyond time. The Unmanifest is not subject to the laws of the Manifest. On the contrary, the Manifest unfolds according to the infinite potential of the Unmanifest, which one might call the Laws of Creation.

Although the calibrated figures derived through kinesiologic testing are not measurable in terms of traditional science, they are clinically experientially reliable, internally consistent, and replicable over time by numerous investigators. The impact on a person's present life and the destiny of their soul is profoundly altered by the change of calibratable consciousness energy; it is therefore more powerful than any temporal physical condition. All that is worldly turns to dust.

It is essential to understand that the nonphysical spiritual reality cannot be understood in terms of ordinary intellectualization or reason. The linear and the nonlinear arise from different paradigms and different contexts. The great value of kinesiologic testing is that it is the only discernible means discovered thus far for crossing over from the linear to the nonlinear because it records and responds based on the invisible, innate quality called 'life'. All scientific instruments, devices, and concepts are by necessity extraneous to the essence of life itself. Science looks at life's consequences and its form. When 'life' is present, the heart beats and brain waves occur. When 'life' is absent, these phenomena stop. Both the heartbeat and the brain waves are merely the consequences of the presence of life; they are not life itself, which is intangible.

When 'life' leaves the physical body, we can still track its presence and state and ascertain that the life of the life energy goes right on, uninterrupted. Life itself is not subject to death. If we track the life energy as it leaves the body, we note that it continues on at its calibratable level, the same as before. The human imagination assumes, of course, that it goes 'elsewhere'. In Reality, there is no 'elsewhere'. Outside time, location, and temporality, there is neither 'here' nor there'; there is neither 'now' or 'then'. If the ego still predominates, the soul will think it is 'located' in a specific realm in accordance with its calibratable level of consciousness. It will therefore 'find' and experience its own definition of reality in a nonphysical realm.

The soul has its own karmic 'buoyancy'. We call its destination the 'inner (nonphysical) realms'. Consciousness is capable of the subjective experience of 'reality' at any level. As we see from the preceding chart, the realms of consciousness beyond physicality are still capable of appearing as form. Form can only be explained by consciousness itself, which is intrinsically beyond form. Form can only be experienced by that which is innately formless. Form can then continue to be experienced as a reality after physical death. There are an infinite number of such nonphysical 'realities' encompassing all possible levels of consciousness. This is in accord with man's collective wisdom throughout the ages. To be enlightened merely means that consciousness has realized its most inner, innate quality as nonlinear subjectivity and its capacity for awareness.

Q: **Is there such a thing as 'collective karma'?**
A: Our research indicates that such is actually the case. Throughout history, mankind has participated in and identified with many group activities by an assent of the spiritual will. History is replete with invasions by great hordes of conquerors, armies of men, occupational choice, and other group identifications. We are subject to that with which we identify. The vibrational pattern of choice and identification is recorded in the field of consciousness itself. To ascribe to a group potentiality subjects one to the karma of the group. Thus, entire groups appear and disappear over time and then reappear later in different garb and social expression.

   The influence of the context of consciousness attracts and repels certain behaviors or proclivity to be reborn into certain tribes, nations, classes, gender, races, occupations, etc. We see that over time numerous disasters simultaneously befall groups of individuals who share the same karmic destiny.

Q: **What is the subjective reality of the sage?**
A: The Self is beyond, yet innate, in all form—timeless, without beginning or end, changeless, permanent, and immortal. Out of it arise awareness, consciousness, and an infinite condition of 'at home-ness'. It is the ultimate subjectivity from which everyone's sense of 'I' arises. The Infinite Reality does not even know itself as 'I' but as the very substrate of the capacity for such a statement. It is invisible and all present. In ordinary terms, it is more like a quality that is devoid of any innate content but is capable of any content. It is the quality that makes experiencing or

witnessing possible. The source of the Self is the reality of Divinity. Although it is the source of existence, it is not subject to it nor is such a term applicable.

Q: What is the meaning of the term "God's grace"?

A: God's grace could be understood as the absolute certainty of the karmic coherence of the entire universe in all its expressions as realms and possibilities. Grace is the provision within the realm of consciousness for the availability to use all the means to salvation and absolute freedom. By choice, one determines one's own fate. There are no arbitrary forces to be reckoned with. Love chooses love and goes to love. The mechanism of forgiveness affords that very forgiveness. The entire universe is encompassed by compassion, which is available to all. Prayer is effective. God does not 'decide' in some arbitrary manner. The innate qualities of Divinity are mercy and compassion. There are no favors to be sought. It is only necessary to accept that which already exists as a given. Grace can only be accepted or denied. An individual soul may deny acceptance because it does not feel it deserves it, but "'Judge not,' sayeth the Lord." Otherwise, one would be at the mercy of the positionalities of the ego.

Q: What about Judgment Day?

A: Man extrapolates the ego's qualities to God and then fears God. Judgment Day is every day; it is already here and is constant and unending. (The calibrated level of this statement is 999.)

Q: In a physical life, when does karma begin?

A: An interesting fact that is probably of great importance for some people to know is that the human soul or spirit does not enter the embryo until the end of the third month of gestation. Consciousness research has verified this fact repeatedly. The embryo is like a house that is being built for a later occupant. Until the end of the third month, there is no intrinsically human occupant as such. If the embryo aborts or dies in utero, the soul has to find another viable embryo in which to incarnate.

Q: **Recent science predicts that eventually there will be an end to this universe. If so, what will become of human destiny?**

A: This physical universe is only one of an infinite number of dimensions. Because of the ego's identification with physicality, time, and place, it imagines its reality is limited to this perceived universe.

Q: **That the spirit does not unite with the body until around the end of the third month of gestation is very interesting. When then does the soul leave the physical body at the end of physical life?**

A: If death is sudden, it leaves instantly. If death is slow, it starts to leave before actual physical death. In cases of senility, Alzheimer's Disease, or progressive, severe disability, the aware aspect of the spirit departs and begins to locate in the spiritual dimensions. Anyone who has worked in nursing homes has observed this phenomenon as commonplace. The family will also say that the person "isn't there anymore." The etheric energy body still remains with the physical body until the end of the physicality, but the mental consciousness is no longer dominant.

When consciousness begins to depart from the physical body, there is a progressive loss of memory, orientation, and the capacity to recognize family members. Cognition and comprehension no longer function. Prior to or concurrently, there may be a period during which the person has 'cat naps', and they report visiting various heavenly realms. The majority of dying persons exhibit a profound sense of peace.

Q: You said before that people do not actually experience their own death.

A: That is true because the sense of 'I' dissociates from the body and the body's death can only be witnessed, if at all. The body is only a past memory, and the awareness of a new reality takes its place. The body is merely forgotten and ceases to be an existent reality of any interest. The new reality at death is overwhelmingly absorbing. This is also confirmed by near-death or out-of-body experiences.

It is reported in spiritual tradition that it takes the spirit approximately three days to complete the total relinquishment of the body. This fact is also confirmed by kinesiologic testing. Therefore, it is traditionally advised to wait for three days after death before cremating the body in order to allow the soul to complete the separation process without residual longing, grievances, or loss.

When the sense of 'I' no longer includes the physical body, there is the cessation of the fear of survival. A multitude of vulnerabilities disappears and is replaced by a profound sense of safety and well-being. A whole myriad of defenses and mechanisms is no longer needed and is therefore dropped, with great relief. In addition, that basic, underlying, unconscious, ever-present fear of physical death that has plagued one's life has gratefully disappeared. The loss of the ego's identification with vulnerable physicality and the illusion that it was the source of existence brings peace.

Q: What reality is there to real death? Is there such a thing?

A: Death means loss of what one identifies with as self. Thus, there is actually a hierarchy of possible deaths. Most basic is the fear of death of the body, subsequent to which is the fear of loss of sensation, memory, and one's life story. Then there is the fear of loss of the emotional body, and so on. The real death that underlies all these, however, and which is actually feared by the ego, is the loss of the ego as a separate, autonomous entity. Unlike transcending the identification of the sense of 'I' with the body, the loss of sense of the reality of the ego as 'I' is experienced as death. In fact, it is the only actual death which can occur.

In this life, although the transition in temporal time probably took less than a minute, when it happened, it seemed to occur at such a profound depth and was beyond control or recall. Like the collapse of a building or an earthquake, once the process started, it progressed of its own momentum and brought with it an associated temporary feeling of terror. It was as though the very structure of all that had been the core of reality was disappearing. But then, in its place shone forth the great wonder of the Infinite 'I' of the Self. For a split second, the last remnants of the disappearing ego were struck dumb with awe. All was wordless and silent in the infinite, all-powerful stillness of the Presence. All existence shone forth as an expression of Divinity, and the truth of God obliterated all illusion and pretense of thought. It was complete and total.

Q: **Is all fear of death then actually the fear of death of the ego's sense of 'I'?**

A: That is true. It is formulated by the mind as the fear of death of the body, which, however, is just a screen. The ego actually fears loss of its own life and identity as 'I', and the basis for its anxiety is its awareness of its own vulnerability. If the ego were based on an absolute reality, it would be beyond fear for it would know it is timeless and invulnerable. In contrast, the knowingness of the real 'I' includes the awareness of the absoluteness of Infinity. The personal 'I' is 'content', whereas the 'I' of Reality is context. By analogy, the cloud is subject to change and dissolution, but the space of the sky is intrinsically inviolate. Weather comes and goes but the sky itself remains unchanged. Enlightenment is merely the shift of identity from the cloud to the sky.

Thus can the sage say "I am that which is before all universes were born and will remain so and as such after they have all disappeared. Timeless am I the Absolute, no longer subject to death or rebirth."

CHAPTER SIXTEEN

THE FINAL DOORWAY

Historical Background

Throughout eons, consciousness has evolved as the 'soul'. It reincarnates in a successive series of lifetimes, physical or otherwise, which are recorded in the awareness level of consciousness as karma. The interaction of the karmic patterns with the totality of the universe is expressed as the details of an identified lifetime. Once the nonlinear Reality becomes manifest as existence, consciousness identifies with the form as the locus of 'I' of a seemingly separate individual. This self claims authorship and believes it is the source of its own existence. As the consciousness of the soul evolves, it eventually seeks to identify and reunite with its true source. Like an orphan who searches for its parents, the orphaned ego/self longs to return to a home but has lost the way.

Although the ego identifies with the linearity of form and time, its source of life stems from the nonlinear. This is intuited as an ephemeral, intangible, indefinable reality or ultimate Source. As civilizations advance, the source is at first thought perhaps to be a specific cause, located in the sun, the stars, or the moon. Later it becomes intuited to be supernatural and invisible and is identified as spirit. Various conceptions of powerful spirits then evolve to a heavenly god who, however, has anthropomorphic, human-like characteristics. In some cultures, whole pantheons of gods and goddesses evolve with specified domains, such as gods of war, gods of fertility, etc. These gods were arrived at by both conscious and unconscious mechanisms.

The myths and legends of man that evolved over time were definitively studied by the Swiss psychoanalyst, Carl Jung, who located their origins in man's unconscious mind and their use as symbols. Many deities turned out to be projections from the unconscious mind and later were given expression in fables and folklore. Man also discovered spiritual entities by other means, such as through dreams, visions, spiritual quests, and the psychic revelations of peyote and other herbs. People also had out-of-body and near-death experiences, shamanistic visions, and altered states of consciousness by communication with other realms and entities who could be contacted only in the trance state.

The collective experiences of mankind summed up to the awareness that there were realms other than just the physical, and that influences from these other realms played a part in human life. The next step was to try to entreat these entities and spirits by chants, worship, prayer, sacrifice, incense, smoke, dance, garb, and ritual. Mankind was like a naïve explorer without a compass or a map. Therefore, superstition, and then various forms of magic and ritual practices emerged. Formulations became codified and segregated people into religions, sects, and cults.

The naïveté of the explorers precluded the awareness that multiple realms were being discovered. The entities that held dominion over some of these realms turned out to be very unpleasant and, in fact, quite fearsome; some were even demonic.

The gods were held responsible for earthly and human events. They were believed to cause earthquakes, floods, fires, famine, and pestilence. Primitive man, therefore, understandably assumed that the gods were angry and redoubled the efforts to appease them with sacrifices of virgins and warriors, food and gold. Guilt and penance gained ground. It seemed that the gods had been affronted.

Even with the advent of monotheism, the anthropomorphic projections from man's unconscious guilt and fear persisted. With monotheism, instead of a whole raft of gods to be appeased, now there was just one super-god. But even this monotheistic super-god had all the basic human failings of the ego—jealousy, partiality, vanity, wrath, vengeance, and judgmentalism. Therefore, the monotheistic god, like the ego, and as a result of the ego, was seen to be limited by positionalities and dualities. It partitioned the wicked and the good, the deserving and the undeserving, the chosen and the condemned. This partialized, impaired super-god then had favorites of chosen races, nationalities, and ethnic and geographic boundaries.

While this monotheistic super-god ostensibly had a good side (love and mercy), that good side was only conditional and actually could not be depended upon. The monotheistic super-god was therefore an admixture of human virtues and faults. At that level, God's love was seen to be conditional, that is, it calibrated below the level of 540, but God was capable of love and therefore calibrated at least at the level of 500.

Inasmuch as the consciousness level of all humanity over the centuries was quite low, the fallacious beliefs easily held sway over the majority of mankind. The god of wrath and destruction seemed believable. Throughout these centuries, only a few enlightened mystics were able to fully comprehend the real nature of God. Their understandings were heard and recorded, but they did not prevail throughout society. (As previously mentioned, the consciousness of mankind at the time of the birth of Jesus Christ was at approximately 100, and at the time and place of the Buddha, it was at approximately only 90.)

Through meditation and insight, advanced spiritual seekers discovered a far different truth of the nature of Divinity than had the masses. While an occasional mystic found favor and schools of teachings survived, many who reached enlightenment stayed in isolation and were unknown to history. Courageously, a very few 'went public' and became the celebrated great avatars of history, out of which arose the world's great religions. Despite the purity of the teachings of the great avatars and enlightened sages, the derogatory depictions of God held sway. Progressively, these contaminations of the ego crept back into the scholarship of the scriptures and obscured the truth.

Because the negative aspects of these distortions of the nature of God were close to the common human experience of the times, they were easily seized upon and exploited to subserve the motives of worldly power and gain that ensued from threat and intimidation. Although the core of truth remained, the ecclesiastic authorities of the times interfered so that the purity and simplicity of the essential truth were distorted and demeaned by being proximate to and included with dissertations that proclaimed the opposite of the truth. Dualistic monotheism was included and portrayed destructive images of God.

For centuries, dark negativism pervaded the Western religions, with the historic period of the Inquisition as its apex. Because of the horrors of the times, secularization of society then became progressive. The destructive positionalities that had been attributed to God had found a ready conversion into the righteousness of nationalism and 'holy' ethnic massacres. Despite the deaths of millions and the destruction of cities and nations, the basic positionality still operates and is reflected in today's endless social and political conflicts. 'Righteousness' is still the basic tenet of totalitarianism, communism, self-rule, religious persecution, ethnic slaughter, racial strife, class struggle, and zealous political groups. These socialized expressions of the dualistic positionality of either/or continue to impair the life of every citizen who has eventually come to accept the loss of freedom, without protest.

Modern civilized societies tend to calibrate in the 400s, which is the level of education, science, and technology; therefore, the intellect is the main arena of focus. Whereas, in an earlier century, the expressions of the ego's dualistic positionalities resulted in barbaric massacres, in a more evolved society, the same ego mechanism persists. To the skeptical intellect, spiritual truth is illogical, unprovable, and therefore irrelevant, in spite of the fact that to the more mature, advanced, and educated intellect, religion and spirituality continue to have an important and legitimate place in life.

The United States Constitution was brilliantly crafted (it calibrates in the 700s) in order to clearly define and separate spiritual truth, upon which the nation is founded, from religion. This document reaffirms the validity of spiritual truth yet precludes political domination by any religion, and in so doing, actually ensures the freedom of religion. This was a subtle discernment in that the founders recognized that past theocracies had always brought suffering and disaster, whereas spiritual truth brought freedom and peace. This was indeed a very enlightened understanding.

The purpose of an historical review is to recontextualize the position of the aspirant who has traversed all these awesome levels of consciousness by spiritual endeavor and has arrived at the very last doorways to enlightenment.

The Final Moment

The last confrontation arises unannounced, and, therefore, it is never too early to be prepared. It can happen to a seeming novice, a 'spiritual idiot', or even an atheist at the point of death. It can happen to a lowly sinner in the depths of hell; it can happen as the car rolls over the cliff from a fatal impact; it can happen just as a devotee is about to give up; and it can happen after decades of seemingly futile spiritual practice.

The 'final moment' opens up in a split instant as an overwhelming illumination, realization, and presentation. The last step can be the consequence of the elimination of all that previously stood in its way by virtue of diligent spiritual practice. There are often preliminary warning flashes of advanced insight, or satori—sudden unbidden moments of absolute stillness and peace in which time stops and the perfection and beauty of Creation shine forth.

The underpinnings of the ego are its illusion that it is a separate self and that the perceptions which its positionality produces are real. When these structures are transcended, the ego brings up its last reserves. These consist of the threat of death or the threat of facing the total void of nothingness or nonexistence. When this arises, it becomes rapidly clear that one is now forced to make a decision and choose. Into this gap in the flow of consciousness there will arrive, beyond conscious recall, the knowingness of the Sage, the Bodhisattva, the Teacher, the Avatar, the knowingness of the Enlightened beings of all times. Instructions will be known: "Hold back nothing; completely surrender life itself to God. Be willing to experience death. Refuse the Void, for it is merely another illusion of the ego and has no reality. Truth has no opposite." Faith in the teachings of those who have realized the truth is crucial. They spring forth into awareness and strengthen the willingness to surrender to and experience the death that is simultaneously the birth of the Self.

By invitation and surrender, death becomes an experiential reality. It can be fearful and intimidating for a brief moment. It is not like the physical deaths that occurred in previous incarnations when one left the body with great relief. This is actually the first and also the last time that real death can be experienced. Therefore, it need be gone through only one time ever. With the courage of conviction and the inspiration of the Self and its teachers, one surrenders to the plunge. For a few moments, the last great fear erupts and one experiences what it really means to die completely as the great door swings open to the Splendor, beyond all comprehension.

The Presence reveals that the Infinite Splendor is actually one's own Self. Innate is the knowingness that one's reality is beyond all lifetimes, beyond all universes, total and complete. One knows the Allness because one is the Totality. There is nothing left to know nor anyone to know about it. The Presence obliterates all but Reality. One is 'home at last'.

In the sudden silence, if karmically destined to do so, the body persists. Amazingly, there is no 'me' to run it. It is discovered to be autonomous. The universe runs it without any help. It proceeds on its destined course and performs on its own, although for a time it may need help from others in order to survive. Whether it does or not, however, is of no interest or importance.

If the body is destined to survive, it is seen to serve some divinely ordained mission. Intuition infers that there was some prior commitment or agreement to that destiny which is, however, beyond recall. The power of the love of God as the Presence precludes any possibility of resistance. Although a return to the world is not likely, when it does occur, it is provided with unbidden assistance that presents itself as though orchestrated to do so.

Q: To the beginner or even the relatively advanced devotee, these instructions may seem too advanced, yet they must be important and relevant or they would not have been provided at this time.

A: It is never too early to hear the truth. One should not embark upon the journey without conviction and courage. It will require all the strength one can muster. The seeking of enlightenment is not an undertaking for the faint-hearted.

To transcend the levels of consciousness, one rejects negativity and thus arrives in the spiritual domain proper at consciousness level 200 (courage and integrity), and then goes on to develop steadfastness, industriousness, and the capacity to focus, perform, and produce. At consciousness level 350, willingness predominates, along with the capacity for acceptance and the re-owning of responsibility. Intelligence, education, and the tools of logic and reason are helpful in mastering the world of form. Although the intellect was a useful tool, it now becomes the barrier. However, the inquisitive intellect becomes interested in and discovers a higher reality. Love and spiritual values replace materialistic goals. Although love is conditional at first, one is no longer satisfied with the barriers and the goal becomes Unconditional Love. At this level, the presence of God as Love begins to transform all life, and spiritual inspiration beckons one onward to the full realization of the Reality that is already present as the Self.

At any phase of this progression of consciousness, the doorway may suddenly present itself. It can open suddenly, even to those who calibrate well below the level of 200, in the realms of hopelessness, depression, and fear, as well as the various levels of hell and suffering. It is therefore important to hear of what may seem like premature information. A description of that final doorway may seem formidable and even intimidating to the ego; however, without advance instruction, confrontation of the doorway by those who are unprepared may indeed lead to two important, serious mistakes.

Although it takes serious commitment to reach the final door, the willingness to surrender one's life to God may falter. To turn back at this moment may precipitate a very profound sense of guilt, failure, and serious depression. The feeling that one has failed at the ultimate human endeavor can be crushing. At this point, the ego rushes back in with a full-scale, retaliatory attack. Any remnants of the ego become resurrected. If commitment survives, much help may be needed; however, the inner pain again drives the motive of transcendence and recovery is thus possible, but unfortunately, it can be long and painful.

When the ego has been cleared of identifiable programs, it then faces dissolution since its software or tapes have been erased. However, it has one trick still remaining, a great trap into which even famous spiritual adepts have fallen. This is the great confrontation with the supposed reality of the abyss of the 'Void'. That this is merely a product of the ego rather than Reality is already known to students of these presentations. They will remember that *there is no opposite to the Allness of God.* Nothingness is neither a possibility nor a reality. It is the ego's last desperate bid for survival.

The groundwork for the acceptance and believability of this error has been laid by misunderstanding the teachings of the Buddha. The correct translation of the

Illumined State as "void" actually means "devoid of content, not containing any thing or form." It was misconstrued as meaning "nothingness" as the supposed opposite of Allness. Using reason as a tool, it can be seen that nothingness cannot exist, or be, or represent a valid option.

The paradox of the void of nothingness versus the reality of Allness is the last great positionality to be transcended. Were it not for the presumed authority of certain misinterpretations of the Buddhist teachings, it would have fallen away as an error that is resolvable just by reason. If the nothingness of the Void were the absolute reality, then there would be neither a seeker nor a void to be found. To be truly void, even voidness would not be a realizable option as there would be nothing to realize and no one to realize it.

The Void is not to be feared but refused. The Void is a trap for the aspirant who follows the pathway of negation. It does not present itself as an option to the pathway of affirmation, for to such a pathway, voidness would present itself as total non-love.

Allness versus Nothingness is a classical duality and is the ultimate pair of opposites to transcend. When one follows the strict pathway of negation, the state of Void as such does indeed present itself. This results from the error of avoiding love due to the misunderstanding of love. The attachment to love is really the trap and the barrier to enlightenment. In Reality, love is freedom, but attachment to love is a limitation.

Another error of the pathway of negation is the teaching that one should release all beauty, perfection, and joy. Here again, the attachment to these is the barrier. In actuality, these are the attributes of God. To negate the attributes of God is to facilitate the arrival of the option of the Void.

The Void is indeed very, very impressive. One is beyond karma and all programs. This state appears to be infinite, endless, nonlinear, and forever. It is so profound that it precludes any thought. It is a nonlinearity, devoid of any content. Importantly, however, there is something missing, and that is the presence of Love. This state presents itself as 'beyond Love', and therefore believable to the pathway of negation.

In the experience of that state of Void, simultaneously present was the knowingness that if the Void, or nonexistence, were the ultimate reality, then what still existed in order to witness the nothingness? If the Void were the ultimate, there would be no survival to claim its authenticity. The benevolence of the Self seemed to be the source of the call, but to respond to it took prolonged and intense endeavor.

This final duality of whether the Ultimate Reality is existence or nonexistence had first presented itself in this lifetime at age three. This soul had gone that way before and, as a spiritual adept, had chosen the Void. Thus, at each physical death, consciousness went into the Void because of its belief in its reality, and then it was shocked and surprised to finds itself back in another physicality. If the Void were the Ultimate Reality, no return to consciousness would have been possible. There is no 'knower of the Void' for such a knower would also have been voided. Because the Void is an illusion and not a reality, one cannot stay in the Void. When one realizes the error, one recognizes that what had been experienced had been oblivion. (The calibration level of this explanation of the Void is 1,000.)

Oblivion is not an unwelcome desire of the ego; in fact, many people consciously look forward to the supposed oblivion of death (meaning no more possible suffering). One can be sympathetic to that wish, but Reality is insistent that one return to consciousness, awareness, and the continuation of evolution.

To repeat, there is no opposite to the Allness, Love, and Totality of God. Unless one is unreservedly willing to

surrender one's very life and die for God, then spiritual
purification should be the goal of one's endeavor instead
of enlightenment.

Q: **This brings up an often quoted saying, "Nothing is
    impossible to God!"**

A: That is a paradoxical absurdity. It is not possible for God
    to be non-God, for it excludes the meaning of the word
    "possible." It is usually quoted in the context of an
    argument to justify some positionality. Like the hypo-
    thetical proposition, it has no basis in Reality and is
    merely a semantic game. When used correctly, the
    quotation does try to explain the unlikely or miraculous,
    but it is meaningless unless correctly contextualized. The
    miraculous is a true possibility and therefore does occur.
    Most often, however, the miraculous occurrences are
    known only to the participants.

Q: **What seems to be the meaning of "The Second Coming
    of Christ"?**

A: Because the unenlightened person believes that they are
    a separate physical body, the expectation, therefore, is of
    a physical reincarnation of a Christ with historical
    connection to that appearance of Jesus two thousand
    years ago. The term "Christ," however, generically refers
    to the ultimately possible level of consciousness on this
    plane. The conscious awareness of the Self as Divinity
    manifests as Christ Consciousness, which calibrates at
    1,000.

    The prediction is that Christ Consciousness will prevail
    upon the earth. It could be that, inasmuch as the con-
    sciousness of mankind prevailed for many centuries at
    190 and only very recently jumped to 207, this signals
    the beginning appearance of the dominion of Christ
    Consciousness on Earth (calibrated as "true"). Whether
    or not a physicality is necessary to confirm that reality
    may be seen as relevant or irrelevant. The need of the

majority of humans for a real human personage could be a 'necessity' capable of being granted.

There is always difficulty in interpreting scriptural quotations as to the level of meaning intended, and, therefore, the use of the kinesiologic test for truth can be very informative. For instance, when Christ said to build this church upon this rock, did he mean a physical rock, St. Peter, or the rock of his revealed Truth? A physical rock is only transitory and subject to time, but the rock of Truth is forever sublime and transformative. One would presume that even if a physical rock was referred to, it was meant to be symbolic of the solid ground of certainty. Again, does the word "church" mean a religious organization, business corporation, or an architectural edifice, or does it mean a body of teachings of truth, such as the Scriptures?

Q: **Aside from the traditional practices of spiritual purification, others are recommended, such as the method of self-inquiry taught by the sage Ramana Marharshi. Is this effective or spiritually practical?**

A: The teachings of any sage are valuable. The teachings of Ramana Marharshi calibrate in the 700s. Another value is that he lived in recent times and his sayings, like those of another enlightened sage of his time, Nisargadatta Maharaj, were recorded verbatim. Marharshi taught that there are two main avenues open to the spiritual initiate: (1) Surrender oneself and the will completely to God, or (2), by the practice of self-inquiry, realize the Self. This latter method depends on the spiritual seeker's keeping ever present in their mind the question "Who am I?" The focus of attention is to be withdrawn from the world and directed inward to discover the Inner Presence as the Light of Consciousness. (It may be more effective to inquire "What am I" rather than "Who.")

To use his analogy of the movie projector, the bulb is the light of the Self that shines through the figures on the film, which are the contents of the ego's perceptions, positionalities, and beliefs. The movie is then seen on the screen of consciousness, and the unenlightened believe that they are the figures in the movie.

Marharshi spoke of the importance of locating and being aware of the inner spiritual heart, which is a fruitful focus for meditation. He also taught that it was not necessary to physically withdraw from the world but to practice the method continuously as one went about one's usual daily business. Although he did not go into an analysis of the anatomy of the ego, he did describe the seven spiritual sheaths or bodies that make up the human aura. If a devotee failed to make satisfactory progress, Marharshi frequently sent them off to visit Nisargadatta Maharaj, who was then still teaching and whose style was more brusque and confrontational.

As elsewhere mentioned, when Maharaj became enlightened (he calibrates at 700), he walked away from his business and family and proceeded to walk from Bombay, ostensibly to reach the Himalayas. Along the way, however, he was persuaded by others to return home where he met with visitors in a small attic room above the Bidi Shop. He died in about 1986. His spiritual practice was based on a complete and total faith in the truth of his guru. Interestingly, his translator and close associate over the years, Ramesh Balsekar, became enlightened and later authored a number of books.

At the time of his enlightenment, Ramana Marharshi was not a spiritual devotee but merely followed his ancestral religion to an average degree. Suddenly, while still in adolescence, he felt he was dying, and after experiencing his own death, he was surprised to see that the body was still alive. He did not, however, speak for two years and was kept alive by friends. During the time when he was silent, a local quasi-guru claimed to have been his teacher and apparently signed up a number of followers. During the remainder of his lifetime, Ramana Marharshi never left his ashram. He died in about 1958.

Q: These examples demonstrate that the final doorway to enlightenment can open unceremoniously and unexpectedly at any time.

A: The two sages mentioned above survived successfully. Those who have failed to make it through the door have remained silent. Their experiences, however, would have been helpful to others had they been described.

From consciousness research, we discover that eighty-four percent of those who arrive at the final doorway to enlightenment fail to successfully make the transition. It is therefore in the service of serious students that these teachings are provided and the nature of the condition is described in detail.

Therefore: Be resolute on the level of absolutely no reservation. Avoid the lure of the astral realms. Beware of the wolves in sheep's clothing for they are attracted to the devotee who is making significant progress. Do not accept anyone into your life who does not pass the calibratable level of Truth. Keep your spiritual goal ever in awareness, no matter what the activity. Dedicate all endeavors to God. Remember the true nature of God and avoid any teaching that states otherwise.

All the truth that is necessary to know has already been spoken by actual beings on this planet. All great teachers proclaim the same truth for there is none other. The radiance of the Self within beckons one on and provides spiritual inspiration and strength. The presence of God within is the Source of one's existence; therefore, to seek one's source is in accord with God's will.

The desire to search for God or enlightenment is already evidence of having been spiritually inspired. As the ego vacates, the radiance of the Self uplifts and inspires. Henceforth, it is not possible to be alone. At the critical moment, spiritual commitment and dedication bring forth the unseen help of the great beings who are no longer in physical bodies, yet their energy stands at the great doorway of the final moment when one is sustained by the Holy Spirit and the wisdom of the teachers of Truth.

SECTION FOUR
THE TRANSCENDENCE

CHAPTER SEVENTEEN
THE INNER PATH

Instruction

The straightest way to enlightenment is through devoted introspection, meditation, and contemplation of the inner workings of the ego so as to understand consciousness. The process is energized by intention, dedication, and devotion, and the total effort is supported by spiritual inspiration. The dedication is focused on the process itself as a surrender to God. The focus needs to be intense, and it is energized by fixity and deliberateness of intention. The process is one of discovery and becomes progressively self-revealing.

Every period of focus and practice is equally valuable. Eventually, the tool of 'one-pointedness of mind' becomes perfected, which in itself is quite an accomplishment that requires devotion to the task. The devotion becomes self-fulfilling and rewarding.

The actual focus, as explained elsewhere, can be either context or content, that is, central (like focusing on the eye of a fly) or peripheral. Context is all inclusive of the totality of the person and the process—the mind, the body, the style of the practice, the person, the setting, the room, the building, the city, the county, the state, the continent, the world, the sky, the planets, the galaxy, the universe, and the mind of God. With practice, either style becomes familiar. In fact, one could try both to see which is the more natural. It is also possible to become equally adept at either focus (central or peripheral).

Under ordinary life circumstances, the automatic functioning of the ego/mind is taken for granted and not subject to scrutiny. The very process of studying the mind already begins to diminish the ego's grip. The sense of self begins to shift locus, and the feeling of one's inner 'I' begins to progress through the layers of consciousness.

This simple drill/process/praxis will reveal evermore rarified levels as the ego's 'gravity field' of fascination with mental content, thoughts, feelings, and dialog is transcended. The layers or fields move from the literal, concrete 'thing-ness' and form of the linear domain and begin to shift from specifics to context.

The Progressive Fields of Realization

Content	Context
Form	Awareness
Register	Observer/Witness
Recognition	Light of Consciousness
Watcher/Experiencer	Manifest as Allness/Self
	Unmanifest (Godhead)

As observation moves through the levels, the sense of 'I' and self-definition move with it. The easiest transition is the realization that one is not the focus or content of the mind but the unchanging experiencer/witness/observer. Although the story of life changes, there is always an aspect of consciousness continuously watching and, on a slightly different level, experiencing. The sense of 'I' moves progressively from content to context.

To recapitulate the primary steps: The mind notes a subject of interest that is constituted by form as thought, image, concept, etc. These are registered in consciousness and then trigger the field of memory processes and emotional responses. One will note that memory is filed in its areas of the memory bank according to prior feelings and judgments, such as good/bad, pleasure/pain, okay/not okay, etc. The registration triggers associated emotions that are experienced at the level of the watcher/experiencer. As one positions the observer thusly, it will be found that the sense of 'I' is identifiable as an impersonal quality that functions automatically to merely 'experience'. The shift of identity to this inner experiencer reveals that it functions automatically, no matter what the content of life may be.

The next step (an easy one) is to notice that the source for experiencing is a field called awareness, which is *a priori* to the ability to experience. If awareness is lost (as in sleep or anesthesia), or medically ('going unconscious'), none of the lower fields operates. Without the awareness of the witness/experiencer, there is amnesia, blankness, or oblivion.

The next step is more subtle in that it is the observer/witness who knows whether awareness is present or not. At the level of awareness, thinkingness becomes replaced by the knowingness of the observer/witness as an impersonal function of consciousness. These faculties occur as a function of their own essence and not of a personal self.

The next step is again more subtle. It is important to note that at all times there is the Light of Consciousness, the total field in which awareness is possible.

The final and most subtle step of all is the revelation of the Self as the ultimate Source of Consciousness. The Self then shines forth and reveals its essence as the manifestation of Divinity which, in turn, presents itself as the effulgence of the Godhead—the Unmanifest—the nameless, infinite, supreme, ultimate Source that is infinite context and therefore infinite potentiality and infinite power. The source of Creation is obvious as the manifestation of God as Creator, out of which arises the Light of Consciousness as the Source of life.

The sense of 'I' is an identification and a knowingness that are qualities of the Inner Presence which enable the capacity to know the 'I' as Self. Stripped of all pretenses, the inner sense of 'I-ness' merely knows Itself without any content.

In the state of Oneness, there is no separation between the Presence and the Self, and the self disappears as the light replaces the darkness. The sense of 'I-ness' is one with all existence at the very core of its Source.

Truth is revealed from within as an absolute certainty because that certainty is innate to the Presence. It is radically subjective as the very source and primary core of absolute knowingness. It has no content because there is nothing to know since one's Reality is All That Exists. It is therefore totally silent and devoid of images, words, or concepts.

In its totality, it is the ultimate extreme of pure subjectivity which obliterates all mental functioning. No concepts are possible in the Infinite Light of the glory of God. There is a profound peace, safety, and at-homeness. Completion has finalized. There are no ripples left for they have been dissolved in the infinite gentleness that is innate to the essence of the Presence. To the infinite context, out of which all Creation arises, a multiplicity of universes is only a passing thought, so minute as to be equivalent to a barely discernible fleeting speck. Completion as Perfection and Beauty radiates from the all-present Divinity which is the infinite source of existence.

History and time are products of the ego. In the realm of the Absolute, there is nothing to record.

Q: **This recitation is indeed most profound. We calibrated the level of this information at 999.9. The question arises, if the Absolute is beyond time and form, then how does karma become recorded and therefore trackable by kinesiologic research?**

A: The highest level of the Manifest is Consciousness, which is formless yet capable of registering form. It can only register that which is real and has existence because that which is false is unreal and has no existence; therefore, it fails to register. The kinesiologic test can only recognize and respond to truth. It has no response to that which does not exist or has never happened; thus, it cannot be used to predict the 'future'. The kinesiologic test is not a "yes/no" but only a "yes" response because to that which is untrue, it has no response. In everyday language, we call the lack of response a "no"; in reality, it is merely the absence of a "yes."

Consciousness exists as an energy field without innate form, yet is inclusive of it. Its power is available to the life that it energizes. The amount of power available varies like the intensity of a light that depends on local conditions. By analogy, the closer one is to the sun, the more intense is the light and the energy of radiation.

Spiritual purification is a process whereby obstructions to the light are removed and its unity with the Self is revealed. The analogy of light and darkness is apt. Mankind intuitively understands that meaning. Enlightenment reveals that the Source of existence—the Light which had been sought elsewhere or later—is shining at this very moment.

Q: **There is some variation in the depictions of the Ultimate Reality (God) among the world's religions and between them and the great mystics, enlightened teachers, and avatars. How can these variations be reconciled?**

A: If properly recontextualized, any differences resolve through understanding the levels of consciousness. If we look to the avatars, great teachers, and enlightened sages throughout history, their descriptions of the Ultimate Reality (God) are the same. There is an absolute concordance that Divinity is infinitely compassionate, loving, peaceful, silent, omniscient, omnipotent, omnipresent, and benign. It is obvious to all that the essence of God shines forth as Creation and is the Infinite Totality and Source of all existence. Divinity is without parts or division.

Any depictions of God that depart from these universal truths stem from lower understandings which are products of lower levels of consciousness. The most frequent is the anthropomorphic error in which aspects of the human ego are projected onto God. These distorted views can be easily calibrated and tracked to their historic origins. Because God is the ultimate context of nonlinear Reality, that reality precludes divisions or positionalities.

Within nonduality, positionality is not possible; thus, dualistic perceptions stemming from positionalities are the source of the misunderstandings about God for which, unfortunately, mankind has paid a great price.

From the above, it can be seen quite clearly that God does not 'act' or have 'purposes' and is free of positionalities and programs. Action is a linear concept that requires a subject, an object, and a verb, plus a motive, a means, and an end. If God is beyond action, then there is no basis for the fear of God, who is Essence and not form.

It is to be remembered that the evolution of the consciousness of mankind has been progressive. Many early religious doctrines lacked accuracy, much as navigation did before the advent of the sextant or compass. The real error was in not realizing the limitations of the ego. Because much of ecclesiastic doctrine resulted from positionalities, it lacked inherent authority and substituted authoritarianism. That which is arguable is fictitious because within the realm of Truth, no argument is possible.

Q: **Is all religious argument therefore based on misinterpretations and lack of awareness of the limits of the intellect?**

A: That is so. The dedicated student of today, however, has immediate access to higher levels of truth and, by kinesiologic test verification, can reach their own conclusions. All that is truly of God brings peace, harmony, and love and is devoid of all forms of negativity. A spiritually aware person realizes that they can only carry the message for it is the inner truth that is the teacher.

Q: **Is there some uniform agreement among all religions?**

A: All the great religions are monotheistic; that truth is also confirmed by the absolute, subjective reality of enlightenment.

All spiritual truth stems from within as a revelation. It is not pronounced from without. Its character is that of a profound knowingness. The Infinite Awareness of the enlightened being arises of its own essence and is never received as information or messages from elsewhere or 'others'. All information emanates from the intrinsic Divine state itself (the classical 'Purusha' of the sage), which needs no external information.

Q: **The world is not very sophisticated or educated about religion or spirituality. In fact, it cannot even differentiate between the two. Does that hinder spiritual progress and the advance of the evolution of the consciousness of mankind?**

A: That has been true historically, but it is changing in a positive direction at this time. Until very recently, society lacked the capacity to differentiate a true religion from a fallacious one, such as a cult. Even now, this brings about political conflict when splinter groups take on a political positionality and become a threat to society. This even results in confrontations in the courts of the world's major countries.

Recently, France passed a law to "stop abuse of the state of ignorance or a situation of weakness" because French law sees that it has a responsibility to society to deter perpetration (spiritual rape) by self-serving cults (a cult calibrates below 200). The falsity of supposedly religious yet violent cults is obvious to everyone.

Q: **What is the basis for schism within a true religion?**

A: Different interpretations arise from ignorance or positionalities that stem from the lack of awareness of the nature of consciousness or from which spiritual body the comprehension arises (i.e., higher mental, Buddhic, Atmic, etc.) and from which chakra of the predominant spiritual body (heart, throat, third eye, or crown chakra). An historic example is the Christian dialogue and argumentation (which split the Catholic Church in half) over the validity of the concept of God as Trinity (Father, Son, and Holy Spirit). This concept confirms that God, the Father/Creator is the transcendent reality. It also recognizes that the Ultimate Reality is capable of incarnation and, therefore, God is immanent in human consciousness as God, the Son/Christ consciousness. Not only is God transcendent and immanent but also available to the human soul as the Presence of the Self, or Consciousness (the Holy Spirit).

From our prior discussions, it is obvious that God is not dividedly triune but that the principle of the Trinity makes that which is difficult to comprehend more understandable.

Other religions have approached the same subject, for example, Brahma/Vishnu/Shiva; or as in Buddhism, Avalokiteschvara (the compassionate one); Amitabha (savior); and Siddhartha Gautama (the historic Buddha).

Q: How can error be prevented or corrected?
A: First, one needs to be aware of the qualities that must be inherent for Divinity to be Divinity and to be the Infinity called God, that is, beyond form; beyond duality; beyond human attributes without parts, actions, or motives; complete and total; beyond time and space, without beginning or end, and lacking in nothing. Out of this Supreme arise infinite compassion, stillness, silence, and peace.

Second, one must have a knowledge of the ego, its mechanisms and its structure, which all rely on form and duality. Then, when any variation arises from what is known to be true, as described above, the origins of the error can be diagnosed to a specific ego function which is calibratable.

Third, the veracity of all teachings is subject to confirmation with the method of kinesiologic testing and calibrating the levels of truth. Thus, these errors can be tracked to their origins, which are specifically positionalities and the true bases for the errors.

Fourth, adequate explanation of the teachings of higher truth need to be presented in sufficient detail to prevent misunderstanding. Errors in history have been due to inadequate depth and breadth of explanation, and therefore, the expositions of truth lack the protective buttress of understanding.

Errors arise from concepts because of a lack of clarity about context. They are also purposely promulgated for ulterior motives and control over others. Ultimate truth is realized as pure, radical subjectivity. It is self-revealing and beyond argument.

Finally, of great value would be a reassessment of scriptures and spiritual teachings through the use of kinesiologic calibration research. Deviations can then be explained and resolved.

Q: What is your advice to a spiritual aspirant who is serious about realizing the state of enlightenment?

A: Spiritual commitment simply means to recontextualize the goal and meaning of one's life. This needs to be done totally, all inclusively, so that life does not become segmented into spiritual work versus ordinary life. All life now becomes spiritual practice because context becomes the priority that encompasses every act, thought, or moment. This poised point of view already results in a degree of nonattachment.

From this viewpoint, the emphasis in practice is to observe all the content of evolving life without making any comment, criticism, or judgment. The prevailing attitude can be stated as "That is how it seems to be." The observer/witness becomes detached from commentary about life and is then capable of transcending opinionation, likes, dislikes, aversions, attractions, arguments, or objections.

Life unfolds of its own and does not need commentary. The habit of editorializing about what is witnessed needs to be voluntarily surrendered to God.

Although nonattachment may seem like a point of view, it is really not a positionality but a nonpositionality. We see from the chart of the stratified levels of awareness that the observer/witness is already a step beyond the confines of the ordinary ego. This practice quiets the mind and also results in the progressive withdrawal of the ego's habit of projecting the 'me' into everything that happens. When this is accomplished, life then reveals that it is impersonal rather than personal.

This practice results in a progressive withdrawal of ego involvement in the details of life into which ordinary mind gets trapped and entangled. Peacefulness results from being aware yet uninvolved, and the sense of 'I' moves from identification with content to the experiencer, and then to the observer/witness.

Q: Does that not lead to indifference?

A: It does indeed lead to what has been called 'Divine indifference'. The peaceful mind has no thoughts or opinions. Because the knowingness replaces thinkingness, it will be discovered that no commentary is required to successfully fulfill the requirements of life, and that what had been believed to be necessary (thoughts) is actually superfluous. The spectacular beauty of a sunset or beautiful music is diminished by mentalization.

The prevalence of inner silence is the threshold of the dawning realization that everything is happening of itself and that nothing is causing anything; one becomes aware that such constructions are merely mental entertainment.

Q: When mentation stops, does one not feel lost or unfamiliar?

A: On the contrary, one feels 'found' and at home because the mind lives only on the surface of life. When the mind stops talking, one is aware that one *is* life. One is immersed in it rather than being on the surface, talking about it. Paradoxically, this enables full participation. With dimunition of egocentricity, the joy of freedom and the sheer flow of life sweep one into total surrender. One then stops reacting to life so it can be enjoyed with serenity.

Q: But isn't one supposed to take positions in life, such as protesting injustices, etc.?

A: The mind of the aspirant has to bypass and refuse temptations. Later it will be seen that nothing was lost as that temptation was merely another illusion. The aspirant gives up the vanities of opinionation and the duties of saving the world. One's inner spiritual evolution is of greater value to society than any form of doingness. The level of compassion radiates out and contributes silently to mankind's wisdom.

Q: By nonpositionality, the sense of self moves out of the 'movie' of content and withdraws from its identification with it. It still recognizes form because of the awareness of the observer. How, then, does one transcend identification with the observer?

A: The ascent of the sense of self progresses through the layers of perception to awareness to the realization that consciousness itself is the screen upon which everything is reflected. It is the innate primordial substrate that illuminates the faculty of awareness/witnessing/observing. It is seen as an impersonal, automatic capacity that is ever present and not subject to editing or volitional alteration. It is the formless faculty which just 'is' on its own. It is unaltered by experience or concepts.

   Like the surface of the pond, it reflects but is unaffected by that which is reflected. The surface of the pond makes no selection. When the intrusion of thoughts, positionalities, and opinions stops disturbing the surface, it reflects impartially. The surface does not act

nor does it have purposes or goals. It exhibits no favoritism or oppositions. The reflecting surface does not edit
or distort but is always silent and peaceful. It cannot
suffer loss or profit from gain. It is the reflecting Light of
the Self.

The sense of 'I' is then taken over by the Self as its own.
This is beyond volition and emanates of its own accord.
The Presence is the Revelation of that which allows for
the sense of Self as the priomordial 'I' and is the basis for
all subjectivity. Upon the reflecting surface, there is
neither subject nor object. The Reality that is the very
source of existence is not subject to existence. Its own
substrate is the Unmanifest, out of which arise existence
and life. The absolute truth of Reality is self-evident; it is
beyond is-ness, beingness, or am-ness.

Q: **We hear the phrase "That which is looking is the same
as that which is found."**

A: Actually, that is not correct. Only the self can look. The
Self does not look. When the obstacles of the ego are
resolved, the Self is revealed; it cannot be sought or
found. The clouds evaporate into the sky and the sun
shines forth, but the clouds do not unite with the sun.

Q: **It now becomes clear why the Buddha did not speak of
God.**

A: Quite so. There is only the Infinite Reality which is self-
revealing in the state of enlightenment; therefore, he
strictly taught the way to that state itself. Traditional
religions have numerous descriptions, attributes, and
qualities ascribed to God so that the Ultimate Truth gets
lost in the adjectives. To search for such definitions of
God would lead one astray into theology and ecclesiastic
doctrines. One then gets enmeshed in lengthy discussions and mentations, such as "Is God just," or the claim
of exclusivity to some particular name for God, which is
not even a possibility in the Truth of Reality.

All kinds of positionalities can arise and lead to tautologies, for the only source of Absolute Truth is subjective verification. Thus, the Buddha was a radical realist. No descriptions of sweetness, for instance, can substitute for the actual experience.

To follow the strict pathway to enlightenment is a specific discipline and commitment. It is not the same as practicing a religion. While there are many tenets of religion that support the search for enlightenment, there are also many that do not and actually constitute a hindrance. To be pious is one thing; to be enlightened is quite another.

Religions usually have a traditionalist faction as well as a liberal one. The conservative wing is usually authoritarian and doctrinaire and tends toward rigidity, and it can also be aggressively judgmental. The 'liberal' wing tends to be more humanitarian and therefore strictly spiritual in the true meaning of the term. Consequently, it is more compatible with the realizations of enlightenment.

Traditionally, dedicated spiritual seekers have formed their own groups and styles of study and meditation. These are usually formed by the followers of a specific teacher or group of similar teachers who reflect the truth of the inner path.

Truly spiritual groups usually have a library available containing the works of the world's great enlightened sages. Although seemingly somewhat slightly different, they are really all the same for there is only one great truth, and the same Self shines forth through each bona fide teacher. There is no doctrine to be followed or forced on others.

With great good fortune, and perhaps as a result of karmic merit, such a committed spiritual group may even have a living, enlightened sage, but that is extremely rare. Truly enlightened sages are few in number and even fewer are accessible.

Q: **Is the experience of the actual presence of such a living sage important to the seeker of enlightenment?**

A: Actually, it is of very great value. The Self of the enlightened sage radiates the energy field of the Presence. The spiritual aura of the seeker receives into itself the power of the field. Historically, the event is termed the "grace of the guru." It is also a karmic documentation, with unseen benefits.

Over time, the Presence, as a Radiation from the enlightened teacher, has been artistically represented as a halo which emanates from the teacher's crown chakra. With research, one discovers that the energy of the halo always calibrates close to 1,000. For instance, at the Last Supper, the transmission of the Divine Spirit to the disciples is recorded as having been the occasion of the receiving of spiritual vision, which then enabled them to see the transfiguration and the spirit of Christ ascending.

Then, as now, directly experiencing the energy field of an enlightened teacher bestows a spiritual benefit. It is an experience to be sought as the opportunities are rare and of great value.

CHAPTER EIGHTEEN
"NO MIND"

Introduction

Concordant with the physical body is the etheric body which is solely energetic in composition. It constitutes the spirit and is the locus of subjective experience. It transmits information to the brain and activates the neuronal circuits. In the out-of-body experience, the etheric body separates from the physical one. In that state, one is still quite able to move, hear, see, and think while the physical body may, at the time, be completely dormant and nonfunctional.

In humans, the etheric body also involves an emotional (astral) body as well as higher (wisdom, abstract thought) and lower (concrete thought) astral 'bodies' (not actually 'bodies' as such but energy fields). Beyond the mental bodies are the spiritual bodies which, over time, have been given various names (causal, Buddhic, Christ, Atmic, etc.). The appearance of the higher spiritual bodies parallels the evolution of consciousness as it manifests over great periods of earthly time.

The early hominids represent the development of the lower mental body and concrete learning accompanied by the production of thought forms and languaging. In Homo sapiens, the higher mental body evolved and represented the capacity for abstract thought with subtleties of meaning and correlation with classes and categories. The degree to which these mental bodies are developed varies widely in the overall population, from mentally retarded to genius.

The degree of development of the spiritual energy systems also shows wide variation in the populous and reflects genetic/karmic predisposition. In many individuals, their spiritual capacities are rudimentary, dormant, or functionally nascent. They become activated by spiritual interest and by association with other spiritually dedicated or motivated people. Therefore, the great teachers throughout history have advised spiritual aspirants to "seek holy company" and avoid those who are nonintegrous.

Spiritual information is stored in the mental body and is educational and useful, but it does not become experiential until the higher spiritual energy fields are activated by the higher frequencies that emanate from the presence of an advanced spiritual teacher. The transmission of the higher frequency energy field is silent and nonverbal (classically referred to as 'grace'). The event is imprinted karmically, and by energizing the higher spiritual bodies, it illuminates so that comprehension then stems from an inner subjective experiential knowingness.

The historical silent transmission of the Buddha was therefore the transmission of the "no-mind" (which is paradoxically referred to in Buddhist literature as "Mind" with a capital 'M'). This illustrates the phenomenon of entrainment which was described in *Power versus Force*. Clinically, this phenomenon is well-known in twelve-step recovery groups, such as Alcoholics Anonymous, in which the aspirant is advised to "just keep going to meetings and you will get it by osmosis." Exposure to the group's aura (at 540) results in the miracle of recovery. It takes a very powerful energy field to overcome the very strong entrapment of addiction. As long as the sober person stays within the protection of the field, sobriety continues, but relapse occurs if they leave unless their own calibrated level of consciousness has advanced to the necessary level of 540.

The door that opens to the advancement of consciousness and spiritual awakening is humility. We note that the consciousness level just below Integrity is that of Pride (the classic meaning of "ego"). It is removed as an obstacle by surrender.

The Search for the Self

Events, including thoughts, come into manifestation as a consequence of intention and prevailing conditions. Mentation is no
exception to the fact that there is no such process as causality
causing the train of thoughts. Dualistic perception includes a
programmed time track that is superimposed on ordinary
experiencing, including the thinking process itself. The mind
then assumes that the thought train evolves as follows:

The→dog→chases→the→cat→up→the→tree.

Time

Actually, what really happens is best illustrated thusly:

The dog chases the cat up the tree.
↑   ↑   ↑   ↑   ↑   ↑   ↑   ↑

Timeless

Each thought arises from a 'space' of nonverbal silence which
is discernible a split 'nanosecond' immediately prior to the
emergence of the thought form. This observation can be
detected by focusing interest on the field of energy out of
which the thoughts arise instead of on the content of the
thoughts themselves. By doing this exercise in contemplation or
meditation, one is focusing on unchanging context instead of
content. This is the field of consciousness called the witness/
observer, without which one would be unable to know or
register what is being thought. The field is autonomous,
nonvolitional, and a quality of consciousness.

The Buddha thought the eternal nonverbal void ('emptiness')
of the Buddha mind (meaning 'no-mind') was discernible
'between thoughts'. The attempt to discern the gap between
thoughts (estimated to be 1/10,000th of a second) is not as likely
to succeed as discerning the reality that is *a priori* to the silent
matrix out of which thoughts arise. It is likely that the Buddha
was referring to the same phenomenon but merely worded it
differently. (Kinesiologic testing confirms that as true.)

It is simple to observe that although there is a 'talking mind' going on at the same time, there is also a silent awareness that is more global and unfocused and operates automatically. Contemplation or meditation that focuses attention on context rather than content facilitates moving one's identity from the transient and volitional (thereby becoming personal) to the unchanging quality of awareness itself. This leads to the discovery that one is the field and not the specifics of the content. This jump in realization can be very sudden, which is a level of satori.

The field of conscious awareness is not time-tracked and it is silent, autonomous, effortless, peaceful, all encompassing, and unprogrammed. It is free, unbound, spontaneous, tranquil, and not subject to birth or death. Discovery of this field is simple, easy, and relaxed. The realization is a consequence of 'allowing' rather than 'trying'. It is surrendered to rather than acquired. As desire for, and the ego's obsession with, control are relinquished, the field presents itself for recognition.

Traditionally, the relinquishment of the ego's programs has been described as arduous and difficult, requiring many lifetimes to accomplish. On the contrary, a profound humility and willingness to surrender all to God at great depth makes it possible for the transition to occur in a split second. Thus, the pathway to enlightenment may be viewed as a slow process or a sudden one.

When realization locates its identity as consciousness itself, the dominance of dualistic perception fades away and the final doorway to Revelation is close at hand.

Q: What is beyond mind?

A: Subjective awareness devoid of content, such as thoughts, feelings, or images—silent, still, unmoving, All Present.

Q: Reality is self-revealing when the ego is removed. How can that be accomplished?

A: There are several simple things. First, accept the fact that the real you is not the mind or anything it believes in or feels. Disengage by seeing that it is an impressive mechanism but not your real Self. Refer to the mind as an 'it' instead of a 'me'. The real 'you' is *a priori* to the mind. The real Self is context.

Like a personal computer, memory has stored up much information and thereby becomes narcissistically overvalued. Actually, it has merely stored up a mass of perceptual programs, none of which is Reality. It is the storehouse of illusions. Devalue it and withdraw energy and interest from it.

Q: Wouldn't that leave one without a personal identity?

A: Yes, that would leave one with a question of "Who or what am I, really?" The old dictum "Know thyself" is misleading because, to most people, it means to simply know the contents of the ego in greater detail.

Q: Why is the ego so difficult to overcome?

A: One becomes addicted to the ego and preoccupied with its contents. It attracts all of one's attention so that one becomes obsessed with the mind and its feelings. If the person believes that the mind and its contents are the real 'me', then the focus is certainly understandable. Basically, this error is due to naïveté. The mind is an amusement park, full of thrills and spills and curiosities. It is also a theater of the absurd for the drama of feelings and social identifications. It is an 'act' in that it is a personal characterization, dramatization, and display.

Q: By 'getting rid of the ego', most people mean getting rid of negativity or pride.

A: That is usually the case. In the beginning of spiritual pursuit, one is often upset to discover negative traits and responses. They can, however, be viewed with detachment by seeing that they are merely just the persistence of animal responsiveness in their human elaborations. The turf wars observed on Monkey Island are identical to the same ones observed as the turf wars of warring nations, with the exception that the monkeys are smarter and retreat when it is obvious that if they persist, they will be defeated. Note that a herd of elephants calibrates at 190, pandas at 185, giraffes at 180, monkey groups at 125, and the current Middle East at 75 (less smart than monkeys).

Q: Is there a simple way to undo the ego?

A: Yes. By commitment to inner honesty, it will become apparent that the underpinning of the ego's responses is the pleasure that is derived from them. There is an inner satisfaction that is the payoff of self-pity, anger, rage, hate, pride, guilt, fear, etc. This inner pleasure, as morbid as it may sound, energizes and propagates all these emotions. To undo their influence, it is merely necessary to be willing to forego and surrender these questionable, inner secret pleasures to God and look only to God for joy, pleasure, and happiness.

Although the mind will at first deny that it gets secret pleasure from suffering, it will reveal upon rigorous self-examination that the reason it clings to its content is for the 'juice' it gets out of its positionalities. With even a little self-honesty, this is a rather easy fact to discover.

Everyone gets a secret pleasure from resentments, from being the martyr or the victim, and from feeling misunderstood, unappreciated, etc. Society and the law even reinforce these benefits with legal and monetary rewards so that one can be compensated for 'having their feelings hurt', for being 'slighted' on the job, for enduring 'stress', for 'feeling uncomfortable', etc.

When the payoff is no longer valued, these feelings disappear. They persist only so long as they serve a purpose. When this 'ego juice' is abandoned, it is replaced with inner peace.

One will also notice that there is a secret vanity associated with this ego game. It is as if the ego is reinforced by proclaiming how much it suffers and how it is such a pitiful victim of injustice and unfairness. Actually, the ego secretly celebrates travail through this secret self-dramatization and its personal and social payoffs. The ego feeds itself and becomes self-propagating to its inner dialog.

To undo the ego, one must be willing to abandon this payoff game, with its grandstanding of emotions and repetitive rehashing of data and stories to justify its positions. One will note that the ego milks every wrong and that it has no greater pleasure than to indulge in 'righteous indignation'. It just 'loves' that juicy positionality which has such a great payoff.

A secondary gain to the ego from taking the position of the injured party is that it now has justification for any actions, no matter how extreme. The ego is sly. It thrives on pain and suffering and all negative emotions. However, one consequence it pays for all this inner, nonintegrous secret gain is an overall sense of guilt, shame, and low self-esteem. Note the tenacity with which people routinely refuse to take positive action. They 'stubbornly' resist all efforts to help them, even though such help is free of charge and widely available. The most common defense is lame excuses. When the problem is severe, that resistance focuses the family or society to intervene with 'tough love' confrontations.

The ego's addiction and survival are based on the secret pleasure of negativity, which cannot be abandoned until it is first recognized, identified, and owned without shame or guilt. One has to see that that is just how the ego, which everyone inherits, operates and recognize that it is not really personal at all.

Q: **Why would such motivations become so tenacious?**

A: It is because it is a distorted substitute for real love and a substitute for God. When viewed for what it really is, this self-reward system is actually a narcissistic, circular self-lovingness; however, it is nonintegrous because it precludes taking the responsibility of admitting the

authorship. Even though the ego is not 'me', it neverthe-
less belongs to one.

This ego game as played out in society depends on an
arbitrary, movable dividing line that separates all
relationships into perpetrator and victim. Actually, this
game originates on the playground of childhood but
becomes current by popularization and media amplifi-
cation, along with the desire for financial gain.

Q: **The examples make the point clear.**

A: They are purposely detailed simply to reveal the mechanism that is self-defeating in the end. Although the ego
gets a temporary inflation, it loses integrity and therefore
power. It is playing the game from weakness. The
confrontational "look what you did to me" game is
supposed to reestablish self-esteem but fails to do so for
it is subverted by the "get even" motive. From a higher
perspective, the whole game is merely a "So what?"

Q: **Why are these self-defeating behaviors so persistent?**

A: The ego responds with anger if its secret sources of self-
feeding are exposed. It can even react with rage or
homicidal fury toward any threat to its dominion. It has
thrived on a secret substitute for God and survived by
short-circuiting love. The ego is therefore unwilling to
give up its surreptitious feeding on itself, as forlorn as
that may sound. Although the ego outwardly protests
suffering, inwardly, it gladly welcomes it.

Q: **This is the sacrifice that one must make in order to
realize the Self?**

A: To the ego, abandoning the self-reward dynamism is
looked upon as a loss. The ego does not trust God and
thereby thinks it has only itself to turn to for sustenance,
survival, and pleasure. The ego has faith in its own
mechanisms and not in God. It should not be faulted for
this error because it has no experiential basis for com-

parison. Its only way out is by faith that there is a better way. It hears a spiritual truth and begins to search for it when the mind becomes disillusioned with its own fallacies and failure to achieve happiness. It finally realizes that the grim satisfaction it squeezes out of pain is a poor substitute for joy.

Q: Then occurs what is called the ripeness for spiritual interest?

A: In the due course of life's events, this becomes the turning point. Even though it may take many lifetimes, it is the 'hitting bottom' of despair and defeat and the inner light that leads one out of hopelessness. Once that point is reached, the ego's days are numbered.

Q: What sacrifice is required?

A: The major step is the realization that there is a source of joy and happiness which is outside and beyond the ego. Then arise curiosity and an interest in how to reach spiritual goals. Belief arises which is then bolstered by faith and eventually by experience. Next follows the acquisition of instruction, information, and the practice of what has been learned. By invitation, the spiritual energy increases, followed by dedication and the willingness to surrender all obstacles. Even the decision to turn one's life over to God brings joy and gives life a whole new meaning. It becomes uplifting, and the greater context gives life more significance and reward. One eventually becomes unwilling to support negativity, within or without. This is not because it is wrong but merely futile. Although the journey to God begins with failure and doubt, it progresses into certainty. The way is really quite simple.

Q: What does "surrender to God" really mean?

A: It means to surrender control and the secret satisfactions of the ego's positionalities. Turn only to love and to God as the source of life and joy. This choice is available in every instant. When finally chosen, the reward is great. By invitation, spiritual awareness illuminates the way. The key is willingness.

Q: How can God be recognized unless one is already well along the path?

A: The first evidence of the presence of God is an awakening curiosity or interest in spiritual matters. That is the crack in the ego's dam. When the person begins to desire or practice spiritual goals or pursue spiritual information, the Presence is already taking hold of one's life.

If the desire arises to surrender all obstacles to love and to God, then God is already present in the form of willingness. When one reaches devotion, there is already quite an advanced Presence that is dissolving the ego and illuminating the way. Spiritual progress and discovery are accompanied by joy, which is the radiance of the Self, and quickly replaces the surrendered ego's positionalities. Spiritual inspiration increases in intensity each step along the way. When the self stops looking to the world or to the ego, it discovers that its source has been the Self all along.

Q: What else is to be surrendered besides the ego's secret payoffs?

A: One has to see through the mind's illusion that it knows anything. This is called humility and has the value of opening the door for realizations, revelations, and intuitive knowingness.

The mind searches for meaning and is therefore circuitous in that it can reach only its own definitions of meaning. In Reality, nothing has any meaning for it has no attributes to be discerned. Everything merely exists as it was created—complete and perfect. Everything fulfills its purpose by merely being what it is. Everything is the fulfillment of its own essence and potentiality. The only 'requirement' for anything that exists is to just 'be'. Its destiny under the conditions of any given moment is already completely fulfilled. Therefore, that which it is represents the completion of all past possibility up to that very moment; everything is the way it is supposed to be. As essence fulfilling its potentiality, it is witnessed by a corresponding level of consciousness. In any nanosecond of observation, nothing is actually changing. What is changing are the position of the witness and the point of observation. Change is merely a process of sequential perception.

Life can be pictured as a series of stop frames, like the flicker pads of childhood. This poses the conundrum: Is it the world that is moving or the mind that is moving?

Q: **Imperfection is then an impossibility.**

A: Everything merely is as it is in its absolute self-identity, but this is an elusive observation because of the ego's propensity for perception and positionality. Thus, the rust on a tin can represents the success and perfection of the oxidative process. Iron exposed to humidity results in the formation of iron oxide, and that is the way it is. It does not 'do' it, it 'is' it, and what is transitory is merely the form of appearance.

Reality is permanent. This is apparent to the eye of the 'I' but not to the 'I' of the personal ego. At any moment of observation, everything is already complete and perfect. Value and meaning are embellishments that are projected by the mind, based on the desirability of certain selected attributes or characteristics. If one desires a wild and natural-looking Christmas tree, then a crooked one is much better than a straight one.

Q: **Can one transcend illusion?**

A: The mind's reality is a fiction. With that realization, it loses its reign as the arbiter of reality. Through the eye of the ego, life is a kaleidoscope of constantly changing attractions and repulsions, fears and transient pleasures.

It bases its security on over-valued positionalities but, with maturity, it progressively looks within for enduring qualities that can be relied upon. Without spiritual direction or information, it does not know which way to look and may merely settle back into basic survival techniques that have had pragmatic value.

Q: How can one survive without the mind?

A: There is 'thinking mind' and 'aware mind'. Awareness is automatic and inclusive of the totality of life's situations. It relies on knowingness rather than on thinking or figuring things out. Its function is spontaneous and silent rather than calculating.

Awareness reflects a different set of operating principles and tends to be more benign and global in its responses. It sees the whole picture and responds in accord. Aware mind is not prone to banal positionalities or judgments nor does it get entrapped in frenetic endeavors. It tends to be easy-going and mellow and prefers to observe rather than to become involved in the world's dramas. Aware mind is not involved in worldly definitions of gain or loss. We speak of that type of relating to the world as 'laid back' or 'philosophical'. While the thinking mind of the ego says "Isn't that awful," awareness knows that it is merely the ebb and flow of life and that, in the end, it is all the same.

Q: That sounds like a passive attitude.

A: To the ego, peace sounds inactive and passive because the ego thinks in terms of 'doing' something, such as seeking control, gain, or avoidance. The ego darts through traffic, pushes the speed limit, and watches for police cars. It fumes at delays and stupid drivers; it tailgates and curses under its breath at slow traffic. It blows its horn and passes on curves. It is driven by the hope of beating time and jumping the line. It shakes its fist at the driver who moves ahead in line and it vows terrible vengeance. While all this is going on, simultaneously, the ego is planning work strategies, talking on the cell phone, and listening to the radio.

In contrast, aware mind flows with the traffic and enjoys being courteous and letting some poor soul into the traffic line in front of it. "Give the guy a break" is okay to the easy-going perspective of awareness.

Q: **Is not such a laid-back attitude ineffective?**

A: It does not rely on actions but on total vision. The ego relies on force; the spirit influences by power. Awareness knows that it is not what you do but who you are and what you have become that counts in the long run. Some persons inflame situations, whereas others calm them.

Q: **But what of success in the world?**

A: The ego sees success as gain and control. Aware mind looks instead to fulfillment, completion, equanimity, and the pleasures of peace and lovingness. To the ego, gains lie without; to spirit, they are internal as the ever present joy of existence, which is independent of content or form. To the spirit, a sunny day or a rainy day are the same. Awareness enjoys qualities rather than grasping at form. Thus, it can enjoy 'being with', without having to own or control. Awareness is not driven by goals but instead values the capacity for equal pleasure in all circumstances.

Q: **Without mentation, how does aware mind get information?**

A: It relies on intuition more than logic, but it also tends to be self-correcting because it does not take positions and therefore is not reluctant to change them or 'back down'. An easy-going attitude allows for changes because there is no stake in any specific point of view. "I guess I was wrong about that" is an easy statement to make from nonpositionality. Many egos would rather have one die than admit it is 'wrong'.

Aware mind values getting the total picture and seeing the options. It is therefore more flexible and adaptable. The ego focuses on specifics; awareness is concerned with generalities and essence. The ego is exclusive whereas the spirit is inclusive.

Q: What is the source of the knowingness of the aware mode?

A: The Presence as Self illuminates the Allness of Reality. Everything is equal by virtue of the divinity of its existence as the Infinite Supreme, out of which all existence and creation arise. There is no selectivity or division; all is of equal value and importance.

In contrast, the ego's focus is narrow and constricted by intention, which is therefore selective. It constantly seeks 'problems'. To the ego, everything can be seen as a 'problem'. As a consequence, the ego's evaluation of situations is often prone to very serious error and miscalculation, with grave consequences to large numbers of people and even entire populations. This propensity to error is a built-in defect of the ego/mind because it selects data that supports its presumptions and positionalities and ignores the data that would suggest contrary conclusions. The ego is rigid, and the collective ego of society is even more so. Awareness is more like the innocence of the child who notes naively that the emperor is not wearing any clothes.

The ego's rigidity and resistance to correction are based on narcissistic egotism, pride, and vanity. The collective egos of whole nations bring about their downfall and destruction. Nationalistic vanities and slogans are inflated by political or righteous religious fervor that feed on whole populations for decades or even centuries. These frenzied, inflated, narcissistic ego positionalities result in the slaughter of millions of people and the downfall of demagogic leaders, and even their entire populations.

Q: **The influence of the ego in national affairs tends to be pernicious.**

A: World history is the record of the cost of egotistic positionalities. Wars continue long after it is obvious even to a child that they have already been lost. Millions more people are destroyed before honesty finally prevails and brings the senseless slaughter to an end. The final days of World War II are certainly a classic example with which most people are familiar. It even took a second atomic bomb to wake up a nation that was blinded by self-delusion; it forced another bomb upon itself.

  The ego is not only unable to correctly assess situations that are fatal but it even willingly sacrifices life for its own ends. The ego is therefore potentially deadly and would rather 'see you dead' than admit it is wrong. The ego is capable of what can only be adequately described as colossal ignorance. Unfortunately, until the late 1980s, it was the prevailing energy that dominated mankind's behaviors. The ego is intransigent in that it fails to learn from its mistakes. Failed policies are reinstated repeatedly, even in the face of major catastrophe, and the justification is almost always a resort to some moralistic catch phrase that serves the political gains of the propagandizers who exploit the gullibility of the naïve public.

Q: **Why is there the persistence of social fallacies in the face of such obvious evidence?**

A: The ego is interested in being seen as right and focused on 'doing something', no matter what the results are. It does not dawn on the ego that there may be social situations for which it has no solutions. They just have to be lived with and accepted as part and parcel of the human condition. The ego relies on force, whereas difficult problems can be resolved only through power that transcends the positionalities of 'good' and 'bad' and sees so-called problems as projects.

Q: Is aware mind primarily a different perspective?

A: The ego conceals, whereas awareness reveals. The answer to many defective ego positions could be subsumed in the commonly overlooked sanity of 'common sense'. The ego is naïve despite its pretentiousness. It pompously demands proof of the obvious, and in doing so, it is slyly nonintegrous. It could be best described as sophomoric in its facile solutions and self-importance.

The ego feels threatened by common sense and piously recites how society has been mistaken in the past. In so doing, however, it does not cite examples of common sense at all but instead cites historical examples of faulty collective-ego positions.

Q: Is 'no mind' then an all-encompassing perspective?

A: That is its great value. The spiritual student is often seeking to transform, overcome, or slay the ego when all that is necessary is to simply abandon it. This requires the development of trust, faith, and confidence in the Reality of God. When the seeking for gain is abandoned, life becomes relatively effortless and peaceful.

Q: Is it not risky to follow the intuition of aware mind?

A: It seems so to the ego; however, we now have a reliable tool with which to assuage the ego's fears and doubts. The kinesiologic test for truth is readily available and reveals the difference between truth and error in a matter of seconds. That test does not require mentation at all; as a matter of fact, it bypasses the mind altogether. The response is totally independent of the mind of the test subject; in fact, the statement does not even have to be vocalized. It can simply be held in mind as can an image. In essence, the whole phenomenon occurs on the level of energies only. The statement is presented as an energy pattern to the field of consciousness which automatically responds to the presence of truth. It is a very common experience for both the tester and the test subject to arrive at an answer that is totally the opposite of their personal beliefs.

This is a rather remarkable gift in that it allows access to advanced levels of consciousness without having to personally go through the long process to arrive at the point where spiritual discernment would reveal the same answer.

Kinesiological testing is pragmatic and valuable because it can verify as a cross-check of intuition. It is a critical tool at times of indecision and doubt as well as being a learning instrument. It is necessary, however, to restate the limitations of the method. It is reliable only if both the tester and the test subject calibrate over the level of 200 and the motive of the question also comes from integrity. This automatically excludes use of the method by egotism or selfishness and limits the use to approximately twenty percent of the current world population.

Q: There seems to be a conflict between thinking mind and aware mind.

A: Gain or loss are merely reflections of perception and have no innate reality. As a generality, one can postulate that what is a gain to the spirit is likely, at least initially, to be viewed as a loss by the ego. The ego holds onto the pleasure and satisfaction of hatred and getting even instead of surrendering to the willingness to forgive and forget. People cling to the familiar, even if it is killing them. Despite their protests, the average person is actually a willing participant in the individual and collective egos. It is resistant to turning down the payoffs of smugly feeling one is better than, more important than, or superior to other people. The satisfaction of spite, revenge, getting even, or 'making them pay' is addictive and self-serving and thus dominates entire nations and areas of the world through endless conflict.

Q: **Is this the basis for all the self-righteous nightmares of 'holy wars'?**

A: These ego positions have been institutionalized in order to guarantee their uninterrupted promulgation and continuance. Catering to the enforced ignorance of the masses brings prestige and power over others and fills the bank accounts of the arms merchants.

The sad/comical fact is that the so-called 'holy lands' are currently some of the most unholy places on Earth. Paradoxically, these legendary pieces of real estate that have cost the lives of multitudes of people over the ages calibrate very low (150). The footprints of the saints have been obliterated over the centuries by the flow of the blood of hatred, cruelty, and suffering. It is better to pray in New York City's Central Park, which at least calibrates at 425, or even on the observation floor of the Empire State Building, which calibrates at 465.

Q: **In a manner of speaking, the kinesiologic test is ruthless in its capacity to rip off the mask of cherished illusions and delusions.**

A: It is ruthless to the ego, deception, and the purveyors of falsity. It is difficult to control and manipulate people who have instant access to the truth. Mankind is gullible, as every politician knows. Whereas statesmen rely on the power of truth, a politician subverts it for gain. This subversion of truth for political gain reached its zenith in the Nazi's Third Reich where Goebbles (calibration level of 30) demonstrated the ease with which even the most ridiculous propaganda can be accepted by the millions. Demagogues distort and emotionalize in order to control; the true statesman utilizes truth to inspire and lead, such as Winston Churchill, who calibrated at 510.

Q: **What is the value of confrontation?**

A: Society hopes that, by confrontation, the victims will lift themselves out of *tamas* into the *rajas* of waking up and taking action. This is the purpose of the law when it confronts criminal behavior. It hopes to provide a motive for change. There are, however, a great many persons who are not capable of change. When we realize that some people are unable to change of their own volition, we begin to see that they are ill or perhaps lack essential critical brain function. Historically, this was called "moral imbecility." Currently, it is referred to as "psychopathic personality." This defect shows up as early as ages two or three through the inability to control impulses or delay gratifications. There is some intrinsic defect in the ability to learn from experience and an intrinsic inability to fear consequences.

Q: **Frankness is not a customary style of religious or traditional spiritual teachers; one expects them to speak and behave in some kind of a pious manner.**

A: Reality is radical in that it does not cater to position-alities which are described as niceness. The Zen of truth is direct and precisely confrontational to delusional fallacy.

When a devotee commits to the pathway of enlighten-ment, then the wheat has to be winnowed from the chaff. This is automatically so because positionalities are based on beliefs. Beliefs disappear in the face of the knowingness of truth. The road to enlightenment is not for bleating sheep. To be offended signifies that one is defended, which, in itself, signifies the clinging to untruth. Truth needs no defense and therefore is not defensive; truth has nothing to prove and is not vulner-able to being questioned for an answer.

Q: **The demand for proof is then a denial of Reality?**

A: That is an astute observation. All proofs are merely constructions. The traditional proofs for the existence of God are epistemologically deficient because of the fallacy that is inherent and intrinsic to the logic process itself; for example, the fallacy of the seeming opposites of objectivity versus subjectivity.

Objectivity is an artificial mental construct that attempts to create an authentic, believable 'reality'; however, it fails to do so because the entire, seemingly logical construction is built entirely on subjectivity and belief. There is no inherent authority of 'truth' to any concept except for the subjective value ascribed to it. Credibility is a subjective decision and purely experiential and indefinable. What is convincing to one person may be dismissed as nonsense by another.

The realization and knowingness of God is radically and purely subjective. There is not even the hypothetical possibility that reason could arrive at Truth. Truth is knowable only by virtue of the identity of being it.

CHAPTER NINETEEN
THE WAY OF THE HEART

Instruction

It might seem that information about consciousness and the structure and function of thought and perception are primarily of value to the spiritual seekers who have chosen the pathway of nonduality (Advaita). These subjects, however, are of equally great value to the aspirant who has chosen the way of devotion of the heart. In practice, however, most seekers combine these pathways, and it is primarily a matter of emphasis or style of practice.

The foremost goal of the pathway of the heart is to reach that level of consciousness called Unconditional Love. The energy of inspiration and devotion facilitates surrender of positionalities and results in reliance upon God's grace. Although this process sounds conceptually simple, as everyone has found by experience, it is often more difficult than one had expected. The sincere devotee discovers that striving for unconditional love has the unpleasant faculty of bringing up the opposite of one's dedicated goal. This is represented in the terse spiritual saying that "Love brings up its opposite."

One must remember that love and peace are the greatest threats to the 'ego' which defends itself by resorting to entrenched positionalities that lie hidden in the unconscious. These nonloving attitudes have arisen from the still present biologic, survival-oriented animal brain which surfaces in childhood where parental and societal pressures force them to go underground by the well-known psychological ego mechanisms of repression, denial, suppression, reaction formation, projection, and rationalization.

These self-serving mechanisms apply to the various subpersonalities as well as to the primary self-identity. Beliefs and emotions then become programmed by the input of society, history, culture, peers, church, school, parents, and now, very importantly, the media. All the above are heavily influenced and either facilitated or hindered by DNA, genetic factors, maternal hormones, and inborn biologic destiny. The range of choices is even aligned with body build as the so-called somatotypes (endomorph, mesomorph, and ecto-morph).

There are also obviously many more factors that influence personality and the content of the ego, such as I.Q. level, socio-economic status, class, health, geography, environment, child-hood nurturance, and others. These factors, however, are visible, and the subject is studied by many branches of science and research.

Perhaps more far-reaching in its total effect is the invisible factor of karmic 'inheritance' and its multitudinous, unsus-pected influences. To be born a human with an ego is already a profound 'karmic event'.

One can view the spiritual ego as the current manifestation of one's karma so that 'undoing the ego' is the same as resolving one's karma because they are operationally one and the same. If the term "karma" is not acceptable, one can use the term "unconscious" instead.

Although the obstacles to be overcome will remain the same whether one considers them from the viewpoint of karma or from the unconscious, one major exception is that the student who has done some research on their own karmic background will be freed from much self-pity, resentment, and anger at the naively assumed 'injustices' of life.

Karmic research is best done when specific answers are needed for clarification. These discoveries can be extremely helpful and save years or even lifetimes of futile spiritual work. The basic value of karmic research is that the information

derived then recontextualizes the problem, places it in the
setting in which it arose, and then facilitates its resolution.

Past-life research often reveals the source of recurrent life
events or themes. The psychological ego mechanisms most
frequently found are:

1. Undoing – one repeats past patterns in order to have the
   opportunity to make better choices this time.
2. Reaction formation – one takes an extreme opposite
   view or positionality in this lifetime to keep its opposite
   repressed and out of awareness.
3. Projection – that which is painful to own about oneself
   is projected onto others.
4. Return of the repressed – in this lifetime, what one did
   to others one now suffers in reverse as the victim.
5. Denial – the motivations and thoughts are completely
   repressed and dismissed as "not me."

While the above may seem to be a simplistic review of basic
psychology, these concepts need to be available for quick recall
as these mechanisms are involved in spiritual purification.
Unless the underpinnings are discovered, it can take great
periods of time to overcome many personality characteristics
that may bring guilt, shame, and suffering to the spiritual
devotee who is going through spiritual purification.

Karmic/unconscious research is also rewarding in that it
reveals that a specific trait or event arose out of a specific
context, time, and place, and it loses its negative energy when
seen anew. At the time that it was recorded in consciousness in
a 'prior life', the ego had jumped to an erroneous judgment
based on a positionality which then persisted unless healed by
self-understanding.

In looking into the past, it is to be remembered that in prior
centuries, the overall level of consciousness of mankind was
below 190, which is below Integrity. Therefore, life was cheap,
violence and brutality were normal, and ignorance prevailed.
At consciousness level 190, mass executions could be readily
rationalized, such as, they were done for the good of the
revolution, the country, the cause, the Church, etc. These same

actions, as well as their lame excuses, would not be accepted so favorably in today's world where the consciousness level has now advanced to 207 overall and tends to be in the 400s in civilized countries.

When one looks at the Scale of Consciousness, it becomes apparent that a specific level implies that what is below one's current level of functioning has been transcended, at least in a major way, and that the upper levels present the material to be comprehended and transcended. For instance, if a person is generally loving and capable of true love (which applies to only five percent of the population), they can then assume that their calibration is at approximately the level of 500. The next step up would be to transform that capacity to love to the level of Unconditional Love (which calibrates at 540).

This would mean looking at the exceptions for loving, which are based on positionalities, such as judgments of good/bad, guilty/innocent, deserving/undeserving, and the general run of resentments. These will reveal pairs of opposites whose positionality is easily discovered. The blocks to learn this will then be discovered to be due to the function of perception itself. Often, inspired seekers try to force themselves to love the unlovable and forgive the guilty. This becomes impossible because the 'bad' people are still perceived as bad; thus, success means transcending the duality created by the positionalities of duality. It is helpful to recall that most people are unable to be different than they are because they are run by endless programs and belief systems.

The reason the mind refuses to own a negative trend is because of guilt and shame. When a trend is understood and recontextualized, it is no longer seen as awful and therefore no longer has to be repressed.

It is interesting to remember biologic heritage and presume that whatever went on in a prior life or time consists primarily of primitive drives, which Freud labeled the "Id." One can then presume that the underlying matrix of much negativity has to do with primordial urges and instincts that are narcissistic, animalistic, crude, and uncivilized. The primitive animal within is, of course, totally untrained and deals in extremes, and its predatory drives are merciless. It thinks in terms of killing, murder, and taking what one wants by violence, rape, violence towards sex objects, slaughtering rivals, and hating whatever frustrates the satisfaction of its drives, which then becomes labeled as the enemy. If the mind perceives that these thoughts and impulses are 'mine', it then reacts with guilt, fear, denial, and projection.

Spiritual work involves not only knowing about God, but also 'knowing thyself'. With adequate understanding, the way of the heart and the way of the mind blend into each other where the terms themselves are merely products of perception. In Reality, there is no separation of heart and mind. It could be said that the heart has a mind of its own, and the mind has a heart of its own. In the end, they are one and the same in the Allness of the Self. (The material in this section was calibrated at 975.)

Q: **Why is it twenty-five points less than in some previous presentations?**

A: It is because the content of this section was positioned from the viewpoint that the ego and its psychological mechanisms are a reality instead of an illusion. The presentation was directed to be helpful to the majority of seekers in whom the ego has to be first accepted as though it is a reality in order to be dealt with before it can be transcended. At the higher levels, the ego is seen to be an illusion, without any innate reality.

The understanding of the ego is therefore useful knowledge which is to be discarded later. To attempt to do so, however, before one can dissolve it through spiritual comprehension would lead to a fictitious stance because the mind readily incorporates all learned material and subtly tries to thrive in a new, disguised form.

A naïve student might hear, for example, that the ego is an illusion and then presume that "I don't believe in the ego. It's just an illusion." At this point, it is actually the student's ego that is making such a statement. Although, in the ultimate Reality, there is no such thing as the ego, until that realization occurs, it is still sufficiently strong enough to kill you in a second if it serves its purpose. Never underestimate its wily strategies. The more realistic position is to respect its capacities and compassionately heal it. Once the ego is docile, it is much more amenable to evaporating into the sunshine.

Q: **The answer you just gave did, in fact, correct that limitation of twenty-five points, and the calibration of the recitation is now up to 999.9.**

A: Your response brings up an interesting point and one that is useful to offset and preclude the development of so-called 'spiritual ego', which has been the Achilles' heel of many an aspirant or even well-known teachers. To offset the vanity of what has been learned, one focuses instead with humility on what is yet to be learned.

The ego is clever. It substitutes spiritual pride for personal pride. It goes right on, undaunted. It takes personal credit for spiritual comprehension instead of realizing that the capacity for understanding itself is a spiritual gift from God. We see from the story of Lucifer that it remains a trap for the unwary.

Q: **The very acquisition of spiritual knowledge is then a risk factor to be watched.**

A: The downside of spiritual education is the buildup of the vanity of 'I know' and the devaluation of people who are 'not spiritual'. Therefore, it is important as a foundation to spiritual training and education to learn how consciousness manifests as the ego and its mechanisms.

If one acquires information and experiences gratitude, then spiritual pride does not gain a strong foothold. It is also meaningless to say that one person is 'higher' than another. It is well to remember that the calibrated levels of consciousness are really measuring the prevalence of illusion and not Reality. It is a measure of one's degree of awareness of the Self as the real 'I'. The levels primarily denote the resistance to one's actual reality.

Spiritual pride can work in two directions, either to augment vanity or, paradoxically, by taking the positionality that one is worse than others. To chant "I am nothing and He (God) is All" is just as far from the truth as the opposite extreme. The position of "I am just a worthless worm" is just a vanity in rags instead of in robes.

Q: What of penance?

A: That is the time-honored mechanism to undo guilt and also try to beseech mercy and forgiveness from God. This is a self-imposed drama based on the lack of understanding the ego. It is a game between positionalities. One 'owes' contrition and confession only to the Self. One 'owes' the undoing of 'sin and guilt' to the Self. One 'owes' the obligation to change one's ways to the Self. One 'owes' it to the Self to give up positionalities. Suffering only serves the ego. Of what use would it be to God, who has no needs, no emotion, and who would in no way be pleasured by human agony?

All suffering is a vanity in which different aspects of the personality play the parts of prosecutor, defendant, judge, and jury. It is hard for people to imagine that Divinity is not a judiciary.

In Egyptian mythology, the soul goes to Hades, where the Lord of the Underworld (Osiris) sits in judgment and weighs the sinner's heart on the scales, whose destiny then hangs in the balance. To understand this depiction (which operates quite mightily in the human psyche), we first note that it is referring to the 'under-world'. This is the judge in the unconscious mind that is self-judging and hands out sentences of guilt, suffering, and self-hatred. This myth is an accurate depiction of the dark side of the unconscious.

On a higher level of consciousness, one would expect that the deity that reigns at the moment of judgment and the weighing of the scales would be a teacher who would educate the soul so that it could learn to do better and thus serve God. On a higher level of consciousness, this drama of the weighing of the scales of justice includes another element, a representative of Divinity who is the intercessor. The privilege of the presence of an intercessor or savior has been earned by spiritual merit, and the intercessor presents the option of accepting God's grace and mercy by turning completely to God. Without the presence of the intercessor or savior, the soul, in its consternation, would not even remember or realize that such an option is always present. The savior is thus indeed a spiritual reality at the gateway to salvation.

In Christianity, on Judgment Day, the intercessor is Jesus, the Christ, who is the witness for the soul's decision for God as the Light of Truth rather than darkness. While Osiris makes one go weak with kinesiology, the intercessor/savior/Christ/teacher of Heaven makes one go strong.

Q: Even if it is eventually revealed that the heart and mind are correlated, what does it matter which one begins with primarily?

A: If the heart opens first, the mind follows; if the mind opens first, then the heart follows. The choice has to do with karmic predisposition and proclivity.

The subjective states open in a seemingly different sequence, depending on which path one primarily follows. When the 'heart' of the spiritual energy bodies goes over consciousness level 600, a profound bliss ensues (traditionally referred to in Sanskrit as Sat-chit-ananda) which may also occur when the spiritual energy (kundalini) reaches the crown chakra (God awareness) of the spiritual bodies. In that state, the devotee may become immobilized and even permanently leave the

ordinary world (fifty percent do). Those who adapt to
and are able to mature in the condition and return to the
world are often viewed as saints (e.g., Mother Theresa).
When this level is reached, the spirit might be said to
seem satisfied for this lifetime, and the consciousness
level tends to remain the same for the balance of the
person's earthly existence. This is also because the
Infinite Love of the Presence precludes any consideration of the progression of consciousness that would
seem irrelevant. The knowingness that is intrinsic to this
state replaces all thinkingness, even to the degree that
speech or verbalization may be impossible for years.
Throughout history and currently, there are such saints
of bliss who are silent but are able to receive visitors and
give them their blessing.

When the pathway through consciousness/mind has
been predominant, Awareness opens up to reveal the
very source of consciousness as the Allness of Divinity
and the Oneness of all Existence as timeless Creation.
This revelation is at first overwhelming and stunning to
the fleeting residue of the disappearing ego/experiencer/
witness which then falls silent. This moment of transcendence of the mind is fleeting, and the light of Divine
Omniscience reveals the Manifest as the expression of
the Unmanifest beyond existence, yet as its source.

The Absolute Self-identity of the Ultimate Reality
reveals God as the Source and confirms the pathway of
Advaita (nonduality), just as the bliss of Sat-chit-ananda
confirms that God is Infinite, Absolute Totality, and
Eternal Love.

When enlightenment occurs, the ensuing state also
completely reconstructs the appearance of the world.
Everything is seen to happen of its own. There is no
longer a 'me' or a personal 'I'. The orientation to the
world is completely altered, and functioning may be
impossible or very difficult. Statistical research shows
that few are able to return to the world at all.

The state of the enlightened sage may or may not seem 'saintly' as the emergence of the enlightened state bypasses the personality. To function again, that ephemeral remnant has to be partially and voluntarily reenergized. The contrast between the saint and the sage would be like comparing St. Francis of Assisi with a Zen Master.

While the Sat of bliss can be expressed by comprehensible description and verbalization, the sage's state of being at one with the ultimate context of Reality is considerably beyond ordinary comprehension. Consequently, the capacity to even language it may take up to thirty years or perhaps even longer in order to be able to coherently describe the experience.

Society reacts differently to the saint in a state of bliss than to the nondetectable state of the sage. The state of bliss is recognizable by others who may respond with reverence or deference. The state of the sage is beyond recognition, and in order to be able to interact with the world, the sage may resort to a communication style which is based on a cryptic sense of humor that plays upon paradox and ambiguity. This is done as a way of recontextualizing perception and liberating options. Thus, it may sound startling to the visitor to hear that a sage has no preference of life or death, winning or losing. There is neither attraction nor aversion.

To both the saint and the sage, survival is of no interest for the Self is eternal and beyond all form. This 'divine indifference' may seem puzzling. These states are also accompanied by physiological changes, such as loss of the startle reflex or a shift of the frequency of the brain's EEG from fast beta waves to slow theta waves.

The level of consciousness of either the saint or the sage generally remains the same for the remainder of their earthly lifetimes. In a very few, the progression of the evolution of consciousness may resume, which then occasions unique difficulties that may again require withdrawal from the world.

Q: **Is society more familiar with the saint than the sage?**

A: The saint is easier to understand and identify with because Unconditional Love is an idealized state. Enlightenment is generally not familiar to the Western world, except as exemplified by the Buddha.

Q: **What about clothing styles or physical appearance that denote a religious or spiritual affiliation—are they appropriate or helpful?**

A: The downside is that they may be used by the ego to denote specialness. If this is watched for, then such garb can actually be appropriate and useful for it makes the devotee more understandable. As a recognized member of a religious or spiritual community, society makes certain allowances and changes its expectations; thus, the garb has a protective function and is an overt statement of spiritual commitment. The devotee may have not only a very different lifestyle but may also go through stages and changes that would not ordinarily be comprehensible.

Q: **What stages occur?**

A: On either pathway, the dedication and devotion can be totally absorbing and lead to the neglect of things the world considers important. There can be a lack of interest in eating, a decreased need for sleep, a need for much solitude, and a loss of interest in ordinary affairs, conversation, or sociability. There may be withdrawal of interest in family and friends, abandonment of vocational interests and financial affairs, and unless correctly perceived, the devotee could be misunderstood as a 'dropout' or as having 'gone over the edge and lost their senses'.

The pathway of the heart takes one through the consciousness level of the 500s. It progresses as the positionalities are identified and transcended. At the level of Unconditional Love (540), the energy becomes quite intense and overwhelming. One then sees nothing but love everywhere and, at a certain stage, 'falls in love' with all that exists. This state results in overwhelming joy; tears frequently occur. The perfection and exquisite beauty of all life as an expression of Divinity are overwhelming and result in ecstasy.

The Presence of God as Love is self-revealing as the duality of perception ceases as a consequence of surrendering positionalities. Love is therefore the doorway between the linear and the nonlinear domains. It is the grand avenue to the discovery of God.

The dissolution of the ego by the Infinite Love of the Divine Presence may be so overwhelming that the capacity to function in the world in ordinary terms may well be lost. Tears of joy can spring forth for long periods out of gratitude for the gift of spiritual vision that transforms all appearance. Beauty stunningly shines forth from all objects. The value of all 'things' is equal by virtue of the intrinsic Divinity of Creation as their existence.

In such a state, a leper is no longer repulsive, and the dying poor on the streets of Calcutta are beautiful and lovable. Unconditional Love pours forth and heals their feeling of separation—such is the miracle. The Self of the devotee recognizes the Self of the dying derelict, and at this moment, they go into a joyful bliss. All fear of death disappears where the Reality of life as God's love shines through.

Knowingness replaces thought, and the Presence precludes all illusion of separation. The love of God is the Self of the Infinite 'I-ness' of existence. In the Presence, there are only stillness, peace, perfection, and beauty. The heart swells with gratitude and pours energy out into the world in response to an unseen need. The miraculous appears unexpectedly and one witnesses the unfolding of the miracle as the Holy Spirit transforms the seemingly impossible.

The Essence reveals that nothing is 'causing' anything else. The Totality reveals its Essence and the transformation is witnessed as miracles that now seem normal and the natural state of affairs. It becomes apparent that all existence is a miracle and that Creation is continuous as the unfolding of the Unmanifest as the experience of the Manifest. Perception sees a different movie of life than is revealed by spiritual vision. It cannot be explained.

Q: In such a state, how can one function in the world?

A: One has to withdraw from ordinary life for a number of years. In the very high 500s, one is overwhelmed by joy, which may mount to ecstasy, but when that ecstasy is transcended, a profound peace prevails in which a slow return to functioning may be possible.

The silence of the Presence is total. Activity is greatly reduced. All needs have vanished. One has to be sure to see that, just like a pet, the body gets fed and cared for. The body may seem irrelevant, not dissimilar from pieces of furniture in the room.

If the state of revelation is destined to continue to evolve, the stages then become more like those that ensue from having followed the pathway of mind. The way of the heart is the pathway of affirmation. By contrast, the way of the mind may appear more ascetic or 'bare bones' in its stringency. The ascetic state no longer needs externals and dispenses with them because the progressive revelations are enthralling and all else is unimportant.

While the world may have the expectation that the life of a spiritually committed person should be holy and tranquil, quite often the opposite may occur. The karma is activated and brought up into awareness. Major changes may occur in the aspirant's life and relationships. For some years, life may appear to be tumultuous as profound inner changes take place. These may involve lifestyle, vocation, relationships, and possessions, all of which may rapidly come and go. Change in geographic location is common. Friends and family in the world may think that the devotee has 'gone mad', 'left reality', and 'gone overboard'.

Q: What other problems may arise for which an aspirant needs to be watchful?

A: The spiritual seeker goes through developmental stages. There is the naïve initiate who is gullible, overly trusting, and vulnerable to persuasion and proselytizing by spiritual politicians and power seekers. In this stage, that which is nonintegrous is not detected, and everyone is seen as trustworthy and lovable. This stage needs to be reminded that unconditional love may blind one to that which is nonintegrous or even destructive. We say "Love is blind," and in the extreme, it may lead to foolishness and serious blunders.

As spiritual progress continues, the naiveté of the aspirant is replaced by greater wisdom and discernment. There is compassion for all ignorance, but the non-integrous are recognized as such. Jesus warned of being naïve (e.g., throwing pearls before swine or the wolves in sheep's clothing). To maintain balance, the spiritual energy needs to flow to the third eye (spiritual vision and awareness) as well as to the heart chakra. It then flows into the crown chakra as revelation unfolds.

Q: How can one prevent the development of a spiritual ego? Each success seems like it would feed into it.

A: Realize that there is no such entity as the doer of deeds or actions. There is no doer/self to take blame or credit. Progress is the result of a quality of consciousness that has been activated by the assent of the spiritual will. Spiritual inspiration becomes the energy that is operating. It does not emanate from the ego/self.

The Self, like the divinity of God, does not 'do' any-thing, nor does it 'act' or 'perform' or 'intend' or 'choose', for it is beyond all volition. The manifestation of God as Existence is void of conditions or positionalities. The purity of Divinity is beyond comprehension by the ego because the ego is limited by form and always assumes a duality of subject and object.

That which is the Ultimate nonlinear Reality is not divisible and is beyond the subject/object duality of the ego's conceptions based on positionality. All spiritual progress is a gift, and humble gratitude precludes pride.

THE RECONTEXTUALIZATION

CHAPTER TWENTY
PERSPECTIVES

For purposes of clarity of expression, the evolution of consciousness has been presented as calibratable, identifiable levels in the style of a progressive chart in order to facilitate comprehension in a manner familiar to the human mind, with its traditionally learned categorization of information. While this style of elucidation is familiar and pragmatic, a progressive chart, however, is an abstraction and not the same as the reality to which it refers. It also appears to artificially separate that which is a wholeness and a continuum into seemingly distinct partitions based on identifiable characteristics.

The calibrated levels represent a perspective, an arbitrary point of observation, which is significant only in relationship to the whole. Each selected level is therefore the viewpoint from an arbitrary perspective. It does not denote a different reality but instead shows how such a reality is experienced or perceived. Thus, it is not that reality 'is' that way, but that it 'feels' or 'looks' that way.

To a fish, water is 'reality' in that it is innate to its total life conditions. To observe and be aware of 'water', the fish would have to experience 'non-water', or air. To the fish, water is friendly and represents reality. To the human, the same water could be deadly and result in drowning. Although air is deadly to the fish, it is essential for the life of the human. These are two different perspectives. Even to the fish, water is only beneficial so long as it stays within a certain temperature range. If it turns to ice or steam, the water, which had formerly sustained life, now threatens it because it has changed form and taken on new qualities. Likewise, the energy of consciousness sustains life and serves as the source of life energy. Like water to the fish, the energy is supportive of life.

Consciousness at its highest frequencies permits awareness beyond the linear physical to self-revelations of its essence, yet at the lowest frequencies, it is insufficient to even support physical life, which then sickens and dies in exhaustion and apathy. At the lower energy levels, life is too weak to even feed itself and respond to light. If we totally transcend duality, there is neither 'destructive' nor 'constructive'. Instead, there is only that which supports life in its fullest evolution and that which does not. Therefore, there is neither 'good' nor 'bad', which are terms that mainly describe degrees of desirability.

If any desired end is surrendered as a positionality, then 'constructive versus destructive' again merely represents points of view and the polarity of the opposites. If there is no desired end or objective, then life would be seen as just 'being what it is'. Philosophically, this could be viewed as a nihilistic position, that is, 'life is absurd or life is nothing'; however, with no yardsticks by which to judge (such as 'meaning' or 'significance'), then reality reveals itself to be the Allness in which all potentiality becomes fulfilled as the evolution of its essence. From the viewpoint of 'everywhereness' and timelessness, omniscience witnesses nothing as 'happening'; therefore, there is nothing to praise or condemn. From that perspective, there is only ultimate Peace.

Q: **What is the difference spiritually between perception and perspective?**

A: Actually, both represent a point of view. Perspective implies a more general witnessing, with an implied nonselectivity in a wide spectrum. The perspective of New York City from the top of the Empire State Building is quite different from that down on the street level.

Each level of consciousness denotes both a calibrated level of power as well as an implied range of possible viewpoints due to the qualities of that given level. The range of observation from the top of the Empire State

Building also depends on the weather and time of day. Conditions impede or assist vision.

The 'I' is the ultimate perspective, for it is the nonlocalized reality of the Allness, which is beyond either 'now' or 'then' or 'here' or 'there' because, from nonpositionality, what appear to be opposites linguistically turn out to be comparative qualities.

All words and languaging contain an unstated positionality and an implied context. In Reality, all is radically only as it is and nothing can be said about it or added or subtracted. Even the statement that 'that is' is a misnomer. 'Is-ness' or 'existence' are deductions and intellectual conclusions, and even to state that 'all is' is again an abstract statement.

There is no need for an intransitive verb except for the purpose of languaging. That is why the mystic may say nothing at all for years about the radical subjectivity of 'Reality', which is beyond description. Because no languaging of the state of enlightenment is actually possible, a Zen Master may just suddenly shout "Hah!" and hit you with a stick. What is hoped for is a sudden flash, during which the inexplicable Reality stands revealed.

Over the centuries a variety of 'techniques' have developed to outwit the wary stream of thinkingness, such as bells, gongs, incense, chanting, recitation of mantras, martial arts, or even the Zen of catching chickens in the henhouse. In that infinitesimal moment, the 'no mind' of eternity is glimpsed and recognized as the Self—beyond 'transcendent', beyond 'immanent'. Such ideas are concepts which attempt to categorize that which is beyond categorization.

Q: **You often use the term "state" or "condition" to describe the subjective reality of enlightenment.**

A: That is because words are being used. The energy behind the words exists independently of the verbalization and reveals itself only as Awareness. In that 'condition', there is neither subject nor object. The Ultimate is only itself, without any external reference. From the human viewpoint, that is a condition or state of 'no mind'. To not be located in any possible position in space or time means to be continuously equally present everywhere, which is beyond present or 'not present'. No 'person' can be enlightened as the state precludes all that is implied by the very term "person."

Enlightenment means that the former personal identity and all that had been believed about it have been erased, removed, transcended, dissolved, and displaced. The particular has been replaced by the universal, qualities have been replaced by essence, the linear has been replaced by the nonlinear, and the discrete has been replaced by the unlimited. Position in time or space has become Allness and Foreverness. Intention has been replaced by spontaneity, and the limiting perception of duality has been removed as the Radiance of Oneness illuminates the Reality and the Truth of nonduality. The essence of Divinity stands forth in its Self-revelation. Mentation has ceased, and in the Silence, the Knowingness of Omniscience radiates forth unasked. Emotion has been replaced by Peace. The exquisite gentleness of Infinite Power is deftly soft and invisible because it is the very Source and substrate of all that appears to exist. By analogy, it is like a shadow which is replaced by a sunbeam. The shadow does not become the sunbeam.

Seeming 'cause' or 'change' are replaced by the unfoldment of Creation. All is the perfect expression of the potentiality of essence. Nothing is acting on anything else. Aesthetic harmony and concordance are innate to the perfect safety that is intrinsic to existence. The stop frame of form is replaced by the continuity of universal essence. Nothing is incomplete, undone, or unfinished. All is continuously complete as total self-identity. The essence of all that appears to exist is Divinity. All is God in the fulfillment of the potentiality of Creation.

The universe is self-creating spontaneously. Nothing is causing it to express itself. The Unmanifest of the Godhead is the Infinite potentiality of Infinite context and all possibility. The universe is spontaneously autonomous; even the thought of 'existence' is merely a notion. The term "ineffable" is appropriate and a close approximation. It is an attempt to language the intrinsic nature of radical Self-identity. God is the universal 'I-ness' of manifestation. Behind even the universal 'I-ness' of God is the Supreme as the Unmanifest, which is unnamable.

Q: One hears the statement that everyone is already 'enlightened'. How is that to be understood?

A: It means that the Self is present and potentially discoverable as the basis and essence of one's existence. The statement is actually an impossibility because it incorrectly defines the understanding of enlightenment, and it also presents the fallacy of the hypothetical. To be enlightened is to know the Truth; consequently, the statement that there is a knowingness of Truth in that which does not know the Truth is an incorrect statement. What could be said to be realistic about the statement is that the ultimate Truth awaits within to be discovered.

If seen for what it really is, all languaging is a paradox because nothing can actually be as it is said to be. Revelation is a revealed knowingness. It is understood without words or concepts, such as "meaning" or "significance," which are merely abstractions.

Neither the universe nor anything in the universe 'means' anything. Its existence *is* its meaning. The mind is accustomed to obtaining, getting, deriving, or discovering meaning or information. In the state of enlightenment, all is self-revealing of its essence as its existence. Everything already *is* what it 'means'.

Truth is the radical solution to epistemology. Ultimately, everything is knowable only by virtue of the identity of 'being it'. The conundrums of epistemology can be solved only by the elimination of thought because all languaging is paradox. One can take any word and trace it to its roots. How does the word originate? From where? Is the word the same thing as its meaning? By asking such questions, one is eventually confronted with the ultimate paradox of duality. The radical Reality is that to understand the essence of anything is to know God. One might say that all languaging is a substitute for God.

Q: Of what use then are knowledge and learning? Are they just blocks to enlightenment?

A: The ego (as the illusory self) propagates itself so that it can continue to be the 'me'. One of its techniques is to try to 'learn about' or 'understand' things. Realize that if you *are* something, there is nothing to understand about it. Reality is the ultimate in simplicity.

Man thinks, but thinking is a two-edged sword. The bird flies about enjoying its life and does not need to study ornithology or even know that it is a bird. It doesn't need to understand or know anything because it *is* a bird. The sun doesn't need to know it is the sun; it just *is*. Grass never even heard of chlorophyll and just goes on being green. Truth is the radical simplicity and obviousness of God. It is unity. The word "unity" signifies the completeness of the Self-identity of existence. All is complete by virtue of being itself. No descriptions or nominal designations are required; they are all distractions. Even to just witness requires no thought. There is no necessity to mentalize Reality; it does not enhance what *is* but instead detracts from it.

All existence has an intrinsic aesthetic quality. Appreciation of beauty requires no mentation. To analyze beauty is to attempt to cross over the spontaneity of experience and obscure it with mentalism. Perfection and beauty are innate to all that exists. All is equally beautiful to the innocence of awareness. All form is an aesthetic experience, and its beauty is obvious when all qualities, intentions, or desires are relinquished. Enlightenment is the ultimate aesthetic awareness for it allows the beauty of creation to shine forth with stunning clarity.

Q: **The Buddha traced the ego to sensory experience and the resulting attachments. Have you any comment about that teaching?**

A: The starting point to unravel the ego was such as described in the experience of Gautama Buddha, but it could be started anywhere. For example, we have already mentioned that in-depth study and immersion into the roots of epistemology and the phenomenon of knowingness is one such avenue. Aesthetics is another. The source of mentation is another. To trace any human experience to its ultimate roots will always end up at the same root. There are only different branches by which to uncover one's Source. We could therefore just as easily choose sensation. The limitation in doing so is the creation of the belief system that it is the *only* approach. That just happened to be the one that attracted the Buddha's intention. It is not necessary to start from sensation, although, in the end, its part in the formation of the ego becomes apparent. To understand one branch is to understand all of them. Even with sensation, it is not the sensation itself but the attachment or aversion to it, or the pleasure or aversion which ensues.

Any approach will reveal that attachments are the core problem to be overcome through relinquishment. The problem is not money, or sex, or pleasure but the attachment to them, plus the illusion that the source of happiness is external, which brings up the fear of loss. Asceticism is the practice of dissolving attachment to sensory experience and thus may be of great learning value at some point in the process of spiritual inquiry.

However, it can itself become an attachment and lead to excess rather than enlightenment.

Sensory detachment can also be seen as a consequence of enlightenment and not a prerequisite condition. The real attachment is to the positionalities that create the polarities of the opposites and the resultant duality. If one examines sensory experience, the question arises of who or what is experiencing the senses. At first, it seems that the body is the experiencer, but then one asks who or what is experiencing the body. This leads to the observation of experiencing itself. Then arises the awareness that experiencing goes on by itself and is a quality of consciousness not requiring the presence of an imaginary 'experiencer'.

One can realize the Self as the primordial, irreducible Reality from any starting point. It is not the starting point that is important but the dedication to relentlessly pursuing it to its very roots. To unravel the nature of experiencing leads to one's Source. Any leg of the elephant leads to the elephant.

Q: Is it the all-pervasiveness of attachment that is the obstacle, no matter where one starts self-inquiry?

A: All serious inquiry eventually uncovers the obstacles to realizing the Self. To examine attachment or its corollary, aversion, is a time-saver; it is ubiquitous, pervasive, and the core element of every obstacle. We can look at it and ask what is the intention of attachment. There is an illusion or fantasy associated with all of them—security, survival, success, pleasure, and so on. That pervasive quality of attachment has an origin or root that can be uncovered. The mind is attached to or identifies with what it values, including its hopes, dreams, and illusions.

Attachment is a very peculiar quality of the ego. It can be totally undone in all its pervasive and multitudinous forms of clinging by simply letting go of one's faith in it or belief in its value as a reality. This one giant step is a confrontation to being unaware of one's attachments. The attachment to 'self' or 'me' or 'I' is a basic trap. One can seek out its fantasy value—the self gets attached to what it values. We note that attachment requires and is sustained by an energy and an intention. *The mind is attached to the very process of attachment itself as a survival tool.* Letting go of the ego is based on the willingness to surrender attachment to it as a substitute for God and just another illusion.

The developmental road of attachment is clinging. The infant clings to its source of comfort and survival, which it experiences as being 'out there'. It then becomes attached to not only externals as the source of survival and happiness but to the very act of clinging itself. This can be seen in baby monkey experiments where the frantic fear of abandonment is greatly lessened by cloth surrogate mothers.

The ego clings to the familiar as the known. Therefore, to let go is to face the uncertainty of the unknown, which brings fear. Thus, to cling is to avoid fear. The infant is nurtured, not so much by the maternal actions but by the intention and nurturing exemplified by the mother's love. Although the infant reaches for the linear, its survival is coming from the nonlinear. At this point, this basic lesson is either learned or not learned. The source of love and survival becomes associated with a person and, therefore, attachment is an attempt to possess and control the perceived source of survival and happiness. The ego then chooses between the linear materiality of possessiveness or the nonlinear reality of trust and love.

During the London blitz of World War II, infants were sent to countryside institutions for safety. Although all their physical needs were well met by scientific standards, they failed to thrive. Instead, they became listless, failed to nurse, became weak, lost weight, and exhibited miasma. The mortality rate was high. Scientific investigation failed to find any medical, nutritional, or infectious reason for the moribund condition of the infants. Some professional nannies were then called in who began to fondle and hold the infants, giving them attention, caring, and love. Miraculously, the infants began to nurse and gain weight and the death rate dropped.

This is interesting because it demonstrates the limitation of the scientific model, which excludes the very essence of life. Love is neither definable nor measurable; it cannot be weighed or located in time or space, yet, to the human infant, it is crucial.

In normal infant development, the loving mother is introjected or incorporated into the developing psyche. The result is the capacity in later life for healthy self-esteem, self-care, and self-love, as well as the capacity to value and return love. The love-deprived child is thus ruled by negative emotions that lack a counterbalance of positive emotions. The adequately loved infant is capable of autonomy; however, the love-starved child is described as 'needy' and prone to attachment and anger. In psychiatry, the unresolved need for adequate infant love leads to so-called "attachment disorders" and dependencies in later life.

Q: Does the pathway to enlightenment consist primarily of the constant relinquishment of attachments?

A: The attachments can be to either content or context, as well as to intended or hoped-for results. To undo a difficult positionality, it may be necessary to disassemble it and then surrender its elements. The payoff that is holding an attachment in place may be that it provides a feeling of security or pleasure; the pride of being 'right'; comfort or satisfaction; loyalty to some group, family, or tradition; avoidance of the fear of the unknown, etc.

When belief systems are examined, they turn out to be based on presumptions that are prevalent in society, such as right versus wrong or good versus bad. For instance, "I have to have chocolate ice cream" (content) "and then I'll be happy" (context) is based on another positionality, that the source of happiness is outside oneself and has to be 'gotten' (in overall context). All these propositions indicate a series of dependencies (e.g., the Buddha's Law of Dependent Contingencies or Dependent Origination), and when they are surrendered, the source of happiness is found to be in the joy of existence itself, in this very moment and, beyond that, in the source of one's existence—God.

Attachments are to illusions. They can be surrendered out of one's love for God, which inspires the willingness to let go of that which is comfortably familiar.

Q: **What about unpleasant attachments that bring such feelings as guilt, fear, or anger?**

A: They also arise from clinging to a point of view. Interestingly, the feeling itself is often the payoff. It is hard to accept that they are unconsciously sought or valued. It is a belief of the mind that one 'should feel' that way and 'deserves to'. Some of these are conditioned responses. To get free of them, one can examine how other people might react differently and begin to see that there are options.

The mind is caught between desires and aversions, both of which are binding. An aversion is also innately an attachment to a conditional perception, and it is disassembled by acceptance.

It is sometimes helpful to see mental mechanisms as an automatic, learned game and the mind as a game board. It plays win/lose, feel good/feel bad, and right/wrong. One could see loss as being set free and winning as being encumbered. It is important to note that emotional consequences are not compulsory but are merely options. There are many 'ought to feel that way' hidden underpinnings to some emotional responses and belief systems. By disassembly, an entire set of belief systems can be surrendered at one time because they have a common basis. Development of the capacity to do so increases with practice. Eventually, one lets go of the entire thinking compulsion in one deep surrender of the whole apparatus. One can then just observe and 'be' with everything as it is, letting God be the sponsor of life. It is helpful to get rid of preoccupation with details and decide on one's total relationship to life instead of its specific expressions.

Q: That sounds philosophical.

A: It is just that. A philosophic position arises from an enlarged context of meaning. It is a position that resolves many lesser ones, enabling one to progressively surrender that context of philosophic abstraction. It serves to pinpoint previously unobserved positionalities. The other value of so-called philosophic positions is that they are more easily accessed for reflection and easier to release because they are much less personalized.

Q: Can you give an example?

A: "It's not worth arguing about" is a common one. It signifies that one has chosen the value of peace above conflict and the promise of winning the win/lose game. To let go of a whole game or melodrama is always an option but one that is often overlooked. That is the purpose of the tongue-in-cheek epigram "I can't decide whether to commit suicide today or go to a movie."

Humor is a means of detachment or recontextualizing the events of life. It is a way of being light-hearted and 'wearing the world like a loose garment'. It leads to compassion for the totality of human life and reveals the option that one can play at life without getting involved in it as though it were an exhausting life-and-death struggle.

Q: **But can't that lead to indifference?**

A: Humor is inclusive of life and is a level of compassion. Indifference, in contrast, is exclusive of life. Humor allows for participation; indifference leads to nonparticipation. Humor enjoys while indifference yields flatness and ennui.

Be passionate for God, not for belief systems. That is the only real decision that has to be made and can be applied to any and all situations. The question is always whether to be at the effect of the world or aligned with the Truth of God instead. The search for enlightenment is different from that of seeking worldly success.

Q: **Often you speak of various qualities as if they are abstractions rather than personal attributes.**

A: To see life as the interaction of qualities is freeing. There is no necessity for a personal pronoun. Positionalities are programs and not the real Self. The world holds an endless array of positions that are arbitrary presumptions and totally fallacious. One can observe them and respect how they are seen and valued by others without personally subscribing to them. One can appreciate how the world sees but not be entrapped by it.

One is free to subscribe to a quality or position. It is important to see that there is freedom. All positionalities are voluntary. As spiritual inquiry progresses, one is faced with evermore primary and seemingly axiomatic positions. Eventually, the core of the belief systems and presumptions begins to appear and, finally, even the reality of the self as an independent, autonomous reality presents itself for examination. The disassembly of every belief system will eventually lead to the question of 'what' holds to that position, what it is that believes it, what it is that chooses it and then becomes run by it. With progress, the prior sense of self turns out to be an identification with the operation center of the mentalization.

The imagining 'who' is really a 'what.' It will be found that it is merely a function and not an independent, circumscribed entity at all. It is a belief system and, actually, all the qualities are operating autonomously. Thinking and feeling happen on their own. Mentation, in its various styles, occurs unasked and unbidden. An independent, autonomous entity called 'I' is a presumption. All is happening of its own, including the central operations center that coordinates the human functions. This operations center automatically identifies, classifies, sorts, remembers, compares, evaluates, files away, observes, and records like a transistor processor unit. This central unit is subscribed to and identified with as being the real 'me'. It then becomes the object of credit, blame, and fear, as well as worry and concern about survival. It becomes associated with the emotions, for better or worse. Options become associated with consequences and potentialities for pleasure or pain, and these automatically influence choices.

In the end, even though all this is understood, it takes great faith, fortitude, and trust in God to surrender the very core of the known to the unknown. At the final moment, the last vestiges of doubt and existential fear may surface from the depths. At that point, faith in the teachings of the masters that direct us to "Walk straight ahead, no matter what" arises and proves to be correct, for the glory of God awaits on the other side of the last great barrier.

Q: How can one prepare for such a final moment?

A: Having heard this, you are already prepared. One has to be willing to walk through the illusion that death of the self results in obliteration of existence. If one is holding the belief that "death is an illusion that I don't believe in," at the last moment, one will be confronted with who it is that thinks so. Then one discovers there really is no 'I' who thinks so, and that illusion dissolves or the fear of death arises to be faced. Only the spirit can walk through the final door; the ego is left behind and cannot pass.

Q: At that point, is there fear about the body?

A: In this particular case, that was not the problem at all. It was the core sense of 'I' that was overwhelmingly threatened. It seemed as if one's very basis of existence was at stake, and the ego feared nonexistence as the only possible alternative to its demise.

With compassion, one realizes that the structure of the ego is such that it cannot know what lies beyond. At best, it hopes that the familiar 'I' will still survive but somehow become 'enlightened'. It does not know nor can it know that only after its own demise, the Infinite 'I' instantly shines forth in its stead. In this particular case, the last nonverbal knowingness was the ancient sages' teaching to "go straight ahead, no matter what," but then, as the familiar identity of self dissolved, so did its capacity for memory, and only consciousness, naked of all props, remained as the Ultimate Reality.

Q: Then what remains to speak of the event?

A: Consciousness has multiple capacities. It may choose to speak again, or not, and in many cases, it does not. In that case, no word is heard, but an imprint is left in the field of consciousness so that someday, another advanced soul will again appear at the doorway and just suddenly 'know' what needs to be known. Not everything can be explained but it can be implied or alluded to. Any baggage has to be left at the doorway.

Q: So the final surrender is not of the self as the core of the ego, but one's attachment to it?

A: That is a serviceable way of expressing it. It is the attachment to the belief that the personal 'I' is the core of one's existence and is the source of life and the sense of 'I'. When that illusion is surrendered despite all obstacles, it is discovered that the sense of 'I-ness' had originated all along from the universal, impersonal 'I'. It is like a sunbeam which thinks that its light originates from itself and then discovers that all the while, the source of its illumination was really the sun. With this discovery, there is a giant relief.

Q: **These descriptions are encouraging and helpful.**

A: From a certain manner of description, the teachers of enlightenment are really the survivors of the death of the ego. Their words serve as guideposts and inspiration to the uncertainty of the spiritual student. There is nothing to gain from speaking about Truth, nor is there anyone to whom such gain would accrue. The words occur by the grace of the Self.

The attachment to the 'I' core of the ego is the belief that it is the source of one's life, so it seems as though one is surrendering life itself to God. That it is safe to do so is reinforced by faith, conviction, and the words of those who have done so. Therefore, it is essential that one verify for themselves the calibrated level of any teachings to which one is entrusting one's life and spiritual faith.

There are two kinds of teachers. There are the integrous, intelligent teachers who have learned of the truth and accurately report it but have not yet completely experienced it. Such teachers are often in the high 200s to the 500s and are excellent instructors. In that case, the level of truth that is being taught will differ numerically from the calibrated level of the teacher; however, such teachers are of great service because they are good at teaching and informed on teaching certain spiritual practices. Similarly, there are excellent ski instructors who have not necessarily skied all the difficult runs. There are great skiing adepts who are very poor teachers. Beethoven was a great composer but unlikely a great piano teacher. Thus, there are also enlightened sages who are not gifted with pedagogical skills. Their brief teachings may be cryptic and insufficiently fluent to be easily comprehended.

The second kind of teacher is one whose enlightenment can be authenticated to everyone's satisfaction. Some of these are not fluent but speak through assistants who are able to explain the teacher's words.

Teachers who have survived the death of the ego may not even be able to speak of the Infinite Reality for many years. A few are able to return to the world, but most are not.

Q: **There is confusion about the state of enlightenment and about the 'individual' to whom it 'happens' or who is it that has become enlightened. There is a common saying that the truly enlightened being does not 'claim' to be enlightened, so anybody who states that they are must be in error.**

A: There is great difficulty in describing a condition that is not within the experiential reality of the ego, and especially in answering a question the asking of which stems from the dualistic paradigm of reality of the questioner. An enlightened being *is* their condition; thus, there is no purpose to make a 'claim'. That is an ego view. Now, with kinesiologic testing, any state can be confirmed.

The personal self does not become enlightened or transformed but instead is assimilated, silenced, and replaced by a different condition altogether. By analogy, if one looks through the lens of a movie projector from one side, they see a movie as it appears on the screen. However, if one looks backwards from the other side of the lens, one sees only a brilliant light. Therefore, what is the reality of the function of the lens?

Another simple analogy is that a shadow does not become a sunbeam but is replaced by it. The ego is the shade; enlightenment is the consequence of the light of the Self that replaces it.

Implied in the common saying that we are discussing is the belief that to disclaim being enlightened is a form of modesty. This is a projection of the spiritual ego of the originator of such a statement for in the condition of enlightenment, no egotism remains. The state is merely a simple fact; it is not an achievement. It has no merits or anything which is laudatory that would require the posture of psuedo-humility. In the naïve spiritual community, there is much adulation, charismatic glamour, and importance attributed to 'enlightened masters', and the like. These are projections. To the enlightened being, the state is merely the natural condition of how it is.

At its onset, the state of enlightenment may seem spectacular or dramatic to the fleeing remains of the disappearing ego. Then peace prevails and there is really nothing to say because the state exists beyond all words. It would not be possible to refer to it in a manner that would have any meaning to other people.

In this case, nothing was said about it for more than thirty years, during which time there progressively arose the capacity to dissimilate as normalcy and function in the world. There was no one to whom such a condition would be comprehensible. Only twice were there meetings with known sages who comprehended the condition. The first was Muktananda, and later, Ramesh Balsekar. There was another such meeting on the streets of New York City that was mutually anonymous but total and complete.

Only slowly over the years did a method of making states of consciousness comprehensible come about. The kinesiologic phenomenon appeared to be the tool to cross over from the linear world of the ego and form to the nonlinear spiritual Reality that lay beyond.

Historically, all enlightened beings have described their state, and by doing so, proclaimed rather than claimed it. None have denied it or pretended that it did not exist.

The Buddha proclaimed the magnificence of the state of enlightenment which eventually became known as "Buddhahood." Jesus described his own condition as the "Christ of the Father in Heaven, Almighty God." Krishna described the Self as the "Supreme." To not acknowledge the Presence of God would be to negate the Allness and Divinity of God; this is not possible for an enlightened being.

By inference, the common saying that is being discussed implies that enlightenment is so rare that to 'claim' it would be a delusion. Because of the number of false teachers who have abounded over the centuries, that, indeed, is a possibility. However, we now have an objective and consensually verifiable test of the levels of consciousness with which to verify states of enlightenment and authenticity of teachings.

The false teacher is one who makes a claim in order to obtain some gains, such as fame, adulation, or followers. There are such entities and they often have enthused followers. We have discussed that problem previously.

Lastly, the expectations of the naïve spiritual seeker lead them to believe that an enlightened being will exhibit an array of mystical, magical, or mythical signs and behaviors, extending even to having bumps on their head or forehead. The naïve seeker expects to meet someone who is 'special' in appearance and demeanor. They are disappointed to find out that the genuine sage is essentially quite ordinary and without theatrical trappings. Because of religious art and icons over the centuries, the naïve seeker expects to see flowing robes, etc. In reality, the only intrinsic, real distinction of the true sage is the quality of the teachings and the power of the energy field of the consciousness that accompanies him. There is, however, an invisible aura, the energy field that supports the advancement of consciousness, and there is a connection between the aura of the visitor and that of the teacher which is facilitated by the intention of the seeker.

Q: What of the 'miraculous'?

A: If the karma of the visitor is 'ripe' and merely needs the catalyst of a higher energy to manifest, then such a potentiality may actualize. It is neither intended nor willed by the sage but happens spontaneously. Often, even the sage does not realize it has happened until witnesses report it later. It is not viewed as special any more than an apple's falling off a tree. It is seen as the natural course of events as they unfold in the manifest world.

 Healings take place of their own accord, and in a true healing, whether the affliction disappears or not is relatively immaterial because the actual healing occurs from within. Consciousness is a state of knowingness that transcends the physical. What is often relieved is not necessarily the physical or mental affliction but the suffering that has accompanied it. The miracle occurs as a transformation of context. The actual 'event' is within consciousness itself, and thus, the transformation of the afflicted person's consciousness brings about a self-healing which may or not be exhibited externally.

Q: Is the statement "I am enlightened" possible for a true sage?

A: The question reveals a well-advanced understanding. The answer is no. The errors that would be involved in such a statement are several. To say "am" is already a divergence from Absolute Truth. It is an intransitive verb (like 'being' or 'is-ness'). The word "enlightened" in that sense would be in the form of a descriptive term that implies an added-on attribute or quality. The 'I' of Absolute Reality is a Self-identity and the complete and total statement. In the statement "I am that," both "am" and "that" are superfluous and misleading. In actuality, enlightenment is neither a state nor a viewpoint, yet it is both, and there is no statement about it that is completely accurate.

A cat is just one hundred percent a cat; it doesn't need the word "cat" and doesn't even need to know that it 'is'. The word "cat" is an invention of language, which is valuable as a pragmatic convenience. The reality of self-existence, self-completion, and self-identity is already complete in the cat's being a cat (i.e., existence).

To be enlightened is merely to be like the cat; the reality is total and complete and is not an additional condition. It seeks neither recognition nor validation because such things are irrelevant.

The term "enlightenment" is semantically correct. It is the recognition and realization that one's reality is the light of the Self and that it stems from within as an awareness and profound, self-evident Reality.

Q: Is doubt the reason for questioning the authenticity of enlightenment as a possibility?

A: That is an important observation. There is a form of realistic doubt that merely seeks confirmation and is therefore rational and part of wisdom.

This is in contrast to what might be called a form of pathologic doubt, which is the expression of the grandiosity of the narcissistic ego of the questioner that sees its imaginary omnipotence as negated and challenged by the possibility of the Real. This sometimes takes the form of severe psychopathology and the megalomania of malice and hatred.

Historically, we note that many great leaders of truth, equality, peace, and spiritual reality have been assassinated, such as Jesus Christ, Mahatma Gandhi, Abraham Lincoln, Answar Sadat, Martin Luther King, John F. Kennedy, Jr., and others. In addition to the successful assassinations of many presidents and other well-known leaders, there have also been many attempts (such as on the current Pope) that were thwarted before they became finalized. Unconsciously, these psychotically delusional entities seek to kill God, so to speak, to prove that their own grandiose, narcissistic ego is greater than God. We also note historically that great works of art, such as the *Pieta*, were attacked by mad men. A local sand sculptor repeatedly had to replace the heads of Jesus and the Apostles in his creation of *The Last Supper* due to their nighttime destruction. He finally just abandoned repairing the display and, in fact, dismantled it.

The desire to desecrate beauty is seen in the displays of graffiti. There are many people who hate beauty, in a sense, and take delight in degrading and even killing young children. The serial killer hates the beauty of the feminine and seeks to desecrate it by mutilation. The wanton killer or the killer in every act defies the authority of God. The grandiose psychotic is the biggest threat to presidents and other persons who threaten the ego of the zealot.

Famous spiritual leaders have also been poisoned 'to see if they would die'. Sometimes these psychotic acts become politicized, such as the bombings of the Federal Building in Oklahoma City and the World Trade Center Towers in New York City. The more grandiose the setting, the greater the pleasure of the attacker who seeks the attention of the public. The jealous megalomaniac seeks to prove that (in the core of the ego) they are greater than God. The lower astral realms are populated by many such entities. They hate the sovereignty of God because it jeopardizes the sovereignty of their own inflated egos and challenges their authenticity.

Evil is not the opposite of God but simply the denial of God, just as falsity is not the opposite of truth but its refusal. The deification of the self does not lead to Godness but to the grandiose delusions of egomania and religious psychosis.

CHAPTER TWENTY-ONE
SPIRITUAL RESEARCH

Q: **Historically, most spiritual teachers have represented the flowering of a lineage, a spiritual tradition, or a school of teaching. What would you describe as your spiritual roots or spiritual foundation?**

A: The Presence of the Self is the inner teacher. In this lifetime, there was exposure to traditional Christianity as a child. During adolescence, however, this turned into a long period of agnosticism which lasted for twenty years. This was followed by some searching for truth by browsing through Buddhism and Zen, but all this searching was given up as futile. In the end, it was discarded and abandoned.

Although there had been intense, inner spiritual experiences in childhood and adolescence, plus a near-death experience, their significance had not been comprehended. During young adulthood, there was the completion of four years of classical psychoanalysis which was very successful in reaching its objectives. Despite the psychological success and all the gains in the view of the ordinary world, there was an inner core within consciousness that was desperate to reach some greater truth.

Attempts at developing true spiritual awareness turned out to be discouraging. In fact, with intensification, spiritual endeavor led to a deeper and deeper black despair that culminated in the crisis of a descent into the lower depths of hell where there was obliteration of all hope of deliverance. There was emergence in total spiritual darkness and the agony of existential terror and aloneness. While in the timeless depths of hell, there arose an inner voice that said, "If there is a God, I ask Him for help."

Following that request, an oblivion of unknown duration occurred. It was perhaps a day later when the oblivion suddenly disappeared and was replaced by the stunning splendor of the Light of Divinity that shone forth as the radiance and essence of Allness. The Infinite stood forth as the all-encompassing Reality. The Self shone forth as the essence of pure awareness for there was neither subject nor object. The state of the Self was and is the radical subjectivity of the Presence and is not different from the Supreme, which is beyond all categories. By analogy, the sunlight that illuminates the stratosphere is no different from the sunlight that illuminates the Earth. One is not 'transcendent' and the other 'immanent'. They are only points of view that originate from a positionality. No positionalities are possible in the total completeness of Allness. The Infinite is equally present and fully expressed as both a grain of sand and in the totality of the universes.

Q: **The term "Self" is not a familiar term in traditional Western religion.**

A: It is a term that originates from the state of enlightenment that emerges at the consciousness level of approximately 740. There are much misunderstanding and lack of authentic information about the states of enlightenment.

To begin with, there are not just two contrasting states, such as enlightened or unenlightened. The realizations of enlightenment formally and classically begin at calibrated consciousness level 600, which is beyond the state of bliss experienced in the high 500s and is incapacitating. Surrender of the bliss state to God opens the revelation which marks consciousness level 600, where incapacitating bliss is replaced by infinite peace, stillness, and silence.

**Q: If there are not two contrasting states, such as enlight-
ened versus unenlightened, then what is the correct
understanding of the term "enlightened"?**

A: There are stages or levels of enlightenment that are
progressive. We can calibrate them so as to calibrate the
different terms that have been used over the ages. These
are not levels of Reality but levels of the degree of
awareness of Reality.

The levels do not denote 'better than' lower levels but
only the position of perspective, much as one might
describe the appearance of the world from different
levels of the stratosphere, or the characteristics of the
oceans at different depths below sea level.

The following calibrations were determined during an
investigative workshop:

Sainthood	Very close to enlightenment	575
Bliss	"Sat-chit-ananda"	575+
Enlightenment	Bliss replaced by peace, stillness, and silence	600
"I Am"	Awareness of the "I" as beingness or is-ness	650
Self	As Existence	680
Sage		700
Sage	Self as God Manifest	740
"I" (as a total statement)	As the Ultimate Reality; the Supreme	740
Self	As beyond Existence or Nonexistence	840
Avatar		985
Buddhahood	At-oneness with God Manifest and Unmanifest	1,000
Krishna/Christ Consciousness	At-oneness with God Manifest and Unmanifest	1,000
"I"	As the Ultimate Reality beyond this dimension transcending dimensions	1,100

"I"	As Essence of Creation	1,200
Archangel		50,000+
Divinity		Infinite

Q: **The calibrated levels of consciousness serve as a point of reference and are not really distinct levels of Reality as such?**

A: Calibrations are merely a shorthand means of denoting a level of consciousness that specifies both context and content. Each level has its own view of what is real and meaningful. This results in differences in motivation, value, lifestyle, or spiritual positionalities. Each level indicates a transcendence of what has preceded it and also indicates the tasks that lie ahead. It could be compared simplistically to school grade levels. Eighth-grade material is beyond seventh-grade but not yet ninth-grade material. Spiritual evolution is similar in that the higher levels of consciousness are comparable to college, post-graduate, doctoral, and then post-doctoral research and discovery.

The difference between spiritual work and academic study is that the subject of spiritual study is the self of the student, and as desired truths are discovered, the student transforms and evolves until the self disappears and is replaced by the Self. By spiritual inspiration, the Awareness of the Self may continue to evolve to an ever expanding context that eventually transcends dimensions as expressions of the Reality of God. The seeming realities of the ego are transcended at consciousness level 600, which denotes the transition from the Newtonian linear paradigm of reality to the nonlinear domain of spiritual truth.

Q: **The idea that a higher level of consciousness is better than one below it is therefore just a projection of egotism?**

A: That is correct. No calibrated level is better than another; it merely denotes different subject matter. Although, throughout history, mankind has been impressed with the state of enlightenment, from the viewpoint of the ultimate possibility of God, it is only a beginning. Comparably, to a high school student, a college degree seems very advanced, but to a post-doctoral researcher, it is merely a bare-minimum requirement.

While consciousness level 600 is rare and 1,000 rarer still, archangels calibrate at or over 50,000. Although not discernible from our dimension, such enormously high energies influence all life in all its expressions. We might say that what is considered a spiritual master within the human dimension is, in turn, an evolving student in much higher dimensions. Each spiritual student is therefore a teacher to those who are behind and a student of those who are ahead.

To be effective, a teacher has to be suitable for the audience that is being addressed. An avatar is the founder of a religion and therefore one who has the teaching capacity to be meaningful to large numbers of people over great expanses of time. There have been very evolved beings on the planet who did not verbally teach because that was not their talent or destiny. To influence the consciousness level of mankind, it is not necessary to actually language one's realization.

Enlightenment is therefore a progressive realization and does not represent a finished product, or a final end, or the completion of the evolution of spiritual possibility. The great spiritual masters of the past were speaking to a human population that calibrated at only 100 or below. The consciousness level of mankind has now made the critical, enormous leap to 207, which means that a much different field of consciousness now prevails.

There are an infinite number of dimensions in which there are an infinite number of infinitely expanding universes emerging into infinite possibilities. The actualization of each potentiality automatically energizes the creation of an infinite number of evolutions of potentialities that then become the nuclei of a subsequent series of infinite progressions, namely, the infinite potentiality implied by Quantum Theory. Due to languaging, this description lacks perfection, but it tries to convey a sense of the information. Because the essence of God is the catalyst of Creation, all that is created contains that same quality. Therefore, the ultimate context of God is an infinite progression of infinite potentialities and possibilities, each of which then creates a further infinite progression of infinite progressions. Although not really satisfactory, the explanation is the view from the perspective of Self as at one with the Creator.

As one can see from calibrated level 600 and over, and especially beyond 1,000, there is no longer concern about the ego, which is finally seen as the residual problems of mankind in its effort to transcend its animal-origin qualities. Humankind is only one potentiality of the Unmanifest becoming manifest. Transcending the ego is therefore probably like kindergarten to consciousness levels 1,000 and up.

Mankind develops progressively in all areas of science, technology, industry, physics, and medicine, so it is not surprising that spiritual awareness would also keep pace. It may, in fact, be the catalyst for the further evolution of mankind in all areas. In evolution, each species reached its ultimate potential and stopped there. From the trunk of the evolutionary tree, the next more highly evolved species then rose anew. This was also true in the evolution of the primate species. Homo erectus and Homo sapiens were different branches and not just the further evolution of either Cro-Magnon or Neanderthal Man. The nature of truth and the universe does not change, but man's comprehension of it progressively advances in all areas.

Q: Can this be affirmed?

A: The appearance of a means of discovering truth from nontruth (falsehood) signaled the onset of a new potentiality. To be unable to tell truth from falsehood is such a staggering limitation that it precluded further development of consciousness, and that ignorance kept mankind in the dark for millennia. Without any reliable test for guidance or ascertaining direction, man has been able to advance only by means of his directionless, basically animal curiosity. Like the curiosity of the animal, the intelligence of mankind sniffed here and there, poked into this and that, and came upon endless discoveries. Then came the curiosity about what these discoveries meant. What were they for? Religion tried to supply some guideposts but even they were frequently quite faulty, misunderstood, or simply ignored by the masses. When spiritual values were negated, massive destruction to humanity ensued and millions perished as a consequence of spiritual ignorance. The Dark Ages still prevail in large areas of this world.

Q: **Is this last decade the beginning of a new era?**

A: The potentiality has advanced and has already manifested as the elevation of the collective consciousness from 190 to 207. What is important about that jump is not that it is just seventeen points, although that in itself is quite sizeable, but that it crossed the critical line at 200, which totally changed the characteristics. Consciousness level 207 has totally different qualities from those at 190. It would be comparable to water in that when it reaches the boiling point at 212 degrees, it suddenly turns into a gas, at which point it is no longer a liquid but a vapor and capable of totally different effects in the universe.

Q: **From the perspective of an advanced consciousness level, there is an awareness of a multiplicity of dimensions. Is there any bridge between that awareness and what is already known to human science?**

A: That potentiality is suggested as a possibility by the so-called "string theory" of advanced theoretical physics. That possibility would also be suggested if it was discovered that over great eons of time, the so-called "alpha constant" reveals even the most minute variation. Comprehension of such vastness requires the expansion of parameters that tax the limits of intelligence.

Q: **Would not even the concept of an infinite number of dimensions be a positionality?**

A: Yes. That is an astute observation signifying that the listener has understood these discourses. The Ultimate Reality is neither subject to nor limited to dimensions, levels, or domains but instead transcends and yet *is* all of them as Allness.

Humanity is merely one expression of that potentiality. Mankind identifies itself as intelligence, which is its capacity to comprehend and formulate. Beyond intelligence is a higher level of reality that is beyond formulation or definition. It is also beyond witnessing, observing, or experiencing. It is beyond beingness or existence. It is neither manifest nor unmanifest. The Source of the Infinite itself is infinite.

Q: **What is the expression of the Self in other dimensions?**

A: Self has what could best be described as seemingly different prevailing qualities at various levels of consciousness. Below 600, self is experienced as ego. Beyond 600, self becomes the Self of the Love of God. At that level, the luminescence of the Presence is exquisite bliss, which then progressively dissolves into a primordial peace and stillness that encompasses and is the Divine Essence of all Existence. Beyond that, the predominant quality of the Presence is its Radiance as the existence of Allness. Further on, the Reality is beyond existence or manifestation, and beyond that, the *anlag* of the Self reveals itself as the ultimate omnipotentiality of the Unmanifest prior to consciousness itself, yet including it by virtue of being its essence.

An entire universe or dimension can arise out of a single thought. There are, therefore, infinite universes, dimensions, and planes within dimensions because every potentiality creates an infinite number of potentialities, all of which, in turn, create an infinite series of potentialities, and so on.

Q: That is beyond comprehension.

A: That is the knowingness of Self-knowingness as the essence of Creation. All is spontaneous and self-creating. The essence of Divinity is present in all Creation as Creation itself. The infinite infinity of the infinite diversity of Allness is self-creating.

Universes are not created by something outside of them but by that which is innately within their essence. Universes, domains, and dimensions are self-creating and self-evolving because of the omnipresence of Divinity.

The Supreme could be likened to an intrinsic quality or capacity for potentiality and existence. Therefore, the Ultimate is described as beyond form or existence or manifestation; beyond is-ness or beingness; beyond consciousness or awareness; beyond Allness or Void, and beyond all qualities, descriptions, or definitions. Language is an attempt to indicate that which cannot be languaged but which can be known only by virtue of being it.

Q: Are these truths innately discoverable?

A: Yes. Students say they struggle to stay in the 'now'. The answer is that one does not have to look for what is already present and is the only reality possible. The complaint is that "my mind is always either in the past or anticipating the future." They are talking about the content of the mind. Even if the mind is looking at the past or the future, it can do so only in the present moment. It is only because consciousness is constantly present that one can elect to review the past or anticipate the future.

Time is merely a positionality and not Reality. The awareness comes from identifying with what it is that identifies itself with time and discovering that it is merely perception, and that the qualities of consciousness are timeless and impersonal. If you think about China, that does not mean that you are in China, because the Self is always 'here'. The positionalities of 'here' and 'now' tend to prevail. They are independent of content. Even to believe that one is 'in this universe' or even 'of it' is a positionality. It is a mistake to identify with time, space, or dimension as it is a limitation. The Self does not experience 'now' at all but instead realizes its foreverness, its 'always-ness'.

There is no 'you', and it is not 'here' or 'here now', nor is it in 'this dimension'. The Ultimate Reality supersedes even existence or a descriptive term such as "consciousness" or "awareness." The Self is neither present nor is it not present. Enlightenment is neither a state nor a condition, neither a level of consciousness nor a realization, yet it is all of them.

Q: Until the present time, the human nervous system has been capable of handling the energy of consciousness level 1,000.

A: The human body is not yet biologically equipped to handle the process without considerable discomfort. Even 2,500 years ago, the Buddha described going through the same process of being racked with pain as though his bones had cracked; Christ sweat blood and also went though physical pain and agony. That seems to be a byproduct of the evolution of consciousness through the 800s and 900s.

Q: What accounts for such an evolution of consciousness?

A: One can postulate karma, commitment, dedication, devotion, and willingness to be of service to God and mankind. One is also assisted from 'on high' (by archangels). Consciousness of its own nature keeps advancing until it meets an error that has to be corrected. Perseverance resolves the positionality into a knowingness.

This is an unusual occurrence. More often, as consciousness reaches level 600, it stops there and remains so for the rest of the lifetime. This occurs because each level of revelation is so complete and self-fulfilling that the sense of completion brings the evolution of consciousness in that individual to a halt. That is why most enlightened beings stop once they cross the line to 600. The bliss is total and it does not seem that there could possibly be anything 'more'. It is not even plausible that there could be anything further, and from a certain viewpoint, that conclusion is correct. Each level is total and complete in itself. That sense of completeness, finality, and totality is characteristic of every level beyond the high 500s. Therefore, there is neither curiosity nor any sense of incompleteness, nor is there any tendency toward further investigation.

Characteristic of the evolution of this consciousness, however, was that at each level, an openness still persisted. There was an awareness that it was not a complete but an ongoing process. Perhaps there was also a willingness which the Self utilized for further evolution of the expression of its own essence and potentiality. The essential element was the willingness to surrender to that process, which was happening on its own. Creation expresses its potential when conditions are favorable.

Q: What is the understanding of Jesus Christ's saying "I came with a sword"?

A: Truth is a sword that cuts away ignorance and the barriers of the ego, along with its proclivity for deception and denial. This quote has been distorted to justify the use of force and physical wars.

Q: From a certain viewpoint, each spiritual teacher in history has had a specific effect and, from the common viewpoint, a purpose. Is there any such identifiable intention to these teachings?

A: The purpose is clarification and explanation so as to recontextualize and accommodate comprehension and understanding. Many paradoxes and misinterpretations have arisen in the history of religion which have left mankind with doubt and misunderstanding. These misinterpretations and confusion have resulted in large numbers of people's dismissing religion because of its ambiguities, lack of clarity, and lack of adherence to its own teachings. With the tools of spiritual research now available, clarification is possible for everyone merely for the asking. The purpose of the calibrated levels of consciousness and the kinesiologic test is to provide a means to understand truth and verify and document it in terms that are open to consensual validation.

No accurate navigation or mapping of the world was possible before the advent of the compass and the sextant; no real knowledge of the cosmos was obtainable without the telescope; and no knowledge of bacteria or sickness was available without the invention of the microscope. The discovery and harnessing of electricity transformed the world and human life. Each discovery expands man's knowledge and, similarly, spiritual research and discovery are now possible and available to all.

When looked at from an historical viewpoint, ex-tremely high consciousness levels seem remarkable, but if that phenomenon is recontextualized in the possibility of the future, it will probably be looked back at from a future time as quite rudimentary, just as we look at the earliest airplanes as antiques.

Q: The kinesiologic test is limited to use by only those people who calibrate over 200 and with motivation that is in integrity.

A: That is apparently its innate safeguard. Only integrity has access to truth.

Q: That does not seem 'fair'. A test of truth is denied to those who need it the most!

A: But that *is* what is 'fair' to the universe! One has to

discern the difference between 'rights' and 'privileges'. All so-called rights are merely privileges that are granted by societal agreement. To understand that concept spells the difference between gratitude and arrogance. The illusion of 'rights' is an ego inflation which can lead to a narcissistic positionality of entitlement, with its hostile, demanding, unappreciative, and paranoid attitudes. One cannot acquire rights by oneself; they are an earned gift from a free society. All rights are also subject to the limitations of context, such as civil rights in times of war or the right to hike in the woods during a drought.

Monarchs used to claim the 'divine right of kings' to justify trampling the masses and denying any more responsibility. Note that any so-called rights can be obliterated by a mere stroke of the pen. The United States Constitution (which calibrates at over 700) states that the equality of all citizens stems from the divinity of their Creator. To be created by God is not a right but a gift. The government and citizens are then expected to conduct themselves in a manner in accordance with that spiritual reality.

Even the Constitutional rights to life, liberty, and happiness can be lost as the result of committing a crime. Then, again, the rights of the accused are subject to interpretation and legal argument. Americans are shocked to hear that in many foreign countries, the accused have no rights at all. Even in America, the right to a trial by a jury of one's peers is not an actuality but an ideal. DNA tests have revealed that multitudes of innocents have been executed. Prosecutors and witnesses deliberately falsify evidence, and many juries consist of persons without the necessary intellectual capacity to even understand the facts presented. It is interesting to note that the concept of rights calibrates at 240, whereas that of privilege calibrates at 520—a very large difference.

Q: **Do the calibrated levels indicate levels of truth or reality?**

A: No. The calibration is only an indication of the degree of awareness or understanding. What seems like truth varies from level to level, as does the capacity for comprehension or adherence to aligning one's life and choices that are concordant; for example, the person hears of the truth but does not practice it.

Q: **Can you give an example of ordinary spiritual research as is done by a spiritual research group?**

A: Very decisive and critical information can be discovered which then explains otherwise ambiguous observations. For instance, the mantra "Om" calibrates at 740. On the other hand, the mantra "A-u-m" calibrates at only 65. There are probably many individuals and groups around the world that are reciting the mantra "A-u-m" and wondering why they don't become enlightened.

There are all kinds of religious practices and beliefs that are not only ineffective but are actually deleterious and have an effect exactly opposite to the one desired. There are spiritual-sounding shibboleths originating from astral realms that are channeled through mediums who become widely quoted with much significant eyebrow raising as if to give them an aura of some high master's secret teaching. Many such quotes are nonsense, but naïve believers are readily seduced and impressed. All so-called masters or teachers, as well as practices, methods, techniques, breathing exercises, chants, or any other supposed spiritual truth or practice should be examined and calibrated. As in many human endeavors, the high value of that which is genuine attracts an invasion by fraudulent imitations. This is especially so in the field of spirituality

Q: **You have taught some people spiritual 'first aid'. How does that work?**

A: To terminate an upset, do the following:

1. "Thump the thymus." The thymus gland is located behind the upper breastbone. Thump that area with a closed hand and say, at the same time, "Ha-ha-ha" rhythmically three times, and then, after a pause, do it three more times. Smile while doing that and picture something or someone that you love. That could be a divine figure or even one's favorite pet. (The thymus is the controller of the acupuncture energy system and is related to one's overall immune health, which is prone to suppression by stress.) This method was originally taught by Dr. John Diamond. (See Suggested Reading.)

2. Then breathe spiritual energy from the base of the spine up to the crown chakra. On each inhalation, picture it as Light. It flows from the base of the spine to the crown of the head. Even a few breaths done in this way will cause a very noticeable effect.

3. While doing the breathing, think or sound the syllable, "Om," as you proceed with the above. (The "O" is pronounced like the name of the letter "O", i.e., "ō")

4. Picture someone you love.

5. While involved in this process, find within yourself the willingness in your heart to surrender anything and everything to God and recommit your devotion above all else.

The above instructions will lift one quickly and easily out of the arena of conflict and distress. It does not take practice and the results are obvious, even on the first try. This can be followed up by prayer and meditation that focus attention on the whole picture (peripheral vision) of what one is witnessing, rather than getting stuck and involved in details. Equanimity is retained by relating to a total situation instead of to any of its parts. This tends to keep one at the level of witness rather than at the effect of the details with attachment to outcome.

Q: **How can one diminish the upset that sometimes arises from the spiritual work of soul searching?**

A: We can learn from the experience of classical psycho-analysis in which there was the rule, "Always approach the patient's problems first from the side of the super ego (conscience) before beginning the uncovering process of what lies in wait in the unconscious." This means to first soften the conscience, make it more reasonable, and diminish its capacity to be rigid and judgmental with black-and-white, right-and-wrong attitudes and judgments. Unattenuated, the super-ego or conscience can be extremely cruel and savage unless domesticated. It is from this area of the ego that self-hatred and even suicide caused by guilt can result.

A rigid person who is prone to black-and-white judgmentalism has to be educated to see things in context as part of being human. One has to develop a more benign, forgiving, and compassionate attitude. The rational ego has to become more easygoing and accept-ing because, in the deepest layers of the unconscious, there are the forbidden impulses that originate from the animal mind. The deeper layer of the unconscious, the "Id," thinks in extremes and uses extreme symbolism. It doesn't just hate its enemies, it frankly wants to kill them.

In spiritual work, likewise, the education about the intrinsic nature of the ego and its evolution and struc-ture helps one to see that it is an inherited, impersonal mechanism that has to be softened. It is important for the seeker to realize that the human mind has no capac-ity to differentiate truth from falsehood. Before plumb-ing the depths, the capacity and willingness for forgive-ness, love, and compassion need to be strengthened.

Ignorance is an inborn human inheritance. In addi-tion, the majority of mankind is extremely naïve. In the Western world, for instance, people are not even aware of their karmic inheritance or its profound influences.

They think there is only a personal 'me' of this lifetime who is making choices or decisions. Similarly, there is a prevailing ignorance of the difference between religion and spirituality.

To understand that the mind operates by means of positionalities tends to obviate guilt and self-attack. The spiritual aspirant also needs to attenuate self-blame by realizing that human consciousness tends to be dominated by the collective consciousness and energy fields.

By its very nature, the pathway to God is not easy. It requires considerable courage, fortitude, willingness, and forbearance. It is strengthened by humility and a benign conscience.

Q: **Before starting serious self-examination, can one tell in advance how potentially 'dangerous' their own conscience (super-ego) might be?**

A: Yes, one can just simply calibrate it. If this is not possible or acceptable, then one can pretty well evaluate what is present by looking at what punishments one thinks that evil-doers and society deserve for this is the same fate that your conscience holds in abeyance for you. If you think evil-doers deserve death, then that is the very same sentence that you have already pronounced on yourself.

The 'downside' of human history remains alive and merely concealed within the unconscious. One has to realize early into self-discovery that one is likely to find negativities that may be upsetting. To ameliorate the reaction, it is necessary to realize that this material is not the real you and yet needs the light of day to be extinguished. At its roots, the ego is the extreme of selfishness and is completely lacking in all ethical principles.

As will be remembered from the famous Zen ox-herding pictures, the ox is wild and needs to be tamed before it can safely be ridden. At all times, remain aware that the real you is not the ego. Refuse to identify with it. One can practice this awareness when one watches television, reads the paper, or watches a movie. Observe that society is merely the stage upon which the ego is demonstrated for all to see. This educational observation leads to nonattachment. It is not really necessary to subdue the ego but merely to stop identifying with it. Although, in the depths of the ego there is the desire to kill one's enemies, that is not the real you but one's animal inheritance as it exists in the human brain and the collective consciousness.

Q: What if one is unable to use the kinesiologic method?

A: There are many people who do know how to use the test. There are charts of levels of consciousness, many web sites, and many holistic practitioners who use kinesiology and are willing to teach it. The simple "yes-no" response can even be elicited with any naïve child as a test subject. There are also classes, workshops, and videos that demonstrate the techniques. The books by Dr. John Diamond spell it out in detail. The easiest procedure is to follow teachings that have already been calibrated and authenticated.

Refuse to be impressed or mystified by the bizarre, the secret, the truths that have to be paid for; avoid the throngs that flock to the novelties. Remember that the lower astral realms, which are the source of psuedo-spiritual tricksters, are the realms of those who have denied God. Their purpose is to waylay and ensnare the naïve and vulnerable. One of their favorite tricks is to sound pious and cite ancient religious figures in order to convey an aura of authenticity. Note that the truly realized individuals do not state that their awareness stems from any external sources, entities, 'ancient masters', or persons. The Presence of God is solely its own authority and requires no confirmation.

CHAPTER TWENTY-TWO
APPLICATIONS

T ruth is radical pragmatism. An understanding of the nature and mechanisms of consciousness and its inner 'laws' is the very essence of ultimate practicality. It bypasses the arid, circuitous sophistry of intellectualism as well as the egocentricity and narcissism of emotionality.

Like the X-ray or CAT scan, the delineation of the elements of the field of consciousness in any situation lays bare its bones and reveals the core elements at work. It is a strict discipline, unadorned and not obscured by sentimentality or the ego's distortions.

Emotional and intellectual errors, as well as religious and political errors, are perpetrated by distortions of either content, context, or both. Sentimentality and emotionalism are presented as justifications to violate even the basic rules of logic. The damaging consequences of these lapses of integrity to society are enormous. They block and impede progress in major areas of life. Major social disasters go on for centuries before the fallacy of their basis is exposed. The serious seeker of spiritual truth cannot afford such deceptions. The way to Truth is via radical honesty.

True asceticism means stringent adherence to truth, and it means of the spirit and not the body. To become a pious, ragged, semi-starved, skin-and-bones entity is a self-indulgence and has nothing to do with Reality. The focus on 'purification of the body', with all kinds of 'cleansings' to get rid of 'toxins' and 'poisons', is a distraction

Purification means to purify the mind of its illusions, attachments, and parroting of supposedly spiritual clichés.

Heaven is not restricted to vegetarians. It is better to eat meat and be enlightened than to piously avoid it as 'not spiritual'. The human body *is* meat. Any lion knows that.

Whether to 'eat meat' or 'have sex' or 'work for money' are all classic life "koans" (puzzles, paradoxes) which present themselves to the spiritual initiate. They are valuable because they unearth numerous belief systems for examination. They involve looking at meaning, significance, values, propositions, and attachments. It is rewarding to give up the attachment to the glamour of 'being spiritual', 'holy', or 'special'. Truth has no trappings. Many false teachers indulge in theatrical self-presentations which are merely lures and self-gratifications of being 'special'.

The Absolute Reality of Enlightenment is complete and total. It has no role or function to fulfill, no purpose to serve, and no rituals to perform. The condition is anonymous and without name or title. If asked, it states the truth of what it is to the degree that such a condition can be verbalized. The state of enlightenment is invisible, and the truly enlightened pass about unnoticed in ordinary life. Neither is there anything about which to be humble or prideful. The field of consciousness of the state of enlightenment is a nonpersonal emanation radiating from the essence of the state, and what the world considers remarkable is merely ordinary to the Self.

The ego, or more accurately, the belief that one *is* the ego, obscures the Realization of the Reality of the Self as the Oneness of All That Is. The dissolution of the ego results in liberation from the bondage of the illusions that create suffering. These illusions are susceptible to fearless scrutiny that reveals the underlying fallacies. The only tool needed is the willingness to unreservedly surrender all beliefs, opinions, and attitudes to God.

To surrender what one thinks they are to God does not leave one as 'nothing', but quite the contrary. It leads to the discovery that one is everything. Every identification is a limitation. Upon examination, every 'am' turns out to be merely a 'doing'. Even the belief that one's true self is an 'is' or an 'am-ness' is an illusion.

If all actions are taking place spontaneously and not being caused by an inner doer, then the emergence of the ego is a spontaneous and impersonal phenomenon. Like any other expression of life, the belief in the independent, self-existent, autonomous 'I' arose of its own—unasked, unwilled, unchosen, unbidden, and impersonal.

Even one's name was chosen by circumstances. It is an arbitrary, nominal designation for purposes of identification, like a license plate on a car. It is well to disidentify with that name. To adopt a new spiritual name is to merely perpetuate the illusion and give it a holier implication (which is probably more of an ego trap than being content with one's name as Tom or Betty). To identify with a personal name is a limitation. The family name also signifies attachments to subtle identifications. Reality has no name; it is merely a linguistic designation for purposes of communication, similar to the term "God."

Any self-designation or description is illusory. Even the statement "to be enlightened" is misleading and not a reality. The state is beyond 'being' anything and there is no one to 'be' that condition. The words "state" or "conditions" are chosen as being closest to the describable truth but again merely allude to what is not able to be accurately captured in words.

Q: If the ego arose spontaneously, then when did it arise? If one is personally not the author of one's ego, then what is its origin?

A: One will first discover that its origin is beyond recall. No momentous decision or making of a conscious choice can be discovered. Like a mushroom that pops up overnight seemingly out of nowhere, the ego also popped up from the hidden spores of karma. That karma is, in essence, the karma of consciousness unfolding and emerging once again as its own continuance. The sense and belief of 'I am' is the spore. The elaborations and identifications are merely added on later.

This rebirth of the ego/self/I occurs again every morning upon awakening. With observation, one can see that awareness returns at first as merely the return of conscious awareness. As the identifications slowly reappear, one becomes aware of location, but the awakening mind doesn't even know what day it is. Then it slowly again identifies with the world, place, time, and name, and all the past identifications return from memory.

Q: **Without memory, how would the self know who or what it is?**

A: It is useful to pretend that one has no memory.

Q: **Then, who is one?**

A: To refuse memory, which is the vast storehouse of illusions, leads to a clear approach to self-inquiry. It leads to the discovery that there is no actual 'who'; there is only awareness.

Q: **What is it that remembers? What if one refuses to identify with memory at all?**

A: Amazingly, the Self has no memory. Its emergence as the Ultimate Reality is shorn of all past identifications. It is like the newborn child who looks around in wonderment. It is born complete, total, and all-knowing and thus needs no memory. The Self knows, by virtue of its essence, all that exists beyond time and therefore beyond memory. Later, it utilizes the former memory but does not misidentify with it as the self but instead as a record of what was once believed. It utilizes data but does not identify with it. If recall is necessary, it is deliberate, and one is no longer at the effect of memory. Memory leads to the continuance of illusions and a record of how the false sense of 'I' arose.

Upon awakening in the morning, the first realization is the nonverbalized knowingness of consciousness itself; then, that one exists, and that is all. The awakening body resumes actions and performs what it has been programmed to do. In animals, we call that propensity 'instinct'. The senses guide the body's movements. With the awakening of the mind, selection begins to take place which leads to thought and planning. The activity of the mind gradually awakens and takes precedence.

Q: How does the experience of thought occur?

A: To fully comprehend any phenomenon requires the relinquishment of the belief in 'cause' as it is commonly understood. In contrast, there is what is best termed "simultaneity," or the Jungian term "synchronicity." Creation unfolds according to the laws of consciousness. An influence which is invisible and situated within the nonlinear has consequences; it becomes visible in the world of form as the unfolding of consequences which are seen in the visible world as sequence. To the dualistic perception of the ego, the sequence appears to represent causality.

To understand human events, it is necessary to realize that awareness is a quality of consciousness. Brain function occurs as a biologic consequence of neuronal activity, but awareness occurs within the etheric body, which is generally concordant (isomeric) with the physical organ. This fact is clear to people who reach higher levels of consciousness, and also to people who have past-life recall, out-of-body, or near-death experiences.

Thus, there is a series of spiritual energy bodies associated with the physical which are not within the realm of traditional science. There are segments of the scientific community that are even quite hostile to any possibility of a nonlinear reality, and they put forth efforts to discredit it. The method that is used for such a purpose could be called 'the fallacy of mimicry'. The orientation of scientific fundamentalists is biologic material reductionism. For example, if stimulating part of the brain creates an experience similar to those of spiritual states, then the inference is supposed to be that spiritual experiences are therefore unreal and merely a brain reaction to anoxia or some other stimulus.

To disprove this fallacious hypothesis, one can now just calibrate the energy fields involved to identify the real from the mimicry. With brain stimulation, the consciousness level remains the same, but with a near-death experience, it significantly escalates and the person is permanently transformed.

Similar irrelevancies are used to imitate spiritual phenomena as though the fact that the Real can be imitated disproves the real (which is a non sequitur). The basic fallacy of such attempts to discredit valid spiritual experience is that the cited evidence is from a different domain and not even applicable (such as looking for spirits with a Geiger counter). The fact that a computerized model can closely imitate actual human life does not prove that human life is a fallacy.

Q: **The terms "synchronicity" or "simultaneity" seem to explain many phenomena of life far better than does "linear causality."**

A: It is more inclusive and holistic. The spin of an electron on one side of the universe does not 'cause' the spin of an electron on the other side of the universe; instead, they are both responding to an unseen force outside the field of perception.

In *Power versus Force,* this third element, which is outside the field of observation of a seeming pair of events, is the actual explanation. "ABC" held in consciousness unfolds in the observable, perceptual world of form as A-B-C. The mind then impugns causality and supposes that what is happening is A → B → C. That is the basic illusion of the perceptual world of form. In personal life, the ego makes the same mistake, thinking that there must be a central, independent 'I' or 'me' that is causing 'events'. This is the classical, logical fallacy of *ad hoc ergo propter hoc.*

Q: **Is the problem then the misidentification of Creation as causation?**

A: It is even more subtle and important than that, for to make this basic error precludes an understanding of the ongoing presence of God as the ever present source of All That Is, and its ongoing, ever present Essence as continuous Creator. The world thinks that if a sequence of events is observed, each element in the sequence now becomes the source or the cause of the next event. The world imputes a causal sequence of A → B → C. The apparent sequence is actually due to the invisible thought form of ABC in consciousness which unfolds in the visible domain thusly:

$$A \quad B \quad C$$

The important and critical point to understand clearly is that if the thought form, ABC, should suddenly disappear in the middle of the perceptual appearance of A → B → C, the sequence would stop at "B" and not complete the "C" at all. Therefore, the cause of "A's" appearing in the world is the thought form, "ABC." The cause of "B's" appearing in the world is still "ABC," and the cause of "C's" appearing in the world is also "ABC."

This perceptual illusion is like a prism that breaks up a beam of sunlight into a color spectrum, but then it would be like the ego's assuming that the color of the spectrum is the cause of the next. Appearance is not causation; that is the error.

Although this understanding may sound academic, it is actually critical to understanding the ever ongoing presence and absolute continuity of God, who is the never ending source of every instant of Creation.

The mind sees God as 'first cause', shown in the arguments for proof of the existence of God from theology such as that of Aristotle and St. Thomas Aquinas. This concept creates the limitation of conceiving of God as the great 'roller of the dice', subsequent to which everything has been a linear succession of sequential causes, like endless billiard balls. Thus, God gets projected backward into the long-distant past. This limitation loses site of God as the Ultimate Reality and Source of every instant of Existence. It is obvious that the Source of Existence is not transferred from God only to A, which then assumes a God-like capacity to cause B, which then transmits the God-like power of causation to C, and so on.

The limitation of the intellectual proof for the existence of God as first cause is this: The proof starts with the presumption that in a series of causes, there would have to be an irreducible, first or primary cause, namely, God. God is thus implied to be the necessary "First Cause." However, this fails to discern that the explanation for a class originates from outside the class.

The primary in a sequence of causes is therefore not a cause, but changes class, that is, to Source or Creator. Seeing 'causes' in the paradigm of form is an epistemologic error. A self-existent, verifiable reality, a 'First Cause' God, would be an effect and not a source. (As an example, one cannot trace back all existent matter to a 'First Matter' that is the 'cause' of all the rest of the universe's matter.) The conundrum is resolved by the realization that the source of the linear is the nonlinear, that is, a different intrinsic quality. Reductionist explanations lead one to epistemological positionalities wherein lie the fallacy.

The truth is that the totality of the expression of God as the entire universe is what creates "A." God Manifest as the entire universe then creates "B," and again, it is the Presence of the Reality of God that accounts for the appearance of "C," that is, every seeming event in the universe has exactly the same Ultimate Source.

Thus, there is only the same sunlight behind the appearance of each color in the spectrum. It is the continuous presence of God that is the Source of the continuous presence of life in all its expressions. To rephrase this statement, Creation is the continuous and ongoing expression of the unfolding Reality as manifestation in timelessness, which is only perceived by the ego as 'this instant'.

The common misconceptions about the existence of God are that (1) He appears briefly as a mysterious creator who sets the dice rolling somewhere back in distant, ancient time; (2) God then disappears and the world unfolds according to biologic reductionism on its own, for better or worse; and, (3) while all this is occurring, God waits elsewhere (in the human mind, heaven is 'up there') and appears again only in some very distant future as the great, feared judge of woeful Judgment Day.

All that occurs between his brief appearance as Creator in the long-distant past and his reappearance again on Judgment Day is assumed to be a sequence of dependent causes to account for all the phenomena of the universe. During all the ensuing eons, God apparently is assumed to have disappeared to an invisible 'elsewhere' (up there in heaven) where he sits on a throne, awaiting the arrival of souls that tremble and fear at their wickedness and sins that were caused by the fall of man in the Garden of Eden long, long ago. The fate of man is then seen as blighted from its very onset, and this event then runs through an endless chain of assumed causes down to the present time.

The basis for sin is thus ascribed to the inability of the human mind to discern truth from falsehood. Blinded by ignorance, man was vulnerable to the temptation of curiosity. He then bit into the apple of dualistic perception (the polarity of the opposites of good and evil).

Having lost the innocence of the Oneness of nonduality, the human was then saddled with a defective ego/mind that was without protection from error due to its inability to recognize the presence or the absence of Truth. The mind's limitation of dualistic perception marked the nature of the fall from Grace.

Instantly, the birth of the ego was labeled as sin since it marked the loss of the innocence of nondualistic vision, which is represented by the innocence of the Garden of Eden. The basis for human suffering is seen to be the birth of the ego via the onset of dualistic perception which operates with the impairment of positionalities. This results in the illusion of the pairs of opposites which culminates in suffering, sickness, and death.

Q: **What is the reality of the seeming opposites of good and evil?**

A: They are not opposites but alternates and merely gradations along a common basis of choice. Like temperature, there are only degrees. There is no such thing as cold versus hot; they are not opposites but only gradations. At some point along the temperature scale, because of human preference for comfort, the terms are used arbitrarily, depending on the desired conditions; for example, 55 degrees F. is cool, or even cold, but if a refrigerator registers 55 degrees F., it is considered to be too warm to store food safely.

Evil represents not the opposite but the absence of Love. The Scale of Consciousness indicates the degree of the presence of Love.

An analysis of the nature of consciousness reveals that redemption occurs as the result of the return of consciousness to its original pristine state of nonduality. It can do this only by the 'obedience' of surrendering the dualities of will and willfulness of the ego to the nonduality of God's Truth. The return from the duality of the ego to the nonduality of the spirit is so difficult and unlikely that only by Divine Grace is it even possible. Thus, man needs a savior to be his advocate, inspiration, and the fulcrum of his salvation from the pain and suffering of the ego.

The 'tempter' is thus man's curiosity, which is a basic weakness. When it is coupled with the inherent defect of ignorance, (the inability to discern truth from falsehood), then entrapment by the lower levels of consciousness ensues. When curiosity leads the innocent consciousness of man into the worlds of duality, he becomes entrained and entrapped and is captured, like a person who is addicted to watching soap operas. Entranced by the melodrama of illusion, the ego merges and identifies with the drama. Thus, awareness of the Self is lost to the movies which preoccupy the self. Attachments then arise to all the faults, identifications, and objects of attraction.

Few people are motivated to emerge from this morass, and fewer still even suspect that such a condition has befallen them. Even less discover the way out of the trap of the ego. The world of the ego is like a house of mirrors through which the ego wanders, lost and confused, as it chases the images in one mirror after another. Human life is characterized by endless trials and errors to escape the maze. At times, for many people, and possibly for most, the world of mirrors becomes a house of horrors that gets worse and worse. The only way out of the circuitous wanderings is through the pursuit of spiritual truth.

Q: Is the Scale of Consciousness the map showing the way out of the house of mirrors?

A: The desire to know and adhere to God's Truth is the only way out of darkness.

Q: Was the ego born out of opposition to God's will?

A: The 'violation' is the choosing of the ego instead of surrendering to God. The ego is baited with pleasures and satisfaction, such as the enjoyment of hate and revenge or greed and selfishness.

Q: How do you define "evil"?

A: Evil is the denial of God and therefore of Love. It is primarily selfishness, which is the egocentricities and narcissistic positionalities of the ego's satisfactions. The megalomaniac ego tramples over the lives of millions of duped citizens and leads them to their death, doing so only for its own gratification. We call that degree of selfishness "evil."

Greed grasps at gain without thought for the lives or happiness of others. This can clearly be seen in the rapist, the murderer, the robber, the liar, the abuser, the hostile and sarcastic, the rude, and the avaricious, all of whom are enthralled with themselves and dedicated to satisfying their endless wants, at whatever costs to others or the world.

The greed for pleasure, even if at the cost of the suffering and the lives of others, is described as cruel, sadistic, and self-centered. It is immune to the world in that it is a self-rewarding trap. It is an addiction to the transient gratifications and pleasures of ego satisfaction. The lust for power, revenge, position, and money then leads the ego ever deeper into the house of mirrors.

To get what it wants, the ego resorts to force and then discovers to its dismay that force triggers the release of counterforce. The terrorist eventually brings ruination not only to himself but ultimately to his whole country. The ego of the terrorist (which calibrates at 70) is not only indifferent to the suffering of others but sadistically enjoys it, as can be seen in the serial killer. This pleasure in the suffering of others is the hallmark of true corruption and what can be correctly termed "degeneracy."

Q: How, then, can the observer not condemn and judge against evil, that is, become polarized into a duality?

A: That is a difficult problem for the spiritual aspirant. It helps to realize that 'evil' is infantilism, primarily selfish greed and grandiosity associated with animal instincts. These are, therefore, major spiritual defects and the earmarks of ignorance. The animal instincts in the terrorist partake of intelligence in order to become the ultimate predator who kills for pleasure. Such animals exist in nature; one can observe weasels or dog packs that go into a killing frenzy. They are not hungry nor do they even bother to eat the prey but continue to kill the whole flock of ducks, chickens, or any other susceptible prey. The killing frenzy results in the throats of the prey being ripped out, and in the morning, the pen is found to be littered with dead bodies, none of which has been eaten.

We see the same bloody frenzy among savage barbarian hordes of ancient times, and in more recent times in the raping of Nanking and other wartime slaughter of the innocents. We see it also in the serial killer who repeatedly stabs and mutilates the victim.

Q: **How should we view such horrific examples of degeneracy, such as the serial killer, the terrorist, or the megalomaniac dictator?**

A: They are like rabid dogs that have gone insane by refusing to accept God. They draw their energy from the lower astral domains. One can detachedly observe the drama but not get drawn into its emotionality or polarity. There still remains the option to choose the pure and refuse the impure. To remain detached is an inner choice. We have the ability to decline the negative option of choosing positionalities. The best position is to stand firm and refuse to participate or 'go there'. One can see that the repudiation of the love of God has severe, grave consequences. These accrue by the nature of the level of consciousness that has been summoned forth. To say "yes" to hate is to join that level of consciousness and become its victim. Hate merely engenders more hate.

Q: Does Christ's alleged saying about turning the other cheek apply in a world-conflict situation?

A: Although that is often cited, it is misinterpreted as meaning that passivity is the only correct spiritual response. However, Jesus also said, "Render unto Caesar that which is Caesar's, and unto God that which is God's." This quotation refers to the fact that there are different realms and that one should not confuse levels of reality. The laws of war are different from the laws of everyday life, and spiritual laws signify spiritual intention and acts of the will. To stand firm with the sword of Truth against the onslaught of destructive forces is different from hating them and seeking revenge.

In the everyday world of form, as in the animal world, the predator/prey response is observable. Nonattachment does not mean passivity or nonaction; thus, one can take a stance in the world to defend innocence as a commitment to the integrity of truth. As we saw prior to World War II, the passivity and naiveté of Neville Chamberlin invited Nazi aggression to 'pursue the rabbit'. In mountain country, everyone knows that to run from the mountain lion invites its attack.

If life is sacred, then to defend life is aligned with the will of God, and it is not intrinsically an act of aggression. Karma is determined by the act of the spiritual will, which is aligned with motive and intention.

Purgatory is a dimension of consciousness that includes the entire strata, from the lowest to the highest, in which all choices are possible. Only the ego goes there where it works out its own salvation by finding itself in a realm where all choices are possible and can be externalized by acting them out.

On this planet are examples of the most savage, degenerate, and cruel acts. Also in mankind are the highest levels of life as represented by the saints, or even those who are enlightened. Thus, between the two extremes, innumerable choices are possible, plus the appearance of 'time', during which error and correction have room for the potentiality to be experienced. At every instant, one is really making a choice between heaven or hell. The cumulative effect of all these choices determines the calibrated level of consciousness and one's karmic and spiritual fate.

Purgatory would then represent a place of learning, correction, and opportunity. In such a realm, the spirit is free to work out its own fate through decisions and options. The growing soul consistently learns to surrender poor choices and choose wiser ones. The choices are made repeatedly and the lessons are learned until the more mature spirit reaches the certainty that it is going in the right direction. The evolving spirit then moves closer and closer to God and the calibrated levels correspond.

At first, spiritual purification seems difficult, but eventually, it becomes natural. To consistently choose love, peace, or forgiveness leads one out of the house of mirrors. The joy of God is so exquisite that any sacrifice is worth the effort and seeming pain.

The inner 'high' of righteous indignation, being 'right', or hating enemies turns out to be disappointing in hollow illusions of victory. The mature spiritual aspirant is one who has explored the ego's options and false promises of happiness. The ego's final song, after examination, is represented by a famous singer's poignant song, "Is This All There Is?" It is interesting that if we use kinesiology to affirm the hypothesis that human life on this planet is merely one of the realms of purgatory, we get the answer "yes."

Q: **Is the ego thus both victim and perpetrator?**
A: That is correct. The ego is the victim of itself. With rigorous introspection, it will be discovered that the ego is really just

'running a racket' for its own fun and games and survival. The real 'you' is actually the loser. The ego has an endless storehouse of prizes on which to feed. It greedily pounces on sentimentality, on the virtue of being right, on the prize of being the victim, or on the martyrdom of loss and sadness. It also offers the excitement of winning or gain as well as the pain of frustration. It offers the ego inflation of getting attention or sympathy. One can see that each emotion is, in and of itself, its own payoff.

The ego clings to emotionality, which is intimately connected with its positionalities; it pretends to think that it has no other choices. To 'surrender to God' means to stop looking to the ego for solace and thrills and to discover the endless, serene joy of peace. To look within is to find the underlying, ever present Source of the illumination of the mind itself. It is like finding the Source of Light, behind which is enabled the expression of that light as the colored spectrum. By introspection, one can see that there is that which changes and that which is changeless. That which changes thereby identifies itself as illusion.

Q: Is the puzzle of the house of mirrors that the mind does not know whether it is the author or the recipient of its experiences?

A: That is a good way of expressing the dualistic dilemma. The way out is simple: Direct one's focus inward to the absolute subjectivity of all experiencing. Examine the nature of the sense of subjectivity that accompanies every expression of life. Without labeling, note that at all times, in every instant, in every moment, in every circumstance, there is always present the ultimately irreducible, underlying substrate of subjectivity. It never changes. The essence of experiencing, in all its forms (thinking, feeling, seeing, knowing, etc.), is the presence of this subjective quality. Then look further to find out what this subjective experiencing is that is ever present. Without it, there would not be the possibility of knowing that one exists.

Ask "How am I aware or even know that I exist?" That question is the best that can be acted upon for it leads directly and nonverbally to the ever present Reality. Identify with that quality, capacity, or condition of ever present subjectivity which is experienced as an underlying awareness. It is consciousness itself. Identify with that consciousness instead of with the 'what' it is conscious about. That is the direct route to the Self. It is actually the only practice that leads directly through the doorway. There is nothing to know, to learn, or to remember. It is merely necessary to focus, fixate, meditate, contemplate, look at, and realize that the substrate and source of existence is the radical subjectivity of the Presence of God as the Light of Consciousness.

Subjectivity devoid of content, subject/object illusion is the Self. The subjective 'I' of the Self is independent of content or form, beyond all thought or concepts. It is not feelings or thoughts that are important but only the subjectivity that underlies their seeming importance.

Paradoxically, it is radical subjectivity that leads to the amazing discovery of the only possible true 'objectivity'. The only fact that can be objectively verified in all times and places and under all conditions by anyone anywhere is the absolute, irreducible fact of subjectivity.

Even radical scientific inquiry leads to the discovery that without subjectivity, nothing is knowable nor could it even be said to exist. The awareness of awareness, the awareness of being conscious, and the awareness of content all depend on rising out of this subjectivity.

The subjectivity of consciousness is the illumination of the Self as the universal 'I' of Reality. It is the Eye of God. That 'I' is the Essence of All That Is and includes the totality of the Presence as the ever present Source of

Existence, beyond all time or place. It has no beginning and no end. Creation and the Creator are one and the same. To describe God as Manifest or Unmanifest, or as transcendent or immanent, are only arbitrary points of view. Reality is beyond all such attempts at description.

CHAPTER TWENTY-THREE
HOMO SPIRITUS

Although human history has been documented as to times, persons, places, and events, it is still lacking a comprehensive contextualization that embraces the totality of this great phenomenon and extracts overall meaning and significance. The material reductionist sees history as merely a "biologic evolution with survival as its primary goal." This mechanistic, 'hard-core' scientific view believes that life spontaneously arose in some unknown manner as a fortuitous convergence of matter and energy.

The linear Newtonian paradigm is based on the notion that intrinsic to evolution, there is a mysterious intention or cause. It is also teleological in that it presupposes that evolutionary events accrued 'in order' to bring about a specific end or purpose, such as survival. How a nonthinking organism could have a purpose, intention, or desired end is not explained. This materialistic explanation satisfies the average person since it sounds 'scientific'. However, Darwin and the Theory of Evolution calibrate only at 405 (simplistic reasoning) which is insufficient to penetrate or elucidate the mysteries of life.

The tentative explanations of science are also made attractive by the historic fact that they are current and easily available. The only alternative historically was the religious doctrine of Creation which, when viewed by modern scientific man, sounds rather antiquated and unconvincing and therefore is credible primarily to those who consider the Bible to be the highest truth. Although Genesis calibrates at over 600, it is unfortunately included with the rest of the books of the Old Testament, all of which (except Psalms and Proverbs) calibrate below 200.

Q: **If the mechanistic view of human evolution is insufficient, and the Biblical view is of questionable accuracy or credibility, then what viewpoint might elucidate the real significance and essence of the development of mankind that is verifiable?**

A: Inasmuch as historical analysis and reviews are couched in the language and viewpoints of the ego, the positionalities expressed in philosophical interpretations appear to be arbitrary at best. Although erudition represents elegance of intellection, it still calibrates only in the high 400s. The Great Books of the Western World, which include the writings of the greatest thinkers in history, calibrate at 474.

We can survey the evolution of human life from its biologic origins and track its development by documenting the progression of consciousness over great periods of time. This is likely to be fruitful because we now have a means of tracking a nonlinear domain as well as that of form and materiality.

Essential to an in-depth understanding of the evolution of life is the subtle but critical comprehension which is axiomatic to higher awareness: The manifest world of form is intrinsically devoid of power. It is not capable of cause; it is an outpicturing, a consequence, an effect, a result, a product, a display in manifestation of the effects of power which originate and reside within the nonlinear domain. Life originates only from preexistent life. Life is the unfoldment of the potentiality of the unmanifest, infinite power of God. Evolution is the progressive unfoldment of Creation as it manifests its potentiality as form (i.e., material, physical existence).

The changes that are seen in the world of form are the consequence of a progression within the invisible, nonlinear domain of the power of consciousness. This is the locus of the enigmatic, sought-for 'missing link'. That was first described in *Power versus Force* as follows:

"Another useful concept is Rupert Sheldrake's notion of morphogenetic fields, or M-fields. These invisible organizing patterns act like energy templates to establish forms on various levels of life. It is because of the discreteness of M-fields that identical representations of a species are produced. Something similar to M-fields also exists in the energy fields of consciousness, underlying thought patterns and images—a phenomenon termed 'formative causation.' The idea that M-fields assist learning has been verified by wide-scale experimentation."

The perceptions of the ego are a limitation and result in the misinterpretation of sequential transformations of form as being due to 'cause'. The change is a result of the consequence of visible progression in a visible domain in which the material world is ruled by unseen energies of enormous power. To misperceive this is to be like the naïve aborigine who sees a movie for the first time and thinks the figures on the screen are causing the action of the movie. It is analogous to thinking that puppets have the ability to interact with each other and ignoring the fact that they are merely reflecting the consciousness of the puppeteer.

The light of the consciousness of Divinity irradiated materiality and thus spawned life. Note that 'life' has a completely different essence, quality, capacity, and characteristic from inert material. It is not even in the same logic class or category as materiality. The energy of life has an innate, critically essential quality that is totally absent from inert matter. It has intelligence, the capacity to learn, adapt, assimilate, accumulate, and utilize information. It is of a domain altogether different from matter. It has a unique essence and potentiality that are not shared by matter. Matter is analogous to a copper wire that is inert and has no actual function until an electric current courses through it, at which time it becomes a 'live wire'.

The forms of life showed progression over millions of years as a consequence of the consciousness that is innate to the presence of the energizing factor of the power of life itself. Consciousness observes, records, recombines, bifurcates, juxtaposes, and sorts information because it has the capacity to record events on the level of mute, but alert, awareness. That innate quality is exactly what enables the kinesiologic test to discern the truth of anything that has ever occurred anywhere in time or space.

It is important to note that the Newtonian materialistic paradigm is rigidly ordered, limiting, and predictive. It is not capable of explaining creativity or evolution, which requires operational possibilities that are only inherent in nonlinear chaotic systems that occur between disorder and order. True creativity and evolution require chaotic attractors that allow for unpredictable transitions and novel chaotic energy trajectories in the infinite quantum potentiality, free of constraint systems. Thus, the nonlinear source of creativity is unlimited within itself but its expansion takes place with the limitations of existing conditions. When viewed from the material world, these observations create an illusion of linear causality. An analogy is that music can be written which is beyond the capacity of existing musical instruments to play. The constraint is therefore not on the creative origination but on its appearance in a physical domain, that is, not all that can be imagined is suitable for production.

Truth is actuality; nontruth is false because it never existed and therefore was never recorded, which is why it exhibits a 'false' (absence of truth) response to testing. Consciousness only responds to what 'is' or 'has been' in Reality. The source of consciousness is the Absolute Reality, classically called Truth. The ultimate basis for the kinesiologic test, which accounts for its uncanny accuracy, is that it originates from a quality of Reality itself. It is the only absolute yardstick for truth yet discovered.

Biologic evolution is the result and consequence of the innate capacity of the energy of consciousness to learn, modify, adapt, and progress in complexity and elegance of design, including esthetics and even 'scientific' discovery (the kingdom of fishes learned how to manufacture electricity eons before man made the same discovery). Immobile creatures were then surpassed by mobile life forms that adapted to land, sea, and air. Life even survived in subterranean regions at high heat, such as the magma within the Earth.

The mammalian kingdom is relatively very recent in emergence. Primates appeared much later than that and represented a progressive capacity for intelligence and adaptation. Like the animal forms that had preceded it, the primate was driven by animal instincts geared to survival. The mind and intellect emerged as effective tools for survival and were based on the basic mechanisms necessary to animal survival: to grab, run, hide, plan, store, acquire, manipulate, guard, attack, defend, club, kill, intimidate, capture, enslave, fecundate, and control. The primate developed more sophisticated techniques, including memory, cognition, group/pack formation, and establishment of boundaries and dominion. The inner animal still growled and howled with rage at conflict and territorial battles for mates and the ruling of domains. The animal brain fears, hates, rages, seduces, dissimilates, camouflages, and puts on purposefully intimidating displays.

To the primitive mind, enemies were seen as 'out there', and 'others' were divided into friend/foe, edible/poisonous, wanted/not wanted, pleasant/unpleasant, and finally, good/bad. To the animal, all these distinctions were critical to survival; however, as a result, the 'polarity of opposites' was deeply imprinted in the primate psyche. These progressive styles of categorization were recorded in the primate field of consciousness and became the basic karmic pattern of the human ego of today.

If we examine the qualities of consciousness levels below 200, we can see that, aside from pride and vanity, which are more specifically human elaborations of the alpha male and female, the rest are primarily animal reactions and patterns. Because of the neural complexity of the human brain, these basic animal instincts later became more sophisticated, complex, and elaborated as human characteristics and societal structures. These patterns and instincts became institutionalized in the elaboration of structures, cities, institutions, the judiciary, and the structures of government, as well as in the creation of nations, territorial boundaries, and the hardware and technology of war and the military.

Although the core of animal instincts is the biologic basis of survival, with the evolution of the human brain, the capacity for self-observation appeared. The 'self' of the evolving psyche became the focus of attention and importance. With the birth of the capacity for self-reflection emerged truly human vanity and pride. Their payoff was the feeling of greater strength and prowess. The ego swells with pride and feels bigger and more powerful than it really is. This ego inflation was then incorporated as a survival mechanism; the 'swelling up' display had already been a survival mechanism in earlier animal species and also specifically in anthropoids. This is used to intimidate potential enemies and to attract mates. Because the temporary inner effect is pleasant, ego expansion became an end in itself. To 'look one's best' is still the basis of the whole fashion industry. The male version is the big house, the big automobile, and 'who I am' expanded to include possessions and symbols of worldly power, including titles, positions, and wealth. Success in sports was also a direct exhibition and socially sanctioned display of prowess, with its culmination as 'the hero'.

Because of the body's requirements and its vulnerabilities, the human being has had to give it importance and devote much time, thought, and energy to its survival. To do this requires determined planning, the control of impulses and instincts, and the capacity to delay gratification. The body requires houses, automobiles, and medicine. The intellect greatly expanded human power because it allowed for symbols and abstract thought to be easily manipulated at a distance from objects. The emerging data banks could store enormous bits of information and file them in categories. Modern man emerged with the birth of the intellect, which had the unique capacity to reason, anticipate, and pose hypotheses that furthered knowledge and discovery.

While the survival technique of the animal instinct/ human ego was sufficient for the survival of the individual and provided basic drives for the survival of the species, a new element appeared within the higher animals—the pack, the maternal bond, nurturance, family affection, and lovingness. The capacity for caring relationships emerged, and with it, the valuation of others as love objects. This led to the formation of the family, the group, the tribe, the settlement, and the village, and it supported trade and barter. Out of the maternal bond arose companionship and long-term pairing in addition to the capacity for attachment as well as grief and mourning at loss. Relationship engendered the positionality of 'us' and 'them', which escalated the great cultural ravages and wars of history. (It is interesting to note that both the cat's purr and the dog's wagging tail calibrate at 500, so, strangely, some of the animals emerge with an even greater capacity to love than many humans.)

As consciousness evolved, each aspect of animal nature reached its fullest expression in the human ego, which expanded these survival instincts into full expression as the structure of society. Alignments created cultures, trades, nations, industries, and advanced technologies.

During only very recent development periods did personal romantic love evolve in importance and expression. At first, the male-female relationship was primarily based on lust, desire, and possession, which led to craving and control. Eventually, the male was required to defend and support the family, and pair bonding, affection, mutual support, and love emerged as progressively important.

Among the monarchies and ruling classes, marriages were traditionally arranged for alliances of gain and power, and love was not even considered a necessary element. It was presumed that love would be covertly found elsewhere. Among the populous, women began to place requirements on male mating privileges and so learned to barter sex for love and permanence.

Romantic love did not appear as a valued human capacity until only a few centuries ago. Initially, love was viewed as passion and possession, but as it became romanticized, to 'sacrifice for love' became a noble ideal. The flowering of womanhood lifted her image from drudge/sex object/nanny to valued friend, partner, and lover. This marked the real daily-life recognition of the human spirit as a quality that attracted and supported love. Affection expanded love as the primary motif of ongoing, long-term relationships, and fidelity appeared as both a virtue and a mainstay to permanency. Prior to that, the daily lives of men and women were quite separate. They spent very little time in each other's company. The men went off to hunt, to war, and to brawl, and the women gathered together to attend to domestic duties. Men bonded with other men but mated with women.

The originally animal curiosity evolved in man and led to the search for explanations and meaning. This resulted in the accumulation of information that was later compiled to form the basis for education. Besides the external world, man's curiosity turned within and he developed theories about human nature. The mechanisms of the ego, however, had already been structured on the fulcrum of the polarity of the opposites, and the resultant perceptions saw the pairs of opposites both within and without. Therefore, man's perception of 'reality' became dualistic.

Because of dualistic perception, the mind could no longer discern the abstract symbol from reality. The road to error was open and inviting, and opinion held sway as the mind had no innate mechanism to discern truth from falsehood. As a result of dualistic mentation, the mind had developed the capacity for repression and denial so that it could remove obstacles to achieving its goals. The mind discovered that it could deny ownership of an unwanted side of a pair of opposites and project it onto the world. Thus were born not only politics but also the well-known psychological mechanisms of splitting, repression, denial, and projection. This capacity turned out to be a fatal mechanism in that even when faced with dire results, the ego relentlessly pursued the same mistakes.

Except in small, personal affairs, the mind was not constructed to readily learn from its mistakes. The idea that one can win by repeatedly attacking one's enemies is as virulent in today's world as it was many centuries ago. The primitive, barbaric patterns of attack and counter-attack of ancient times persist in today's society and constitute each day's newspaper headlines.

There was really no means by which to stop the unmitigated onslaught of the ego in either personal or worldly affairs over the many centuries. The purpose of sheer survival through social control arose to set limits and rules. Laws emerged and were backed up by threats of force and terrible consequences. At one time, there were close to five hundred different offenses that were punishable by a gruesome and horrific death through execution. (It is questionable whether or not the crime rate decreased.)

The individual, as well as collective ego, represented force, and force was extended to its fullest expression in the dark history of the human race. The ego held sway and dominated the consciousness of the masses; they were then easily manipulated between greed and fear. Control was thus uneasily maintained by governments which themselves were periodically challenged by the collective egos of dissenting parties, leading to factionalism, revolution, and civil war.

Many governments throughout history and even up to today have been more murderous and cruel than the citizens they were meant to control. Government and law relied on force to combat the negativity of the individual and the collective egos of mankind. Like all wars, force had to be constantly fed energy in the form of gold, human lives, and manpower. Eventually, resources dry up and force meets a greater force, so all rulers, empires, and great civilizations have come and gone. Even the greatest of them all, the great Roman Empire, which ruled for many centuries, finally dissolved into history, fragmented from overexpansion.

From its first appearance, and continuing until very recent times, humankind represented the extravagances of the unimpeded, unbridled ego, whose only counter was the collective ego-based institutions. Both government and religion lacked sufficient influence to control the masses, so they aligned themselves for mutual gain, prestige, and worldly power. To accomplish that end, religion had to modify the teachings of its founders and give them a secular rationalization that was enforced by fiat of ecclesiastic authority. The Church then usurped the authority as the author of truth from the great avatars (e.g., Christ, Buddha, Krishna) from whose teachings it ostensibly drew its prestige and authenticity. In some countries, the fusion was made complete as a theocracy in which the head of state and the head of religion were one and the same. This precipitated the great historic revolutions and schisms within religions and nations as exhibited by massive oppression, such as that shown by the Islamic countries of today. In some countries, religiosity merged into nationalism, and the political philosophy of militant nationalism and the worship of the 'great leader' reached their peak. This was an expression in World War II that still proceeds unimpeded in Third World countries today.

The ego thus reigned supreme, century after century, but despite its relentless grip, love had opened a crack in the ego's armor. In many areas of the world, despite the ego's oppositions and attempts to stamp it out, love and integrity gained ground and was later reinforced by reason and intellect as the development of ethics and moral responsibility.

Although a few thousand years ago seems remote from a current viewpoint, in the evolution of consciousness, it signifies only very recent times. The intellectual ego, however, was limited by the duality of perception; thus arose the illusion of linear causality, plus the inability to tell truth from falsehood. Man looked without to find the 'causes' of nature as well as human events. Man looked at the stars and the heavens. Seers and prophets appeared. Horrific gods were invented and their myths were propagated as legends and supposed truth. In a world where superstition and ignorance abounded, the illiterate masses were easily impressed with mystery and imaginary tales drawn from astral visions, dreams, hallucinations, delusions, inflated narcissistic egos, demagoguery, and, peculiarly, the persuasive charisma of egomaniacs.

These multiple sources collectively contributed to fabled mythologies whose control was then taken over by the emergent priesthood. It thereby obtained prestige, power, and control and was able to intimidate and extract submission from the masses. They sought influence over government, land, and wealth. The great temples arose, constructed at the cost of the bodies and sacrifice of the populous that was in awe of the priest caste, with its striking edifices and glamorous displays as well as control of secret mysteries, rituals, and impressive ceremonies.

Because they claimed authority from the unseen and therefore mysterious, nonlinear domain, the priest caste collected a composite of myths, legends, prophetic pronouncements, and spiritual and religious expositions from a variety of sources. They declared them to be authoritative, calling them 'holy scriptures' in which supposedly resided all truth and deistic authority. Although purportedly divine in origin, the structure and mechanisms of the ego glared out through these apocryphal stories. Throughout these writings, however, moments of spiritual truth suddenly appeared that tended to counterbalance some of the error. These historic legends, however, did provide the needed comfort of some kind of explanation for the existential uncertainty and unknown origins of human life.

During this same historic period, however, there were individuals of true spiritual genius who were uniquely inspired and gifted. In contrast to ordinary mortals, they looked within instead of without to find truth and undertook the knowledge of the inner pathway. These were the great, enlightened mystics, such as the fabled Aryan Hindu gurus of the *Vedas*. They represented the results of the process of inner purification and revealed that when the ego is transcended, the ultimate Realization shines forth.

Those for whom the Light of Truth had replaced the ego were termed "enlightened." Thus arose the great yogas. Although infrequent, the periodic recurrence of that remarkable phenomenon on the Indian continent led to India's becoming the legendary home of the holy men who sought God through austerity and relentless purification of the ego in order to reach the ultimate awareness of the Supreme. To this day, their teachings calibrate from the high 700s on up to those of Krishna at 1,000.

Great mystics also appeared in the Middle East and elsewhere. Gautama, the Buddha who became enlightened in Nepal, launched one of the world's greatest religions which, incidentally, has declined the least in calibrated level from its inception at 1,000 to the present time where it still remains in the high 900s. Five hundred years later emerged the great Jesus Christ, who also calibrated at 1,000; and in Arab lands, there was also the prophet Mohamed (early calibration level 740) who became the founder of Islam. (At age 38, however, his calibration level dropped to 130 although the Koran remains at 700.)

It is of considerable importance to appreciate that it is consciousness itself which is the source of life, and that innate to that consciousness are the qualities of creative growth and evolution which appear to seek a return to its Source. Although consciousness evolves from the 'bottom up' in evolution, it was sourced from 'above to below'. An analogy is sunlight, which pours energy onto the Earth upon which life progresses upward from the simplest to the most complex, and finally, through man who, through enlightenment, again returns to the Source of Life itself.

The collective ego levels below 200 do not value the source of life and consider spirituality to be a threat to their dominion. Over the centuries, negativity dominated mankind. Although its domination met islands of resistance in spiritually advanced subcultures, it managed to sweep aside spiritual values by submerging them into such subcultures as nationalism and 'righteous' ecclesiastic and legal dictums or to distort their meaning so as to make them ineffective.

Human civilization was the ego's relatively unimpeded stomping ground. It handled resistance by means of subversion. If a real threat occurred, such as Christianity, it managed to invade the enclave of truth by sending clever missionaries of its own. The lower ego simultaneously envies and fears the power of Truth because Truth relies on no vulnerable, external sources. The only energy that has more power than the strength of the collective ego is that of spiritual truth. The nonintegrous ego has only force, and it knows that that force cannot stand against power.

The ego therefore escapes to other domains and rules in other dimensions where its major players assume the titles and rules of psuedo-gods. Interestingly, the lower astral domains are ruled by those who actually deny God. They thus hate and envy the souls who have chosen the evolutionary path back to God and have acknowledged God as their Source.

Any sage who has reached the higher levels of consciousness attests to the experience of having had numerous attacks and visits by the entities who look for a vulnerability. They try flattery, seduction, promises of power (their version of it), prestige, control over multitudes, glamour, riches, or even paradises filled with objects of lust, such as gold and even "seventy virgins."

Surprisingly, these tempting offers are sometimes made via an actual 'entity' that suddenly seems to displace someone who is speaking; in fact, often a supposed teacher. This overshadowing personality then boldly presents a proposition.

One telltale and reliable sign of such an 'unclean spirit' is that it launches into a diatribe that can only be described as utterly "stupid" in the full meaning of that term. Such an entity will suddenly say, for example, that "money is a greater good than all the teachings of Christ or Buddha," or that "Christ and Buddha and all the great teachers of history were just astrals."

The temptations are expressed so crudely that one wonders how anyone with any spiritual understanding at all could be deceived. However, apparently many are, as the history of fallen gurus attests. The negative entity looks for any residual impurity and appeals to that weakness. Vanity is the great classic pitfall, along with greed and lust.

While doing research, an interesting discovery was made. Many world-famous spiritual teachers actually calibrated at quite low levels, and some even calibrated below 200; yet, their earlier writings by which they became well-known calibrated quite high (at least in the 500s). This presented a quizzical paradox: How could such relatively advanced teachings originate from teachers who currently calibrate in, or before they deceased, calibrated in the low 200s, or some even well below 200?

A pattern then emerged, namely, a semi-enlightened being becomes famous, sought after, and attracts many followers whose adulation feeds the spiritual ego. The waiting 'dark forces' attract the vulnerable spiritual ego and seduce by sophistry and clever argument. Although the content of the seductive concepts may sound convincing, it is the context which is out of integrity. Examples include the following: "Your fame and fortune are the means to salvation for the many"; "Secular and holy are one and the same; therefore, own power over others for their own good"; "Now that you are beyond karma, own power"; and "Love is only a trap and an attachment." The temptation (which is luciferic) is to try to obtain the power of God without also accepting that God is Love. From the luciferic viewpoint, Love would preclude and temper the ego's greed for power and riches and therefore be seen as a limitation from that perceptual distortion.

Although the luciferic fall occurs as a result of the desire for fame, wealth, and power, the satanic temptation also fells the previously saintly beings who then succumb to sexual lust with followers or even children. The lust may be hidden behind supposedly 'mystical' rituals and esoteric rationalizations. (For example, God created sex, sex is holy; therefore, let's have holy sex and worship God by having sacred sex.)

In homes and ashrams around the world, one sees pictures of gurus being worshipped, prayed to, meditated upon (complete with candles, incense, and gifts of flowers and fruit) who calibrate at even less than level 190. Such is the state of affairs.

The energies which we call negative stem from the lower astral realms that were already in existence at the time of the appearance of life on earth. They dominated animal life but not vegetable life. As animals evolved, however, they roughly divided into two classes. There were rapacious carnivores that continued to be dominated by lower astral forces and reached their greatest expression during the age of the dinosaurs that calibrate at 70. They lived at the cost of the life of others. The dinosaur expressed in form and character the essence of the lower astral realm. After the disappearance of the dinosaurs, progressively peaceful animals appeared on Earth (herbivores) that did not live by killing others and that were not dominated by the lower astral forces; instead, they were killed and eaten by them. These two contrasting types of energy then prevailed in mankind as well, where the masses became the prey of the rapacious.

One expression of the lower astral domain is cleverness and expertise at disguise. It preys on the spiritually naïve, among whom lower astral forces seek to acquire followers by means of disguise as 'holy persons'.

Because the seekers of truth had no means to discern truth from falsehood, they were extremely vulnerable to mystification by that which they did not understand. The most stunning example of this in human history is the Book of Revelations, which calibrates at 70 and was the lower astral vision of a man named John, who also calibrates at 70. (Similar "end times," hallucinations, and lower astral scenarios recur over the ages, including the present time.) It is from that negative antithesis of God's truth that the far-right 'fundamentalist' wing of modern religion launches its aggressive and sadistic attacks on the spirit of the vulnerable. (Modern-day Islamic fundamentalists calibrate at 70.)

In the modern world, the disguises are more sophisticated and enormously seductive. For instance, by seducing man into intoxication, the negative energies create an opening into the psyche of the addict and attract by pleasure. The current most ingenious ruse is by means of the carrier wave that accompanies much of modern music. Naïve critics think that the negativity is represented by the lyrics, but that is not where the negative messages lie. As cited in previous writings, if the sound of such music as heavy metal is occluded by white-noise headphones so that the music cannot even be heard, the listener instantly goes weak when tested with kinesiology. The test subject calibrates below 200 and subsequently stays at that level for a period of time. The psyche of the captured victim has now been enslaved by an energy frequency that dominates via the well-known phenomenon of entrainment. An entrained psyche is now open, vulnerable, and easily influenced toward destructive activities and group identifications with whole subcultures that worship violence and vulgarity. They dominate the airwaves and entertainment media aimed at the young people, who are the most naïve and easily seduced by pleasure and glamour.

The motive of these energies that are threatened by spiritual truth is to counter truth by subverting it. At the present time, the greatest entrance onto this planet of lower astral forces is through the media—television, movies, music, and especially video games—which blatantly glamorize evil in the forms of violence, seduction, and the denigration of spiritual symbols that are purposely mocked for shock value.

In the past, it was expected that devotees would avoid such pitfalls by strictly following the rules of the great teacher/enlightened sage and would thereby be prevented from falling off the path into seductive snares. To assist in this safety measure, followers were encouraged to 'stay with holy companions', avoid 'evil' and not be drawn into combat with it, which is also a favorite ruse of the negative energy systems (as described in a recent video game popular among young people that deals with the hierarchies of the entities of the astral realms).

The world of the great avatars was not pervaded by the mass media, and so group adherence afforded safety. Now, however, the open arenas of mass communication are pervasive. At the same time, the overall energy level of mankind is evolving more and more toward spiritual reality, and spiritual values are now appearing even within the integrous corporate culture.

The description of the various evolutionary branches of the hominid tree has given us the Latin designations of the interesting developmental offshoots that were based on anthropologic criteria of form and function. The recently emergent Homo sapiens not only walked erectly but was capable of reason and abstract thought. From within that level of consciousness arose the capacity to transcend the domination of the ego-based animal instincts and evolve past selfish self-interest to companionship, affection, and concern for others. These evolved not only into love but even unconditional love and compassion. Thus, the domination of the lower astral regions over humanity was superseded by the appearance of the evolution of consciousness as spiritual awareness.

These advanced, evolving states of spiritual conscious-ness were enormously more powerful than their ego-based predecessors and, in fact, had the prerequisite power to discern, undo, and absorb the lower levels of ego positionalities. The illumination of the radiance of the inner Self could thereby dissolve the ego and displace it as the sense of 'I-ness'. The appearance in humanity of the realization of God as the ultimate Reality, substrate, and source of Existence and Creation marked the beginning of the emergence of a new, evolutionary branch of mankind called *Homo spiritus.* The term "Homo spiritus" refers to the awakened man who has bridged the evolutionary leap from physical to spiritual, from form to nonform, and from linear to nonlinear. The awakened man realizes that it is consciousness itself which constitutes the core of the evolutionary tree in all its seemingly stratified and evermore complex expressions as the evolution of life. Thus, life transforms from the relatively unconscious linear to the fully conscious nonlinear, and Creation reveals itself to be the ongoing unfolding of the Unmanifest becoming Manifest. The capacity to reach the condition or state classically called Enlightenment represents the fulfillment of the potential of consciousness in its evolutionary progression.

There is only one Divine, Absolute, and Supreme Reality that transcends all potentialities, dimensions, realms, and universes and is the source of life and existence. Enlightenment is merely the full, conscious recognition that innate truth is the core of one's own existence, and that God as Self is the illumination whereby that realization is made possible. The Infinite Power of God is the manifestation of the power of Infinite Context. The Unmanifest is even beyond Infinite Context.

The Glory of God shines forth as the Source of Existence and the Reality that is knowable by the subjective awareness of the Self as the Infinite 'I'.

Gloria in Excelsis! Deo!

APPENDICES

APPENDIX A

CALIBRATION OF THE TRUTH OF THE CHAPTERS

APPENDIX B

MAP OF THE SCALE OF CONSCIOUSNESS

God View	Life View	Level	Log	Emotion	Process
Self	Is-ness	Enlightenment	700-1,000	Ineffable	Pure Consciousness
		↑			
All-Being	Perfect	Peace	600	Bliss	Illumination
		↑			
One	Complete	Joy	540	Serenity	Transfiguration
		↑			
Loving	Benign	Love	500	Reverence	Revelation
		↑			
Wise	Meaningful	Reason	400	Understanding	Abstraction
		↑			
Merciful	Harmonious	Acceptance	350	Forgiveness	Transcendence
		↑			
Inspiring	Hopeful	Willingness	310	Optimism	Intention
		↑			
Enabling	Satisfactory	Neutrality	250	Trust	Release
		↑			
Permitting	Feasible	Courage	200	Affirmation	Empowerment
		↓			
Indifferent	Demanding	Pride	175	Scorn	Inflation
		↓			
Vengeful	Antagonistic	Anger	150	Hate	Aggression
		↓			
Denying	Disappointing	Desire	125	Craving	Enslavement
		↓			
Punitive	Frightening	Fear	100	Anxiety	Withdrawal
		↓			
Disdainful	Tragic	Grief	75	Regret	Despondence
		↓			
Condemning	Hopeless	Apathy	50	Despair	Abdication
		↓			
Vindictive	Evil	Guilt	30	Blame	Destruction
		↓			
Despising	Miserable	Shame	20	Humiliation	Elimination

APPENDIX C

CALIBRATION OF THE LEVELS OF CONSCIOUSNESS

General Information

The energy field of consciousness is infinite in dimension. Specific levels correlate with human consciousness, and these have been calibrated from '1' to '1,000'. (See appendix B: Map of the Scale of Consciousness) These energy fields reflect and dominate human consciousness.

Everything in the universe radiates a specific frequency, or minute energy field, that remains in the field of consciousness permanently. Thus, every person or being whoever lived, and anything about them, including any event, thought, deed, feeling, or attitude, is recorded forever and can be retrieved at any time in the present or the future.

Technique

The kinesiologic response (muscle testing) is a simple "yes" or "no" response to a specific stimulus. In holistic health, it is usually done by the subject's holding out an extended arm and the tester pressing down on the wrist of the extended arm, using two fingers and light pressure. Usually the subject holds a substance to be tested over their solar plexus with the other hand. The tester says to the test subject, "Resist," and if the substance being tested is beneficial to the subject, the arm will be strong. If it is not beneficial or has an adverse effect, the arm will instantly go weak. The response is *very quick and brief.*

This test has been done by thousands of practitioners all over the world for many years, and the reliability and accuracy of the results have been well studied and documented. (See Suggested Reading.) **It is important to note that both the tester and the one being tested must calibrate over 200 in order to obtain accurate responses.**

For many years, the test was thought to be a local response of the body's acupuncture or immune system. Later research, however, has revealed that the response was not a local response to the body at all, but was instead a general response of consciousness itself to a substance or a statement. That which is true, beneficial, or pro-life gives a positive response which stems from the impersonal field of consciousness that is present in everyone living. This positive response is indicated by the body's musculature going strong. For convenience, the deltoid muscle is usually the one best used as an indicator muscle; however, any of the muscles of the body can be used, such as the gastrocnemias, which are often used by practitioners such as chiropractors.

Before a question (in the form of a statement) is presented, it is necessary to qualify "permission"; that is, state "I have permission to ask about what I am holding in mind." (Yes/No.)

If a statement is false or a substance is injurious, the muscles go weak quickly in response to the command "Resist." This indicates the stimulus is negative, untrue, anti-life, or the answer is "no." The response is *fast and very brief* in duration. The body will then rapidly recover and return to normal muscle tension.

The test requires two people: the tester and the test subject. A quiet setting is preferred, with no background music. The test subject closes their eyes. ***The tester must phrase the 'question' to be asked in the form of a statement.*** The statement can then be answered as 'yes' or 'no' by the kinesiologic response. For instance, the incorrect form would be to ask "Is this a healthy horse," rather than correctly as in the statement, "This horse is healthy," or its corollary, "This horse is sick."

After making the statement, the tester says "Resist" to the test subject who is holding the extended arm parallel to the ground. The tester presses down with two fingers on the wrist of the extended arm sharply, with mild force. The test subject's arm will either stay strong, indicating a "yes," or go weak, indicating a "no." The response is *very short and immediate.*

Calibration of Specific Levels

The critical point between positive and negative, between true and false, or between that which is constructive or destructive is at the calibrated level of 200 (see chart). Anything above 200, or true, makes the subject go strong; anything below 200, or false, allows the arm to go weak.

Anything past or present, including images or statements, historical events, or personages, can be tested. They need not be verbalized.

Numerical Calibration

Example: "Ramana Marharshi's teachings calibrate over 700." (Y/N) Or, "Hitler calibrated over 200." (Y/N) When he was in his 20s. (Y/N) His 30s. (Y/N) His 40s. (Y/N) At the time of his death. (Y/N)

Applications

The kinesiologic test cannot be used to foretell the future; otherwise, there are no limits as to what can be asked. Consciousness has no limits in time or space; however, permission may be denied. All current or historical events are available for questioning. The answers are impersonal and do not depend on the belief systems of either the tester or the test subject. For example, protoplasm recoils to noxious stimuli and flesh bleeds. Those are the qualities of these test materials and are impersonal. Consciousness actually knows only truth because only truth has actual existence. It does not respond to false-hood because falsehood does not have existence in reality. It will also not respond accurately to nonintegrous or egoistic questions such as should one buy a certain stock, etc.

The kinesiologic response is therefore, accurately speaking, either an "on" response or it is merely "not on." Like the electrical switch, we say the electricity is on, and when we use the term "off," we just mean that it is not there. In reality, there is not such thing as "off-ness." This is a subtle statement but crucial to the understanding of the nature of consciousness. Consciousness is capable of recognizing only Truth. It merely fails to respond to falsehood. Similarly, a mirror reflects an image only if there is an object to reflect. If no object is present to the mirror, there is no reflected image.

To Calibrate A Level

Calibrated levels are relative to a specific reference scale. To arrive at the same figures as in the chart in Appendix B, reference must be made to that table or by a statement such as, "On a scale of human consciousness from 1 to 1,000, where 600 indicates enlightenment, this _____ calibrates over _____ (a number). Or, "On a scale of consciousness where 200 is the level of Truth and 500 is the level of Love, this statement calibrates over _____. (State a specific number.)

General Information

People generally want to determine truth from falsehood. Therefore, the statement has to be made very specifically. Avoid using general terms such as a 'good' job to apply for. 'Good' in what way? Pay scale? Working conditions? Promotional opportunities? Fairness of the boss?

Expertise

Familiarity with the test brings progressive expertise. The 'right' questions to ask begin to spring forth and can become almost uncannily accurate. If the same tester and test subject work together for a period of time, one or both of them will develop what can become an amazing accuracy and capability of pinpointing just what specific questions to ask, even though the subject is totally unknown by either one. For instance, the tester has lost an object and begins to say, "I left it in my office." (Answer: No.) "I left it in the car." (Answer: No.) All of a sudden, the test subject almost 'sees' the object and says, "Ask, 'On the back of the bathroom door.'" The test subject says, "The object is hanging on the back of the bathroom door." (Answer: Yes.) In this actual case, the test subject did not even know that the tester had stopped for gas and left the jacket in the restroom of a gasoline station.

Any information can be obtained about anything anywhere in current or past time or space. By cross-checking, accuracy can be easily confirmed. It is normal to be skeptical at first. To anyone who learns the technique, however, more information is available instantaneously than can be held in all the computers and libraries of the world. The possibilities are therefore obviously unlimited, and the prospects breathtaking.

Limitations

Approximately ten percent of the population is not able to use the kinesiologic testing technique for as yet unknown reasons other than that it is due to an "imbalance of their 'chi' energy."

The test is accurate only if the test subjects themselves calibrate over 200 and the intention of the question is also integrous. Inasmuch as only twenty-two percent of the world's population calibrates at 200 or over, the result is that the kinesiologic test method is suitable for approximately only twenty percent of the population.

Sometimes married couples, also for reasons as yet not discovered, are unable to use each other as test subjects and may have to find a third person for a test partner.

It is not advisable to try to calibrate oneself because one can see that the ego almost automatically gets in the way.

A suitable test subject is a person whose arm goes strong when a love object or person is held in mind, and it goes weak if that which is negative (fear, hate, guilt, etc.) is held in mind (e.g., Winston Churchill makes one go strong and Bin Laden makes one go weak).

Occasionally, a suitable test subject gives paradoxical responses. This can usually be cleared by doing the "thymic thump" as was discovered by Dr. John Diamond. (With a closed fist, thump three times over the upper breastbone, smile, and say "ha-ha-ha" with each thump and mentally picture someone or something that is loved.)

The temporary imbalance will then clear up. It can be occasioned by recently having been with negative people, listening to heavy metal rock music, watching violent television programs, playing violent video games, etc. Negative music energy has a deleterious effect on the energy system of the body for up to one-half hour after it is turned off. Television commercials or background are also a common source of negative energy.

Explanation

The kinesiologic test is independent of personal opinion or beliefs and is an impersonal response of the field of consciousness which, like protoplasm, is impersonal in its responses. This can be demonstrated by the observation that the test responses are the same whether verbalized or held silently in mind. Thus, the test subject is not influenced by the question as they don't even know what it is. To demonstrate this, do the following exercise:

The tester holds in mind an image unknown to the test subject and states, "The image I am holding in mind is positive." (Or true, or calibrates over 200, etc.) On direction, the test subject then resists the downward pressure on the wrist. If the tester holds a positive image in mind (e.g., Abraham Lincoln, Jesus, Mother Theresa, etc.), the test subject's arm muscle will go strong. If the tester holds a false statement or negative image in mind (e.g., Bin Laden, Hitler, etc.), the arm will go weak. Inasmuch as the test subject does not know what the tester has in mind, the results are not influenced by personal beliefs.

Correct Kinesiologic Technique

Just as Galileo's interest was in astronomy and not in making telescopes, the Institute for Advanced Spiritual Research is devoted to Consciousness research and not specifically to kinesiology. The video, *Power Versus Force*, demonstrates the basic technique. More detailed information about kinesiology may be found in the following references:

Internet

Search for "kinesiology." Numerous references are provided, such as the College of Applied Kinesiology (www.icak.com), and other educational institutions.

Note: The author and publisher are unable to answer personal questions or requests for calibrations.

APPENDIX D
QUANTUM MECHANICS

T he contrast between Newtonian and Quantum paradigms of reality can be stated in generalities for the purpose of the spiritual reader. For the scientifically minded, the evolution of mathematical understanding of advanced theoretical physics requires a progression through its development.

Beginning in the late seventeenth century, the deterministic system of Isaac Newton's classical mechanics was expressed in the differential and integral calculus. In the late nineteenth century, James Clerk Maxwell elucidated the electrodynamic discovery of the wave nature of light.

In about 1900, Max Planck's "Black Body Radiation" experiment quantified variables of atomic oscillation and specified the famous "Planck's Constant" (as about 6.625 x 10^{-34} joule/sec). By 1905, Einstein had analyzed the photoelectric effect and clarified light as composed of particles. In 1913, Niels Bohr quantified the H atom radiation.

In 1923, Compton defined the light particles as photons. By 1927, Davisson, German, and Broglia had clarified that both light and electrons could be either wave or particle. By 1930, the microscopic physics of quantum mechanics had evolved from the combined work of Heisenberg, Shroedinger, Born, Bohr, and Dirac.

Comprehension of advanced theoretical physics is subject to interpretation of the basic epistemology involved in the philosophy of scientific thought. One of the most important philosophical implications of quantum discovery involves the breakdown of the causality principle in subatomic phenomena.

There are certain basics to understanding quantum mechanics that are at some variance with customary beliefs that arise from the usual familiarity with more conventional macroscopic physics. The underlying state to be ascertained is variable and depends on position, momentum, time, potential, kinetic energies, angle, and nonsubstance qualities such as the act of human observation itself, namely, consciousness (the famous Heisenberg Uncertainty Principle).

What is important for the spiritual student to grasp is that the various substratum of what we assume to be reality are profoundly affected and alterable by the mere act of human observation.

Aside from the mathematics, a student of quantum theory may conclude that what one discovers is a product of intention in that what one discovers depends on what one is looking for.

The most often quoted example which demonstrates the implications is the following: When an atom of matter encounters an atom of antimatter, there is an emission of two photons that fly off in different directions. At the time of their emission, there is no rotation to the photon. If one of the photons is looked at by a human observer, however, it instantly begins a rotation. At the same instant of time, the other photon simultaneously begins to rotate in the opposite direction. The phenomenon does not begin of its own but only as a consequence of human observation. This implies that there is an underlying matrix/lattice field underlying both the subjective consciousness of the human and the phenomenological world of matter.

Explanation

The discoveries of Quantum Mechanics required innovations of epistemologic and philosophic comprehension to explain the impact of human observation and participation in scientifically studied events. In 1927, the Copenhagen Solvay conference addressed the problem subsequent to which there were differing interpretations by Bohr, Einstein, Dirac, von Neumann, Wigner, and others to answer the problem that the famous Schroedinger's equations were insufficient in not specifying the effect of the observer. This was later termed the Heisenberg choice. (See Stapp, H., for discussion.)

This is the threshold of the jump from the linear to the nonlinear domain. It is interesting that Einstein refused to make the transition and rejected the inclusion of consciousness as an integral element essential to explaining events (this correlates with his calibration level of 499, which is the same as Newton's).

In the explanation given previously of the kinesiologic test, it was noted that the test is a response that indicates "yes" or "not yes." Its correlate in Quantum Theory is called the "von Neumann formulation" in which a complete comprehension of events in Nature requires recognition of two simultaneous processes, called Process I and Process II. Process II is limited to the physical properties while Process I includes the human consciousness elements of intention and selection; that is, what we discover has already been influenced and preselected by the nature of the question itself and its underlying intention.

The problem that confronts the science and consciousness researchers is basically the comprehension of the relationship of context and content and how this relates to brain function in which content and function are dominated by the field effect of context. Choices are thereby open to possible "yes" answers or precluded by "not yes" exclusion.

It is interesting that the intellect's attempt to create a quantum theory of consciousness, (i.e., experience is a consequence of the collapse of the wave function), runs into the "glass ceiling" of the limits of its own dimension and cannot progress farther without a paradigm jump (i.e., consciousness level 500). It then opens into the paradigm of reality of the mystic.

It could be said that the quantum physicist is the expert of content, and the mystic is the expert of context. This interface is the locus of the jump from the linear to the nonlinear, from ego to spirit, and from "knowing about" to "knowing by virtue of identity with" reality.

The purpose of the spiritual work of transcending identification with the ego by its disassembly facilitates the transformation necessary to the dissolution of the limitations of paradigm. The knowingness of self shifts from limited content to unlimited context, and the journey is then complete with the realization of the source of existence itself—the Infinite "I" of radical subjectivity.

Discussion

Quantum Mechanics provides a rationale to explain such phenomena as the occurrence of the miraculous, the efficacy of prayer, and the exercise of free will in which choice alters potentiality by altering context that, in turn, influences outcome, but not by resort to force, which would be necessary if the sequence were due to an implied causality.

If the universe were limited to deterministic causality (i.e., Newtonian), all events would occur as a consequence of force and would result in an endless chain of dependent causes for which there could be no spiritual accountability or freedom. In Reality, all acts are simply limited to a change of conditions, and subsequent phenomena are merely reactions or responses that are expressions of their own essence and not derived from any external source.

Thus, we can see that the presumed observed perception of a seeming chain of events is, in reality, stimulus and response, within which human consciousness is free to choose among a multitude of possible responses. For example, nobody can 'make' another person angry or 'cause' them to do anything.

In Quantum Mechanics, therefore, it is importantly noted that the discoveries of Quantum Theory lead to a breakdown of the causality principle. This clarifies that 'causality' is a mentation and an operative theory and explanation rather than a provable reality.

We can demonstrate the usefulness of this crucial understanding by using the example of 'the idea whose time has come'. The idea is the content and the 'time has come' is the context. The context is actually comprised of millions of components; then, at a critical degree of balance, intensity, and density (e.g., socio-political, economic, geographic, etc.), the idea may be activated into a reality.

The mechanism of activation is not due to 'cause' but depends on the volition of the populace and shifting winds of human proclivities. A hit movie can suddenly popularize a bygone era, and suddenly, all kinds of music, décor, clothing styles, and attitudes reemerge. For example, the events of

September 11, 2001, reactivated the display of the American flag.

Symbols can be content, context, or both and have subtle but powerful and widespread influence on values, behaviors, and priorities. Whole empires can crash from a public scandal. Thus, we can see that general, nonspecific conditions (context) can increase or decrease the likelihood of the appearance of innumerable potentialities. Therefore, the integrity of prevailing political, economic, sociologic, and spiritual attitudes is of profound importance as they constitute the social context in which innumerable choices are made that influence decisions and actions which have far-reaching consequences.

To further elucidate the interaction of the universe and consciousness, it is necessary to clarify the seeming relationship between 'content' and 'context'. In so doing, it will quickly become obvious that both are actually arbitrary selections of focus of attention. Both terms basically denote a mentalization and a point of view rather than different categories or conditions.

In a field of objects, any one or several can be selected for attention or examination and the remainder become termed 'context'. If we change the selection to another object, then the objects originally selected now shift in terminology from 'content' to constitute part of the new 'context'. For example, if we focus on the planet Earth (content), then the rest of the universe becomes context. However, if we select the planet Mars to examine, then planet Earth becomes part of the context of the rest of the universe.

Thus, we can see that there is no actual discrete divisibility of the Allness of the Totality of Creation except in mentalizing about it via arbitrary perceptions and points of observation. There are only observables and no actual provables, and the observed is a consequence of arbitrary selection within the mind itself.

By a mere shift of focus of attention, content becomes context linguistically and vice versa. Thus, the seeming scintillation of the universe and its descriptions in 'time' and 'events' are 'sequence', and 'cause', 'antecedent', 'consequent', 'here', and 'there' are inherently really depictions of mentalizations rather than representative of some hypothetical 'objective reality'.

All knowledge rests upon and arises out of an epistemological matrix that of itself forms the very context of comprehension. The context of epistemology is in turn the nonlinear qualities of consciousness. Thus, all information systems require a comprehension of the nature of consciousness to reach their full understanding. Ever deeper research inevitably leads to the realization that all knowingness is purely subjective and actually only possible at all because the Self of the investigator already includes all that exists or it would not be capable of the quality and faculty of knowingness in the first place.

The witness of any mentally selected event is thus simultaneously both content and context and therefore trapped in the epistemological dilemma of duality itself. The mind can therefore only 'know about' rather than truly comprehend essence, which is a nonverbal realization in which consciousness and essence are united as Oneness.

From the above analogy and examples, we derive a better understanding of the nonlinear domain: An infinite number of complex, interacting components constitute a field which, in an infinite number of unidentifiable ways, potentiates an infinite number of possible responses, all of which are themselves subject to an infinite number of possibilities. Thus, we can see that the hypothetical 'cause' of anything that can be perceived or is invisible is the entirety of the whole universe in its collective totality throughout all time. It thus proceeds out of the totality of all Creation which continues to expand in infinite dimensions more rapidly than the speed of light.

Thus, to believe that the human mind can actually discern a 'cause' of anything at all is really a colossal delusion and a pomposity of egotism. The infinite context of all that exists and of all possibility is obviously God.

SUGGESTED READING/VIEWING

Amaroso, R. L. 1987. "Consciousness: a Radical Definition: The Hard Problem Made Easy." *Noetic Science Review* 1, 1.

Amoroso, R.L. 1998. "An Introduction to Noetic Field Theory: The Quantization of Mind." *Science and the Primacy of Consciousness.* Orinda, Calif.: Noetic Press.

Anonymous. 1996. *A Course in Miracles.* (Combined Vol., 2nd Ed.) Mill Valley, Calif.: Foundation for Inner Peace.

Arehart-Traichal, J. 2002. "Adult Criminality May Be Rooted in Troubling Childhood Behavior." *Psychiatric News.* Jan. 4.

Balsekar, R.S. 1989. *Exploration into the Eternal.* Durham, NC: Acorn Press.

———. 1989. *A Duet of One: The Ashtavatra Gita Dialogue.* Calif.: Advaita Press.

———. 1988. *Experiencing the Teaching.* Calif.: Advaita Press.

Carney, T. 1996. *Synopsis and Study Guide to "Power versus Force."* Sedona, Ariz.: Veritas Publishing.

———. 2003. *Synopsis and Study Guide to "The Eye of the I."* Sedona, Ariz.: Veritas Publishing.

Davies, F. 2002. "Policymakers, Public at Odds on Immigration." *Arizona Republic.* December 18, A:4.

Diamond, J. 1979. *Behavioral Kinesiology.* New York: Harper & Rowe.

———. 1979. *Your Body Doesn't Lie.* New York: Warner Books.

"Dog Packs Terrifying Neighborhoods." *Arizona Republic.* Dec. 2, 2002.

Frattaroli, E. 2001. *Healing the Soul in the Age of the Brain: Becoming Conscious in an Unconscious World.* New York: Viking, Penguin Putnam, Inc..

Gahanter, M. 1999. *Cults: Faith, Healing, and Coercion.* 2nd ed. New York: Oxford University Press.

Gunther, M. 2001. "God and Business." *Fortune.* May, 58-80.

Hawkins, David R. 2002. *Consciousness: Understanding Self, Mankind and the Nonlinear Domain.* Series of 12 six-hour lectures. (Video/audio cassettes) 1. *Causality: The Ego's Foundation;* 2. *Radical Subjectivity: The I of Self;* 3. *Levels of*

Consciousness: Subjective and Social Consequences; 4.
Positionality and Duality: Transcending the Opposites; 5.
Perception and Illusion: Distortions of Reality; 6. *Realizing the
Root of Consciousness: Meditative and Contemplative Tech-
niques;* 7. *The Nature of Divinity: Undoing Religious Fallacies;*
8. *Advaita: The Way to God Through Mind;* 9. *Devotion: The
Way to God Through Heart;* 10. *Karma and the Afterlife;* 11.
God: Transcendent and Immanent; and, 12. *Realization of the
Self: The Final Moments.* Sedona, Ariz.: Veritas Publishing.
————. 2002. *Power versus Force: An Anatomy of Consciousness.*
(Rev.). Carlsbad, Calif., Brighton-le-Sands, Australia: Hay
House.
————. 2001. *The Eye of the I: from Which Nothing Is Hidden.*
Sedona, Ariz.: Veritas Publishing.
————. 2000. *Consciousness Workshop.* Prescott, Ariz. (Videocassette) Sedona, Ariz.: Veritas Publishing.
————. 2000. *Consciousness and A Course in Miracles.* California. (Videocassette) Sedona, Ariz: Veritas Publishing.
————. 2000. *Consciousness and Spiritual Inquiry: Address to
the Tao Fellowship.* (Videocassette) Sedona, Ariz.: Veritas
Publishing.
————. 1997. *Research on the Nature of Consciousness.* The
Landsberg 1997 Lecture. University of California School of
Medicine, San Francisco, CA. Sedona, Ariz.: Veritas Publishing.
————. 1996. "Realization of the Presence of God." *Concepts.*
July, 17-18.
————. 1995. *Power vs. Force: An Anatomy of Consciousness.*
Sedona, Ariz.: Veritas Publishing.
————. 1995. *Quantitative and Qualitative Analysis and
Calibration of the Levels of Human Consciousness.* Ann Arbor,
Mich.: VMI, Bell and Howell Col.; republished 1999 by
Veritas Publishing, Sedona, Ariz.
————. 1995. *Power Versus Force; Consciousness and Addiction;
Advanced States of Consciousness: The Realization of the
Presence of God; Consciousness: How to Tell the Truth About*

Anything. Undoing the Barriers to Spiritual Progress. (Video-cassettes) Sedona, Ariz.: Veritas Publishing.

———. 1987. Sedona Lecture Series; *Drug Addiction and Alcoholism; A Map of Consciousness; Cancer (audio only); AIDS;* and *Death and Dying..* (Audio/Videocassettes) Sedona, Ariz.: Veritas Publishing.

———. 1986. Office Series: *Stress; Health; Spiritual First Aid; Sexuality; The Aging Process; Handling Major Crisis; Worry, Fear and Anxiety; Pain and Suffering; Losing Weight; Depression; Illness and Self-Healing;* and *Alcoholism.* (Audio/ Video-cassettes) Sedona, Ariz.: Veritas Publishing.

———. 1985. "Consciousness and Addiction" in *Beyond Addictions, Beyond Boundaries.* Burton, S., Kiley, L. San Mateo, Calif.: Brookridge Institute.

Hay, L. 1987. *You Can Heal Your Life.* Carlsbad, Calif.: Hay House.

———. 2002. *Meditations to Heal Your Life.* Carlsbad, Calif.: Hay House

History and Culture of Buddhism in Korea. 1993. Seoul, Korea: Dongguk University Press.

Huang Po. 1958. *The Zen Teachings of Huang Po: On Transmission of the Mind.* John Blofield, trans. New York: Grove Press.

Ironson, G., Soloman, G., et al. "Ironson-Woods Spirituality/ Religious Index is Associated with Long Survival-Low Cortisol People with HIV/AIDS." *An. Behav. Med.* (1) 34-48.

Jackell, R. and Hirota, J. 2000. *Image Makers.* Chicago: University of Chicago Press.

James, W. 1929. *The Varieties of Religious Experience.* New York: Modern Library, Random House. (Longman's Green and Company).

Jung, C. 1973. *Synchronicity as a Causal Connecting Principle.* R.F. Hall, trans. Bollington Ser., v. 20. Princeton: Princeton University Press.

Kandler, K.S. 2001. "A Psychiatric Dialogue on the Mind-Body Problem." *Amer. J. Psychiatry,* July, 158:7.

Kaufman, S.A. 1993. *The Origin of Order.* New York: Oxford University Press.

Korean Buddhism. 1996. Seoul, Korea: Korean Buddhist Chogye Order,. (Ox-herding pictures, 116-117.)

Krishna, Gopi. 1985. *Kundalini: the Evolutionary Energy in Man..* Boston: Shambala

———. 1971. *Kundalini.* New York: Shambala.

Lamonick, M., Dorfman, A. 2001. "One Giant Step for Mankind." *Time.* July 21, 54-61.

Lamsa, G. (trans.) 1957. *Holy Bible from Ancient Eastern Manuscripts.* Philadelphia: A.J. Holmes Co.

Larimer, T. 2002. "Why Japan's Terror Cult Still Has Appeal." *Time,* June 10.

Lewis, B. 2001. *What Went Wrong: Western Impact and Middle Eastern Response.* London: Oxford University Press.

———. 2002. "What Went Wrong." *Atlantic Monthly.* Jan. 289:1, 43-45.

Lewis, J.R. 2001. *Odd Gods: Now Religions are the Cult Controversy.* Amherst, NY: Prometheus Books.

Losada, M. 1999. "The Complex Dynamics of High-Performance Teams." *Mathematical and Computer Modeling.* 30, 179-182. Amsterdam: Elsevier Science (Perganon).

Maharaj, Nisargadatta. 1982. *Prior to Consciousness.* Dunn, J., ed. Durham, NC: Acorn Press.

———. 1982. *Seeds of Consciousness.* New York: Grove Press.

———. 2001. *The Ultimate Medicine.* Powell, Robert, Ed.

———. 2001. *The Nectar of Immortality*

———. 2001. *The Experience of Nothingness.* San Diego, Calif.: Blue Dove Press.

———. 1973. *I Am That.* Bombay: Chetara.

Maharshi, Ramana. 1972. *Day by Day.* San Diego, Calif.: Blue Dove Press.

———. 1975. *Be As You Are* (D. Godman, Ed.). San Diego, Calif.: Blue Dove Press.

———. 1953. *Who Am I.* San Diego, Calif.: Blue Dove Press.

———. *Advaita Buddha; Deapika; Dual Knowledge; Lamp of Now; Talks.* San Diego Calif.: Blue Dove Press.

McGeary, J. 2002. "Why A Civilization Declined." *Time,* July 18.

Mendelero, D. 2002. "Thank God for Upbeat Teenagers: Religious Youths Happier." *Rochester (New York) Democrat and Chronicle,* as reported in *Arizona Republic,* Dec. 13: A-4.

Miller, W.R., and C'de Baca, J. 2001. *Quantum Change: When Epiphanies and Sudden Insights Transform Ordinary Lives.* New York: Guilford Publishers.

Monti, D., Sinnett, J., et al. 1999. "Muscle Test Comparisons of Congruent and Incongruent Self-Referential Statements." *Perceptual and Motor Skills,* 88; 1019-28.

Nicholas, G. 1995. *Introduction to Nonlinear Science.* New York: Cambridge University Press.

Ostling, R.N. 2002. "Religiosity High in U.S. Worldwide Survey Says." *Arizona Republic.* December 20, A-11

Patanjali. 1978. *The Yoga Sutras of Patanjali.* Satchinananda, Sri S., trans. Buckingham, Va.: Integral Yoga Pubs.

Paxon, J. (quoted by Keyworth, J.) 2002. "Fire Neither Good nor Bad." *Payson* (Ariz.) *Roundup,* 13:72, Sept. 6.

Peck, M.S. 1983. *People of the Lie: The Hope for Healing Human Evil.* New York: Simon & Schuster.

Pediaditekis, N. 2002. "Borderline Phenomena Revisited: A Synthesis." *Psychiatric Times.* Feb., 37-38.

Pontari, B., Schlenken, B., and Cristopher, A. 2002. "Excuses and Character: Identifying the Problematic Aspects of Excuses." *J. Social and Clinical Psychology.* 26:5, 497-516

Rosband, S.N. 1990. *Chaotic Dynamics of Non-Linear Systems.* New York: John Wiley and Sons.

Ruelle, D. 1989. *Chaotic Evolution and Strange Attractor: The Statistical Analysis of Time Series from Deterministic Nonlinear Systems..* New York: Cambridge University Press.

Sangioneti, V.R. 1999. *Landscapes in My Mind: Origins and Structure of the Subjective Experience.* Madison, Conn.: Psychosocial Press (International University Press).

————. 2002. "The Subjective Experience: Crucial Keys to Therapy and the Human Mind." American Psychiatric Assn. Annual Meeting, Philadelphia.

Satinover, J. 2001. *The Quantum Brain: The Search for Freedom and the Next Generation of Man.* New York: John Wiley and Sons.

Sheldrake, R. 1981. *A New Science of Life*. London: Victoria Works.

———. 1981. Essay in *New Scientist* 90. June 18, 749, 766-768.

———. 1981. "Formative Causation." Interview in *Brain/Mind Bulletin* 6, August 3: 13. Los Angeles.

Scherer, R.A. 2002. "President's Commission Calls Mental Health Care System 'A Maze.'" *Psychiatric Times* 19 (12) 1-5.

Stapp, H.P. 1993. *Mind, Matter, and Quantum Mechanics*. New York: Springer-Verlag.

———. 2003. "Attention, Intention, and Will in Quantum Physics." Berkeley, CA: National Laboratory, University of California.

———. 2003. *The Mindful Universe* (in pub.). For draft, see http://www-physics.lbl.gov/-stapp/stappfiles.html.

———. 2003. The Lucerne Lecture: "Quantum Theory of the Human Person." Jan. 19. See http://www.pysics.lbl.gov/~stapp/LUCERNE.doc.

Stevenson, J., Goodman, R. 2001. "Adult Criminality and Childhood Behavior." *Brit. J. Psychiatry*, July, 158:7.

Stewart, H.B., and Thompson, J.M. 1986. *Nonlinear Dynamics and Chaos*. New York: John Wiley & Sons.

Strogatz, S.H. 1994. *Nonlinear Dynamics and Chaos: Physics, Biology, Chemistry, and Engineering*. Boston: Addison-Wesley.

Sullivan, A. 2002. "Lacking in Self-Esteem? Good for You!" *Time*, October 14, 107.

Watson, P. 2002. "How the East Didn't Win." *Times On Line*, June 13.

Weinstock, M. 2002. "Physicists Learn to Turn Back Time." *Discover* 23:12 (December) p. 12.

ABOUT THE AUTHOR

D r. Hawkins is an internationally known author and speaker on the subject of spiritually advanced states of consciousness and the Realization of the Presence of God as Self.

His published works, as well as recorded lectures, have been widely recognized as unique in that a very advanced state of spiritual awareness occurred in an individual with a scientific and clinical background who was later able to verbalize and explain the unusual phenomenon in a manner that is clear and comprehensible.

The transition from the normal ego state of mind to its elimination by the Presence is described in the trilogy of which this book is the third and final volume. The preceding two books, *Power versus Force* (which won praise even from Mother Theresa), and *The Eye of the I* are already well-known and have been translated and are available worldwide in foreign editions. Reviews (such as those on the Internet at Amazon.com) have given five stars.

The trilogy was preceded by research on the Nature of Consciousness and published as the doctoral dissertation, *Qualitative and Quantitative Analysis and Calibration of the Levels of Consciousness* (1995), which correlated the seemingly disparate domains of science and spirituality. This was accomplished by the major discovery of a technique that, for the first time in human history, demonstrated a means to discern truth from falsehood.

The importance of the work was given recognition by its very favorable and extensive review in *Brain/Mind Bulletin* and at later presentations such as the International Conference on Science and Consciousness. Many presentations were given to a variety of organizations, spiritual conferences, and church groups as well as at conferences of nuns and monks nationally and in foreign countries. In the Far East, Dr. Hawkins is a recognized "teacher of the way to Enlightenment."

In response to his own observation that much spiritual truth
has been misunderstood over the ages due to lack of explanation, Dr. Hawkins has been presenting monthly day-long
seminars that have been recorded on videocassettes. Detailed
explanations that are too lengthy to describe in book format
are now available, along with questions and answers that
provide additional clarification.

The overall design of this lifetime work is to recontextualize
the human experience in terms of the evolution of consciousness and to integrate a comprehension of both mind and spirit
as expressions of the innate Divinity that is the substrate and
ongoing source of life and Existence. This dedication is signi-
fied by the statement "Gloria in Excelsis! Deo!" with which his
published works begin and end.

Biographic Summary

Dr. Hawkins has practiced psychiatry since 1952 and is a life
member of the American Psychiatric Association and numerous other professional organizations. His national television
appearance schedule has included *The McNeil/Leher News
Hour, The Barbara Walters Show, The Today Show*, science
documentaries, and many others.

He is the author of numerous scientific and spiritual publications, books, video tapes, and lecture series. Nobelist Linus
Pauling coauthored his landmark book, *Orthomolecular
Psychiatry*. Dr. Hawkins's diverse background as researcher and
teacher is noted in his biographical listings in *Who's Who in
America* and *Who's Who in the World*. He was a consultant for
many years to Episcopal and Catholic Dioceses, The Monastery,
monastic orders, and the Zen Monastery.

Dr. Hawkins has lectured widely, with appearances at
Westminster Abbey, the Universities of Argentina, Notre Dame,
and Michigan; and Fordham and Harvard Universities. He gave
the annual Landsberg Lecture at the University of California
Medical School at San Francisco. He is also a consultant to
foreign governments on international diplomacy and has been

instrumental in resolving long-standing conflicts that were major threats to world peace.

In recognition of his contributions to humanity, Dr. Hawkins became a knight of the Sovereign Order of the Hospitaliers of St. John of Jerusalem which was founded 1077. This ceremony was officiated by Crown Prince Valdemar of Denmark at the San Anselmo Theological Seminary in 1995.

For a list of available audio and video cassettes
and other publications on consciousness
and spirituality, please contact:

Veritas Publishing
P. O. Box 3516
West Sedona, AZ 86340 U.S.A.
Phone (928) 282-8722
Fax (928) 282-4789
www.veritaspub.com